Think of your first day in Manhattan, when it was hard to go to sleep because of the traffic outside. Now think of those noises—honking, wind, people talking—and what they mean to you now. Do you still notice them? If you do, you probably won't be here long. If those noises are the sort of background music that waves are to a beach town, then welcome home, if only for a while.

People will tell you there are better cities, and go on and on about whatever's special about them, but none of their cities is as complete a city as this one, New York, both an ideal and a reality. It's an ideal because New York is everything a city could be. From its start as a Dutch port to the financial capital of the world, New York accommodates everything from the best art to the most money, with little conflict and room for all in between.

New York's a reality because of what most people talk about when they talk of New York—the pace, the loneliness, the lights, the excitement. It's a mixture of the feelings you get when you ask New Yorkers for directions and, without stopping, they point, tell you the exact cross streets, and disappear. Now you're standing there, on an avenue you've probably heard of, buildings rising straight-faced around you. You're on your own, it seems you now have a destination, and the adventure starts.

Inside New York 2002

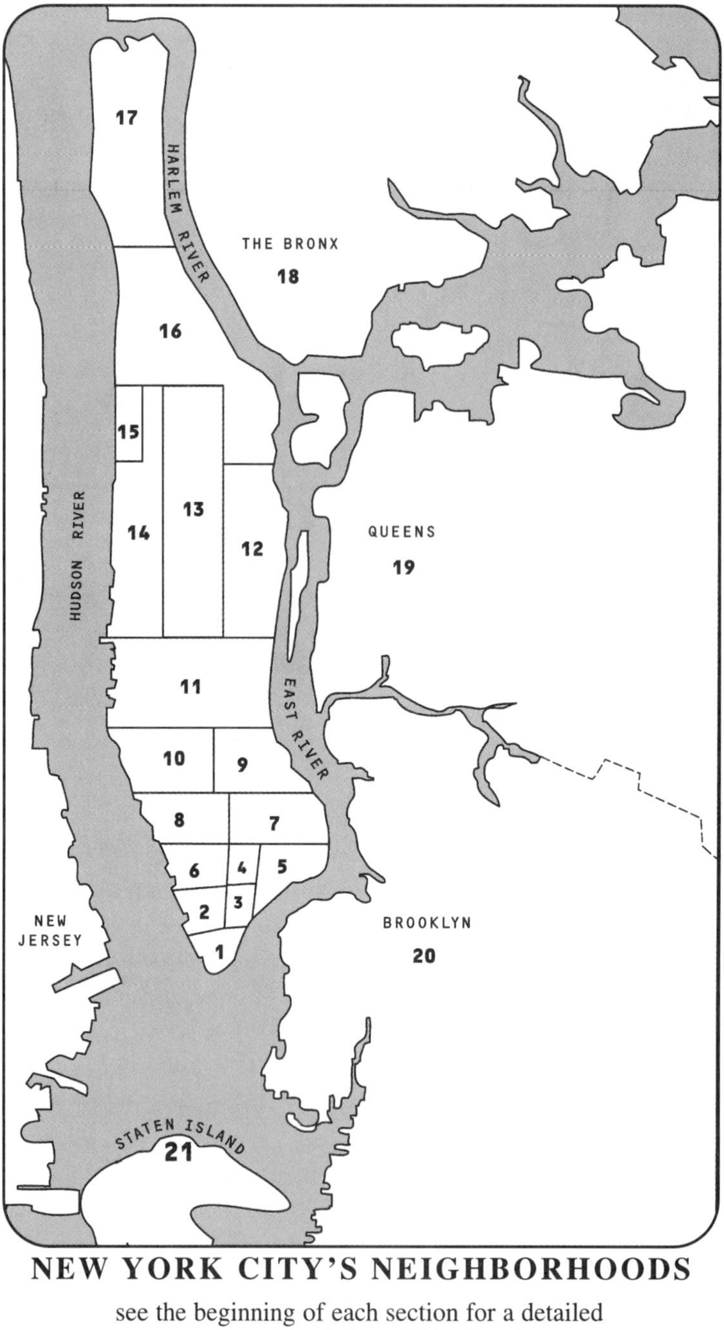

NEW YORK CITY'S NEIGHBORHOODS

see the beginning of each section for a detailed street map of the neighborhood

INSIDE
New York

2960 Broadway, MC 5727
New York, NY 10027
Phone: (212) 854-2804
Fax: (212) 663-9398

Publishers
Robert H. Polsky
Elizabeth H. Sosnov

Editor-in-Chief
Alexander P. de Lucena

Layout and Design
Nell J. Miller

Shopping and Recreation Editor
Ashley Fenwick-Naditch

Nightlife Editor
Erica C. Grieder

Dining Editor
Lydia Grunstra

Arts Editor
Sophie Lam

Director of Sales
Noha Elbaz

Contributors
Miles Berger
Harold Braswell
Jonathan Brody
Alison Folland
Lauren Fritz
Steve Hofstetter
Abby Jacobs
Christy Lai
Marykate Locantore
Corinne Marshall
Jenny Mousa
Rochelle Thomas
Andres Zuleta-David

Copy Editor/Fact Checker
Joseph Fischel

Photographers
Polly Aurit
Alex Kosicki

Printed by: Hamilton Printing
Cover Photo: Polly Aurit
Cover Design: Paul de Lucena

Special thanks to:
The staff and administrators at the Center for Career Services, Pat Macken, Noreen O'Hara, Sue Mescher, Columbia University, Steve Feuer, Boris and Tanya Polsky, Steven and Amy Sosnov, Sandy Miller and Evy Leonard, Holly, Anthony, Leah, Jeff, Paul, Dell Computers, the stellar staff of INY.

CONTENTS

City Living

Neighborhoods

Features

City Living

City

January & February

♦ New Year's Day Beach Walk
On Rockaway Beach, Jones Beach, and Sandy Hook; bring your own loved one to make out with, champagne and cookies provided.
(718) 634-6467

♦ Chinese New Year
February 12
Celebrate the dawning of the Year of the Horse in Chinatown. Parades, fireworks, and food make it worth the crowds (pg. 44).
ⒷⒹⒻⓆ *to Canal St.*

♦ International Motorcycle Show New York
First weekend in February. Hogs, speedsters, Ninjas and BMWs. The men who love them and the women who pose on top of them, all under the lights of this monster of a convention center.
Eleventh Ave. between 34th and 39th Sts. (212) 216-2000 or www.javitscenter.com.

♦ Tisch School of the Arts
Free theater in February from the students of the best acting and film school in the country.
NYU Tisch School of the Arts (212) 998-1850.
ⒶⒷⒸⒹⒺⒻⓆ *to West 4th St.-Washington Sq.*

♦ Black History Month
Black History Month is celebrated throughout the city in the month of February, with readings, concerts, theater events, etc.
Consult The New York Times and call museums of interest for more specific information.

♦ Empire State Building Run-Up
Third Wednesday in February.
The 23rd annual mad dash to the 86th floor, for those looking for some sort of personal victory or celebrating finally being done with cigarettes.
New York Roadrunners Club, Inc. (212) 860-4455 or www.nyrrc.org.

March & April

♦ Art Expo New York
Second weekend in March
The world's largest trade show in the art business-comes to the Javits Center. The expo features landscapes, posters, sculptures, decorative arts and more.
Eleventh Ave. between 34th and 39th Sts. (212) 216-2000 or www.javitscenter.com.

♦ St. Patrick's Day Parade
March 17th, 10:30am to 4pm.
The smell of beer and the sound of bagpipes fill Fifth Ave. as all New Yorkers get drunk, become Irish or both.
Fifth Ave. at 44th St., ⒷⒷⓆ *to 42nd.,* ❼ *to Fifth Ave.*

♦ Symphony Space's "Wall to Wall" Marathon
End of March or beginning of April, 11am-1am.
The 24-hour music marathon features a multitude of performers and a different theme each year (pg. 199)
Symphony Space, 2537 Broadway (at 95th St.) (212) 864-5400 or www.symphonyspace.org ❶❷❸❾ *to 96th St.*

♦ The Annual English Handbell Festival
A sort of migraine come to life in a beautiful, melodic way, features 100 ringers from New York plus guest choirs.
Riverside Church, 490 Riverside Dr. (at 122nd St.) (212) 870-6722 ❶❾ *to 125th St.*

♦ Easter Parade
Easter Sunday.
Once something sacred, now a place where six-foot tall men in heels and bunny ears prepare for Wigstock.
Fifth Ave. (a 49th St., heading up to 59th)

♦ Opening Day at Yankee Stadium
A few baseball legends always show up to see if the winningest team in baseball can do it again.
(718) 293-4300 ⒷⒹ❹ *to 161st St.-Yankee Stadium*

♦ The Cherry Blossom Festival
Last weekend in April.
A great reason to see what's in bloom at the Brooklyn Botanic Gardens.
1000 Washington Ave. (718) 623-7200 or www.bbg.org ❷❸ *to Eastern Pkwy-Brooklyn Museum*

Calendar

May & June

♦ **Bike NY: The Great Five Borough Bike Tour**
First weekend in May.
No near death cab experience as the city closes off streets so you can bike all five boroughs!
(212) 932-0778 or www.bikenewyork.org.

♦ **AIDS Walk New York**
Third Sunday in May.
This annual 10K walk raises money to fight AIDS and for the Gay Men's Health Crisis.
(212) 807-WALK.

♦ **Martin Luther King Jr. Parade**
Celebrate the legacy of Dr. King in May.
Fifth Ave. from 60th to 86th Streets.

♦ **Ninth Avenue International Food Festival**
Mid-May.
Food galore from around the world — pick what you eat carefully because there is a staggering amount to choose from! Also jewelry, music, and vendors too.
Between 37th and 57th Sts.

♦ **Memorial Day Concert at the Cathedral of St. John the Divine**
Memorial Day at 8pm
The Philharmonic performs at the Cathedral of St. John the Divine *Amsterdam Ave. (at 112th St.)* 1 9 *to Cathedral Parkway (110th St.)*

♦ **Fleet Week**
On Memorial Day weekend, the city's harbors fill up with naval vessels while the streets and bars fill up with sailors. Land ho!

♦ **Belmont Stakes**
Early June.
A circus of cheap suits, high stakes and fun at the longest, and final, Triple Crown leg.
Call for information. (718) 641-4700.

♦ **Puerto Rican Day Parade**
A Sunday in early June.
Jennifer Lopez, Marc Anthony, Salsa Music, dancing in the street, food and booty everywhere.
Fifth Ave. to 86th St.

♦ **Met in the Parks**
Ten nights in mid-June. Shows start at 8pm.
The Metropolitan Opera gives performances at parks in the city and New Jersey.
Call for schedule (212) 362-6000, ext. 4.

♦ **JVC Jazz Festival New York**
Begins in June.
Well-known performers give free outdoor concerts in Bryant Park and at venues all over the city.

♦ **The HBO/Bryant Park Film Festival**
Monday nights in June and early July (pg. 79).
A chance to see everything from Casablanca to modern classics, on the big screen, in the open air .
Sixth Ave. (at 42nd St.). Call for information (212) 512-5700.

♦ **Mermaid Parade**
Late June.
Coney Island boardwalk season opening is commemorated with a show of kitsch and fun. People of all ages dress as mermaids or whatever else makes them happy.
B D F *to Stillwell Ave.-Coney Island*

♦ **The Lesbian and Gay Pride March**
Late June.
The annual Gay Pride Parade is a celebration of Gay culture and reaffirmation of the rights New YOrk's Gays have fought too hard for (pg. 105)
Starts at 52nd St. and Fifth Ave.; goes to Waverly Pl.

♦ **Midsummer Night Swing Dance Festival**
June through August.
Dance the night away under the stars and tango around the Lincoln Center fountain; also jazz, zydeco, swing — prices start at $11. Dance lessons start at 6:00pm (pg. 194)
1 9 *to 66th St.-Lincoln Center*

City

July & August

♦ **New York Philharmonic Time Warner Concerts in the Parks**
The New York Philharmonic gives concerts in various city parks.
(212) 875-5709 for schedule.

♦ **Macy's Fourth of July Fireworks on the Hudson**
Oooh and aaah at the gala fireworks on display over New York Harbor. Find a spot in Battery Park or call on a friend with a downtown view.

♦ **Concerts in the MoMA Sculpture Garden**
Classical music concerts at the foot of Rodin's and other world-renowned sculptures.
11 West 53rd St. (212) 708-9400.

♦ **Harlem Week**
A slew of cultural activities, including concerts, outdoor fairs, and workshops throughout Harlem.

♦ **U.S. Open**
Late August through early September.
The premier tennis championship in the United States. Tensions run high as the right people are always unexpectedly knocked out while someone unheard of shines. Flushing, Queens (pg. 142).

September & October

Information at (718) 760-6200 or www.usta.com.
7 *to Willets Point-Shea Stadium.*

♦ **Washington Square Outdoor Festival**
First weekend in September, noon-7pm
Great Art outdoors and all for free!
A B C D E F Q *to West 4th St.-Washington Sq.*

♦ **Broadway on Broadway**
See the stars of the hottest shows on the Great White Way belt out their signature tunes.
Broadway and Seventh Ave., (bet. 43rd and 48th Sts..), N R S 1 2 3 7 9 *to 42nd St.-Times Sq.*

♦ **The Medieval Festival in Fort Tryon Park**
September
Fort Tryon Park transforms into a New York that never was with falconers, jesters, knights, fair maidens, medieval food, and music.
(212) 923-3700 A *to 190th St.*

♦ **West Indian-American Day Carnival and Parade**
Crown Heights is lined with food, floats, & shopping.
2 3 *to Eastern Pkwy-Brooklyn Museum*

♦ **The Downtown Arts Festival**
Art education, events, and performances at New York galleries and performance spaces. Contemporary and experimental performances. Call headquarters *(212) 243-5050 or visit www.simonsays.org.*

♦ **San Gennaro Festival**
Little Italy's yearly bash, with or without Vinnie the Chin.
B D Q *to Grand St.*

♦ **Atlantic Avenue Antique Festival**
Vast, multicultural street fair in Brooklyn in September
Call for more information. (718) 875-8993.

♦ **Columbus Day Parade**
Cheer on Christopher's "discover." every october
Fifth Ave from 44th to 86th Streets.

♦ **New York's Village Halloween Parade**
What used to be a carnival of subversion has become a parade of drunken innocents, but it is Halloween, after all, and the goblins do turn out in

Calendar

November & December

♦ The New York City Marathon
First Sunday in November
30,000 runners gallop 26 miles through five boroughs as friends, family, and strangers line the streets and cheer them on their epic journey.
Call (212) 423-2240 or www.nyrrc.org.

♦ George Balanchine's "The Nutcracker"
Late November
New York City Ballet and students from the School of American Ballet unite to perform this beloved Christmas classic.
Call the New York State Theater (212) 870-5570.

♦ Macy's Thanksgiving Day Parade
Beware of a giant Bullwinkle loosing his tether and wear your mittens, other than that it's the kind of PG13 fun you never get over.
B D F N Q R *to 34th St.*

♦ Holiday Lighting Ceremony at the World Financial Center Winter Garden
Over 100 thousand lights lit right after Thanksgiving.
Call for more information (212) 945-0505.

♦ Holiday Windows Along Fifth Avenue
New York outdoes itself with whimsy and holiday cheer, especially Saks Fifth Ave.
Fifth Ave. in the 50s

♦ Rockefeller Center Tree Lighting
Gather around the city's favorite tree for the ceremonial lighting and celebrity ice-skaters at the ice rink. B D F Q *to 47th-50th Sts. - Rockefeller Center*

♦ Park Avenue Tree Lighting and Carolling
First Sunday of December at 6:30pm
Over 45 blocks of trees light up at the flip of a switch at the Brick Presbyterian Church.
Park Ave. (at 91st St.) (212) 289-4400
4 5 6 *to 86th St.*

♦ New Year's Marathon Reading
Held at the Paula Cooper Gallery, the reading begins on December 31st and ends when the book ends. Celebrity writers show up.
534 West 21st St. (bet. Tenth and Eleventh Aves.), (212) 255-1105

♦ Times Square New Year's Eve Countdown
Dick Clark is ageless, New Yorkers become warm and fuzzy, and the City counts down in delirious unison waiting for that ball to drop. It's epic every year.
N R S 1 2 3 7 9 *to 42nd St.-Times Sq.*

Year Round Fun

♦ Films at MoMA
See avant-garde and classic films during MoMA's pay-what-you-wish Friday, starting at 4:30pm
53rd St. (bet. Fifth and Sixth Aves.)
(212) 708-9480 B D F Q *to 47-50Sts.-Rockefeller Center*

♦ Tour Grand Central
Wednesdays at 12:30pm
Learn about the design and features of one of the nation's most important urban landmarks, Grand Central Station.
Meet at information kiosk at the Main Concourse of Grand Central Station (42nd St. at Park Ave.) (212) 935-3960 S 4 5 6 7 *to 42nd St.-Grand Central Station*

♦ Moonlight Ride
First Friday of each month at 10pm
Join other bikers for a safe ride through Central Park in the peace and quiet of the starry night.
Meet at Columbus Circle entrance to Central Park. (212) 802-822 A B C D 1 9 *to 59th St.-Columbus Circle*

♦ Urban Park Rangers
Walk with the Urban Park Rangers in NYC Parks for entomology, ecology, ornithology, and plain old fun.
Saturdays and Sundays at 11am and 2pm
Call for more information 1-800-201-PARK.

Transportation

There's a good reason that many lifelong New Yorkers never set foot on a gas pedal. They trust subways, buses, cabs, ferries and, many times, their feet to get them where they need to go. Public transportation runs everywhere all the time and is, for the most part, clean, safe, and cheap. If the subway's off its tracks and the buses are on the blink, though, cabs run everywhere too, but they'll cost you more money and cause mild distress as they turn tight city corners at 60 miles an hour and narrowly evade an old woman pushing a cart. Our advice: pay a $1.50 and go underground.

SUBWAYS

The subway is the quickest and most efficient way to navigate the city, especially during rush hour, when aboveground traffic is stopped dead. While the subway has a few bad points — trains and stations get unbearably hot in the summer and overcrowding can make a subterranean trip unpleasant — keep in mind that, for a $1.50, Coney Island, Yankee Stadium, and Kennedy International Airport are all within reach.

Start by acquainting yourself with a subway map. Each subway line is assigned a color and a number or letter. The 1/9 line, for instance, is red and runs North/South along the west side of the island from Riverdale (242nd Street station) to the southern tip of Manhattan (South Ferry station). These numbers or letters appear on station signs, subway platforms, and the trains themselves. The conductor usually announces the direction and terminus of the train: In Manhattan, "Bronx-bound" or "Queens-bound" means it's heading uptown; "Brooklyn-bound" means it's heading downtown.

Of course, a universal New York experience is getting lost once or twice — if this happens, don't panic. Ask someone on the train how to get back on course; New Yorkers are eager to help — really! If you're headed downtown instead of up, or vice versa, get off at a station where you can transfer underground. Don't be afraid to yell over the turnstile to the token-booth clerk. They've heard it all before, and aren't easily bothered. Consult your map or the maps posted in each station, stay calm, and the right train will arrive in no time.

Though subway crime has decreased dramatically, it's still not always comfortable to ride the train alone after 11pm. For those who must, wait in the designated after-hours areas, and stay in view of the token booth. Avoid taking the long underground tunnels to transfer between trains; late at night, these can be deserted and potentially dangerous. Stay away from the entrances with no token booths, marked by a red light above ground.

A general note on subway safety: keep all valuables hidden, and make sure your wallet and money are buried away in a deep pocket. Most of all, look like you belong and stay in close proximity to other people — they are your best security system.

BUSES

Buses are slower than the subway, but offer a

more scenic trip. Also, buses reach some far stretches of the city that subways don't, like the College Point section of Queens, the Belmont section of the Bronx and JFK. They stop every three or four blocks along most avenues (i.e. north/south streets), and every block on crosstown (east/west) trips.

Stops are marked either by a glass shelter or a street sign which lists the lines servicing them. Posted schedules at stops are useful when traveling in the evening or on weekends, when buses run less frequently.

All buses are identified by numbers, which are preceded by a letter that denotes the predominant borough of its route:

- M for Manhattan
- Q for Queens
- B for Brooklyn
- Bx for the Bronx

The M5 bus, for example, runs North/South along the west side of Manhattan. Most buses run continuously from 7am to 10pm; after that, service slows. Past midnight on weeknights, many lines run as infrequently as once an hour.

To switch bus lines, ask the driver for a transfer (or "add-a-ride") when you first get on, then present it to the driver of the next bus, or simply use a MetroCard, which automatically takes the transfer into account.

PAYING YOUR FARE

Buses take tokens, MetroCards, or exact change ($1.50 per ride—COINS ONLY), while subways take only tokens and MetroCards, both of which may be bought at token booths in subway stations. (They can also be found along with bus and subway maps at various stores and kiosks around the city.)

Sleek, small and handy, a MetroCard resides in the wallets of all real New Yorkers. Slide a

floppy Pay-Per-Ride card through the sensors on turnstiles and bus-fare boxes; do it again in two hours or less, and it's free! That's right, transfer with a MetroCard from bus to bus, bus to subway, or vice versa, and get a free ride.

MetroCards come in a few different flavors. First, there are Pay-Per-Rides:

- a $15 Pay-Per-Ride card buys you one free extra fare
- a $30 card gets two, etc.

When all the fares are used up, take the card back to the token booth and pay cash to have more added.

Another option, the Unlimited Ride MetroCard, lets you ride all you want for a set price on subways and non-express buses. Here are the options:

- A 7-Day MetroCard costs $17
- A 30-Day MetroCard costs $63

As the MTA is fond of telling you, "the more you ride the less each ride costs." Do the math to figure out which version is most cost-effective for you.

MetroCard also offers the Fun Pass, which, for $4, gives you unlimited access until 3am the next morning. Aimed at tourists, The Fun Pass is also useful for those with an isolated day full of treks around town.

While the Pay-Per-Ride and Unlimited Ride MetroCards are available at all subway booths, the Fun Pass can be purchased only at select vendors. To find out where to pick one up, look up www.metrocard.citysearch.com

CABS

Taxi-Cabs (Giuliani-sanctioned yellow sedans) are a pricier way to go, though there's less hassle. Head out into the street and wave an arm — a yellow cab will come to a screeching halt. If one drives on by, don't be insulted; it was probably off duty or already taken. (Look at the lights atop the cab: if it has passengers, the lights will be off; if it's empty, the lights in the middle will be on; if the driver is off duty, the "off duty" lights will be on as well.)

Rates for yellow cabs have been steadily climbing over the years and are currently $2 for the first fifth-mile, 30¢ for each additional fifth-mile or 20¢ for seventy seconds stopped in traffic. There's an additional 50¢ charge after 8pm. These rates cover all passengers; legally, the driver can carry up to four passengers at a time (though ask nicely for a fifth person and it's usually fine).

Drivers can't refuse service to any destination in the city, whether

it's only a few blocks or an outer borough. Expect to pay significantly more for destinations outside the city. Fares to Kennedy International and Newark Airports from Manhattan are fixed at $30, with a $5 tip.

OTHER CAR SERVICES

Car services and gypsy cabs also provide private service; in the outer boroughs, they are the only form of taxi consistently available. Although theoretically restricted to telephone orders, these cars — predominantly Lincolns or other large American sedans — often cruise for fares.

Always agree on a price before entering the car. While fares are comparable to yellow cab service in the outer boroughs, the cost for a car service in busy districts of Manhattan can be exorbitant. Drivers prey especially on tourists in busy parts of town (e.g. the Theater District)

Internet

Though wits and wiles should be your primary tools for navigating New York, the Internet age has swept through the city and left in its revolutionary wake some helpful, insightful sites. Here are the ones we think you'll find most useful.

TRANSPORTATION

Metropolitan Transit Authority (MTA). www.mta.nyc.ny.us.
The starting point for any New York transportation search. Detailed information about all NYC public transit — subways, buses and trains — and the maps, schedules, and fare information you need to make transportation painless and simple.

MetroCard Online. metrocard.citysearch.com.
Yes, the amazing MetroCard is now available online. With a few mouse clicks and a credit card, you can bypass the line at the subway token booth. Instead, arrive armed with a ready-to-swipe MetroCard in hand.

MEDIA

The New York Times Online. www.nytimes.com.
An exhaustive news, entertainment, sports, and cultural resource, the newspaper of record is available free online. The personal info they require is a fair swap for the depth and breadth of information available, especially the arts reviews and listings.

The Village Voice Online. www.villagevoice.com.
As exhaustive and interesting as the *Times*, the *Voice* speaks with an edgier tone and from a younger perspective. The publication also features consistently excellent arts coverage and listings, and the city's best classified ads.

MULTI-PURPOSE CITY GUIDES

New York Convention and Visitors Bureau. www.nycvisit.com.
The official line on visiting the Big Apple, this site can point you to the appropriate hotel, the most intriguing neighborhood, or the week's most happening events. A good launch pad into the rest of the city's cyber-galaxy.

CitySearch: New York. newyork.citysearch.com.
Still the most handy guide to New York events, accommodations, and entertainment, this site also now offers links to TicketMaster and other online ticketing agencies, plus a link to the must-have online MetroCard site. The events information is updated

MUSEUMS
Metropolitan Museum: www.metmuseum.org
American Museum of Natural History: www.amnh.org
Museum of Modern Art: www.moma.org
Guggenheim: www.guggenheim.org/new_york_index.html
New York Public Library: www.nypl.org

THEATERS AND CONCERT HALLS
Carnegie Hall: www.carnegiehall.org
Lincoln Center: www.lincolncenter.org
Madison Square Garden: www.thegarden.com
Radio City Music Hall: www.radiocity.com

PERFORMANCES
New York City Opera: www.nycopera.org
New York City Ballet: www.nycballet.com
New York Philharmonic: www.nyphilharmonic.org

RESTAURANTS
Zagat's Dining: www.zagat.com
Kosher Dining: www.shamash.org/kosher
CuisineNet: www.cuisinenet.com

SPORTS
New York Yankees: www.yankees.com
New York Mets: www.mets.com
New York Knicks: www.nba.com/knicks
New York Giants: www.nfl.com/giants
New York Jets: www.nfl.com/jets
New York Rangers: www.newyorkrangers.com

RECREATION
Central Park: www.centralpark.org
New York City Parks and Recreation: www.nycparks.org

TICKETS
Ticket Depot: www.ticketdepot.com
TicketMaster: www.events.ticketmaster.com
TicketWeb: www.ticketweb.com

Transportation

COMMUTER TRAINS

MTA Metro-North Railroad (212) 532-4900
Metro-North services Westchester, Putnam, and Duchess counties in New York state, and Fairfield and New Haven counties in Connecticut. Its three major lines (Hudson, Harlem, New Haven) each extend about 70 miles from the City, departing from Grand Central Station (Park Ave. and 42nd St., S4567).

Long Island Rail Road (718) 217-LIRR
The LIRR, as it is called, originates at 34th St.-Penn Station (ACE1239) and at the Atlantic Ave. subway station (DQ2345). It services both Nassau and Suffolk counties.

Port Authority Trans Hudson (800) 234-PATH
The PATH departs from the Manhattan Mall at 33rd St. (BDFNQR to 34th St.), a block east of Penn Station, and is the best buy for transportation out of the city. For a dollar, travelers can ride and transfer among this subway's four lines: 33rd St.-Journal Square and Newark-World Trade Center every day, day and night; and weekdays during the day and evening: 33rd Street-Hoboken and World Trade Center-Hoboken. The lines originating from 33rd also stop at 23rd, 14th, 9th, and Christopher Streets, making transportation cheaper than the MTA subway.

LONG-DISTANCE BUSES

Out-of-state buses leave from Port Authority at 42nd St. and Eighth Ave.; the station also houses the ACE lines and is connected to the 42nd St.-Times Sq. subway stop on the NR12379S lines by an underground tunnel. Heavily-traveled routes, such as those to Boston and Washington, D.C., have regularly-scheduled departures; round-trip tickets go for roughly $50 to these cities. Be sure either to buy tickets in advance or show up at least an hour before scheduled departure, or find out the hard way that a ticket in hand does not necessarily guarantee a seat.

Many companies, such as Peter Pan Trailways (800) 343-9999, do not sell tickets for a specific departure time, just for a particular route. For Greyhound (800) 231-2222 treks to other cities, you are restricted to a specific destination and time of departure after purchasing the ticket.

For information on bus transportation to all three airports, the Meadowlands, and Six Flags Great Adventure Park, call Port Authority at (212) 564-8484.

LONG-DISTANCE TRAINS

Train travel along the eastern seaboard is cleaner and more pleasurable than the bus, but not necessarily faster: bus travel from New York to Boston clocks in at four and a half hours; the train takes more than five, due to the number of stops in between. The train is also markedly more expensive.

Amtrak (800) USA-RAIL runs regularly-scheduled trains out of Penn Station (34th St. and Broadway, ACE1239) to locations all over the country. Reservations are available, but these seats tend to be more expensive, especially on holidays.

Prices may depend on whether a route is local, making many stops, or express. They also depend on

to & from the City

availability and the class in which you choose to ride. Amtrak also operates an express, the Metroliner, to Washington D.C., running throughout the week; reservations are required.

AIRPORTS

There are three main airports accessible from Manhattan:

- La Guardia Airport
  (718) 533-3400 in Queens
- Kennedy International Airport
  (718) 244-4444, also in Queens
- Newark International Airport
  (973) 961-6000 in New Jersey.

All are accessible by cab for a flat fee from Manhattan:

- $30 plus tolls to Kennedy and Newark
- $25 to La Guardia

A $5 minimum tip is recommended for all routes. For less money, you can get to the airports by shuttles (about $14) or public transportation:

- Olympia Trails (908) 354-3330 runs a shuttle bus from Port Authority, Grand Central Station, Penn Station, and the World Trade center to Newark for $10 in each direction.

- The M60 bus hits points in uptown Manhattan (near Columbia University on the West Side) and stops at each La Guardia terminal, all for $1.50 EXACT CHANGE (coins only) or with a MetroCard

- The A line subway goes to Howard Beach-JFK Airport, where a shuttle stops every 20-30 minutes and then stops at all terminals.

Be sure to leave tons of time if making a flight. It takes more than an hour from Manhattan.

> "It is an ugly city, a dirty city. Its climate is a scandal. Its politics are used to frighten children. Its traffic is madness. Its competition is murderous. But there is one thing about it - once you have lived in New York and it has become your home, no other place is good enough."
>
> - John Steinbeck

Media

♦ NEWSPAPERS

The New York Amsterdam News
A historic black-owned newspaper, providing an insightful perspective on New York's African-American community. (212) 932-7400

New York Post and New York Daily News
New York's tabloids that brashly headline everything lurid. These rags provide a certain hometown pride you can't find anywhere else. (212) 930-8000 (Post); (800) 692-6397 (Daily News)

El Diario la Prensa
New York's award-winning Spanish-language daily dishes out the same coverage as its corresponding English local dailies, but with an eye to Hispanic issues. (212) 807-4600

The New York Times
Excellent coverage of metropolitan and international issues, as well as the goings-on in the Arts. Friday's Weekend section and the Sunday Times are most popular. (212) 556-1234

The Wall Street Journal
A financial paper geared toward the business world, with extensive coverage of economic and corporate news; no pictures, only drawn portraits of people in the news. (800) 568-7625

Manhattan Spirit
What the city would rely on were it stranded about 200 miles to the north. Still, a useful read amidst the hubbub and the hype. (212) 268-8600

New York Press
This weekly contains columns that read like journal entries, and the writing is among the city's best; the mail never fails to amuse. (212) 244-2282.

Resident
Several Residents are published throughout Manhattan, each covering a different neighborhood. (212) 679-1850.

Village Voice
The bastion of liberal politics, this free weekly keeps its readers abreast of the machinations of city politicians and provides good coverage of gay and lesbian concerns. Snatch up a copy on street corners Tuesday nights (and then throughout the week). (212) 475-3300

♦ MAGAZINES

Black Book
Provocative and offbeat, with a sharp focus on the hipper-than-thou downtown subculture. Articles are arranged as if in an address book. (212) 334-1800

Free Time
This monthly gives comprehensive listings for all events in New York that are free or under $5. Available at some newsstands throughout the city or by subscription for $1.25 per issue. (212) 545-8900

New York Magazine
Check out this glossy for the latest juice on New York celebs. Comes out Mondays for $2.95. (212) 447-4749

The New Yorker
A literary staple featuring fiction and poetry by heavyweights like Munro and Brodsky. Film reviews and weighty journalistic exposes too. Available everywhere every Monday for $2.50. (800) 825-2510

Paper
The shiny bible of the downtown scene, dishing out monthly pronouncements on the latest in fashion, entertainment, and lifestyle. The perfect accessory for every hipster's coffeetable. (212) 226-4405

TimeOut
The most comprehensive listings for entertainment in the city, as well as short articles on different aspects of all things social and cultural in New York. (212) 539-4444

♦ RADIO

More interesting and less predictable than commercial radio, the city supports a number of college and public radio stations:

WNYU, 89.1, *New York University*'s radio station, shares its frequency with **WFDU**, *Fairleigh Dickinson University*. NYU's format varies from hard rock to jazz, and their new music show is every weekday afternoon. WFDU leans towards more alternative programming.

WSOU, 89.5, *Seton Hall University*, plays metal, hard core, and punk throughout the day, more than any commercial station.

WKCR, 89.9, *Columbia University*, is the WNYC of college radio, programming jazz, classical, country, world music, and an evening news broadcast.

WFUV, 90.7, is public radio from *Fordham University*. Programming covers various genres, but leans toward college rock.

WFMU, 91.1, *Upsala College*, programs everything from the latest in underground and indie rock to specialty shows like the Hebrew music show.

WNYE, 91.5, programs for *New York public schools* and also broadcasts "Radio France International" late nights and early weekday mornings. On weekends, the station programs a Hellenic broadcast and various talk shows.

WNYC, 93.9, New York's *National Public Radio* Station, programs mostly classical, but runs a number of weekly programs of world music, new age, and other modern instrumental genres. Besides NPR, WNYC also broadcasts "A Prairie Home Companion" and works in conjunction with Symphony Space.

Radio Stations

am

Adult Contemporary	**WALK 1370**
Adult Contemporary	**WICC 600**
Adult Contemporary	**WPAT930**
Big Bands/Talk	**WLIM 1580**
Christian Music	**WWDJ 970**
Ethnic	**WWRV1330**
Gospel/Talk	**WWRL 1600**
Korean Language	**WZRC 1480**
Music	**WNYG 1440**
New/Talk	**WGBB 1240**
News	**WBBR 1130**
News	**WCBS 880**
News	**WINS 1010**
News/Sports/Talk	**WEVD 1050**
News/Talk	**WNYC 820**
Nostalgia	**WRHD 1570**
Oldies	**WHLI 1100**
Pop Standards	**WMTR 1250**
Pop Standards	**WQEW 1560**
Religion	**WMCA 570**
Spanish Language	**WADO 1280**
Spanish Language	**WKDM 1380**
Sports/Talk/Mets	**WFAN 660**
Talk/News	**WABC 770**
Talk/News	**WOR 710**
Talk/Nostalgia	**WVOX 1160**
Westchester News	**WFAS 1230**

fm

Adelphi University	**WBAU 90.3**
Adult Contemporary	**WALK 97.5**
Adult Contemporary	**WBLI 106.1**
AdultContemporary	**WEBE 107.9**
Adult Contemporary	**WFAS 103.9**
Adult Contemporary	**WHFM 95.3**
Adult Contemporary	**WKJY 98.3**
AdultContemporary	**WLTW106.7**
Adult Contemporary	**WPAT 93.1**
Adult Rock	**WEHM 96.7**
Barnard College	**WBAR 87.9**
Big Band/Nostalgia	**WRTN 93.5**
C.C.N.Y.	**WHCR 90.3**
C.W. Post Campus	**WCWP 88.1**
Classic Rock	**WXRK 92.3**
Classic Rock	**WMXV 105.1**
Classical	**WNYC 93.9**
Classical	**WQXR 96.3**
Columbia University	**WKCR 89.9**
Comedy/Rock	**WPLR 99.1**
Community Services	**WNYE 91.5**
Contemporary Jazz	**WQCD 101.9**
Easy Listening	**WEZN 99.9**
Fordham University	**WFUV 90.7**
Hofstra University	**WRHU 88.7**
Jazz	**WBGO 88.3**
Light Contemporary	**WBAZ 101.7**
LightContemporary	**WHUD 106.7**
Light Contemporary	**WMJC 94.3**
Multi-ethnic	**WNWK 105.9**
Music/Public	**WFDU 89.1**
Nassau Comm. Col.	**WHPC90.3**
Oldies	**WCBS 101.1**
Oldies	**WKHL 96.7**
Oldies	**WLNG 92.1**
Progressive Rock	**WDRE 92.7**
Rock	**WAXQ 104.3**
Rock	**WBAB 102.3**
Rock	**WDHA 105.5**
Rock	**WNEW 102.7**
Rock	**WRGX 107.1**
Seton Hall Univ.	**WSOU 89.5**
Stony Brook Univ.	**WUSB90.1**
Top 40	**WHTZ 100.3**
Top 40	**WPLJ 95.5**
Top 40	**WPSC 88.7**
Top 40/Urban	**WQHT 97.1**
Top 40	**WRCN 103.5**
Urban Contemp.	**WBLS 107.5**
Urban Contemp.	**WRKS 98.7**
Varied	**WBAI 99.5**
Varied	**WFMU 91.1**

Financial District

This is where the money's made. The Hudson's on the west. Cross town, the Brooklyn Bridge lies down over the East River. Once the Brooklyn Bridge was the tallest structure in New York, now it's just the most beautiful bridge in the city. The view from the boardwalk running down the middle of the bridge inspires anyone from a strolling couple to a speeding bike messenger.

For tourists, the Financial District is home to New York's biggest cliches—save maybe Times Square—the Statue of Liberty and very tall buildings. There's more to it though. The Financial District is the most historically rich of New York's neighborhoods. The first Dutch settlements were founded here in 1624, on the beaches now turned skyscrapers.

When the British took over from peg-legged governor Peter Stuyvesant in 1664 they built the Battery, at that time a fortress, on the island's southern end. Buildings, like the Battery, Trinity Church, on and up to the World Trade Center, tell the story of New York's growth. A proposed new Guggenheim museum, right on the tip of the Financial District, promises to be the new building to point at and a sign of where the city will go next.

During the day, the District's as fast as New York gets. Handshakes and messages are traded faster than the computers that decided them. The mayor shows up early at his City Hall office. Analysts arrive even earlier at their Wall Street firms. Trucks from New England head back from their deliveries to the Fulton Street Fish Market.

By six in the evening the bars are packed with high fives and desperation. On weekends the District's empty, really empty, except for the crowds of tourists getting off at South Ferry, squeezing into a boat, and climbing twenty-two claustrophobic flights of stairs. From the crown of the Statue of Liberty it's all pictures and contemplation. Someone puts their arm around the shoulder of the person they're with, motions at the view, and says, "It really is beautiful."

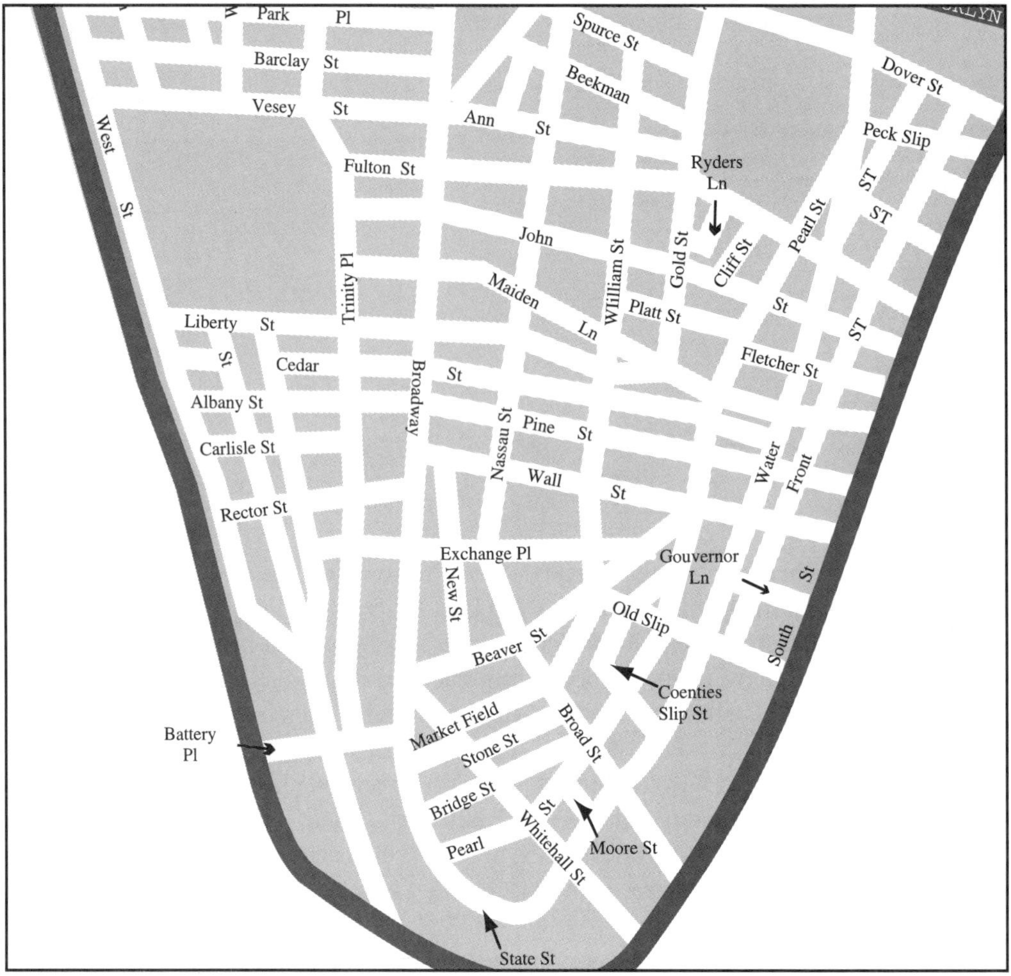

Dining

♦ RESTAURANTS

Bridge Cafe

Even if you're not a part of the city's political machine, the attentive staff will provide you with reliable standards at this adorable eatery just south of City Hall, one of former mayor Ed Koch's favorite haunts. Mostly a middle-aged crowd of spin doctors and other politicos.

Financial District, 279 Water St. (at Dover St.), (212) 227-3344, www.bridgecafe.com. Open Su-M 12pm-9:45pm, T-F 12pm-11:45pm, Sa 5pm-11:45pm, MC, V, AmEx, Entrées: $12-$24, ❹❺❻ to Brooklyn Bridge-City Hall. ♿

14 Wall St. Restaurant

Join stockbrokers and investment bankers carrying on the legacy of J.P. Morgan by puffing cigars and sipping scotch in his old library, the closest thing to a private dining room in the city. The breakfast room overlooks the Harbor.

Financial District, 14 Wall St. (bet. Broadway and Broad St.), (212) 233 2780, www.14wallstretrestaurant.com. Open M-F 7am-7:30pm. MC, V, AmEx, DC, D. Entrées: $20-$25, ❷❸ to Wall St. ♿

Harbour Lights

The food is second to the view here. Go on a beautiful day and give your eyes a treat while your legs rest after having explored South Street Seaport all day. It may be overpriced, and a little touristy, but the view makes it seem worthwhile.

Financial District, South St. Seaport, Pier 17, 3rd fl. (at Fulton St.), (212) 227-2800, www.harbourlts.com. Open M-Su 10:30am-12am. MC, V, AmEx, DC, D, Entrees: $25-$40, ❹❺❻ to Fulton St. ♿

Harry's at Hanover Square

If you're in the mood for suits, cigars, and meat, this Wall St. hangout is the place. Order a martini and scan the great wine list as you enjoy one of Harry's excellent

steaks. Not known for its feminine touches, it's not the place for "ladies who lunch." Like the stock market, it's closed on weekends.
Financial District, 1 Hanover Sq. (bet. Pearl and Stone Sts.), (212) 425-3412. Open M-F 11:30am-10:30pm. MC, V, AmEx, DC, D, Entrées: $14-$30, N R to Whitehall St.-South Ferry.

Hudson River Club
Advertising that this Wall Street professional haven "specializes in food from the Hudson" might not seem too smart, but the seasonal seafood masterpieces are delectable. Gorge on artfully prepared shellfish while Lady Liberty gazes stolidly in the distance.
Financial District, 4 World Financial Center, 250 Vesey St. (at West St.), (212) 786-1500. Open M-F 11:30am-2:30pm, 5pm-10pm, Sa 5pm-10pm. MC, V, AmEx, DC, D, Entrées: $28-$36, 1 9 to Cortlandt St., C E to World Trade Center.

Mangia
Gourmet Mediterranean cuisine and friendly waitstaff at this lunch restaurant make it a culinary hot-spot for the surrounding working worlds of businesses, galleries and museums. Mangia's diverse array of pastas, sandwiches, and entrées — including an "antipasto table," with a wonderful selection of foods ranging from paella to rare tuna — is sure to quench anyone's desire for a gastronomic thrill. In a rush? Stop at the café downstairs for equally delicious take-out dining.
Financial District, 40 Wall St. (bet Nassau and Broad Sts.), (212) 425-4040. Open M-F 7am-6pm. MC, V, AmEx, DC, D, Entrées: $11-$15, N R to Rector St.

Wave
Enjoy this Japanese restaurant's outdoor terrace. The stunning views of New York Harbor and the Statue of Liberty are the perfect backdrop for some of the finest sushi around. With the breeze off the water, and shade from the trees, there's no better place to chill on a hot summer day.
Financial District, 21 South End Ave. (at Battery Park), (212) 240-9100. Open M-F 11:30am-3pm, 5pm-10:30pm, Sa-Su 12pm-10:30pm. MC, V, AmEx, DC, Entrées: $7-$18, 1 9 to Rector St.

PLACES TO GO:

The Statue of Liberty and Ellis Island
The most universal symbol of freedom and democracy and the first stop of the immigrants who made up what is now New York.

Battery Park City
Built on the landfill created to construct the World Trade Center this home of the rich has one of Manhattan's prettiest, most laid back parks.

South Street Seaport
Sure tourists flock, but it's still a great place for great views and mediocre food that will fill and never fail.

♦ CAFES

Seaport Café
The menu at this open-air café features fresh pastas, sandwiches, wraps, and gourmet coffees and desserts. It's perfect for casual diners who don't want generic fast food but don't want to pay a fortune at one of the seaport's finer restaurants. The outdoor table area is great for people-watching, and ensures that diners won't miss any of the action on the lively pier area.
Financial District, 89 South Street (at Pier 17), (212) 964-1120. Open Su-R 8am-2am, F-Sa 7am-3am. MC, V, AmEx, DC, D, J M Z 2 3 4 5 to Fulton St.

Sushi-Tei
An oasis in the middle of a fast food desert, Sushi-Tei offers a variety of ready-made sushi and maki, as well as noodles and other hot dishes, made-to-order. Take your meal back to the office, or take a break from shopping in their upstairs seating area--it's one of the few places in this new shopping mecca where one can escape the surrounding frenzy.
Financial District, 5 World Trade Center, (bet. Church and Vesey Sts.), (212) 912-9328. Open M-F 11am-9:30pm, Sa 11am-6pm. MC, V, AmEx, DC, D. N R 1 9 to Cortlandt St.

Shopping

♦ CLOTHING & SHOES

Ann Taylor
One of many stores at South Street Seaport, Ann Taylor is a pit stop for the the sophisticated woman. Taylor's designs are neat, humble, and classic. But, like most good things, they come with a hefty price, so come armed with the plastic.
Financial District, 4 Fulton St. (at South St. Seaport), (212) 480- 4100. Open M-Sa 10am-8pm, Su 11am-7pm. MC, V, AmEx, D. ❹❺ *to Fulton St.* ♿

Burlington Coat Factory
Why pay more? With six floors of discount coats, suits, shirts and casual sportswear, you're sure to find what you need at the right price.
Financial District, 45 Park Pl. (bet. Church St. and West Broadway), (212) 571-2630, www.coat.com. Open M-F 8am-7pm, Sa 10am-6pm, Su 11am-5pm. MC, V, AmEx, D, ❷❸ *to Park Pl.*

Century 21
A hit or miss across the street from the World Trade Center, this department store has everything for the whole family at 25%-75% off retail prices. Regulars can sometimes root out $100 Armani suits among last year's polyester rejects. On weekends, be prepared for large crowds and diehards trying on items in the aisles.
Financial District, 22 Cortlandt St. (bet. Broadway and Church Sts.), (212) 227-9092, www.c21stores.com. Open M-F 8am-8pm, Sa 10am-7:30pm, Su 11am-6pm. MC, V, AmEx, D, ⓃⓇ *to Cortlandt St.* ♿

♦ BOOKS, MAGAZINES & RECORDS

Shakespeare & Co.
One of four locations left after the recent demise of the Upper West Side store, offering a diverse selection of books, and the soul of an actual bookstore too.
Financial District, 1 Whitehall St. (bet. Stone and Bridge Sts.), (212)742-7025, www. shakespeare-nyc.com. Open M-F 8am-7pm. MC, V, AmEx, ⓃⓇ *to Whitehall St.-South Ferry.* ♿

South St. Seaport Museum Shop
Any wannabe sailors who pride themselves on knowing how to tie knots can learn the rest from one of the many books about ships, port histories, and New York City from the colonial period to the 19th Century.
Financial District, 12-14 Fulton St. (bet. South and Front Sts.), (212) 748-8663, www.southstseaport.org. Open M-Su 10am-6pm. MC, V, AmEx, ⒿⓏ❷❸❹❺ *to Fulton St.* ♿

Where the Money's Made

♦ New York Stock Exchange
Literally where the money's made, and lately, lost.

♦ American Express Building
Where credits are ruined and debts piled up. Don't leave home without it.

♦ Federal Reserve Bank
One third of the world's gold for some reason in one place.

♦ World Trade Center
The observation deck makes for the sort of view that screams "wow" or "jump."

♦ Morgan Guaranty Trust Building
Still bears the scars of a 1920 Italian anarchist attack that exploded a cart full of dynamite outside.

♦ World Financial Center
Center piece of the neighborhood and the ultimate expression of a city within-a-city

♦ The Commodities Exchange
An amazing free floor show of high hopes and predictable disappointment.

The Strand Book Annex

As if "eight miles of books" wasn't enough, here's another 15,000 square feet (2-3 miles) of Strand, with wider aisles, more windows, and a generally less cluttered feel.

Financial District, 95 Fulton St. (at William St.), (212) 732-6070, www.abebooks.com. Open M-F 9:30am-9pm, Sa-Su 11am-8pm. MC, V, AmEx, D, J M Z 2 3 4 5 to Fulton St.

♦ GROCERY, GOURMET & SPECIALTY

Ecce Panis

A bread store with an ecclectic (and expensive!) flair, they most definitely have bragging rights to the best chocolate bread in NYC. Go for the generous selection of free samples.

Financial District, 5 World Trade Center- Concourse Level (bet. Church and Vesey Sts.), (212) 432-2820. Open M-F 7am-8:30pm, Sa 9am-6pm, Su 10am-4:30pm. MC, V, AmEx, D, N R 1 9 to Cortlandt St. ♿

Godiva Chocolatier

When you need a chocolate fix and Hershey's just isn't cutting it, head to Godiva's. But be prepared, you won't find Hershey's prices here; a candy bar goes for two bucks. All real chocolate-lovers concede it's well worth the price.

Financial District, 21 Fulton St. (at South St. Seaport), (212) 571-6965. Open M-Sa 10am-9pm, Su 11am-8pm. MC, V, AmEx. 4 5 to Fulton St. ♿

World Trade Center Greenmarket

With a handful of vendors selling fresh fruit, juices, breads and jams, the WTC market sticks out in the shadows of the Financial District. Stroll by or actually shop, this farmer's market juxtaposes the New Yorker personality with a homegrown attitude. It's open every Thursday from 8 to 5 and Tuesdays June through December.

Financial District, Church and Fulton Sts. C E to World Trade Center

♦ MISCELLANEOUS

Sephora

Customize your face. Experienced sales people help customers weed through an inventory deeper than Santa Claus' sack. The idea is you shouldn't be focusing on brands but what colors work best for you. If a brand doesn't have your color they make colors for you and, hours later, you leave, your face covered in the person you always knew you could be.

Financial District, 204 World Trade Center Mall- concourse level, (212) 432-1311, www.sephora.com. Open M-F, 8am-8pm, Sa 11am-6pm, Su 12pm-5pm. MC, V, AmEx, D, N R 1 9 to Cortlandt St. ♿

Arts & Recreation

♦ LEISURE

The Mall at the World Trade Center

Although the mall claims "exotic finds," "worldly treasures" and "uncommon discoveries," you won't find much more here than your local Gap and Hallmark stores. Still an interesting find at the foot of the Twin Towers, if you're a suburbanite at heart, you might be at home. There's a mix of middle price stores to dress all ages, plus a large variety of quick lunch stops.

Financial District, World Trade Center. Open M-F 8am-7pm, Sa 10am-6pm, Su 11am-5pm. 1 9 A E N R to World Trade Center.

Heaven Day Spa at the Manning Institute

This holistic spa with incredible views and great décor aims to heal as well as pamper the skin. The Weleda facial is extraordinary and includes a scented footbath, leg massage, facial cleansing, eye treatment and arm massage, plus a refreshing elixir accompanied by relaxing music in the background. Heaven Day has many other exceptional exclusive services; even some major celebrities are among their clientele.

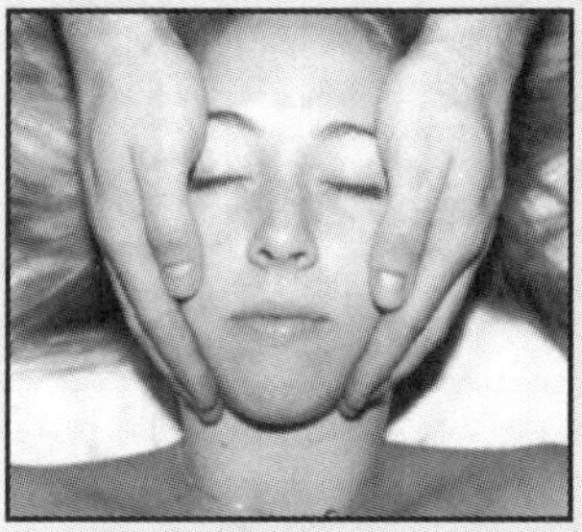

Financial District, 47 West St. (off the West Side Highway), (212) 785-0330. Open M 11am-8pm, T 1pm-9pm, R-F 10am-6pm, Sa 10am-3pm. 1 9 to Rector St.

South Street Seaport

Over 120 retail shops, restaurants and eating establishments now color the trading port dating from the 1600's. Spectacular views of the Brooklyn Bridge and historic cobblestone streets allow visitors to forget for an afternoon or lunch hour that this is the heart of the Financial District. Street performances and musical concerts as well as the South Street Seaport Museum, the Pier 17 Pavilion and the Fulton Market make South Street Seaport seem more than just another mall.

Financial District, Pier 17, 89 South Street (bet. Fulton and South Sts.), (212) 732-7678. 2 3 4 5 J Z M to Fulton St. 1 9 to Rector St.

Wall Street, 1987

Michael Douglas won the Oscar for playing Gordon Gecko, a Wall Street investor as intriguing and inherently evil as Milton's Satan. The story follows the illegal back alleys of money making in the 80s and its rise into ridiculous riches and down sadly, but predictably into poverty. Charlie Sheen plays the main character in, arguably, Oliver Stone's best movie.

♦ SITES

Federal Reserve Bank of New York
Occupying an entire city block, this edifice holds one-third of the world's gold. Don't get any funny ideas: security cameras watch from every possible angle. Free tours of the vaults are available; make reservations one week in advance.
Financial District, 33 Liberty St. (bet. William and Nassau Sts.), (212) 720-5000, 2 3 to Wall St., ♿

New York Stock Exchange tour
Bull or bear, there's always action at the NYSE. Come watch NYC's high rollers from a bird's eye view as they buy, sell and contemplate suicide on the trading floor. You'll have to know the right people to get beyond the Interactive Education Center, however– and if you're lucky enough to get a private tour of the floor, men have to wear jackets at all times. Upstairs admission is free to all plebians.
Financial District, 20 Broad St., 3rd fl. (212) 656-3000, www.nyse.com. Open M-F 8:45am-4:30pm, 2 3 4 5 to Wall St.

Statue of Liberty
The symbol of inspiration to many generations of immigrants, the Statue of Liberty is a great trip for tourists and New Yorkers alike. She is 151 feet tall from the base to the top of the torch and weighs 450,000 pounds. To enter Lady Liberty's crown, visitors must climb 22 stories. But the long walk is worth the terrific view of the Manhattan skyline visible from its 25 windows. The statue is accessible only by ferry; watch out for the long lines. The ferry also stops at Ellis Island, giving a rich sense of history of American immigration.
Financial District, Battery Park and Liberty State Park, (212) 269-5755. Ferry is $8; $6 seniors; $3 children 3-17. Ferries depart 8:30am-4:30pm every 30 minutes. Cash Only, 1 9 at South Ferry

World Financial Center
The centerpiece of Battery Park City houses American Express, Merrill Lynch and Dow Jones, among other financial institutions, in its four postmodern towers. The Winter Garden is the focus of the center, with palm trees, sweeping views and the Mall at the World Trade Center.
Financial District, West St. (bet. Liberty and Vesey Sts.), (212) 845-0505, A C E to World Trade Center, ♿

World Trade Center
Look down and marvel at what capitalism has wrought. Ride the elevator to the 107th floor observation deck, then walk up further to the open-air deck 110 stories high, where you can see 55 miles in every direction. It may not have the romance of the Empire State Building, but there's a sense of achievement you get from knowing you can't get higher than this.
Financial District, 2 World Trade Center (at Church St.), (212) 323-2340, www.wtc-top.com. $13; $11 students; $9.50 seniors and military; $6.50 children under 6. Open M-Su 9:30am-9:30pm, June-Aug 9:30am-11:30pm. MC, V, C E to World Trade Center

♦ PARKS

Battery Park
Like SoHo and the Lower East Side, Battery Park City is another slowing gentrifying Manhattan neighborhood. The beautiful greenery and views of the East River make this the ideal location for afternoon strolls and community events. There is also a flea market every Friday beginning at 8am.

Greatest Bar on Earth
Fight your way through herds of Wall Streeters and avert your eyes from the decor (a queasy melange of the tacky and the hallucinatory) to get to the windows. Perched on the 107th floor of the World Trade Center, this bar commands a breathtaking view. Watch the tourists on the roof of WTC 2 and gloat: you get both cocktail and view for less than their price of admission. No T-shirts, no sneakers, no jeans.

Financial District, 1 World Trade Center (at Church St.), (212) 524-7000. Open M-T 12pm-12am, W-Sa 12pm-1am, Su 11am-10pm. MC, V, AmEx, DC, D, C E to World Trade Center, N R 1 9 to Cortlandt St. ♿

Financial District, Bound by Chambers and West Sts., Pier A and the Hudson River. ❶❾ *to Rector St.*

♦ MUSEUMS & CULTURAL CENTERS

The National Museum of the American Indian

The Old Custom House contains this extensive, well-curated museum, one of the few Smithsonian Institutions outside of Washington. The exhibits are fine North, Central and South American Indian artifacts such as clothing, weapons and jewlery. All of it is fascinating. The federal architecture and the beautiful rotunda alone merit the trip.

Financial District, 1 Bowling Green (at Battery Park), (212) 668-6624, www.nmai.si.com. Open M-W, F-Su 10am-5pm, R 10am-8pm. Admission: free, ❹❺ *to Bowling Green,* ❶❾ *to South Ferry.* ♿

New York Unearthed

Archeology and New York may seem like strange bedfellows, but this small museum does the juxtaposition justice: cannonballs, bones and everything an excavation could dig up as well are on display. The Lower Gallery offers the chance to watch conservationists working busily behind glass.

Financial District, 17 State St. (at Water St.), (212) 748-8628. Open M-F 12pm-6pm. Admission Free, ❶❾ *to South Ferry.* ♿

St. Paul's Chapel, Parish of the Trinity Church

Just a short walk from the gargantuan buildings of the financial district lies the Gothic revival Trinity Church. It is the third church on this site; the first built in 1698 and destroyed by the great fire of 1776. The magnificent interior showcases high Gothic arches and elegant stained glass windows, which can be further appreciated during the noonday concerts of classical music. The exterior provides solemnity from the district's commotion; an idyllic cemetery – home to the grave of Alexander Hamilton – surrounds the church.

Financial District, 74 Trinity Pl. (bet. Broadway and Fulton St.), (212) 602-0800, www.trinitywallstreet.org. Open M-Su 8am-4pm. ❷❸❹❺Ⓙ Ⓜ Ⓩ *to Fulton St.*

South Street Seaport Museum

This museum boasts property on land and water: here you'll discover detailed exhibits on maritime history in New York's past and present in the museum's gallery, or on their restored ships. Go for the walking tours of Manhattan's many harbors, or see the gallery's collection of watercolors and model ships. The Melville Library also houses impressive archives on port business.

Financial District, 207 Front St., (212) 669-9400, www.southstseaport.org. Open M-W, F 10am-6pm. Admission $5 and free to members. Melville Library by appointment only (212) 748-8648. ❷❸❹❺Ⓙ Ⓩ Ⓜ *to Fulton St.* Ⓐ Ⓒ *to Broadway Nassau* Ⓔ *to World Trade Center.*

Nightlife

♦ BARS

North Star Pub

For the true pub grub fan: this is where limeys go to dine. Great ales, cheerful ambience and an astounding variety of single-malt scotches are the draws here. Be sure to take the tasting tour of Scotland.

Financial District, 93 South St. (at Fulton St.), (212) 509-6757. Open M-Su 11:30am-1am. MC, V, AmEx, DC, Ⓙ Ⓜ Ⓩ ❷❸❹❺ *to Fulton St.* ♿

♦ CLUBS

New York Dolls

Located on the edge of Manhattan's financial district, New York Dolls is where single young male bankers go to relax. Coincidentally enough, it's also one of the few bars remaining in the city which features topless dancers. From noon to 2pm on weekdays, the girls have to compete with the free buffet for attention.

Financial District, 59 Murray St. (bet. Warren St. and Park Pl.), (212) 227-6912. MC, V, AmEx, Cover: $5-$10, ❶❾Ⓐ Ⓒ *to Chambers St.*

♦ MUSIC

Orange Bear

A good after-work bar if you're in the area. Most performers are unknown locals working on their acts. On some Sundays, the space is used as an art gallery and for poetry readings.

Financial District, 47 Murray St. (bet. Church St. and Broadway), (212) 566-3705. Open M-Sa 11am-4am. MC, V, AmEx, Cover: free-$5, ❶❷❸❾ *to Chambers St.,* Ⓝ Ⓡ *to City Hall.*

Tribeca

TriBeCa was invented by real estate developers in the seventies. Basically, what had once been a cemetery of warehouses showed residential potential and the Triangle Below Canal became TriBeCa. First came the artists, then came the bars, then came the near brawls, community board meetings and plenty of pouting as rich people took over.

The neighborhood's beginnings can be traced to the 1813 opening of the fruit and produce market, Bear Market. By the mid-19th century, the area was a major point of transfer for the increased shipping and commerce moving through lower Manhattan. Its cast-iron facades and spacious five-and-six story buildings—housing stores, factories, and storage facilities—helped to make it a thriving light manufacturing zone.

By 1939, Bear Market and the surrounding areas were renamed Washington Market, which did more business than all other markets in New York combined. It remained a vital part of the city's produce industry until most companies made an exodus from the city in the early 60s and were quickly replaced by real estate developers. The Washington Market Urban Renewal Project was launched almost immediately and office buildings, institutions such as the Borough of Manhattan Community College, and public parks sprang up in the neighborhood. In the 70s alone, the area's population jumped from 243 residents to more than 5,000.

Now Donna Karan-clad moms push strollers and shop for gardening tools or baby clothes that would swallow most peoples' daily salary. Washington Market spills over with school kids around 2pm, while at night, Wall Street sends its suits and gold cards up a few blocks to descend upon the clutch of restaurants along Hudson and Franklin Streets. Robert DeNiro, the neighborhood's most famous resident and restaurateur, finances upscale eateries like Tribeca Grill, which, along with Bouley Bakery and Nobu, help define this starlit scene.

Despite TriBeCa's increasing ostentation, the Knitting Factory, a powerful presence on the TriBeCa scene, hosts everyone from Naked City to folk and roots rock to marginalized drama. CityKids, a grassroots organization that promotes youth-to-youth communication, still flourishes. But whether or not the socially conscious and the avant-garde can coexist with the nouveau riche is anybody's guess.

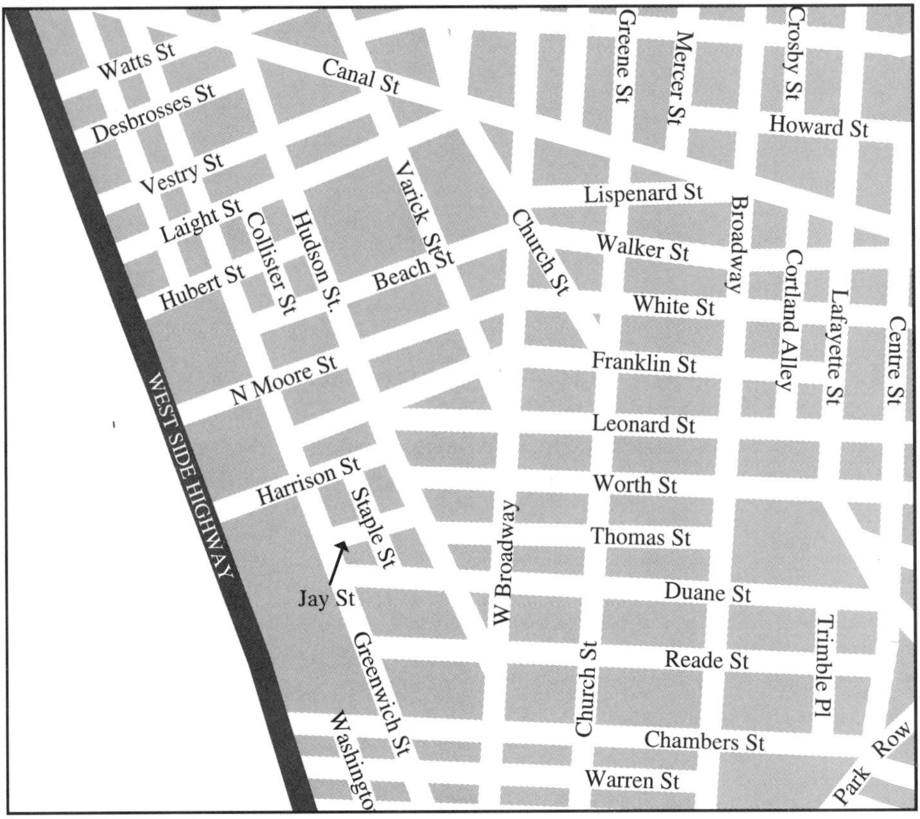

Dining

◆ RESTAURANTS

Bouley Bakery
Reserve well in advance for what many consider to be "the perfect meal." The white walls, curved ceiling, and green stone floors all work to create an ambiance that is both elegant and casual. Bouley Bakery maintains the Bouley reputation for excellence by using the finest regional ingredients, and taking great care with each meal served. The waitstaff will help you order, so sit back and relax.
TriBeCa, 120 W. Broadway (bet. Duane and Reade Sts.), (212) 964-2525. Open M-Su 11:30am-3pm, 5:30pm-11:30pm. MC, V, AmEx, Entrées: $28-$35, 1 2 3 9 to Chambers St. ♿

Bubby's
Forego the fancily named sandwiches, which don't merit their prices, in favor of the sturdier main fare like quesadillas served with great salsa. Gorgeous ceiling-high windows afford people-watching, and the wooden floor and benches evoke the comfort level of an unpretentious, rather rustic, cafe. Great brunch.
TriBeCa, 120 Hudson St. (at N. Moore St.), (212) 219-0666, www. bubbys.com. Open M-R 8am-11pm, F 8am-12am, Sa 9am-12am, Su 9am-10pm. MC, V, AmEx, Entrées: $7-$15, 1 9 to Franklin St. ♿

Café Noir
A trendy spot for late-night dining, the bar is generally inundated with well-dressed, air-kissing types looking for fun. The atmosphere is Spanish-Moroccan, as is the food. Eschew the more expensive entrées in favor of lighter fare like sandwiches and tapas, which combine simple ingredients to perfection. Use the difference in price to splurge on a good bottle of wine from their extensive list of French vintages.
TriBeCa, 32 Grand St. (at Thompson St.), (212) 431-7910. Open M-Su 12pm-4am. AmEx, Entrées: $12-$18, A C E to Canal St.

Chanterelle
One of the city's most highbrow restaurants, serving elegant cuisine in a lovely high-ceilinged dining room. The prix fixe lunch is superb, and the most affordable option.
TriBeCa, 2 Harrison St. (at Hudson St.), (212) 966-6960, www.chanterellenyc.com. Open M 5:30pm-11pm, T-Sa 12pm-2:30pm, 5:30pm-11pm. MC, V, AmEx, DC, D, Entrées: $20-$30, 1 9 to Franklin St. ♿

PLACES TO GO:

Nobu
The best sushi anywhere.

The Flea Theater
Experimental and avant-garde plays that are actually good.

Knitting Factory
One of the last homes of original music in New York. The Knitting Factory keeps everything varied and real.

White Street
The last stand of what TriBeCa was before it sold out.

Duane Park Café
For quiet conversation and delicious food in a relaxed atmosphere, this place can't be beat. The soft shell crabs and roasted Bartlett pear are musts. Best of all, you can actually get a table without a reservation.
Tribeca, 157 Duane St. (bet. Broadway and Hudson St.), (212) 732-5555. Open M-F 12pm-2:30pm, 5:30pm-10pm, Sa-Su 5:30pm-10pm. MC, V, AmEx, DC, D, CB, Entrees: $15-22, ❶❷❸❾ to Chambers St.

El Teddy's
Known for its crazy, amusement-park facade, this TriBeCa favorite specializes in Tex-Mex cuisine and legendary margaritas. Bar scene is mostly Wall Streeters and neighborhood types during the week, a chi-chi crowd picks things up late at night.
TriBeCa, 219 W. Broadway (bet. White and Franklin Sts.), (212) 941-7070. Open M-W 12pm-3pm, 6pm-11:30pm, R-Sa 12pm-3pm, 6pm-1:30am, Su 6pm-11pm. MC, V, AmEx, DC, Entrées: $15-$23, ❶❾ to Franklin St., ⒶⒸⒺ to Canal St. ♿

Layla
For authentic food from a trendy restaurant with beautiful decor, this is as good as it gets. The menu is a mix of standards like tabouleh and new creations centered around fish and lamb. Even when the food isn't incredible, the beautiful setting is enough to compensate.
TriBeCa, 211 W. Broadway (at Franklin St.), (212) 431-0700, www.myriadrestaurantgroup.com. MC, V, AmEx, Entrées: $19-$27, ❶❾ to Franklin St. ♿

Nobu
One of the hottest and best restaurants in the city, offering exquisite L.A.-style Japanese cuisine served in a pristinely decorated, lofty, and uncluttered space for the rich, famous, and gourmands. Reservations must be made 30 days in advance, leaving you plenty of time to eagerly anticipate the meal.
TriBeCa, 105 Hudson St. (at Franklin St.), (212) 219-0500, www.myriadrestaurantgroup.com. Open M-F 11:45am-2:15pm, 5:45pm-10pm, Sa-Su 5:45pm-10pm. MC, V, AmEx, DC, Entrées: $20-$30, ❶❾ to Franklin St. ♿

The Odeon
After many years, this place remains one of the most stylish eateries around. Its secret lies in maintaining a classically stylish, rather than trendy decor, and serving excellent brassiere food for the late-night dining crowd. More suitable for making the scene with a group than an intimate dinner for two.
TriBeCa, 145 W. Broadway (bet. Duane and Thomas Sts.), (212) 233-0507. Open M-R 11:45am-2am, F 11:45-3am, Sa 11:30am-3am, Su 11:30am-2pm. MC, V, AmEx, DC, D, Entrées: $15, ❶❷❸❾ to Chambers St. ♿

TriBeCa Grill
This flagship of the DeNiro mini restaurant empire is a haven for those who like to enjoy a little celebrity watching with their meal. Movie industry big shots from the nearby TriBeCa Film Center can be found sharing the spacious, dark, wood and brick dining room with plenty of other notables and, of course, some commoners all there to enjoy New American cuisine delicious enough to distract you from your gape-eyed staring.
TriBeCa, 375 Greenwich St. (at Franklin St.), (212) 941-3900, www.myriadrestaurantgroup.com. Open M-R 11:30am-3pm, 5:30pm-11pm, F-Sa 5:30pm-11:30pm, Su 11:30am-3pm, 5:30pm-10pm. MC, V, AmEx, Entrées: $18-$28, ❶❾ to Franklin St. ♿

♦ CAFES

Basset Coffee and Tea Co.

Coffee and tea are a foregone conclusion; the secret attraction here is the eats. What the locals call "that dog place" dishes out gourmet comfort food like garlic mashed potatoes and homemade mac-and-cheese cafeteria-style, but without the hairnets.

TriBeCa, 123 W. Broadway (at Duane St.), (212) 349-1662, www.bassetcafe.com. Open M-F 7:30am-10pm, Sa-Su 9am-6pm. MC, V, AmEx, DC, ❶❷❸❾ *to Chambers St.*

Pennsylvania Pretzel Company

If you're tired of the ubiquitous pretzel vendors found on the streets of Manhattan, head on down to this place. Instead of the hard exterior/soft interior variety that are often found on the streets, these pretzels are soft and chewy and come in a variety of flavors from plain to cinnamon. Choose from a number of different dipping sauces from cheese to pizza sauce all for only $1.75.

TriBeCa, 295 Greenwich St., (212) 587-5938. Open M-Su 8am-8pm. MC, V. ❶❷❸❾ *to Chambers St.*

Yaffa Tea Room

Alice in Wonderland stumbles out of the rabbit hole and finds herself in New York. Burgundy velvet and antique crystal chandeliers make you feel like a cosmopolitan Queen of Hearts sipping her tea. Reservations required for high tea ($20), served Monday through Saturday 2pm-5pm. Remem-ber to point your pinky like a lady.

TriBeCa, 19 Harrison St. (at Greenwich St.), (212) 966-0577. Open M-Su 8:30am-1am. MC, V, AmEx, DC, D, ❶❷❸❾ *to Chambers St.* ♿

Shopping

♦ CLOTHING & SHOES

Anbar Shoes' Steal

The southeastern corner of TriBeCa is a bargain shopper's paradise, and this is by far the best outlet for shoe deals. Name-brand footwear goes for close-out prices and the selection is remarkably good, especially for those seeking sizes other than a 7 or 8. Perfect for finding cheap and stylish accessories to match an end-of-season clothes purchase in an unusual color.

TriBeCa, 60 Reade St. (bet. Church St. and Broadway), (212) 227-0253. Open M-F 9am-6:30pm, Sa 11am-6pm. MC, V, AmEx, DC, D, Ⓐ Ⓒ *to Chambers St.* ♿

Carla Behrle

Carla Behrle's sexy leather apparel has appeared in film, TV, and on the backs of celebrites trend-setters. The fame wasn't enough for Ms. Behrle who decided all people should have the benefits of her leather. Treat your inner dominatrix to a decadent leather mini-dress crafted by the same hands that brought us Pamela Anderson's deliciously flesh-grabbing body suit from *Barb Wire*.

Tribeca, 89 Franklin St. (bet. Church St. and Broadway), (212) 334-5522, www.behrlenyc.com. Open T-Sa 12pm-7pm. MC, V, AmEx, D, Ⓐ Ⓔ Ⓒ *to Canal,* ❶❾ *to Franklin St.*

A Day-in-the-Life of TriBeCa's Senior Citizen Robert De Niro

9:00am: Call up young model friend and ask her if she needs the Italian Fervor. She says no.

10:00am: Eat Corned Beef and New Balance sneaker for upcoming role as Middle School Principal in 1940s Sheepshead Bay.

11:00am: Call Ben Stiller and tell him he's a wuss.

2.30pm: Meet Joe Pesci for lunch. Hit him with candelabra for, "Not knowing how to eat okra like we did in the old country."

4.00pm: Sipping Shirley Temples.

4.15pm: Drunk on ego.

6:00pm: Stop by one of my many five star restaurants. Hit waiter with large piece of okra for "handling candelabra like a mama luc."

8:00pm: Ray Liotta serves me dinner at local diner. He asks for job. I tell him to walk outside and down dark alley.

9:00pm: Marty and I talk about how great we are.

10.30pm: Yes! Yes! The Italian fervor!

10.45pm: I realize there's no difference between Al Pacino and I, then quickly repress the thought.

1:15am: Losing and gaining weight for same role.

2:30am: "Mirror Exercises" and sleep.

Syms
Originally a men's suit warehouse, today Syms offers complete lines of men's, women's and children's designer clothing at heavily discounted prices. With items from over 200 brand labels in stock, and a convenient color-coded price tag system to tell you what's in your price range, Syms is a great place for both apparel aficionados who crave the ultimate bargain and novice shoppers who just need a nice, cheap ensemble to impress mom on their next trip home.
TriBeCa, 42 Trinity Pl. (at Rector St.), (212) 797-1199, www.syms.com. Open M-W 9am-6:30pm, R-F 9am-8pm, Sa 10am-6:30pm, Su 12pm-5:30pm. MC, V, AmEx, D, N R 1 9 *to Rector St.*

♦ BOOKS, MAGAZINES & RECORDS

Manhattan Books
This store caters mostly to students at nearby Stuyvesant High School, so you'll find textbooks and required reading works here. There's a large number of SAT workbooks and Regents reviews and a fair assortment of popular books and an extensive magazine section.
TriBeCa, 150 Chambers St. (bet. W. Broadway and Greenwich St.), (212) 385-7395. Open M-Su 10am-6pm. MC, V, AmEx, D, 1 2 3 9 *to Chambers St.*

Sufi Books
If there's such a thing as your average neighborhood spiritual book store, this is TriBeCa's. Sufi Books has a quiet atmosphere with a soft-spoken staff to match, and contains a wealth of Eastern religion resources and smaller sections on Judaism, Christianity, Islam, and Sufism to feed spiritual quests of any ilk.
TriBeCa, 227 W. Broadway (bet. Franklin and White Sts.), (212) 334-5212, www.sufibooks.com. Open M 11am-7pm, T-F 11am-9pm, Sa 11am-6:30pm. MC, V, AmEx, 1 9 *to Franklin St.*

♦ GROCERY, GOURMET & SPECIALTY

A.L. Bazzini
Brazil nuts, pine nuts, peanuts, more nuts, big nuts. This is what you'll find at Bazzini's, that and dried fruit and gift baskets and a bunch of other specialties. For cheap fun, stop by for a look around and treat yourself to an ice cream cone.
TriBeCa, 339 Greenwich St. (at Jay St.), (212) 334-1280. Open M-F 8pm-7pm, Sa 8:30am-6pm, Su 9am-5pm. MC, V, AmEx, 1 2 3 9 *to Chambers St.* ♿

Duane Park Patisserie
Get an entire cake — those peddled by trendy TriBeCa restaurants for $7 per slice — for less than $20. Perfect for impressing dinner guests or, if gluttony is your thing, treat yourself.

Leviathan, 1992

While this wonderful Paul Auster novel of literary espionage features many different New York neighborhoods, it specifically forecasts TriBeCa's role as an upscale artists' haven when describing love interest/photographer Maria's move to a Duane Street loft.

TriBeCa, 179 Duane St. (bet. Greenwich and Hudson Sts.), (212) 274-8447, www.madeleines.net. Open T-Sa 8am-6:30pm, Su 9am-5pm. MC, V, AmEx, ❶❷❸❾ to Chambers St. ♿

Morgan's Market

Although there are already a slew of small grocery stores in Manhattan, Morgan's is the only one of its kind in the TriBeCa area. It is a combination speciality gourmet store; think Dean & Deluca meets your neighborhood deli.

TriBeCa, 13 Hudson St. (at Reade St.), (212) 964-4283. Open 24 hours. V, AmEx, ❶❷❸❾ to Chambers St. ♿

♦ MISCELLANEOUS

J & R Music and Computer World

Sick of being shuffled from sales rep to ignorant sales rep at popular electronic stores? Take a trip down to J & R. This technical empire has divisions to fill any electronic, audio, video, or computer need. With a massive (and reliable) inventory, knowledgeable staff, and (most importantly for the electronically inept among us) a comprehensive technical support department. They also have a whole floor of jazz music.

TriBeCa, 23 Park Row (bet. Beekman and Anne Sts.), (212) 238-9000, www.jandr.com. Open M-Sa 9am-7pm, Su 10:30am-6:30pm. MC, V, AmEx, D, ❷❸ to Fulton St., Ⓐⓒ to Broadway/Nassau St., ⒿⓂⓏ to Fulton St., ⓃⓇ❹❺❻ to City Hall/Brooklyn Bridge.

Arts & Recreation

♦ LEISURE

Gotham Bikes

A good place to buy or rent a bike without being intimidated by a staff of gearheads trying to push an Italian racing model when you just want to ride through the park like Mary Poppins.

TriBeCa, 112 W. Broadway (bet. Duane and Reade Sts.), (212) 732-2453, www.gothambikes.com. Open M-Su 9am-6:30pm. MC, V, AmEx, ❶❷❸❾ to Chambers St. ♿

The Screening Room

A place to catch independent and foreign film hits or classics like *Breakfast at Tiffany's* (shown every Sunday). The unique seating makes it feel as comfy as a Blockbuster night, without the Bud Light and the remote. Diners at the restaurant next door get seated first for shows, so take a dinner-and-movie date.

TriBeCa, 54 Varick St. (at Canal St.), (212) 334-2100, www.thescreeningroom.com. MC, V, AmEx, D, ❶❾ to Canal St. ♿

TriBeCa Bodyworks

The largest Pilates center in New York City also has a physical therapy office and offers both private and group classes. Set in a renovated loft, this place has got style: go on and make an appointment while you still can.

TriBeCa, 177 Duane St. (bet. Hudson and Greenwich Sts.), (212) 625-0777, www.pilatesnyc.com. Open M-Su 7:30am-8:30pm. ❶❷❸❾ to Chambers St.

♦ PERFORMANCE

Flea Theater

The home of the Bat Theater Company, you'll be pleased to find both experimental productions of classics and recent, more avant-garde plays. Plays usually run for a week or two, so catch them while you can. You'll also find poetry readings at the theater.

Tribeca, 41 White St. (bet. Broadway and Church St.), (212)226-0051. V, MC, ❶❾ to Franklin St. ⓃⓇⒶⒸⒺ to Canal St. ♿

SoHo Repertory Theatre
Home for anything new and compelling, from freshly adapted literary works to personal dramas. Well known for excellent casting choices, the theater generally offers several overlapping runs from which to choose.
TriBeCa, 46 Walker St. (at Church St.), (212) 334-0962, www.sohorep.org. MC, V, AmEx, A C E *to Canal St.* ♿

TriBeCa Performing Arts Center
Inconspicuously housed in the main building of the Borough of Manhattan Community College, this large venue is easy to miss. That would be a shame since the programming is excellent, offering multicultural music, dance, theater from around the world, and urban youth-themed performances consistent with the diverse student population. The college connection means cheap student-rate tickets.
TriBeCa, 199 Chambers St. (bet. Greenwich St. and the West Side Hwy.), (212) 346-8510. MC, V, AmEx, 1 2 3 9 *to Chambers St.* ♿

Worth St. Theater
Begun as a small-time theater company on its namesake Worth St., it's since grown into bigger digs on Laight St. and remains a testing ground for new productions that larger companies lack the freedom to attempt. A fine place to catch several one-acts that all fit into a grander theme, satisfying the urge for consistency without putting all your eggs in one basket.
TriBeCa, 13-17 Laight St. (at Varick St.), (212) 604-4195. MC, V, AmEx, D, 1 9 *to Canal St.*

♦ SITES

White Street
Typical of TriBeCa's architecture mélange: juxtaposed alongside Federal-style buildings are 19th Century cast-iron warehouses. Number 10 is notable for its creative stonework. Numbers 8 and 10 feature shorter stories on the upper levels, a design intended to make the building look taller.
TriBeCa, White St. (bet. Church St. and W. Broadway), 1 9 *to Franklin St.,* ♿

♦ PARKS

Washington Market Park
Pick up a copy of the TriBeCa Tribune and chill out on the grass with a mix of hordes of students and corporate types. From the park, you have a good view of the Twin Towers, Stuyvesant High School right across the West Side Highway, and the Borough of Manhattan Community College. For river views, stroll across the West Side Highway.
TriBeCa, Chambers St. (at Greenwich St.), www.nyc-parks.org. 1 2 3 9 *to Chambers St.* ♿

♦ GALLERIES & LIBRARIES

Apex Art C.P.
Off the beaten path of art and into a fresh perspective, Apex is one of the best places to find innovative work; appreciating it comes easily also, since the staffers are far less aloof than most of their SoHo counterparts. Shows tend to feature a combination of efforts by a few different artists and include both painting and sculpture.
TriBeCa, 291 Church St. (bet. Walker and White Sts.), (212) 431-5270, www.apexart.org. Open T-Sa 11am-6pm. 1 9 *to Franklin St.* ♿

SoHo Photo Gallery
One of the most well established photography galleries in town, with shows highlighting many different styles. Additionally, they offer classes on the history and work of various photographers, and to help people learn and improve artistic skills.
TriBeCa, 15 White St. (bet. Sixth Ave. and W. Broadway), (212) 226-8571, www.sohophoto.com. Open R 1pm-8pm, F-Su 1pm-6pm. 1 9 *to Franklin St.* ♿

Nightlife

♦ BARS

Anotheroom
As the name implies, this beer and wine bar is deliberately anti-thematic and not particularly striking on the interior. They have 40 bottled beers, ten on tap and a good selection of imported wine. The beers, however, are only good quality, so those looking for just "another room" to drink Bud in are not in luck.
Tribeca, 249 W. Broadway (bet. Beach and N. Moore Sts.), (212) 226-1418. Open M-Su 5pm-4 am. MC, V, AmEx, D, ❶❾ to Franklin St., ⒶⒸⒺ to Canal St.

Bar Odeon
Bar Odeon serves standard café fare like fries and burgers. The crowd and the drinks lack even this much creativity, and the staff is often too busy to hear you shouting your order. You'd be better off going to the original Odeon across the street.
Tribeca, 136 W. Broadway (bet. Duane and Thorn Sts.), (212) 233-6436. Open M-Su 11:30am-12am. MC, V, AmEx, DC, D, ❶❷❸❾ⒶⒸⒺ to Chambers St.

Bubble Lounge
The banking and "Beemer" set here can get a little tiresome at times, but the bar's selection of champagnes and sparkling wines, arguably the city's best, more than makes up for it. The posh interior provides a great setting to impress a first date with some champagne and caviar, so long as you don't mind dropping mucho dinero.
TriBeCa, 228 W. Broadway (at White St.), (212) 431-3433. Open M-Sa 5:30pm-4am, Su 5:30pm-1am. MC, V, AmEx, D, ❶❾ to Franklin St. ♿ 🚬

Church Lounge
One bartender describes it confidently as the "cultural, sexual, cocktail center of Tribeca-the town hall." Yet, it seems more like a tourist stop in "I'm cool, I swearville." Ironically, you'll be laughed at if you order a Cosmopolitan (they're so over!). Drinks are expensive, too: martinis cost $12.
Tribeca, in the Tribeca Grand Hotel, 2 Sixth Ave. (at White St.), (212) 519-6600. Open M-Su 12pm-3am. MC, V, AmEx, DC, D, ❶❾ to Franklin St.

City Wine and Cigar Co.
Catering to celebrities, Wall Street suits and others arrivistes. This luxury lounge is firmly onboard the cigar bar bandwagon. Venture in only if you think you can, and want to, pull it off.
TriBeCa, 62 Laight St. (at Greenwich St.), (212) 334-2274. MC, V, AmEx, DC, ❶❾ to Canal St. ♿ 🚬

Grace
A sophisticated, corridor-like watering hole where young professionals en route from the PR firm to the clubs stop to schmooze. The dining room in back serves up tasty dishes until four AM..
Tribeca, 114 Franklin St. (bet. W. Broadway and Church St.), (212) 343-4200, grace.citysearch.com. Open M-Su 11:30am-4am. MC, V, AmEx, ❶❾ to Franklin St.

Ice Bar
Climb into this glacial tunnel of a bar way, way out west and dig the undulating white ceiling either from the white bar or one of the sleek white couches. Yes, everything here but the frosty-blue accent lighting is white. However gelid in name and appearance, Ice Bar is hardly that in atmosphere. There's attitude-free service and never a velvet rope.
TriBeCa, 528 Canal St. (at Washington St.), (212) 226-2602. Open T-Su 7pm-4am. MC, V, AmEx, ❶❾ to Canal St. 🚬

Liquor Store Bar
Huge front windows, an oak bar and sidewalk seating render this bar utterly irresistible. The charming, slightly motley group of locals welcomes newcomers as a fresh victims for their stale jokes. Heaven for any true bar lover.
TriBeCa, 235 W. Broadway (at White St.), (212) 226-7121, www. liquorstore.net. Open M-Su 12pm-4am. Cash Only, ❶❾ to Franklin St. ♿ 🚬

Lush
Lush is a lounge with upscale standards: the crowd is extremely well-dressed and good looking, as are the waitstaff and bartenders. Everyone exudes a sort of frosty air that goes well with the cold cosmo you're sipping. Sit back, enjoy the downtempo grooves and stay a bit to people watch.
Tribeca, 110 Duane St. (bet. Church St. and Broadway), (212) 766-1275, lush.citysearch.com. Open T-F 5pm-4am, Sa 8pm-4am. MC, V, AmEx ❶❷❸❾ⒶⒸ to Chambers St.

Rubber Monkey
John Waters slept here. Actually, he didn't, but it's swanky enough that he wishes he did. Velvet curtains frame a mini cabaret stage with a lush multilevel seating area, while the downstairs houses a secondary bar and dance floor.
Tribeca, 279 Church St. (at White St.), (212) 625-8220. Open M-F 5pm-4am, Sa-Su 9pm-4am. MC, V, AmEx, D, ⒶⒸⒺ to Canal St.

♦ CLUBS

Vinyl
This alcohol-free club is ground-zero for serious dance enthusiasts. Expect to hear uplifting house, hard house, garage, and Latin. And expect to dance. Vinyl is home to Body and Soul, the famous Sunday afternoon party where the vibe is inclusive and attitude unheard of.
TriBeCa, 6 Hubert St. (at Hudson St.), (212) 343-1379. Cash Only, Cover: $12-$20, ACE to Canal St. 19 to Franklin St.

♦ MUSIC

Knitting Factory
One would be hard pressed to find a more original, more eclectic, or more New York venue than the Knitting Factory. With four performance spaces, a record label, and a reputation for knowing what's good versus what's popular, this is one of the few venues in town where a visitor can justify spending the entire night.
alternative, avant-garde, blues, punk, jazz, klezmer, rock, world
TriBeCa, 74 Leonard St. (bet. Broadway and Church St.), (212) 219-3006, www.knittingfactory. com. Open: M-F 5pm-3am, Sa-Su 6pm-3am. MC, V, AmEx, Cover: $6-$30, 19 to Franklin St.

Shine
It would be tough to tell someone which night to show up to this eclectic venue. The Tuesday night drum and bass party? The Wednesday night DJ cook-off? The weekly Friday and Saturday late night freakouts, with, for example, fire jugglers, trapeze artists, burlesque, and cabaret? Maybe you should just catch an early band and go from there.
alternative, hip-hop, percussion, rock, R&B
TriBeCa, 285 W. Broadway (at Canal St.), (212) 941-0900 www. shinelive.com. Open M-Su 9:30pm-4am. MC, V, AmEx, Cover: $8-$15, ACE to Canal St. 21+

Wetlands
Bands play upstairs and downstairs at the same time, usually spacing their breaks so there is always music happening somewhere. Wetlands music is jammed out and full of the "I don't know where this is going, but I like it" kind of solos. Worth the trip just to see the VW bus parked inside the lobby, from which merchandise is sold.
acoustic-rock, jam-bands, reggae, rock
TriBeCa, 161 Hudson St. (at Laight , St.), (212) 386-3600, www.wet landspreserve.org. Open 8pm-4am. Cash Only, Cover: $5-$20, 19 to Canal St. 18+

TENNIS

Sure there's tennis in New York, it's just been designated to specific places. A walk crosstown from Tribeca is a good warm up before you get to the Wall Street Racket Club. It can be expensive and sometimes there's a wait, but where else do you get to argue if the ball hit the line with the Brooklyn Bridge and the Hudson one court over.

♦ Wall Street Racket Club
Piers 13 and 14 (at Wall St.), (212) 422-9300

Other Courts Include:

♦ USTA National Center
Flushing Meadow Park, (718) 592-8000), the site of the US Open.

♦ HRCS Tennis Courts
110 University Pl. (bet 12th and 13th Sts.), (212) 989-2300

♦ Central Park Tennis Center
West 96rd St. and Central Park West, (212) 280-0205

♦ Tower Tennis
1725 York Ave. (at 89th St.), (212) 860-2464

♦ Columbus Tennis Club
795 Columbus Ave. (at 99th St.), (212) 662-8367

♦ Stadium Racket Club in Mullaly Park
11 East 162nd St., (718) 588-0077

♦ Long Island City Indoor Tennis
50-01 Second St., Queens, (718) 784-9677

Gay and Lesbian in New York

That summer night in 1969 a curious thing happened at a West Village bar called Stonewall when the police went in to close the place down because it was operating without a liquor license. It wasn't only the missing license that prompted the cops to bust into Stonewall: The police also had the nasty habit of harassing and beating up the gay patrons.

The cops cleared out the place but a crowd gathered and began shouting and trying to push over the paddy wagon that held the five people arrested in the bar. The police called for reinforcement and were barricaded inside the Stonewall, with the crowd outside throwing things and screaming. By this time the crowd had reached nearly a thousand. The police were able to clear the street but it had already begun. The newspapers carried the story and ran headlines. A movement that had long existed was given the attention it long deserved, and has since held onto.

In the early days of the 20th century, a burgeoning community was establishing itself in Greenwich Village. Stewart's and

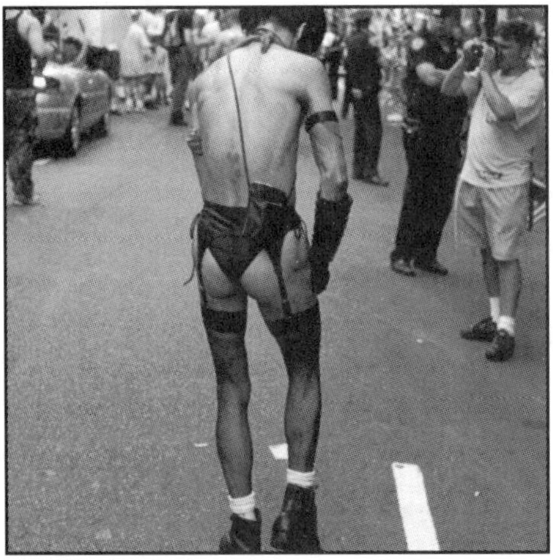

Life Cafeterias, now defunct but formerly located on Sheridan Square, were well-known gay hangouts, serving essentially as halfway houses where young gays could come out and gather with other out friends.

The East Village and the more upscale Greenwich Village became magnets for artists eager to make their mark. The numerous gay playwrights, actors, painters, sculptors, novelists, poets, photographers, and musicians who flooded into the Village contributed to the area's bohemian flair and intellectual prowess, and made it the city's most famous gay enclave.

Before emigrating to Paris, a young James Baldwin penned *Giovanni's Room* while living in a $100 per month apartment on Horatio Street. Playwright Edward Albee, very much a part of the Village gay scene in the late 50s, walked into the restroom at The Ninth Circle, a now-extinct bar he frequented, and found "Who's Afraid of Virginia Woolf?" scrawled across the mirror. He later used the question as the title for his most famous play.

Djuna Barnes, best remembered for her novel Nightwood, lived the last reclusive years of her life in a small apartment at Patchin Place, and some of the century's most accomplished poets, Allen Ginsberg, Frank O'Hara, and W.H. Auden, lived in the perennially nonconformist East Village.

Today the streets and avenues of New York City house more gay bars, restaurants, cafes and clubs that most other cities combined. Walking down the street in downtown Manhattan it's not uncommon to see men walking hand in hand or women with their arms interlaced. Whole sections of this city are mostly gay and it's strange to think that all this wouldn't have even been a thought to most gay people only thirty-odd years ago. Remember, homosexuality was considered an official mental illness until 1973.

Greenwich Village remains the same core of the gay community as it was one hundred years ago. Many political organizations have offices in the area, and help organize and publicize local goings-on. Chelsea is also a predominately gay area, with many young gay professionals calling it home. Every June is Gay History Month, and fun, informative events and celebrations abound. In addition to two popular film festivals, the most anticipated event is, of course, the Gay Pride Parade.

Although Manhattan is the "gayest" of New York City's boroughs, and is home to most of the city's exciting clubs (as well as its quaint coffee houses and its entertaining cabarets), many gays and lesbians call Brooklyn and Queens home and have created their own gay enclaves in Park Slope and Jackson Heights.

If you're gay, lesbian, bisexual, transgender or just plain curious or confused, this is the place to move to find out who you are and meet others who are doing the same thing. Or if you just want to find bars where you can flirt, cruise and mingle with cuties of the same sex, this is where many on the East Coast flock. And why? Because New York is the place where the closet is only where you hang your clothes.

Whatever religious fundamentalists and the conservative press choose to think, homosexuals and organized religion are far from mutually exclusive. The many gay and gay-friendly congregations that march every year in the Gay Pride Parade signal not only their existence, but the desire that many gays and lesbians have for a spiritual community. The following is a modest sampling of these organizations:

Metropolitan Community Church of New York
Founded in the late '60s by Reverend Troy Perry, the MCC welcomes all individuals and is an interdenominational fellowship.
212-629-7440

Congregation Beth Simchat Torah
This lesbian and gay synagogue lies in the heart of Greenwich Village, the epicenter of NYC's gay community.
212-929-9498

West-Park Presbyterian Church
The day after the General Assembly of the Presbyterian Church struck down amendments that would have sanctified same-sex relationships, this progressive church defiantly flew the rainbow flag.
212-362-4890

Saint Paul the Apostle
This Roman Catholic parish has a gay and lesbian ministry.
212-265-3495

Chinatown

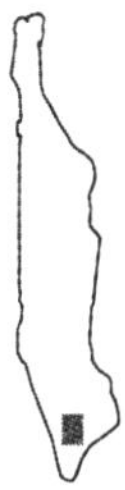

Fish eyes stare up at pedestrians, the smell of ripe fruit and deep fry like a brick in the air. Chinatown, where soft Chinese rock ambles out of windows and drips down laundry lines to the crooked alleys below. Barber shops here, tea parlors there. Sundays, under the Manhattan bridge, vendors hawk Chinese style crullers with hot soy milk; store fronts sell counterfeit everything; and, the drug store on Grand Street still weighs out deer antlers and "dragon's eyes" with brass hand scales.

It's not the typical residential community. Over one third of New York's 300,000 Chinese live here, and the community grows each day. The first documented Chinese immigrants arrived in 1825 and settled within the borders of Bowery, Canal, Worth and Mulberry Streets. Now the neighborhoods growing population edges past the boundaries of Soho and flirts with the skyscrapers of the Financial District. Chinatown is the largest Chinese community in the Western Hemisphere. Refugees from Vietnam, Cambodia, Thailand, Malaysia and other Southeast Asian countries change the make up everyday: a Thai restaurant sits down next to a Chinese noodle shop, asks it if it could move over a bit, an Indonesian restaurant follows the lead.

Most tourists gather around Mott and Pell streets, the oldest part of Chinatown. But the oldest part is changing too as shop owners move to the suburbs and mom and pop stores become chains. Since Hong Kong's repatriation, businessmen are transferring funds from abroad, turning Chinatown into what some have described as "a little Hong Kong." The constant change makes for a potential no other New York neighborhood can claim.

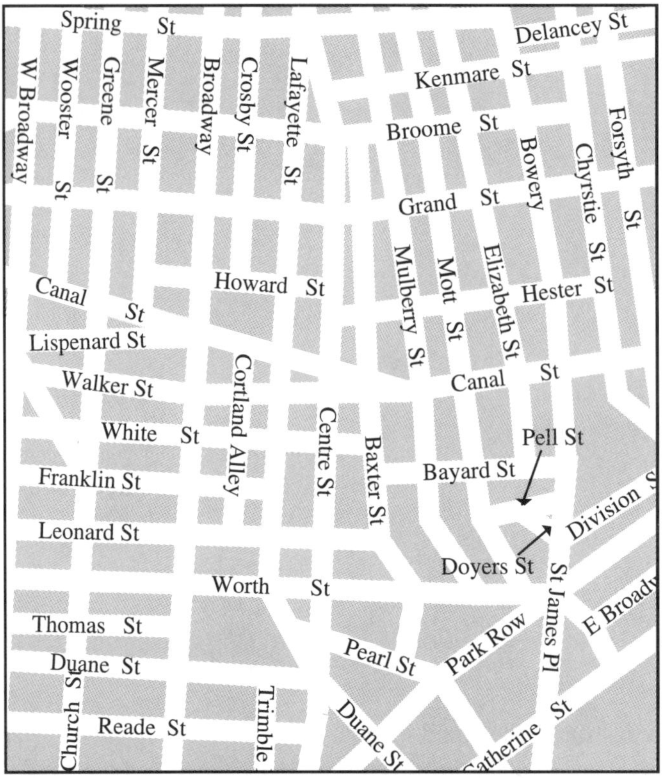

Dining

♦ RESTAURANTS

Bo Ky
Seafood variations served over rice and noodles are the staples of the Chinese menu. The central location attracts both tourists and locals on a lunch break. Efficient service moves patrons in and out in a hurry.
Chinatown, 80 Bayard St. (at Mott St.), (212) 406-2292. Open M-Su 8pm-9:30pm. Cash Only, Entrées: $5-$13. J M N R Z 6 to Canal St. ♿

Golden Unicorn
Cleaner and more polished than most Chinatown dim sum houses, this chandeliered restaurant has become especially popular among tourists and local businessmen hosting lunch meetings. Delicious dim sum (7 days a week, 9am-3:30pm) is served Hong-Kong style, stacked on metal carts piloted by vigorous employees.
Chinatown, 18 East Broadway (at Catherine St.), (212) 941-0911. Open M-F 9am-8:30pm, Sa-Su 8:30am-10:30pm. MC, V, AmEx, DC, D, Entrées: $8-$11, B D Q to Grand St.

Joe's Shanghai
Joe's crabmeat buns are deservedly famous and tourists, locals, and suburban Chinese flock here year round for it. Friendly service and the savory quality of the rest of the fare keeps customers coming back for more.
Chinatown, 9 Pell St. (bet. The Bowery and Mott St.), (212) 233-8888. Open M-Su 11am-11:15pm. Cash Only, Entrées: $5-$18, J M N R Z 6 to Canal St.

New York Noodletown
Away from the tourist center of Chinatown lies this affordable and cozy restaurant where you're guaranteed to find a dish to excite your taste buds. In-season seafood specials, the crab in particular, are a definite must-try, as is the barbecued chicken/duck/pork combo. The ultra-accommodating service will make sure that you leave both full and fully satisfied.
Chinatown, 28 Bowery (at Bayard St.), (212) 349-0923. Open M-Su 9am-4am. Cash only, Entrees: $8-12, B D Q to Grand St.

Onieal's Grand Street
A turn-of-the-century tavern, rumored to have been frequented by Teddy Roosevelt during his tenure as police commissioner. Onieal's retains its old-world charm for the bankers, architects, models and celebrities who come for the flavorful dishes. New American with Italian overtures, it

also features a traditional Irish breakfast, while at night it transforms into a popular late night lounge.
Chinatown, 174 Grand St. (bet. Baxter and Mulberry Sts.), (212) 941-9119. Open M-Su 6pm-1am. MC, V, AmEx, DC, Entrées: $17-$25, BDQ to Grand St., JMNRZ6 to Canal St.

Pongsri Thailand Restaurant
Practically adjacent to the municipal court houses, Pongsri delights jury-duty sufferers with its tasty and affordable lunch specials. Standard noodle and curry dishes are all fabulous,timesmbers and tomatoes piquant with lemon juice and chilies, will make you shudder in ecstasy.
Chinatown, 106 Bayard St. (at Baxter St.), (212) 349-3132. Open M-Su 11am-11pm. AmEx, Entrées: $5-$10, JMNRZ6 to Canal St.

Vietnam Restaurant
A basement location nestled in the crook of elbow-shaped Doyers Street, Vietnam Restaurant would be hard to find if it were not for the blazing sign above the doorway. The menu is hit-or-miss, but when it hits, it hits hard. The daily specials continue to astonish, as do the fish sour soups, caramel pork, and the strange-sounding but absolutely delicious "shrimp paste grilled on sugar cane."
Chinatown, 11 Doyers St. (bet. The Bowery and Pell St.), (212) 693-0725. Open Su-R 11am-9:30 pm, F-Sa 11am-10:30pm. AmEx, Entrées: $4-$8, BDQ to Grand St., JMZ to Bowery.

♦ CAFES

Chinatown Ice Cream Factory
If chocolate and vanilla make you groan with boredom, this tiny café will satiate your jaded taste buds. Lick away at flavors like red bean, green tea, taro, and lychee; the ginger is divine.
Chinatown, 65 Bayard St. (bet. Mott and Elizabeth Sts.), (212) 608-4170. Open Su-R 11am-11pm, F-Sa 11am-12am. Cash Only, BDQ to Grand St.

Tai Pan Bakery
The pastries at this extremely popular bakery merit its long weekend lines. Custard tarts and pearl milk tea drinks are sure to please. Fish burgers are for the adventurous.
Chinatown, 194 Canal St. (212) 732-3233. Open M-Su 10am-10pm. MC, V, Amex NR to Canal St.

PLACES TO GO:

P.S. 23
Houses a Museum, Dance Company, Athletic Association, Senior Citizen Center and a handful of other organizations all catering to the Chinese community.

Fun
A club that is literally fun, from the cameras in the bathroom to the movies on the walls.

BLT Supplies, Inc.
Bruce Lee Posters, throwing stars, ninja uniforms and anything else you need to be a vigilante.

New York Noodle Town
Noodles, noodles, noodles and not a tourist to be found.

Shopping

♦ CLOTHING & SHOES

Oriental Dress Company
Step inside and you'll be greeted by bolt after bolt of colorful silk brocade. The in house tailor custom-makes Chinese dresses that fit like a glove for between $100-$250, depending on the type of silk you select. This service is a rarity in the U.S.
Chinatown, 38 Mott St. (at Pell St.), (212) 349-0818. Open M-Su 10am-7pm. MC, V, B D N R Q *to Canal St.*

♦ BOOKS, MAGAZINES & RECORDS

Asian Music and Gift
Who's the Chinese pop equivalent of Mariah Carey? Find out here. Huge selections of the most popular music of Asia, Chinese oldies, LP's for karaoke diehards and American/ Chinese blockbuster smashes, Japanimation, ceramic toys, and oversized cloth posters of Asian teen idols that sell in the blink of an eye.
Chinatown, 151 Canal St. (at The Bowery), (212) 226-6696. Open M-Su 11am-7pm. MC, V, B D Q *to Grand St.*

K & W Books and Stationery
One of the biggest Chinese bookstores, K & W carries Hello Kitty toys and a large selection of books in Chinese and in English on topics like martial arts, bonsai care, Buddhism, and knife throwing.
Chinatown, 131 Bowery (bet. Grand and Broome Sts.), (212) 343-0780, www.kwbooks.com. Open M-Su 10:30am-7:30pm. MC, V, J M N R Z 6 *to Canal St.* ♿

Oriental Books and Stationery
The owners of K & W Books bring you this warehouse of legal pads, paper clips and things to clutter your desk with. They also have one of the area's largest selection of books in Chinese.
Chinatown, 29 E. Broadway. (bet. Catherine and Market Sts.), (212) 962-3634, www.kwbooks. com. Open M-Su 10am-7pm. MC, V, F *to East Broadway.* ♿

Zakka
Do Japanese teenagers feel the same angst as American teenagers? Are they as full of, I don't cares and Mom you don't understands? Gain your insight at this bookstore, boutique and video palace focusing on Japanese pop culture.
Chinatown, 147 Grand St. (at Lafayette St.), (212) 431-3961. Open M, W-F, Su 12pm-7pm, Sa 12pm-8pm. MC, V, AmEx, J M N R Z 6 *to Canal St.*

♦ GROCERY, GOURMET & SPECIALTY

Dynasty Supermarket
One of Chinatown's largest supermarkets, boasting a full herb and medicine counter, an in-house butcher and fishmonger, a beef jerky bar, and best of all, weekly sales.
Chinatown, 68 Elizabeth St. (at Hester St.), (212) 966-4943. Open M-Su 9:30am-8:30pm. MC, V, J M N R Z 6 *to Canal St.,* N R *to Prince St.*

Hong Kong Cake Co.
Don't let the shabby appearance of this kiosk fool you, the long lines are for the delicious treats within. Despite the demand, the owner refuses to expand her one woman gig. Rumor has it her business has paid two sons' college and medical school bills.
Chinatown, Mosco St. (bet. Mott and Pell Sts.). Open W, R, Sa, Su from when she arrives (10:30-11am) until when she runs out of batter (5-ish). J M N R Z 6 *to Canal St.* ♿

Kam Wo Herb and Tea Co., Inc.
Drawers of medicine line the walls in this apothecary shop, filling the space with a cloud of herb smells thick as a brick. Specialty medicinal cookware and a library of health books written by the boss himself, Dr. Leung. Herbs, weighed out on handscales and wrapped in white rice-paper envelopes, will cure any ailment.
Chinatown, 211 Grand St. (at Elizabeth St.), (212) 966-6370. Open M-Su 9:30am-7:30pm. MC, V, J M N R Z 6 *to Canal St.* ♿

Outdoor Markets
Perhaps the most authentic experience Chinatown offers, these vendors line the busy street with a full range of wares. Push through the crowds to view the exotic offerings and

fresh produce. Weekends offer the best selection, but be prepared to elbow your way through packed streets.

Chinatown, Mulberry St. (bet. Bayard and Canal Sts.). J M N R Z 6 *to Canal St.*

Ten Ren Tea and Ginseng Co.

Masters of the ancient but still sophisticated Chinese ritual of tea preparation, the folks at Ten Ren not only sell teas (ranging from $8 to $125 (!) per lb.), but also provide lessons on the proper brewing and enjoying of the venerated green leaf. Superb black teas, jasmine teas, and ginger are also sold.

Chinatown, 75 Mott St. (bet. Canal and Bayard Sts.), (212) 349-2286. Open M-Su 10am-8pm. MC, V, AmEx, J M N R Z 6 *to Canal St.* ♿

♦ MISCELLANEOUS

BLT Supplies, Inc.

Billing itself as "the complete martial arts store," BLT tops its claim with an eye-popping collection of unusual Ninja t-shirts, throwing-star necklaces, samurai swords, and more bizarre weapons. Head to the back and discover kung-fu outfits, instructional videos, Bruce Lee posters, and spears--eight foot long spears.

Chinatown, 77 Mulberry St. (bet. Bayard and Canal Sts.), (212) 732-8388, www.BLTSupplies.com. Open M-Su 10am-7pm. MC, V, AmEx, D, J M N R Z 6 *to Canal St.*

Jade Garden Arts & Crafts Co.

Not one of the humdrum Asian tchotchke-stalls littering Chinatown, Jade Garden sells original and beautiful ceramic tea sets, flower pots, and censers at bargain prices. Here they will carve your name in Chinese characters onto stone stamps for five dollars a syllable. Also sold: hand-calligraphed posters and ceramic boxes depicting ribald scenes of randy emperors propagating the dynasty.

Chinatown, 76 Mulberry St. (bet. Bayard and Canal Sts.), (212) 587-5685. Open M-Su 9:30am-7pm. Cash Only, J M N R Z 6 to *Canal St.* ♿

Pearl Paint

A supermarket of art and decorating supplies, Pearl Paint carries top-of- the line painting and drawing supplies and studio accessories for serious artists and amateur. Other floors carry a wide selection of frames, photo albums, and fine papers.

Chinatown, 308 Canal St. (bet. Church St. and Broadway), (212) 431-7932, www.pearlpaint.com. Open M-F 9am-7pm, Sa 9am-6:30pm, Su 9:30am-6pm. MC, V, AmEx, D, A C E J M N R Z 1 6 9 *to Canal St.* ♿

Pearl River Mart

Sort of like a Chinese Woolworth's, this two-floored department store stocks all the staples that the now defunct Five and Dime Store did, with a twist: bamboo mats, bedding supplies, electronics, video rentals, a minigrocery section, and traditional cookware.

Chinatown, 277 Canal St. (at Broadway), (212) 431-4770, www. pearlriver.com. Open M-Su 10am-7:30pm. MC, V, AmEx, D, J M N R Z 6 *to Canal St.*

Arts & Recreation

♦ PARKS

Columbus Park

There's more asphalt than grass at this bustling niche: pick-up basketball games and bladders share the space with Chinatown's elderly, who gather to play cards and mahjongg, gossip and sun themselves.

Chinatown, bet. Bayard, Worth, Mulberry and Baxter Sts., J M N R Z 6 *to Canal St.* ♿

The Bachelor's Society

The Chinese Exclusion Act (1882-1943) is to date the only non-wartime federal law that excluded people based on nationality. Chinese weren't allowed naturalization and could only come to the country if they had a special work permit deeming them merchant, student or diplomat; worst of all the law prohibited the immigration of the wives and children of laborers.

The Exclusion Act caused an imbalance in the male-female ratio in Chinatown. This resulted in only 150 women for the upwards of 7,000 Chinese living in Manhattan in the year 1900. A "bachelor's society" of opium dens, prostitution and slave girls set in and deepened white antagonism toward the Chinese. In the face of government hostility the neighborhood banded together in their own associations and societies to protect their own interests. The societies protected the rights of illegal and impoverished immigrants, but also warred with each other pretty much up until the Exclusion Act was lifted.

Chinese New Year

February 12, 2002
Bring in the year of the horse at Chinatown's fifteen-day New Year festival. Every block is plastered red and gold to celebrate what in China is the beginning of spring and the start of year 4700. Families start it off with a "sweeping of the grounds", a spring-cleaning to get rid of the old and evil of the year before. Besides a parade featuring the traditional lion dance there are also community events like dumpling making at the China Institute.

♦ PERFORMANCE

Four Seas Players
Deriving its name from the Chinese saying: "within the four seas, all men are brothers," this troupe unites Chinese and Western theatrical traditions. Founded in 1970 in the basement of the Church of the Transfiguration, they have achieved national recognition and now stage two to three full length theatrical productions each year in various theaters around New York.
Chinatown, (718) 831-1998, www. asianweb.net/~4seas/.

♦ SITES

Church of the Transfiguration
Masses in Mandarin, English and Cantonese, this copper-roofed Church, with the help of its adjoining school building, has served immigrant communities for almost two centuries. A relief plaque by the door displays the founder; Father Felix Varela, a Cuban-born priest who fled political persecution in Spain peers out from the façade of stately stone at the masses who've found solace in his sanctuary.
Chinatown, 29 Mott St. (bet. Mosco and Bayard), (212) 962-5157. J M N R Z 6 *to Canal St.* ♿

H.T. Dance Company
"Dance is not only doing your own good work," says director H.T. Chen, "it should have a social value as well." Since 1980, the company's small black-box theater has hosted the Arts Gate Center, which teaches dance, piano, and martial arts to children and adults year round.
Chinatown, 70 Mulberry St., 2nd Fl. (at Bayard St.), (212) 349-0126, www.htchendance.org. Open M-F 9am-6pm, Sa-Su 11am-4pm. Cash Only, J M N R Z 6 *to Canal St.*

Kim Lau Memorial Arch
This arch takes its name from Lt. Kim Lau, who ordered his crew to bail safely out of their faulty plane while he crashed it into the ocean to avoid the residential district below. Erected in 1962 to commemorate the Chinese-Americans who died in WWII, the arch stands at the south-east entry to historic Chinatown.
Chinatown, Chat-ham Sq. J M N R Z 6 *to Canal St.*

♦ MUSEUMS & CULTURAL CENTERS

Asian American Arts Center
As the name suggests, Asian-American artists have top billing at this thriving community arts center, which supports activities ranging from traditional dance performances to the journal on contemporary Asian-American artists, *Arts Spiral*. Around Chinese New Year, the Asia Folk Arts Festival brings traditional arts produced both here and abroad for display.
Chinatown, 26 Bowery St. (bet. Bayard and Pell Sts.), (212) 233-2154. Open Tu-F 12pm-6pm, Sa 4pm-6pm. Admission: free, J M N R Z 6 *to Canal St.*

Museum of Chinese in the Americas
No Chinatown experience is complete without a visit to this community-oriented museum, the first ever dedicated to the history of Chinese Americans. The award-winning permanent exhibition entitled "Where Is Home?" features a moving collection of memorabilia, photographs, and commentary exploring the diverse identities and experiences of Chinese Americans.
Chinatown, 70 Mulberry St., 2nd fl. (at Bayard St.), (212) 619-4785. Open Tu-Sa 12pm-5pm. Cash Only, Admission: $1-3, J M N R Z 6 *to Canal St.*

P.S. 23

Once a school building, P.S. 23 now serves as Chinatown's cultural center. It houses the Museum of Chinese in the Americas, H.T. Dance Company, United East Athletic Association, the Chinatown Health Clinic, Senior Citizen Coalition Center, the Young Lions, and the Chinatown Manpower Project. The ornate grillwork on the banister and large windows add a decorative touch to the institutional architecture.

Chinatown, 70 Mulberry St. (at Bayard St.), (212) 349-0126. J M N R Z 6 *to Canal St.*

♦ GALLERIES AND LIBRARIES

Chatham Square Library

Four stories of books – including the impressive Chinese Heritage Collection featuring classics – keep Chinatown's avid readers busy. Available resources include free computer workshops, art, poetry, pre-college information sessions, live performances, magazines, popular fiction, videos and

Friday-night Internet training classes.

Chinatown, 33 E. Broadway (at Catherine St.), (212) 673-6344. Open M, W 10am-6pm, F 12pm-6pm, Sa 10am-5pm. F *to E. Broadway.*

Nightlife

♦ BARS

169

Early in the night there's nothing special about this Chinatown bar. It's dark, has a pool table and not too full. Then the pool table vanishes, the DJ arrives, the place is packed and it makes sense why they have a velvet rope set up outside. 169 is a great place to dance for a long, long time. It's filled with a mix of hipsters and locals dressed down, getting down, having a good time.

Chinatown, 169 E. Broadway (at Essex St.), (212) 714-8149. Open M-Su 4pm-4am. MC, V, AmEx, F *to E. Broadway.* ♿

Winnie's

So what if it's a dark, low-ceilinged dive with baleful-looking dishes of chips and peanuts scattered across the bar; did you see the big video-karaoke screen in back? That's where the action is. Come to watch and hoot locals singing Asian chartbreakers. A dollar will buy you a song but one caveat: these folk are serious ka-raoke artists and won't hesitate to mock your braying.

Chinatown, 104 Bayard St. (bet. Mulberry and Baxter Sts.), (212) 732-2384. Open M-Su 8pm-4am. Cash Only, J M N R Z 6 *to Canal St.* ♿

♦ CLUBS

Fun

Everything it claims to be, Fun is packed with enough dazzling gee-gaws to make you woozy. Movie clips and live-feed video from the bathrooms project onto the walls. Cocktail waitresses are shuttled to the upper level in a lucite hydraulic lift. Using hidden microphones, the DJs sample crowd voices into their mix. On Tuesdays, hipsters come by to play video games on the 20-foot screen.

Chinatown, 130 Madison St. (at Pike St.), (212) 964-0303. MC, V, AmEx, Cover: None, F *to East Broadway.* ♿

> At the Southern end of Manhattan is the largest Chinese community in the Western hemisphere. The crooked streets of one of New York's oldest ghettos smell of salt and fish and orange peel. This booming, chaotic, little piece of China overflowing with new immigrants, is a remarkably self-contained neighborhood . . . To a degree almost impossible for outsiders to comprehend.
>
> —Gwen Kinkead

Little Italy

The "How you doing," the close talk, the talking with the hands. It's gone. The wise ass, the scammer, the old lady in black, the loud girls. Gone too. And, the mobster, with his entourage, he's not here either. Who knows if he ever was in Little Italy. He would have been outside the Ravenite Social Club, where John "the dapper don" Gotti hung out before he left for jail. The Ravenite's gone, a store now, with suits hanging from the window.

Chinatown approaches from the south and east. Soho stores loom from the north and west. The true Italian communities are in Bensonhurst, Brooklyn or Belmont in the Bronx. What's left is Mulberry Street, lined in Italian flags, lined with novelty shops, some pastry shops and really good restaurants. At Centre and Grand Streets is the old Police Headquarters whose huge dome was once Teddy Roosevelt's office when he was president of the police board in 1895. On West Houston, between Thompson and Sullivan, The Church of Saint Anthony of Padua honors its eponymous saint with an annual festival in June.

Things pick up during the San Genaro festival; dedicated to the patron saint of Naples. Mulberry's a paisan paradise then. Sausage, zeppoles, ices, fried calamari, fresh connoli's. A ball sends an abrasive clown into the pool of water below him. A girl clutches a stuffed bear she won under her arm.

For those ten days it's the Little Italy of Scorcese's *Mean Streets* or Coppola's *Godfather Part II*. The rest of the time it's just Mulberry Street, with the novelty shops and pastry shops. It's 11am. A waiter sits over a blackboard with colored chalk in his hands. Specials: Soup, minestrone; Appetizer, carpachio di monzo; Entrees, porcini mushroom ravioli, veal marsala, osso buco. He takes the sign outside, props it against the wall next to the entrance. Italy in Little Italy lives on.

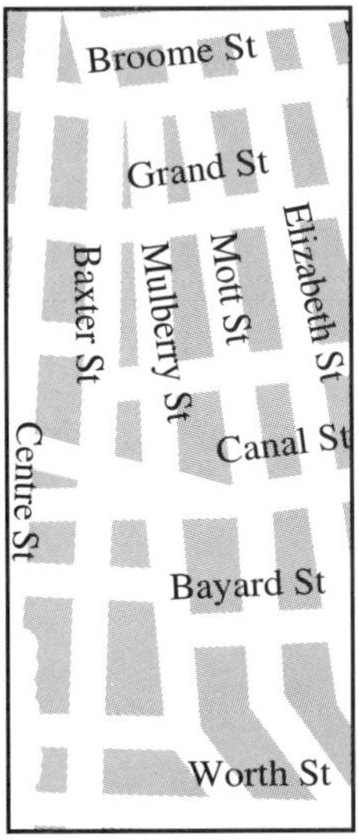

PLACES TO GO:

Luna's Ristorante
The best of Little Italy's many quality Italian restaurants.

Vig Bar
The first of New York's now many lounges still stands as an original to be imitated.

Ferrara Bakery and Café
America's oldest espresso bar and home of the best connoli this side of the Atlantic.

Dining

♦ RESTAURANTS

Buona Notte
Attractive space with seating choices in the front, dining room, and garden. Plenty of mirrors, so you can detect the fettuccine between your teeth before your date does. Nice presentation and delicately seasoned dishes.
Little Italy, 120 Mulberry St. (bet. Canal and Hester Sts.), (212) 965-1111. Open Su-R 12pm-11:30pm, F-Sa 12pm-12:30pm. MC, V AmEx, Entrees: $11-24, N R *to Canal St.,* ♿

Cafe Gitane
France approaches the border of Little Italy, armed with authentic bistro menu and aloof waiters. Perfect ambience for flipping through fashion rags, drinking a cappuccino, and the standard downtown sports of posing and people watching.
Little Italy, 242 Mott St. (bet. Houston and Prince Sts.), (212) 334-9552. Open M-Su 9am-12am. Cash Only, Entrées: $7-$10, N R *to Prince St.*

Luna's Ristorante
Come join The Family at this neighborhood hideaway in the heart of Little Italy where the decor is hip and non-pretentious. The aroma of fresh garlic sizzling in olive oil more than compensates for the lack of hyped-up atmosphere and perfunctory service. Still one of the best buys in Little Italy. *Little Italy, 112 Mulberry St. (bet. Canal and Hester Sts.), (212) 226-8657. Open Su-R 11am-12pm, F-Sa 12pm-2am. MC, V, AmEx,* J M N R Z 6 *to Canal St.* ♿

Positano Ristorante
The slender space and subdued décor make Positano seem less raucous than its Mulberry Street neighbors. A peaceful meal in the heart of Little Italy.
Little Italy, 122 Mulberry St. (bet. Canal and Hester Sts.), (212) 334-9808. Open M-Su 12pm-12am. MC, V, AmEx, N R *to Canal,* ♿

La Mela
The clashing furniture, Christmas lights, and out-of-season holiday decorations will make your head spin before you even drink anything. Like on a street vendor's cart, the menu is hand-scrawled on the outside walls.

Little Italy, 167 Mulberry St. (bet. Broome and Grand Sts.), (212) 431-9493. Open M-Su 12pm-11pm. MC, V, AmEx, Entrees: $31-50, B D Q *to Grand St.,* ♿

Puglia
Like Pasta? Like Elvis? Then you're in luck — spend your time at large communal tables, chugging wine with your new friends as an Italian Elvis works his magic on a little Casio keyboard in the corner. By the time you leave, you'll be arm in arm with half the restarant.
Little Italy, 189 Hester St. (bet. Mott and Mulberry Sts.), (212) 226-8912, www.littleitalynyc.com/puglia. Open M-Su 12pm-1am. MC, V, AmEx, DC, Entrées: $5-$10, J M N R Z 6 *to Canal St.* ♿

♦CAFES

Caffé Roma

Tiny marble-topped tables and an ancient, snorting espresso machine to whisk you into the back alleys of Rome while you enjoy old world cannoli like mama used to make, in portions bigger than mama ever imagined.

Little Italy, 385 Broome St. (at Mulberry St.), (212) 226-8413. Open M-Su 8am-12am. Cash Only, 6 to Spring St. ♿

Ferrara Bakery and Café

America's oldest espresso bar, Ferrara's has been around since 1892 and has been owned by the same family ever since. Everything is homemade!!! Best Conoli this side of Palermo.

Little Italy, 195 Grand St. (bet. Mulberry and Mott Sts.), (212) 226-6150, www.ferraracafe.com. Open M-Su 8am-12am. MC, V, AmEx, DC, D, JMNRZ6 to Canal St.

Shopping

♦ CLOTHING & SHOES

Built By Wendy

Originally called "Built by Wendy and Cake," two new designers teamed up together to make this store, each with one rack to display their collections. Now it's just Wendy displaying mens and womens contemporary clothing and accessories.

Little Italy, 7 Centre Market Pl. (bet. Broome and Grand Sts.), (212) 925-6538, www.builtbywendy.com. Open M-Sa 12pm-7pm, Su 12pm-6pm. MC, V, JMNRZ6 to Canal St. ♿

Calypso

Fun and funkily printed fabrics abound in this boutique which successfully attempts to bring an international-island aesthetic to Little Italy. While the inspiration for the clothing styles may be other-wordly, the prices mirror all-too-closely those of fashion boutiques only blocks away in SoHo. Paradise doesn't come cheaply, after all, for the true fashion elite.

Little Italy, 280 Mott St. (bet. Prince and Houston Sts.), (212) 965-0990. Open M-Su 11am-7pm. MC, V, AmEx, DC, NR to Prince St.

555 Soul, Inc.

The styles here are nothing if not original. The prices on the hip-hop clothes they sell are moderate to expensive, but most would say it's worth it. This store is a cut above the rest in hip-hop fashions.

Little Italy, 290 Lafayette St. (at Prince St.), (212) 431-2404. Open M-Su 11am-7pm. MC, V, AmEx, D. NR to Prince St. ♿

INA

This Little Italy clothing store features fabulous designer vintage for both men and women. They carry current collections, but the real treasures are their vintage designer items.

Little Italy, 21 Prince St. (bet. Mott and Elizabeth Sts.), (212) 334-9048. Open M-Su 12pm-7pm. MC, V, AmEx, NR to Prince St.

Find Outlet

The slashed prices on every tag send adrenaline through the hearts of any power-shopper. The service blends into the concrete floors and white walls – if you don't ask for help, you won't know they're there. A constantly changing inventory and regular Upper East Side customers, make this the trip when you're in the mood to spend or browse, better yet, run to the seasonal clearance sale.

Little Italy, 229 Mott St. (bet. Prince and Spring Sts.), (212) 226-5167. Open R-Su 12pm-7pm. 6 to Spring St.

> We [New Yorkers] were always the best and the strongest of the cities, and our people were vital to the teeth. Knock them down eight times and they would get up with that look in the eye which suggests that the fight has barely begun.
>
> —Norman Mailer

Also at:
Chelsea, 361 W. 17th St. (bet. Eighth and Ninth Aves.) (212) 243-3177. Open R-Su 12pm-7pm . A C E to 14th St.

♦ BOOKS, MAGAZINES & RECORDS

Temple Records
Here they feature enough dance music, on CDs and vinyl, to keep your party hopping for years. New releases and back-catalog records are available. Best of all you can preview your purchases before you buy.
Little Italy, 29 Ave. B (at 3rd St.), (212) 475-7552. Open M-Sa 1pm-9pm, Su 2pm-7pm. MC, V, AmEx, D, F to Second Ave. ♿

♦ GROCERY, GOURMET & SPECIALTY

Alleva Dairy, Inc.
Fourth-generation owner, Bob Alleva, serves up hot and cold sandwiches for under $5, authentic enough to keep the idea of Little Italy respectable. Mozzarella is made fresh daily at the oldest Italian cheese store in America.
Little Italy, 188 Grand St. (at Mulberry St.), (212) 226-7990, 1-800-4-ALLEVA. MC, V, AmEx, J M N R Z 6 to Canal St. ♿

Di Palo Fine Foods
Has everything you'll need when you're planning an Italian feast. The guys who work here are charming and will help you choose the ingredients: fresh mozzarella, sun-dried tomatoes, sausages, bread, etc. for what is sure to be a memorable meal.
Little Italy, 206 Grand St. (at Mott St.), (212) 226-1033. Open M-Sa 9am-6pm, Su 9am-3pm. MC, V, AmEx, J M N R Z 6 to Canal St. ♿

Italian Food Center
An extraordinary Italian grocery for everything from sandwiches to the ingredients you'll need to imitate your favorite Italian restaurant's risotto. They offer delivery throughout Manhattan, and they cater and have a mail order catalog service.
Little Italy, 186 Grand St. (at Mulberry St.), (212) 925-2954. Open Su 8am-6pm, M-Sa 8am-7pm. MC, V, AmEx, B D Q to Grand St. 🚲

♦ MISCELLANEOUS

Language
There is a definite mix of ethnicities in the products offered here, and everything is young and current. This store is all about being hip. They feature furniture, home accessories, and clothing from European, South American, and American designers.
Little Italy, 238 Mulberry St. (at Spring St.), (212) 431-5566. Open M-Sa 11am-7pm, R 11am-8pm, Sa 12pm-6pm. MC, V, AmEx, D. 6 to Spring St. ♿

Arts & Recreation

♦ SITES

Hester St.
A historic monument to the immigrant experience. The street is lined with tenement buildings, some of which are still inhabited. Hester St. used to be a part of Little Italy but with the recent expansion of Chinatown into the area, Hester Street has changed its ethnic alliance.
Little Italy/Chinatown, Hester St. (bet. Chrystie and Centre Sts.). B D Q to Grand St. ♿

Former site of the Ravenite Social Club
Until recently, 247 Mulberry St. (just below Prince St.), was the site of the Ravenite Social Club, a longtime Mafia hangout. Even though the building's façade had been bricked up to evade FBI surveillance, the Feds managed to bug the building and John Gotti was arrested there in December 1990. The ground floor's brick front wall was recently replaced with a shiny glass storefront, and is now a coffee shop.
Little Italy, 247 Mulberry St. (at Prince St.), 6 to Spring St.

♦ PARKS

Elizabeth Street Company Garden Sculpture
Most Manhattanites couldn't even fit these sculptures in their living rooms, let alone any "garden" to which they may have access. However, this patch of green off of Elizabeth Street is the perfect place to escape the bustle of Houston and to dream of the English countryside.
Little Italy, Elizabeth St. (bet. Prince and Spring Sts.), 6 to Spring St.

♦ MUSEUMS AND CULTURAL CENTERS

St. Patrick's Old Cathedral
Though it's difficult to tell now, the church was New York's first Gothic Revival structure, built in 1815 by Joseph Mangin. A fire in 1866 destroyed the historic façade, necessitating Henry Englebert's 1868 renovation. The parish consisted of a predominantly Irish immigrant population after the consecration of the new St. Patrick's Cathedral on Fifth Avenue.
Little Italy, 264 Mott St. (bet. Prince and Houston Sts.), (212) 226-8075, N R to Prince St. B D F Q to Broadway-Lafayette St. ♿

Nightlife

♦ BARS

Double Happiness
Friendly bartenders and an excellent mix of happy house and organic grooves attract a hip, young, and unpretentious crowd nightly to this basement bar. With ample floor-space for dancing, and hidden, candle-lit alcoves, Double Happiness is perfect either for that first date or for a night on the town with a group of friends. The bar menu features pan-Asian cuisine with an Italian accent.
Little Italy, 173 Mott St. (bet. Broome and Grand Sts.), (212) 941-1282. Open M-Su 6pm-4am. MC, V, B D Q to Grand St., N R to Prince St., 6 to Spring St.

Mare Chiaro Tavern
Ooh and aah at the huge photo of Frank Sinatra. Then go get yourself a drink at one of Little Italy's last genuine bars. Also known as "Tony's" in case you want to feel like a real local.
Little Italy, 176 Mulberry St. (bet. Grand and Broome Sts.), (212) 226-9345, Open M-Su 10am-2am. Cash Only, J M Z to Essex St., F to Delancey St. ♿

Vig Bar
Owner Russell has kept this lounge from getting too pretentious, despite the yuppie crowd that flocks in on weekends. Friendly bartenders and great DJs are Vig's greatest draws, and the dimly lit lounge areas are an added bonus. Weeknights are recommended for those looking to relax with a well-crafted Manhattan cocktail. Decent pick-up scene on weekends.
Little Italy, 12 Spring St. (bet. Elizabeth St. and The Bowery), (212) 625-0011. Open M-Su 5pm -4am. MC, V, AmEx, DC, D, N R to Prince St., 6 to Spring St.

How They Took Down the Mafia

Located at 247 Mulberry Street, the Ravenite Social Club was originally the Alto Knights Social Club and the place where old-time mobsters like Lucky Luciano conducted business. Carlo Gambino renamed it in 1957 after his favorite Poem, *The Raven*. About thirty years later, and after he over stepped his authority and bumped off Paul Castellano, the Ravenite was the place mobsters came to pay their respects to new boss, John Gotti.

No windows and strict security made FBI surveillance impossible, or so Gotti thought. After years of shaking their heads the FBI figured they could bug the club's backroom through one of the apartments above it and get the information they needed. They guessed right. John "the Dapper Don" Gotti had a big mouth and three conversations was all it took to put him away for life. His side man Sammy "the Bull" Gravano turned pigeon on just about every one else in the organization and like that a century of extortion and movie material disappeared.

The store that replaced the club.

Avant Art

(read before you head off for some aestheticism)

As of late, the gallery scene in New York City seems to be expanding and moving beyond the perimeters of the Chelsea scene in Manhattan and into the outer boroughs. This is not to say that the crop of Chelsea spaces don't discover new and original artists, as they have done in the past. In fact, Chelsea is the first spot to head to if you are easing into the realm of provocative contemporary American art.

Along West 22nd Street and West 24th Street between Tenth and Eleventh Avenue you may spot an amazing number of galleries that house sculpture, video art and digital photography. A gallery worth a second look is **White Columns**, a beautifully maintained space that consistently astounds both casual viewers and serious art critics. Don't expect any "what the hell is that" art here; you will find technique and creativity in various amalgamated forms.

It is often worth noting that the galleries in Chelsea change with artistic trends; for some reason or another they often all seem to be displaying the same sorts of exhibits at the same time. Browse these galleries until you get the gist of their exhibitions and expand into other neighborhoods.

The **Gracie Mansion Gallery**, in the West Village, houses quirky and colorful sculptures and paintings that may hold some universal, if kitschy, appeal. Some galleries leave you with absolutely no feeling of the gallery or the artist's historical importance; Gracie Mansion Gallery has moved all over the Manhattan island and remains an integral forum for artists to display their work. It remains true to its Warhol, Haring and Basquiat roots by promoting artists with an upstanding repertoire.

The new arts community is in two areas in Brooklyn: D.U.M.B.O. (Down Under

Manhattan Bridge Overpass) and Williamsburg. Expect dynamic performance and installation art in architecturally stimulating warehouse-type galleries, like **GAle GAtes et al.** and the **Galapagos Art and Performance Space**. These galleries have diverse exhibitions that deal with traditional mediums like painting and sculpture.

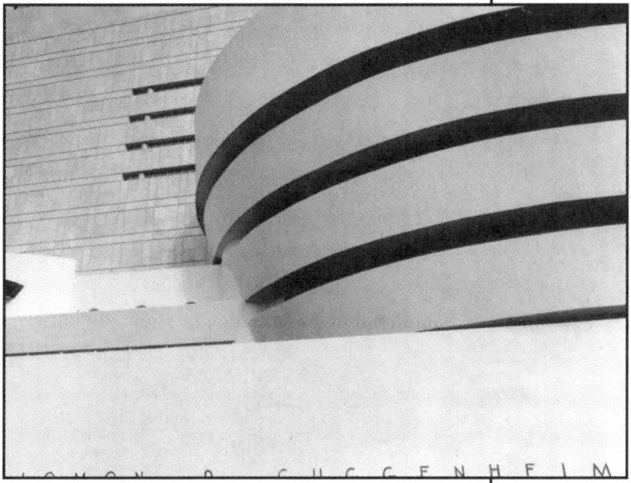

However, you can also venture into the digital world of art through some exhibitions with tweaked photos, experimental film installations and various other screenings. Meet your local favorite artist at the post-exhibition art scene; you can have a drink with them at the numerous bars around the area devoted to hosting such crowds.

Now that you're up-to-date with the hippest stuff in town you can scale back and venture into museum territory. The **Brooklyn Art Museum** offers tours, and has in the past provided many of its visitors endless amusement by showcasing dung-covered art. Although that exhibition is gone, in its place have been eclectic exhibitions, like the audio-visual history of rap music and hip-hop culture.

Other options abound upon a return trip to midtown Manhattan: the Museum Mile and its vicinity are home to the **Modern Museum of Art (MOMA)**, the **Guggenheim Museum** with its many floors (often devoted to one relentlessly detailed exhibit), and the **Whitney Museum**. These spots also offer guided tours and house the likes of Matisse, Kandinsky, Pollock, Balthus, Rothko ...you get the picture.

If you are itching to gaze at some Rembrandt or some vintage-wine caliber art after the rambunctious and heady samplings of the Chelsea galleries, go to the **Metropolitan Museum of Art**. A bit of the old classics never gave anyone a head-banging hangover; so do not miss this spot and its partner museum, **the Cloisters** at Fort Tryon Park (with its incredible medieval tapestries.) Avoid the afternoon clatter of schoolchildren and go on a weekday morning. Did I mention Chelsea? Go there, but dare to venture in other directions. Art awaits.

Lower East Side

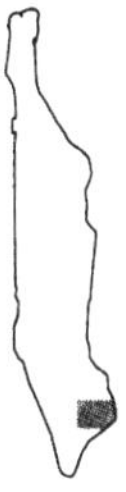

In 1890, Jacob Riis entered the tenements the Lower East Side was most infamous for with a camera. At the time the tenements were home to the most overpopulated neighborhood in the world--five story firetraps, of mostly Jewish immigrants, with an infant mortality rate of 40 percent. Riis's book, *How the Other Side Lives*, was the first of many rallying cries for housing reform that started in New York and affected the whole country. Riis concluded that after seeing the Lower East Side, "you shall come away agreeing with me that, humanly speaking, life there does not seem worth living."

But while the Lower East Side's legacy is one of poverty, its history is as the most concentrated center of Jewish culture in the United States. Yiddish Theater flourished along Second Avenue, area newspapers grew into forums of intellectual debate, and many performers like George Gershwin, Irving Berlin and the Marx Brothers cut their teeth here.

Now the Lower East Side is a center of Puerto Rican culture and many of the old synagogues have been converted to churches. Near the Williamsburg Bridge it's all red- and yellow-bannered bodegas. Many play cards and dominoes on the sidewalk, salsa pours out of cars and windows.

On Ludlow and Orchard Streets it's some of the hippest bars in Manhattan. Some are upscale, but most don't have the gentrified feel of a couple blocks north. Meyer Lansky's old speakeasy, now the Lansky Lounge, on Norfolk, is a trip back to the days when every man, no matter the age, woke up and put on a suit. Ratner's, the deli attached to Lansky Lounge, Katz's Delicatessen, and Kossar's Bakery, are a testament to a Jewish presence that still lingers.

Drugs and other criminal activity hit the neighborhood hard in the 70s, and locals had to pool their strength and resources in order to reclaim the "Loisaida." The Clemente Soto Vélez Cultural Center is testament to the neighborhoods new found stability and champions local Hispanic culture with its theaters, art galleries, and studios for local artists. Thanks to their efforts, combined with those of local block associations, the crime rate and drug traffic have plummeted. More than the two villages above it, the Lower East Side is the place where the working class mingle with the artistic and everywhere, something beautiful comes out of it.

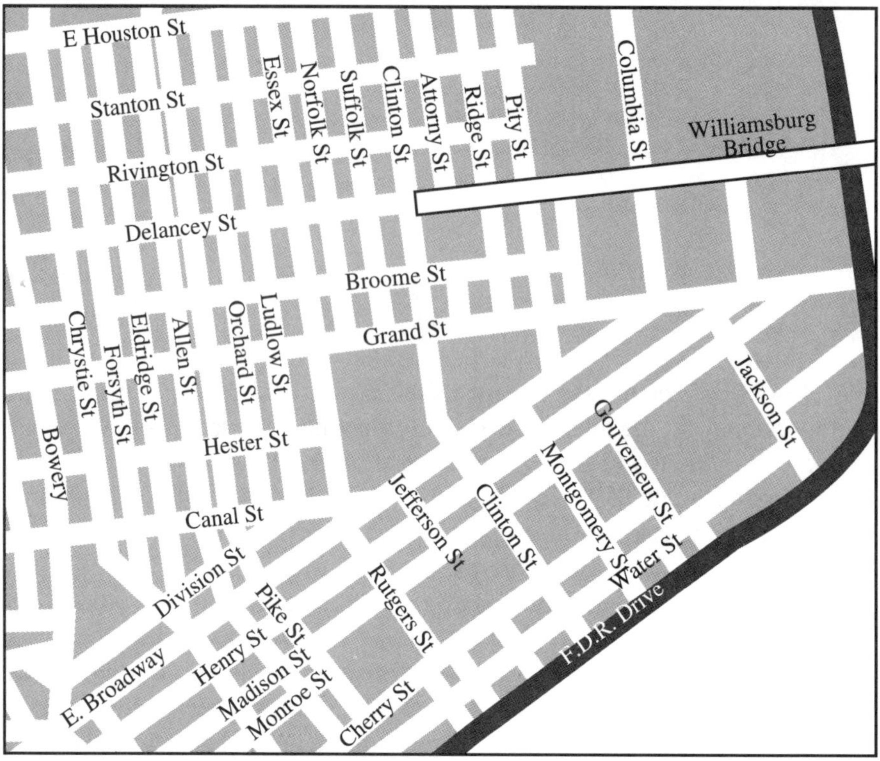

Dining

♦ RESTAURANTS

Casa Mexicana

The food isn't bad and there's a club in the basement, but it's a tad overpriced, and there's not much of a scene. Besides, what's a Mexican restaurant without margaritas?

Lower East Side, 133 Ludlow St. (bet. Rivington and Stanton Sts.), (212) 473-4100. Open M-Su 11am-2am. MC, V, D, AmEx, DC, Entrees: $16-22, F *to Second Ave.* ♿

Castillo de Jagua

A homely but decent Dominican dive in the heart of Loisaida, this place pleases with rice & beans, fried plantains, cafe con leche, and fresh squeezed O.J. served to the beat of loud salsa music.

Lower East Side, 113 Rivington St. (bet. Ludlow and Essex Sts.), (212) 982-6412. Open M-Su 8am-12am. Cash Only, F *to Delancey St.,* J M Z *to Essex St.* ♿

Grilled Cheese

All kinds of combinations of grilled cheese imaginable here, and they're all priced to go. The place is very small, but how long does it take to make and eat a grilled cheese, anyway?

Lower East Side, 168 Ludlow St., (212) 982-6600. Open M-Su 11am-11pm. Cash only, Entrees: $2-$8, F *to Second Ave.* ♿

Katz's Delicatessen

Steaming pastrami, corned beef sandwiches and other artery-clogging delicacies await at this cavernous, superior (non-Kosher) delicatessen, where yellowing paint and curling posters tell patrons to "Send a salami to your boy in the army" Nothing much has changed here in the last 50 years. A dollar tip to one of the gruff, portly attendants behind the counter will beget a sandwich big enough to feed a family of 5.

Lower East Side, 205 E. Houston St. (at Ludlow St.), (212) 254-2246. Open Su-T 8am-10pm, W-R 8am-11pm, F-Sa 8am-3am. MC, V, AmEx, Entrées: $5-$15, F *to Second Ave.* ♿

Le Pere Pinard

This charming French restaurant in the Village might very well have been transported from the south of France, waitstaff and all. Bare wooden tables and eclectically decorated stucco walls add to the rustic, French country ambience but hardly hint at the sophisticated food to come. Especially

PLACES TO GO:

Meow Mix
The hippest and most well known of New York's lesbian bars.

Sammy's Roumanian
Vodka by the bottle and the sort of food that warrants a catherization.

Tonic
Some of the finest sit down and be swept away music in the country.

Grilled Cheese
Every kind of grilled cheese sandwich, from the, "I never thought of that," to the "downright wrong."

delicious are the Raw Tuna and Ginger in Soy Sauce, the Shrimp, Mango, and Asparagus Salad, and the delightfully gooey Chocolate Valrona Cake with coconut sorbet.
Lower East Side 175 Ludlow St. (bet. Houston and Stanton Sts.), (212) 777-4917. Open M-F 5pm-12am, Sa-Su 11am-am. AmEx, Entrees: $12-$18, F *to 2nd Ave.*

Oliva
Oliva – a Spanish gem of a restaurant, where waiters greet regulars with a peck on the cheek – is the perfect spot to dine with a date or an intimate friend. Expect romantic ambience with slow groovy music, chosen by the manager (a local DJ). The food is impeccably presented and savory: choose from an excellent daily selection of seafood and paella on Sundays and Mondays, as well as the sinfully sweet dessert wines. You might leave with your wallet a bit lighter, but you'll be smiling.
Lower East Side, 161 E. Houston St. (at Allen St.), (212) 228-4143. Open M-Su 12pm-4pm, M-F 5:30pm-12am, Sa-Su 5:30pm-1am. AmEx, Entrées: $10-$20, 2 *to Houston St..*

Ratner's
Ratner's has lost its completely kosher menu, but patrons still come for the friendly atmosphere. In its heyday, Ratner's was the place to eat gefiltefish and matzoh balls; today, you'll find hamburgers alongside tasty cheese and pineapple blintzes. For a taste of the original menu, sample the appetizer platter with eggplant and whitefish. The vegetarian cutlet is also worth a taste. Do expect heaping portions of everything!
Lower East Side, 138 Delancey St, (212) 677-5588. Open Su-F 8am-7pm, Sa 8am-4pm. MC, V, AmEx, D, Entrées: $8-$15, F J M Z to Delancey St.

Sago's
This Moroccan restaurant should no longer be a secret; the whole world should know how good this place is. Suggestion: just have one of the pleasant waiters do the ordering for you. She'll probably want you to have some Moroccan wine, get it-it's sweet, goes down easy and compliments the food perfectly. Maybe you'll have a beet salad, or some trout or just a steak; it's all good. Thursdays there's a belly dancer-tassels, beads, smiling-so beautiful the show's worth it if for some unexplainable reason the food isn't.
Lower East Side, 19 Clinton St. (bet. Houston St. and Stanton Ave.), (212) 614-8817. Open Su-R 11am-12am, F-Sa 11am-1am. V, MC, Entrees: $14-$20 F *to Second Ave.*

Sammy's Roumanian
This bustling and lively restaurant hosts rich meals and a loud Yiddish band. Locals and other New Yorkers, none of

whom are dieting, frequent the place. Red meat is a featured menu item. Chopped liver, and lots o' vodka are popular as well.

Lower East Side, 157 Chrystie St. (at Delancey St.), (212) 673-0330. Open Su-W 4pm-10pm, R-Sa 4pm-11pm. MC, V, AmEx, Entrées: $20-$27, F *to Delancey St.,* J M Z *to Essex St.*

Tonic

Natural light pours in through the skylights of this cavernous space, as patrons feast on cheap, eclectic café fare. A former Lower East Side kosher winery, Tonic has a performance space in back, encircled in red velvet; avant-garde and experimental films are played on Monday nights. Most endearing feature is the downstairs cocktail lounge with circular booths built within 2,500-gallon hardwood wine casks.

Lower East Side, 107 Norfolk St. (bet. Delancey and Rivington Sts.), (212) 358-7503, www.tonic107.com. Open M-W 8am-12am, R-Sa 10am-2am. Cash Only, Entrées: $5-$12 J M Z *to Essex St.,* F *to Delancey St.*

Torch

This supper club was one of the first restaurants to descend on the now popular Ludlow strip. Delight in the South American-influenced French cuisine and nightly torch performances, or linger in the lounge area with a cocktail and smoke in hand.

Lower East Side, 137 Ludlow St. (bet. Rivington and Stanton Sts.), (212) 228-5151, www.torchrestaurant.com. Open Su-R 6pm-1:30am, F-Sa 6pm-4am. MC, V, AmEx, DC, Entrées: $10-$20, J M Z *to Essex St.*

Triple Eight Palace

After taking the escalator to the threshold of this Hong Kong extravaganza, you understand how they derived the "palace" part of the name. The multi-roomed restaurant assumes the air of a circus, with families chattering over fried and steamed noodles, shrieking toddlers playing chicken with rolling dim sum carts, and tables of heated woks threatening diners with third-degree burns. The dumplings, buns, and shellfish are all excellent.

Lower East Side, 88 E. Broadway (under the Manhattan Bridge), (212) 941-8886. Open M-Su 8am-10pm. MC, V, AmEx, DC, D, Entrées: $10-$18 F *to East Broadway.*

Shopping

♦ CLOTHING & SHOES

Cherry

All the vintage clothing from the '30s to early '80s is "classy," "elegant," "sexy," and "far out." There is a heavy emphasis on '60s and '70s minimalist styles from swimsuits to night-wear, plus designer pieces by Gucci, Bob Mackie and Rudi Gernreich (a radical '60s designer). You can also find "space-age biomorphic design" furniture and home accessories such as lamps, phones, speakers, and sculpture.

Lower East Side, 185 Orchard St. (bet. Houston and Stanton Sts.), (212) 358-7131, www.erols.com/hotcherry. Open Su-R 1pm-7pm, F-Sa 1pm-11pm. MC, V, AmEx, D, F to *Second Ave.*

TG-170

The most sophisticated of the small boutiques on the Ludlow strip features simple dresses, skirts, and tops in subtle but fashionably retro designs, as well as "phat" bags and wallets; gentrification hasn't hit the relatively cheap prices yet.

Lower East Side, 170 Ludlow St. (bet. Houston and Stanton Sts.), (212) 995-8660, www.tg170.com. Open M-Su 12pm-8pm. MC, V, AmEx, F *to Second Ave.*

♦ BOOKS, MAGAZINES & RECORDS

Bate Records

This thirty-year-old music store carries everything from the hottest new releases to the obscure Latin music you've been searching for. Their extensive catalog selection of music is sure to please.

Lower East Side, 140 Delancey St. (bet. Norfolk and Suffolk Sts.), (212) 677-3180. Open M-Su 10am-7pm. MC, V, AmEx. F

to Delancey St. ♿

♦ GROCERY, GOURMET & SPECIALTY

Economy Candy

Calling itself a "nosher's" paradise on the Lower East Side, this is the best discount store in the city for penny candy, imported chocolates, nuts, sweets, and gourmet savories like mustards, chutney, tea, and spices. Try their dense, chewy, pistachio-laden Turkish delight, the most authentic this side of Byzantium.

Lower East Side, 108 Rivington St. (bet. Essex and Ludlow Sts.), (212) 254-1832, www.economycandy.com. Open Su-F 8:30am-6pm, Sa 10am-5pm. MC, V, AmEx, J M Z *to Essex St.,* F *to Delancey St.* ♿

Hoi Sing Seafood

Be wary of the language barrier, Cantonese is what orders are communicated in. They do carry very good fish, so if your Cantonese is rusty simply extend your index finger and point at your selection until it arrives.

Lower East Side, 126 E. Broadway (at Catherine St.), (212) 964-9696. Open M-Su 9am-6pm. Cash Only, F *to E.ast Broadway.*

Moishe's Kosher Bakeshop

One of a dying breed of old-school Jewish bakeries in the city, Moishe's kosher bakeshop carries all the Jewish goodies, from challah to babke. Enough to make your toughest Babushka smile.

Lower East Side, 181 E. Houston St. (bet. Orchard and Allen Sts.), (212) 475-9624. Open Su-R 7am-6pm, F 7am-4pm. Cash Only. F *to Second Ave.*

♦ MISCELLANEOUS

New York Adorned

The hottest body art in the city is created at New York Adorned. Their jewelry selection is extensive, too, featuring handmade baubles from around the world.

Lower East Side, 47 Second Ave. (bet. 2nd and 3rd Sts.), (212) 473-0007. Open Su-T 1pm-9pm, F-Sa 1pm-10pm. MC, V, AmEx, D. F *to Second Ave.*

Fine and Klein

Featuring the largest selection of leather handbags in the United States, you're sure to find something appealing at Fine and Klein. If for some absurd reason you can't find a purse try a wallet, gloves or anything else from their collection.

Lower East Side, 119 Orchard St. (bet. Delancey and Rivington Sts.), (212) 674-6720. Open Su-F 8:30am-4:30pm. MC, V, AmEx, D, F *to Delancey St.*

Arts & Recreation

♦ LEISURE

Hamilton Fish Recreation Center/Pool

Just $25 per year buys membership to this and many other municipally run pools and fitness centers around the city.

Historic Synagogues

Bialystoker Synagogue

A former church and hiding place of runaway slaves, purchased and converted into a synagogue by the Bialystoker Jews in 1905. It is now designated a New York City Landmark and listed on the National Register of Historic Places.

Eldridge Street Synagogue

The prettiest of the historic synagogues, Eldridge Street boasted a congregation of 1,000 at the turn of the century. Though smaller now the congregation still stands. A Sabbath or holiday service has not been missed since it was built in 1887.

Angel Orensanz Cultural Center

Built in 1849-50, this is the oldest surviving building in New York City built specifically as a synagogue, and the first on the Lower East Side.

Don't expect state-of-the-art equipment or classes; just a workout without an attitude.
Lower East Side, 128 Pitt St. (at E. Houston St.), (212) 387-7687. Open M-Su 8am-9pm. Cash Only, F to Second Ave.

♦ PERFORMANCE

Collective Unconscious
Every possible configuration of campy art and anti-art event takes place at this downtown performance space. The hip, tongue-in-cheek crowd takes nothing seriously — especially not the art world. Popular open mike at Reverend Jen's Anti-Slam, Wednesday nights.
Lower East Side, 145 Ludlow St. (bet. Stanton and Rivington Sts.), (212) 254-5277, www.collective.weird.org. Cash Only, F to Second Ave. ♿

Nada
A storefront theater that in a few short years has acquired a wide-ranging reputation, including an Obie award. Catch one woman stand up comedy or something more serious almost every night.
Lower East Side, 167 Ludlow St. (bet. Houston and Stanton Sts.), (212) 420-1466. Cash Only, F to Second Ave ♿

Surf Reality
"Anything can happen here," boasts one of the regulars at this zany alternative comedy space. The tiny, makeshift stage hosts acts too silly or outrageous for the mainstream comedy circuit. New York's most bizarre performers turn out for Faceboyz Open Mike, Wednesdays, 8pm-3am; $3 to sign up and perform. Once a woman pulled an onion out of her vagina.
Lower East Side, 172 Allen St., 2nd Fl. (bet. Stanton and Rivington Sts.), (212) 673-4182, www.surfreality.org. Cash Only, F to Second Ave.

♦ PARKS

East River Park
Every Saturday and Sunday in the warmer months, the park fills up with families from the nearby projects who come here to barbecue, fish , play ball, bike, or just hang out in the shadow of Williamsburg Bridge. A walk through this riverside park reveals the romantically derelict urban landscapes of industrial Brooklyn. Don't venture here after dusk or on rainy days, when it can get a little sinister.
Lower East Side, Montgomery to 12th Sts. (E. of E. River Dr.), J M Z to Essex St. F to Delancy St. ♿

Seward Park
The first municipal park in the country to be made a permanent playground now has good-sized baseball field, four handball courts, a basketball court, a play area for little kids and a sitting area for the parents and pedestrians. Neighborhood kids flock to the place on weekends, so prepare for screams of joy and the occasional scraped knee.
Lower East Side, Canal St. (at Essex St.), www.nycparks.org. F to E. Broadway. ♿

♦ MUSEUMS & CULTURAL CENTERS

Angel Orensanz Foundation Center for the Arts
This neo-Gothic building with its spectacular vaulted interior and great doors is the oldest synagogue in New York City and was the first synagogue in LES. Spanish sculptor Angel Orensanz bought the synagogue in 1986 and converted it into a hub of education and culture in New York City. Many well-established institutions and independent artists develop educational and artistic projects here, and use the center for theatrical events, gallery shows and special events. A small congregation still worships in the basement.
Lower East Side, 172 Norfolk St. (212)529-7194. Call for admission (varies), F to Delancey St.

Eldridge Street Synagogue
Eastern European Jews erected the Lower East Side's first large-scale building in 1887. With its multi-hued stained glass window, brilliant frescoes and intricate woodwork, the synagogue stood out for many years amidst the notorious Lower East Side tenements. It fell into disrepair during hard times, but in recent years, the Eldridge Street Project

So please when I die . . .
Keep me nearby
Take my ashes and scatter
them thru out
The Lower East Side . . .
—Miguel Pinero,
A Lower East Side Poem

has made significant renovations.
Lower East Side, 12 Eldridge St. (bet. Canal and Division Sts.), (212) 219-0888, J M Z *to Essex St.* F *to Delancey St.*

First Roumanian-American Congregation
A former Methodist Church turned synagogue in 1882, the Roumanian has an elaborate sanctuary and is one of the largest synagogues in the city. This congregation is recognized internationally as a center for cantorial music. They conduct twice-daily, have Orthodox services every day of the year and have an annual "Community Seder" during Passover.
Lower East Side, 89 Rivington St., (212) 673-2835. F *to Delancey*

Lower East Side Conservancy
The LESC is a non-profit organization sponsored by the United Jewish Council of the Lower East Side. It promotes and preserves Jewish culture on LES, particularly historic synagogues. The Conservancy also offers guided minibus and walking tours of synagogues, local delis and restaurants with kosher food and judaica stores.
Lower East Side, 200 E. Broadway #3A, (212)598-1200. Open M-R 9:30am-5:30pm, F 9:30am-3pm. F *to E. Broadway.* ♿

Lower East Side Tenement Museum
The musuem chronicles the era when L.E.S. was the most oppressive and packed immigrant ghetto in the world. The building that houses this unique museum, built in 1863, predates existing housing laws. Bedrooms, typically eight square feet, common rooms of twelve by eleven feet, and apartments with no windows, running water or electric lights are on sad display.
Lower East Side, 90 Orchard St. (bet. Broome and Delancey Sts.), (212) 431-0233, www.tenement. org. Open Tu-F 1pm-4pm, Sa-Su 11am-4:30pm. MC, V, AmEx, Admission: $7-$9, J M Z *to Essex St.,* F *to Delancey St.*

♦ GALLERIES & LIBRARIES

Esso
If there is a mien that suggests I-just-became-legal at a drinking establishment, then the artistic counterpart that suggests I-just-finished-art-school reigns at this funky downtown space, where pop art is reworked for a generation that grew up on the Smurfs and Atari.
Lower East Side, 191 Chrystie St., 6th Fl. (bet. Rivington and Stanton Sts.) (212) 714-8192, www.essogallery.org. Open T-Sa 1pm-6pm. F *to Second Ave.* ♿

Seward Park Library
Fun for all ages, this library provides vintage films and a book collection for adults, and a picture book hour, where volunteers read aloud children's favorites.
Lower East Side, 192 E. Broadway (bet. Jefferson and Clinton Sts.), (212) 477-6770, www.nypl.org. Open M, R 12pm-8pm, T, W, F 10am-6pm, Sa 12pm-5pm. F *to E. Broadway.* ♿

Storefront for Art and Architecture
Only open from March to November, this unique international gallery favors abstract works, and often organizes shows along geographical themes. The name is derived from the gallery's unique facade.
Lower East Side, 97 Kenmare St. (bet. Mulberry and Lafayette Sts.), (212) 431-5795, www.storefront news.org. Open W-Sa 12pm-6pm. 6 *to Spring St.*

Nightlife

♦ BARS

Angel
Late night on weekends, this is a good place to go. The bouncers are mean, the lines big, lots of traffic. Inside it's all hip-hop and everybody grinding away until they're told to leave. The lounge upstairs is a good place to break commandments. Weekdays it's slower and more a bar between bars than a place to stay.
Lower Eastside, 174 Orchard St. (bet. Houston and Stanton Sts.), (212) 780-0313. Open Su-R 7pm-4am, F-Sa 6pm-4am. MC, V, F *to Second Ave.* ♿

Barramundi
The drinks never get sloppy at this mellow den, thanks to some clever bartenders. The back garden is a great place to sip white sangria, a caipirinha or one of many other specialty drinks they offer.
Lower East Side, 147 Ludlow St. (bet. Stanton and Rivington Sts.), (212) 529-6900. Open M-Su 7:30pm-4am. Cash Only, F *to Delancey St.*

Good World Bar
Tucked away down at Orchard Street's southern source, Good World is a true neighborhood bar in an unlikely setting. It draws a mixed crowd from Chinatown and the

> "Everyone ought to have a Lower East Side in their life."
> —Irving Berlin

Lower East Side.
Lower East Side, 3 Orchard St. (bet. Division and Canal Sts.), (212) 925-9975. Open M-Su 4pm-4am. MC, V, AmEx, F to E. Broadway, B D Q to Grand St.

Idlewild
Its airplane-fuselage design has gawking crowds flocking from all over. The gimmick gets old, but, in its favor, the music is eclectic, the atmosphere is loungy and a DJ spins nightly.
Lower East Side, 145 E. Houston St. (bet. First and Second Aves.), (212) 477-5005. Open T-Sa 8pm-indefinite. MC, V, F to Second Ave.

Kush
This relaxed, Middle Eastern-tinged lounge is a good place to, say, meet up with someone you used to date, who you haven't seen in a few years, but for whom you still have some feelings for and you think they might feel the same, too.
Lower East Side, 183 Orchard St. (Bet. Houston and Stanton Sts.), (212) 677-7328. Open T-Sa 6pm-4am, Su-M 8pm-4am. F to Second Ave.

Lansky Lounge
A 20s gangster theme with zoot-suited doormen leading you down a long corridor and through two doors so that when you walk in you really feel like you're in a bar whose existence is illegal. Martinis are the size of a baby's head and there's pretty good food to boot.
Lower Eastside, 104 Norfolk St. (bet. Delancey and Rivington Sts.),(212) 677-9849, lanskylounge.citysearch.com. Open M-Su 6pm-4am. MC, V, AmEx, F to Delancey St.

Ludlow Bar
This dependably cool bar stakes all its seating on minimalist couches. The pick-up scene, however, is most robust around the pool table.
Lower East Side, 165 Ludlow St. (bet. Houston and Stanton Sts.), (212) 353-0536. Open M-F 6pm-4am, Sa-Su 7pm-4am. MC, V, AmEx, F to Second Ave.

Luna Lounge
Lively swarms of boho kids populate this cavernous bar. The front room is eminently nondescript, but if you can push through the back room you have a pretty good chance of catching a local rock act (and maybe a glimpse of rumored regular, Elliott Smith.)
Lower East Side, 171 Ludlow St. (bet. Houston and Stanton Sts.), (212) 260-2323, www.lunalounge.com. Open M-Su 4pm-4am. Cash Only, F to Second Ave.

Max Fish
Hipsters live it up at this bright and lively Ludlow standard, once a hotspot, now just comfortably cool. Play pool with the regulars or spend a week's wages on pinball while enjoying local artists' work hanging on the walls.
Lower East Side, 178 Ludlow St. (bet. Houston and Stanton Sts.), (212) 529-3959, www.maxfish.com. Open M-Su 5:30pm-4am. Cash Only, F to Second Ave.

Meow Mix
Cool kids of all persuasions are welcome at this campy and casual dyke bar. The hub of the queer art scene, it hosts everything from comedy to poetry to performance art. Pick up a calendar, and, if you're lucky, one of the cute, pierced and well-tattooed chicks.
Lower East Side, 269 E. Houston St. (at Suffolk St.), (212) 254-0688, www.meowmixchix.com. Open M-R 7pm-4am, F 5pm-4am, Sa-Su 3pm-4am. Cash Only, F to Second Ave.

Motor City Bar
"Professional creative types" too old to be carded flock to this unlikely Detroit theme bar far south of Houston. The vehicular bric-a-brac adorning the walls may strike some as a little corny. Slicker and a little less funky than other joints in these parts, Motor City is favored by locals "cuz there's elbow room."
Lower East Side, 127 Ludlow St. (bet. Rivington and Delancey Sts.), (212) 358-1595. Open M-Su 4pm-4am. Cash Only, J M Z to Essex St., F to Delancey St.

Orchard Bar
This narrow little strip of nightlife real estate supports a thriving weekend pick-up scene. The music is usually more intelligent than the crowd, but it's a good time. Dan and the other bartenders know how to throw a party nightly, and keep things going late with friendly service and stiff drinks.
Lower East Side, 70 Orchard St. (bet. Houston and Stanton Sts.), (212) 982-BABY. Open M-Su 6pm-4am, MC, V, AmEx, N R to Prince St.

Swim
There's not much seating or, for that matter, much space at all. Still, Swim's crowd of benign hipsters and good music (check out the Tuesday night party) make it worth a visit.

Lower East Side,146 Orchard St. (bet. Rivington and Stanton Sts.), (212) 673-0799. Open M-Su 7pm-4am. MC, V, AmEx, DC, D. Ⓕ *to 2nd Ave.*

Welcome to the Johnson's

Decorated like the Brady Bunch's rec room, WTTJ's is where the shabby-chic go to meet. There are strong drinks at the bar, and they're more for the whiskey-sour set than the martini people. The jukebox, stocked with classic rock and funk, is one of the city's best.

Lower East Side, 123 Rivington St. (bet. Essex and Suffolk Sts.), (212) 420-9911. Open M-Su 3pm-4am. Cash Only, Ⓕ to *Delancey St.*

♦ CLUBS

Chaos

Chaos stridently proclaims total gentrification to the LES. Don't come without a full wallet; this is a bottle club, which means you buy not the cocktail, but the whole fifth (prices start around $90). Seems this rule must encourage heavy drinking, as the chichi crowd is always eager to table-dance to the loud, conventional, house music.

Lower East Side, 225 E. Houston St. (at Essex St.), (212) 475-3200. MC, V, AmEx, Cover: $20-$25, Ⓕ *to Second Ave.*

The Sapphire Lounge

Drink before coming to this claustrophobic den. Sweaty fun awaits anyone who can shove their way to the middle of the dance floor. It's deserted on weeknights, though.

Lower East Side, 249 Eldridge St. (at Houston St.), (212) 777-5153. Cash Only, Cover: $3-$5, Ⓕ *to Second Ave.*

♦ MUSIC

Arlene Grocery

In its few years of existence, Arlene has quickly established itself as one of the premiere showcases for many New York-based independent labels. The bands play for free here to build a fan base, and the sound is great.

acoustic, pop, rock, ska

Lower East Side, 95 Stanton St. (bet. Ludlow and Orchard Sts.), (212) 358-1633, www.arlenegrocery.com. Open 6pm-4am. Cash Only, No Cover, Ⓕ *to Second Ave.*

Best and Worst Bar on Ludlow and Orchard Streets

The last five years have seen the super charged rise of Ludlow and Orchard Streets from junky haven to home of some of the hippest bars. These are the bookends of what lies in between.

Worst Bar

Max Fish

Though one of the first bars on Ludlow this place has become as fun as a family funeral. The tragically hip and the under age commiserate over nothing worth being a part of.

Best Bar

Angel

A little arrogant and real jiggy, this is the sort of dirty, anything can happen place you see in rap videos. Bring the Moet and lose the underwear.

Soho

Recently, lower Manhattan has seen the naming of mini-neighborhoods such as NoHo and NoLita. The process of gentrifying and identifying an area in this way started about 30 years ago with chi-chi SoHo. At that time the area South of Houston was simply seen as the southern edge of the Village; heading farther downtown, industry ruled until you hit the western fringe of Chinatown and then Wall Street.

Attracted by the cheap, huge, well-lit spaces, artists started moving into the area in the 60s. Word of mouth spread quickly, and a colony took root. Early SoHo pioneers liken the community's 'pitch-in-and-help' practice to barn raisings: With the help of friends, artists would install wiring, plumbing, and heating in non-residentially zoned spaces.

The buildings they moved into were legacies from the Civil War. Foundry owners had converted their stock to the production of building materials. The great cast-iron buildings they raised now mark this neighborhood as one of New York's first and finest architecturally rich enclaves.

Eventually, galleries sprang up to showcase local artists work. Outsiders took note of the change, and bigger, pricier galleries opened. Today Broadway anchors a classy retail district of huge emporiums and the biggest names aren't on paintings but on clothing labels.

The gentrification's an old story though; Soho will never be what it was. Now it's the home of the most beautiful people in New York and while it might not be setting the trends in art anymore, it does in lifestyles. If you have a platinum card, are aloof and inaccessible, this is the place for you. Soho is Never, Never Land and while it might cost too much, it never looked so good.

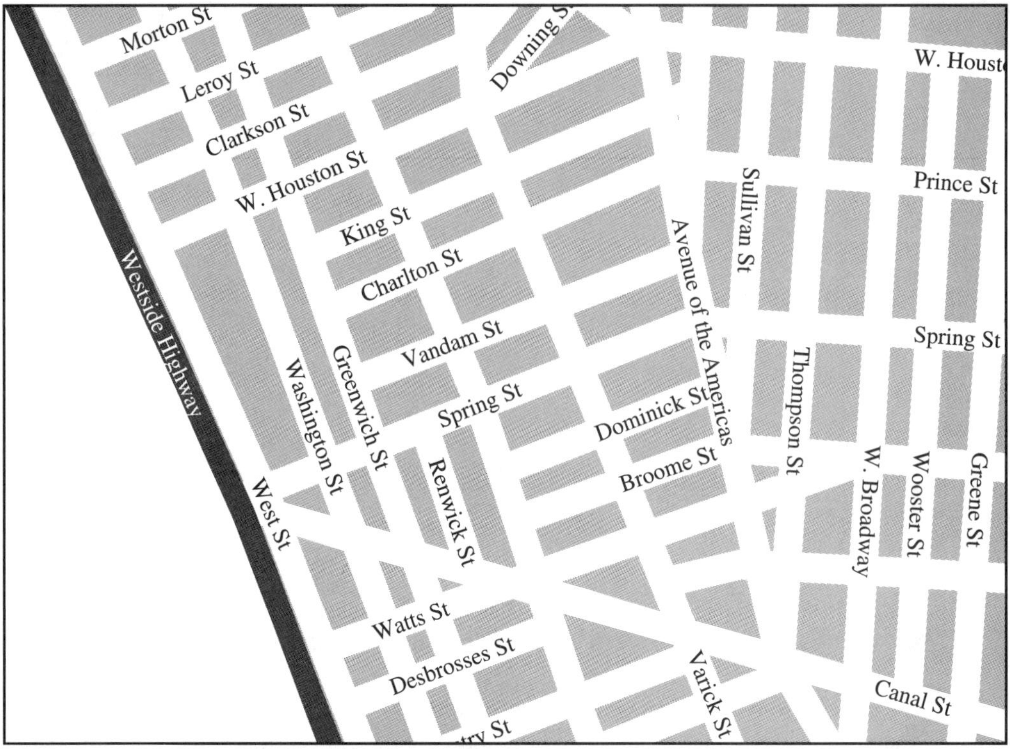

Dining

♦ RESTAURANTS

Alison on Dominick

Small, intimate, and appropriately nestled away in the relatively barren western edge of SoHo, this place is truly unique. The food is flawlessly prepared upscale French Bistro fare and perfectly matched ambience. Ideal for a romantic dinner.

SoHo, 38 Dominick St. (bet. Varick and Hudson Sts.), (212) 727-1188, www.alisondominick.com. Open M-R 5:15pm-10pm, F-Sa 5:15pm-10:45pm, Su 5:15pm-9pm. MC, V, AmEx, DC, Entrées: $28-$38, C E *to Spring St.*

Baluchi's

Named after Pakistan's Balochistan province, this bonafide Indian restaurant does justice to the sultry opulence for which the region is known. Numerous options will satisfy vegetarians, including pallak paneer and Basmati rice.

SoHo, 193 Spring St. (bet. Thompson and Sullivan Sts.), (212) 226-2828. Open M-F 12pm-3pm, 5pm-11pm, Sa 12pm-11:30pm, Su 12pm-10:30pm. MC, V, AmEx, DC, Entrées: $10-$14, C E *to Spring St.*

Bistro Margot

A French treasure hidden in SoHo, gourmet enough to satisfy the upper-crust, older patrons who don't mind the bloated prices. A surplus of two person tables and seductive lighting emphasize its potential as a date restaurant.

SoHo, 26 Prince St. (at Mott St.), (212) 274-1027, Open M-Su 11am-12am. AmEx, Entrées: $5-$13, 6 *to Spring St.,* B F D Q *to Broadway-Lafayette St.*

Blue Ribbon Sushi

Let the simple yet elegant modern Japanese decor draw you into this fashionable SoHo sushi haven and you shall be rewarded with yellowtail and tuna of melt-in-your-mouth freshness. Closed Mondays, the restaurant is open for dinner until 2am but accepts no reservations, so weekend waits can be long, especially taking into consideration the space's diminutive dimensions.

SoHo, 119 Sullivan St. (bet. Prince and Spring Sts.), (212) 343-0404. Open T-Su 4pm-2am. MC, V, AmEx, DC, D, Entrées: $20-$30, C E *to Spring St.*

The Cupping Room Cafe

A wonderful spot with an ambitious, if slightly pricey, brunch. Even at peak hours, there's plenty of space in the large, airy, main room, so the wait is never too long. Portions are generous; try the delicious Eggs Florentine and the variety of pancake options.

Soho was positively awash in hardwood floors, talked to plants, indoor swings, enormous record collections, hiking boots, conceptual artists, video communes, Art book stores, Art grocery stores, Art restaurants, Art bars, Art galleries, and boutiques selling tie-dyed raincoats, macramé flower pots, and Art Deco salad plates.

—Fran Lebowitz

SoHo, 359 W. Broadway (at Broome St.), (212) 925-2898, www. cuppingroomcafe.com. Open Su-R 8am-12am, F-Sa 24hrs. MC, V, AmEx, Entrées: $7-$15, ACE to Canal St.

Fanelli's

One of the last remnants of pre-gentrification SoHo. Everything about this place is unpretentious, from the spare decor to the sturdy pub-style food, which is what keeps it going strong as an alternative to all the other too chic and trendy restaurants in the neighborhood. Be prepared to wait; on weekends they're often packed for hours.

SoHo, 94 Prince St. (at Mercer St.), (212) 226-9412. Open M-Su 10am-2am. MC, V, AmEx, Entrées: $10-$12, NR to Prince St.

Jerry's

A longtime crowd pleaser, Jerry's still has a line out the door for weekend brunch. Try a plate of stellar tuna salad or citrus-marinated chicken — they're all the rage. This hot lunch spot draws a huge art crowd and plenty of celebrities while maintained a down-to-earth atmosphere.

SoHo, 101 Prince St. (bet. Greene and Mercer Sts.), (212) 966-9464. Open M-F 9am-11pm, Sa-Su 10:30am-5pm. MC, V, AmEx, Entrees: $9-$13, NR to Prince St.

Kin Khao

Don't be surprised to see a supermodel sitting down the bench from you here; this place is *very* trendy. However, the atmosphere isn't prohibitive to normal people and once you get inside, the waitstaff is unpretentious and the decor beautiful and comfortable. The food is Thai, and the quality isn't all that consistent; to be safe, stick to one of the noodle dishes that are always delectable.

SoHo, 171 Spring St. (bet. W. Broadway and Thompson St.), (212) 966-3939. Open M-Sa 5:30pm-12am, Su 5:30pm-11pm. MC, V, AmEx, Entrées: $11-$19, CE6 to Spring St.

Kitchen Club

Turquoise curtains, a huge checkered tile floor, and French doors which open out onto the street give Kitchen Club its unique atmosphere. Serving up Continental cuisine with a Japanese twist, this "friendly little place" is as eccentric on your palatte as it is on your eyes.

PLACES TO GO:

Spring Street at Night

If it's a weekend put on your best black and walk East to West on a bar hop of New York's trendiest lounges, clubs and bars.

Yohji Yamamoto

If you are going to go on this bar hop, stop here during the day and pick up all of your black needs, from tight pants to tighter underwear.

Don Hill's

End your night here. The underage and transvestites under one roof. It's good times 80s fun all over the place and a great place to dance.

SoHo, 30 Prince St. (at Mott St.) (212) 274-0025. Open T-Su 6pm-11pm. MC, V, AmEx, Entrées: $16-$22, N R to Prince St., 6 to Spring St.

La Poème

Inside the antique-laden dining room of chef Martine Abitbol's daytime home, aging poets and artists chat around a taffeta-covered table crowded with platters of steaming seafood. The Abitbol family's husky ambles across the dining floor toward the kitchen. Martine leaves her stove momentarily to ask customers how they are enjoying the hearty Tunisian and Corsican dishes.

SoHo, 14 Prince St. (at Elizabeth St.), (212) 941-1106. Open T-Su 11am-11pm. Cash Only, Entrées: $10-$15, N R to Prince St.

Le Gamin

A more successful stab than most at replicating a Parisian café, this neighborhood joint serves crepes, croque monsieur, quiche, and salads to a laid-back, lingering crowd. Family types mix with the downtown chic; the lack of a liquor license encourages people to bring their own beer or wine. A great stopover for a cappuccino while club-hopping or a good setting for more lengthy leisure and a latte. The French menu has English subtitles.

SoHo, 50 MacDougal St. (bet. Houston and Prince Sts.), (212) 254-4678. Open M-Su 8am-12am. Cash only, Entrées: $8-$10, C E to Spring St.

Le Pain Quotidien

The smell of freshly baked bread welcomes you to this cozy Belgian bakery/café featuring a giant communal wooden table and some of the flakiest croissants this side of the Atlantic. Everything from rustic baguettes to country loaves, for which European flour is specially imported, is masterfully prepared and baked on the premises in batches throughout the day. A delicious array of breakfast and lunch dishes are also served.

SoHo, 100 Grand St. (at Mercer St.), (212) 625-9009, www.painquotidien.com. Open M-F 7am-7pm, Sa-Su 8am-7pm. Cash Only, A C E to Canal St.

The Mercer Kitchen

At this cafe specializing in American provinical food, you can sit under the sidewalk on a Soho street in a glass encased dining room and watch people walking above.

SoHo, 99 Prince St. (at Mercer St.), (212) 966-5454. Open M-Su 7:30am-11am, 12pm-3pm, 5:30 pm-12am. MC, V, AmEx, Entrées: $25-$30, N R to Prince St.

Palacinka

"It's anything you want it to be," says co-owner Tariq, but really this BYOB café specializes in serving tired and trendy SoHo shoppers delicious French-style crepes as a light meal or dessert. It's worth a visit just for the unusual, but obviously trendy decor: a smattering of random antiques amid metal tables and chairs that can be easily positioned for a romantic meeting over a cup of coffee. Be prepared to sit a while — crepes are made to order.

SoHo, 28 Grand St. (bet. Sixth Ave. and Thompson St.), (212) 625-0362, Open M-Su 10am-11pm. Cash Only, Entrees: $6-$8, A C E to Canal St.

Balthazar

This SoHo gem already has a reservation line and a ten minute wait. Onlookers rave about the lofty bistro decor and surprisingly arrogance-free staff. The authentic French brasserie "looks just like Paris", and sounds like it, too.

SoHo, 80 Spring St. (bet. Broadway and Lafayette St.), (212) 965-1414. Open M-Su 7:30am-11:30am, M-F 12pm-5pm, Sa-Su 11:30am-3:45pm, MC, V, AmEx, Entrées: $20, 6 to Spring St.

Penang Malaysia

This lively, decked out Malaysian eatery is usually packed on weekends and rightfully so; the food is innovative and tasty and the crowd generally young and hip. To avoid a wait, try eating in the bar downstairs which features a lounge and live music.

SoHo, 109 Spring St. (bet. Greene and Mercer Sts.), (212) 274-8883, www.penangnyc.com. Open M-R 11am-12am, F-Sa 12am-1am, Su 12pm-11pm. MC, V, AmEx, DC, Entrées: $11-$20, N R to Prince St.

Rialto

First-time visitors are consistently wowed; the understated SoHo ambience and first-rate Continental food entice stunning neighborhood folks time and again. Feast on the Chef's Tasting Menu (a 3, 5, or 8 course meal), which includes a potato leek soup infused with roasted garlic, served in a demitasse cup. The staff shuffles back and forth to the magnificent garden out back.

SoHo, 265 Elizabeth St. (bet. Houston and Prince Sts.), (212) 334-7900. Open M-Su 11am-12:45am. MC, V, AmEx, DC, Entrées: $8-$18, N R to Prince St.

Zoë

About as good as SoHo gets: attentive waitstaff, elegant decor, and intricate yet subtle food all await you at this SoHo hot spot. The crowd is a pleasing mixture of downtown denizens and suited professionals on their way home from work. The crowd does get funkier as the evening wears on. Perfect for a romantic date.

SoHo, 90 Prince St. (bet. Broadway and Mercer St.) (212) 966-

6722. Open M 6pm-10:30pm, T-R 12pm-3pm, 6pm-10:30pm, F 12pm-3pm, 6pm-11pm, Sa 12pm-3pm, 5:30pm-11:30pm, Su 11:30am-3pm, 5:30pm-10pm. MC, V, AmEx, Entrées: $18-$28, N R *to Prince St.* ♿

♦ CAFES

Ceci-Cela

Homemade sorbet and café au lait evoke La Cote d'Azur at this charming patisserie perched on the edge of Little Italy. The chat room in back is oh-so-perfect for nibbling on petit-fours and playing post-structuralist salon.

SoHo, 55 Spring St. (bet. Mulberry and Lafayette Sts.), (212) 274-9179. Open M-R 10am-7pm, F-Sa 10am-10pm. MC, V, 6 *to Spring St.* ♿

Cybercafe

Spend serious quality time with computers. Options extend beyond basic Net access to the latest games and sophisticated design and desktop publishing programs. To top it all off, the café makes a mean mocha.

SoHo, 273 Lafayette St. (bet. Spring and Prince Sts.), (212) 334-5140, www.cybercafe.com. Open M-F 8:30am-10pm, Sa-Su 11am-10pm. MC, V, AmEx, DC, D, N R *to Prince St.* ♿

Once Upon A Tart

Delectable pastries, both savory and sweet, at lower prices than the standard coffeecakes served up by Manhattan's corporate chain espresso bars. Everything is made in their own bakery. Try a special that includes a tart and choice of salads.

SoHo, 135 Sullivan St. (bet. Houston and Prince Sts.), (212) 387-8869. Open M-F 8am-8pm, Sa 9am-8pm, Su 9am-6pm. MC, V, AmEx, D, C E *to Spring St.* 🚲

Shopping

♦ CLOTHING & SHOES

555 Soul

In 1989, designer Camella Ehlke gave the hip-hop crowd something that was finally funky enough for them to wear. Now that hip-hop's gone mainstream, her store is more popular than ever, featuring tees and baseball caps jazz-ed up with some of that downtown vibe.

SoHo, 290 La-fayette St. (bet. Houston and Prince Sts.), (212) 431-2404, www.triple 5soul.com. Open Su-F 11am-6:30pm, Sa 11am-7pm. MC, V, AmEx, D, B D F Q *to Broadway-Lafayette St.,* N R *to Prince St.* ♿

Afterlife

T-shirts reign at this trendy unisex shop. Next to its overpriced SoHo counterparts, Afterlife is surprisingly affordable. You might find a cute "Brooklyn" logo T-shirt, or a baggy one that sports a giant "NYC" plus many other colors and styles.

SoHo, 59 Green St. (at Broome St.), (212) 625-3167. Open M-F 10:30am-7pm, Sa-Su 10:30am-8pm. MC, V, AmEx, N R *to Prince St.*

agnès b.

Among the finest in smart, up-to-date women's wear, with a touch that makes you feel like Ingrid Bergman.

SoHo, 116 Prince St. (bet. Wooster and Greene Sts.), (212) 925-4649, www.agnesb.fr. Open M-Su 11am-7pm. MC, V, AmEx, N R *to Prince St.* ♿

Alice Underground

Behind the hippieish exterior is one of Manhattan's biggest and best vintage stores. Skip the bargain bins as there's usually a good reason why the items are being unloaded so cheaply, and shell out a little more for pants and jackets off the racks, where the finds can range from the fabulously unique to solid standards. An excellent selection of winter coats.

SoHo, 481 Broadway (bet. Grand and Broome Sts.), (212) 431-9067. Open M-Su 11am-7pm. MC, V, AmEx, N R *to Prince St.* ♿

Anna Sui

Rock 'n roll style meets the runway and boutique world in this small designer outpost. Leather pants hang alongside sequined dresses and the atmosphere is relaxed enough to allow for trying it all on without feeling conspicuous. It's expensive, but end-of-season markdowns are often high

Ghost, 1990

The renovated Soho loft of Patrick Swayze and Demi Moore's characters is home to the famous scene where Moore makes a pathetic excuse for a clay pot and a Righteous Brother's song is ruined. Aided by, funny for once, Whoopi Goldberg, the couple proves love can be so strong it defies death and make you cry in the process.

enough for a reasonable and well-deserved splurge.
SoHo, 113 Greene St. (bet. Spring and Prince Sts.), (212) 941-8406. Open M-Sa 11:30am-7pm, Su 12pm-6pm. MC, V, AmEx, N R *to Prince St.*

Anthropologie
The grown-up Urban Outfitters. Owned by the same people, with a similar variety of housewares and clothing for women, the bent here is more stylish than trendy, with lots of classic and basic pieces that are of high quality, but prohibitively priced at around $70 and up. The clearance racks generally yield some good finds though, and sometimes paying full price isn't so bad, since the clothes are unlikely to either fall apart or go out of style quickly.
SoHo, 375 W. Broadway (bet. Spring and Broome Sts.), (212) 343-7070, www.anthropologie.com. Open M-Sa 11am-8pm, Su 11am-6pm. MC, V, AmEx, D, C E *to Spring St.*

APC
Clothes so simple and perfect that you simultaneously wonder why they cost so much and how you've lived without them for so long. Classics like jeans and button-down shirts hover around the $100 range, so clasp your credit card tightly — it's hard to resist such flawless incarnations of old standards at any price.
SoHo, 131 Mercer St. (bet. Prince and Spring Sts.), (212) 966-9685, www.apc.fr. Open M-Sa 11am-7pm, Su 12pm-6pm. MC, V, AmEx, N R *to Prince St.* ♿

Betsey Johnson
In your face girly chic means Betsey's not afraid to flaunt lace alongside faux leather, or pair zebra stripes with fuschia fishnets. Straightforward, sexy slip dresses are surprisingly affordable on sale.
SoHo, 138 Wooster St. (bet. Prince and Houston Sts.), (212) 995-5048, www.betseyjohnson.com. Open M-Sa 11am-7pm, Su 12pm-7pm. MC, V, AmEx, N R *to Prince St.* ♿

Canal Jean Company
With its well-known checkered flag visible blocks away, this multilevel specialty in discount brand names (such as Levi's) carries more than enough merchandise to satisfy the picky shopper. Calvin Klein underwear, Lip Gloss dresses, and plenty of vintage clothes and jeans crowd the place. Check out the huge, overwhelming downstairs selection of used clothes.
SoHo, 504 Broadway (bet. Spring and Broome Sts.), (212) 226-3663, www.canaljean.com. Open M-F 9:30am-9pm, Su-Sa 10:30am-8pm. MC, V, AmEx, DC, D, N R *to Prince St.,* 6 *to Spring St.* ♿

Club Monaco
This Canadian Company has transformed New York. They have basics with a trendy kick. Check out their CMX sports line.
Soho, 121 Prince St. (bet. Greene and Wooster Sts.), (212) 533-8930, www.clubmonaco.com. Open M-Sa 11am-7pm, Su 12pm-6pm. MC, V, AmEx, DC, N R *to Prince St.*

Also at:
SoHo, 520 Broadway (at Spring St.), (212) 941-1511, www.clubmonaco.com. Open M-Sa 11am-8pm, Su 12pm-7pm. MC, V, AmEx, DC, N R *to Prince St.* ♿

Cynthia Rowley
Classic and simple designs, executed in extraordinary fabrics. The prices are relatively low for such an established designer, and much of the clothing comes in mix-and-match pieces, making it easy to have a sophisticated look that merges smoothly with your existing wardrobe.
SoHo, 112 Wooster St. (bet. Spring and Prince Sts.), (212) 334-1144, Open M-W, Sa 11am-7pm, R-F 11am-8pm, Su 12pm-6pm. MC, V, AmEx, N R *to Prince St.* ♿

D&G
Walking into D&G is a sight for sore eyes. This two floor unisex store features a variety of styles in colors like fushia, lime green, azure blue. For the more tame at heart there is also conservative wear like black pants and Khaki blazers. If you are looking for accessories, they also have their own line of belts, bags, and shoes. But be careful — like so many SoHo shops, the prices ain't cheap.
SoHo, 434 West Broadway (bet. Prince and Spring Sts.), (212) 965-8000. Open M-Sa 11am-7pm, Su 12pm-6pm. MC, V, AmEx,

DC, BDFQ to Broadway-Layayette St., NR to Prince St.

Each and Them
This dully lit store has great vintage clothing (never used!) and is the place to find vintage Lee's and Wrangler's.
SoHo, 216 Lafayette St. (bet. Spring and Broome Sts.), (212) 925-9699. Open M-Su 12pm-7pm. MC, V, AmEx, DC, D, 6 to Spring St.

INA (Women)
This designer consignment store features a big selection of women's clothing from their current collections. First-time shoppers fast become regulars to the cozy neighborhood store. Find designer items by Prada, Helmut Lang, Agnès b. and Joseph at 1/4 to 1/2 the regular retail price.
SoHo, 21 Prince St. (bet. Mott and Elizabeth Sts.), (212) 334-9048. Open Su-R 12pm-7pm, F-Sa 12pm-8pm. MC, V, AmEx, NR to Prince St., 6 to Spring St. ♿

John Fluevog
Possibly the hippest source of shoes in the city, a Fluevog can be spotted a mile away. Chunky platforms, combat-quality boots, and funky, offbeat colors are all well-represented; end-of-the-season sales can yield amazing bargains on the otherwise expensive footwear, usually priced at around $100.
SoHo, 104 Prince St. (at Mercer St.), (212) 431-4484, www.fluevog.com. Open M-Sa 11am-7pm, Su 12pm-6pm. MC, V, AmEx, D, NR to Prince St. ♿

Kate Spade New York
Neat and minimalist, in a variety of colors from basic black to bright green. A rising star, Spade's attraction is her simplicity of design. Simply timeless.
SoHo, 454 Broome St. (at Mercer St.), (212) 274-1991. Open M-Sa 11am-7pm, Su 12pm-6pm. MC, V, AmEx, 6 to Spring St.

Living Doll
Plenty of throwbacks to the "80s chic" à la Madonna at fair prices; perfect for young SoHo migrants on the east side from Broadway.
SoHo, 123 Crosby St. (bet. Prince and Houston Sts.), (212) 625-9410. Open M-F 11am-7pm, Su 11am-6pm. MC, V, AmEx, 6 to Bleecker St., NR to Prince St.

Marc Jacobs
This store offers a full selection of Jacobs' high-end designer clothing, for men and women. You're better off buying this hot designer's clothes here than in department stores because this store has a wider selection of sizes and styles.
SoHo, 163 Mercer St. (bet. Houston and Prince Sts.), (212) 343-1490. Open M-Sa 11am-7pm, Su 12am-6pm. MC, V, AmEx, DC, BDFQ to Broadway-Lafayette St. ♿

Where to Shop

Soho is the place to look good, which means if you're going to survive here you better have the clothes.

◆ Phat Farm
Russell Simmons opened this store eight years ago to much acclaim. The shorts cost $80, but they look good.

◆ Todd Oldham
MTV's "House of Style" turned this man's store into the place to go for progressive, cool, well-designed clothing.

◆ Afterlife
These aren't the t-shirts that sit in your bureau for eighteen years, these are the t-shirts that replace the clothes you're wearing now and never leave.

◆ D&G
Two floors of top of the line clothes. D&G's fabrics are the sort that will last you ten years or, if you go with the trends, be in the trash by next season.

◆ John Fluevog
Make-up for your feet. If your feet have a complex about the way they look this is how to make them feel better about themselves.

◆ Betsey Johnson
Girly, girly stuff. Women walk out of Betsey Johnson looking like a character from a Japanese anime cartoon.

Miu Miu
Prada's second breakthrough strikes a more contemporary look geared toward a younger crowd.
SoHo, 100 Prince St. (bet. Mercer and Greene Sts.), (212) 334-5156. Open M-Sa 11am-7pm, Su 12am-6pm. MC, V, AmEx, NR to Prince St.

Nicole Miller
This designer is known for her detailed bold silk patterns. They are on everything from eyeglass cases to bow ties to umbrellas. She carries dresses for all occasions with interesting fabrics. While you are there, be sure to check out the sale rack.
SoHo, 134 Prince St. (bet. West Broadway and Wooster St.), (212) 343-1362, www.nicolemiller.com. Open M-Sa 11am-7pm, Su 12pm-6pm. MC, V, AmEx, CE to Spring St., NR to Prince St.

Occitane
The moment you step on the tiled floor of this Provencal boutique, the lavender smells of the south of France surround you. An international chain devoted to body products, the graceful display includes milled soaps, lotions and shampoos, with the staple being moisturizing products made form the plant extract Shea Butter. Think of Occitane as an upscale Body Shop.
SoHo, 146 Spring St. (bet. Wooster and W. Broadway), (212) 343-0109. Open M-Sa 11am-8pm, Su 12pm-8pm. MC, V, AmEx NR to Prince St.

Phat Farm
A hip-hop house of style, where XL is the size of choice and clothing's executed well enough to earn the Farm its SoHo digs.
SoHo, 129 Prince St. (bet. West Broadway and Wooster St.), (212) 533-7428, www.phatfarm.com. Open M-Sa 11am-7pm, Su 12pm-6pm. MC, V, AmEx, D, D to Prince St.

Steven Alan (Men)
Casual sportswear for men, featuring Alan's own label as well as other brand names such as Generic Costume and Filipa K.
SoHo, 558 Broome St. (bet. Sixth Ave. and Varick St.), (212) 625-2541, www.stevealan.com. Open W-Sa 12pm-7pm, Su 1pm-6pm. MC, V, CE to Spring St., NR to Prince St.

Steven Alan (Women)
Coveted labels, often at half price. Expect good deals on creations by the hottest young designers, like United, Bumboo, Sully Penn, and Alice Roy.
SoHo, 60 Wooster St. (bet. Spring and Broome Sts.), (212) 334-

6354, www.stevealan.com. Open M-Sa 11am-7pm, Su 12pm-7pm. MC, V, AmEx, 6 to Spring St., NR to Prince St.

Todd Oldham
One of America's hottest young designers and with good reason: The collections found here key into the young and fresh end of fashion with lots of color, prints, denim and other unstodgy stuff.
SoHo, 123 Wooster St. (bet. Spring and Prince Sts.), (212) 219-3531, www.toddoldham.com. Open M-Sa 11am-7pm, Su 12pm-6pm. MC, V, AmEx, D, CE to Spring St., NR to Prince St.

Yohji Yamamoto
Definitely one of the up-and-coming designers of the 21st century, Yamamoto's signature color is a black that works in many colors and fabrics. Two beautifully poised mannequins carry evening wear at the entrance, showing off the designs that are as luxuriously light as your wallet will be after a purchase here.
SoHo, 103 Grand St. (at Mercer St.), (212) 966-9066. Open M-Sa 11am-7pm, Su 12pm-6pm. MC, V, AmEx, DC, D, JMNRZ6 to Canal St.

Yves Saint Laurent (Men)
All the latest in YSL designs for men, though the "latest" never deviates much from the signature, tireless elegance. In this case, dress up to shop, or even to window shop.
SoHo, 88 Wooster St. (bet. Spring and Broome Sts.), (212) 274-0522, www.yslonline.com. Open M-Sa 11am-7pm, Su 12pm-6pm. MC, V, AmEx, D, NR to Prince St.

♦ BOOKS, MAGAZINES& RECORDS

Housing Works Used Bookstore Cafe
Used books SoHo style. No dingy paperbacks with tattered covers and peculiar odors here. Instead, browse through nearly pristine coffee table art books and hardcover fiction with jackets fully intact, all at low used-book prices. There's also a coffee bar for refueling while settling on what to take home.
SoHo, 126 Crosby St. (bet. Houston and Prince Sts.), (212) 334-3324, www.housingworksubc.com. Open M-W 10am-8pm, R-F 10am-9pm, Sa 12pm-10pm, Su 12pm-7pm. MC, V, AmEx, Ⓑ Ⓓ Ⓕ Ⓠ *to Broadway-Lafayette St.,* Ⓝ Ⓡ *to Prince St.* ♿

A Photographer's Place
New and used books from camera manuals to texts on fashion photography line the intimate wood-paneled walls of this photographer's pit stop.
SoHo, 133 Mercer St. (bet. Prince and Spring Sts.), (212) 966-2356. Open M-Sa 11am-7pm, Su 12pm-6pm. MC, V, AmEx, D, Ⓝ Ⓡ *to Prince St.*

Rizzoli
Get lost in this dark, warm store which, like its uptown counterpart, specializes in beautiful architecture, art, design, and coffee table books. Literature and non-fiction selections are not inspiring.
SoHo, 454 W. Broadway (bet. Houston and Prince Sts.), (212) 674-1616. Open M-Sa 10:30am-8pm, Su 12pm-7pm. MC, V, AmEx, D, Ⓝ Ⓡ *to Prince St.*

Rocks In Your Head
Around since 1978, this store offers an eclectic selection: music from the past 40 years, both indie and major rock titles, with a great techno section and lots of box-sets. Best of all, the staff is very friendly and always willing to help.
SoHo, 157 Prince St. (bet. Broadway and Thompson St.), (212) 475-6729, www.rocksinyourhead.net. Open M-Su 12pm-9pm. MC, V, AmEx, Ⓒ Ⓔ *to Spring St.*

SoHo Books
The best sale tables around await outside this bargain book cavern, which offers everything from slightly outdated editions of *Let's Go* guides to slick Generation X novels for $1.98 each, or three for $5. (Where on earth is Donna Tartt these days?)
SoHo, 351 W. Broadway (bet. Broome and Grand Sts.), (212) 226-3395. Open M-Su 10am-11pm. MC, V, AmEx, Ⓐ Ⓒ Ⓔ *to Canal St.*

♦ GROCERY, GOURMET & SPECIALTY

Dean & DeLuca
One of New York's most revered specialty food stores, it's the Zabar's of downtown. Stop by for a caffeine break at the stand-up espresso bar, pick up some paté for your next dinner party, and ogle the produce section, full of fruits and vegetables suitable for a still-life masterpiece. They also offer specialty breads, meats, cheeses, desserts, and quality packaged foods. If you have to bring a special addition to a dinner or a picky host a gift, come here.
SoHo, 560 Broadway (at Prince St.), (212) 226-6800, www.deandeluca. com. Open M-Sa 10am-8pm, Su 10am-7pm. MC, V, AmEx, D, Ⓝ Ⓡ *to Prince St.* ♿

Gourmet Garage
Formerly a wholesale market for the city's most elite chefs, today the Gourmet Garage shares its sizable inventory of fresh and eclectic delectables with the entire city, offering up a wide variety of produce, meats, breads, and prepared foods, at prices that rival those at a regular grocery store.
Soho, 453 Broome St. (at Mercer St.), (212) 941-5850. Open M-Su 7am-9pm. MC, V, AmEx. Ⓝ Ⓡ *to Prince St.*

♦ MISCELLANEOUS

Depression Modern
Plush, beautiful furniture and retro, refurbished housewares make for great browsing, test-sitting, and daydreaming of a perfectly decorated home for anyone who longs for the era of their grandparents. It's all very expensive, but the people who run it are amiable and tolerant of browsers.
SoHo, 150 Sullivan St. (bet. Houston and Prince Sts.), (212) 982-5699. Open W-Su 12pm-7pm. Cash Only, ① ⑨ *to Houston St.* ♿

Dom
Need some inflatable furniture for your dorm room? Have a fondness for housewares made of neon-colored plastic? All that and plenty more for the home at this trendy decorator hot spot, as well as other junk, from pens to pillboxes. Most of it is inexpensive and equally suitable for gift-giving or feeding your personal flair for home decorating.
SoHo, 382 W. Broadway (bet. Spring and Broome Sts.), (212) 334-5580, www.dom-ck.com. Open M-Sa 11:30am-8pm, Su 11:30am-7pm. MC, V, AmEx, Ⓒ Ⓔ *to Spring St.*

Face Stockholm
With MAC right up the street, the situation seems too close for comfort, though this Swedish based company excels at the basics. Personal attention is easy to come by within the airy boutique; the $9 nail polish selection makes you wish you had more fingers. A favored stop for fashionistas and actresses, you might even spot a celeb or two au naturel!
SoHo, 110 Prince St. (at Greene St.), (212) 966-9110, www.beauty.com. Open M-Su 11am-8pm. MC, V, AmEx, Ⓝ Ⓡ *to Prince St.* ♿

L'Occitane
This small French company has all of the essentials plus

more — great selections of their own perfumes and candles.
SoHo, 146 Spring St (at Wooster St.), (212) 343-0109, www.loccitane. com. Open M-Sa 11am-8pm, Su 12pm-8pm. MC, V, AmEx, DC, CE to Spring St.

MAC
Makeup straight from Canada and cruelty-free to boot, SoHo-ites and cosmetophiles are more than willing to pay the price for the name and the creamy, metallic signature look. High quality, too.
SoHo, 113 Spring St. (at Mercer St.), (212) 334-4641, www.maccosmet ics.com. Open M-Sa 11am-7pm, Su 12pm-6pm. MC, V, AmEx, D, NR to Prince St., 6 to Spring St.

Mood Indigo
This is the first stop on the way to becoming a full-fledged member of cocktail culture. The whole idea is putting some classy retro-style back into drinking, and martinis out of a plastic cup simply will not do. Fortunately, here they offer tons of authentic and unique glasses and accessories from the original cocktail era to choose from. It's all a little expensive, but think of it as investing in some valuable antiques.
SoHo, 181 Prince St. (bet. Thompson and Sullivan Sts.), (212) 254-1176. Open T-Sa 12pm-7pm, Su 1pm-6pm. MC, V, AmEx, CE to Spring St.

Arts & Recreation

•GALLERIES•

Artist's Space
A testing ground where new artists get the chance to cut their teeth, pay their dues, and show their stuff to the gallery world. Shows generally focus on a central theme and contain several new artists with works that fit in. Check out up-and-coming talent in its larval stages.
SoHo, 38 Greene St. (bet. Grand and Broome Sts.), (212) 226-3970, www.artistsspace.org. Open T-Sa 11am-6pm. JMNRZ6 *to Canal St.* ♿

David Zwirner
Whatever the well-known featured artist displays, it's done to near perfection, to the delight of critics and other viewers. The gallery is as stylish and ecelctic as its art. Look for exhibits ranging from neon video installations to conceptual sculpture and photography.
SoHo, 43 Greene St. (bet. Grand and Broome Sts.), (212) 966-9074, www.davidzwirner.com. Open T-Sa 10am-6pm. JMNRZ6 *to Canal St.*

Deitch Projects
No stranger to the art world, this gallery has featured the works of George Condo, Keith Haring and Yoko Ono, to name a few. Look for the installation pieces and the attention paid to balancing the quirky exhibits with the more serious and mysterious.
Soho, 76 Grand St. (bet. Wooster and Greene St.), (212)343-7300. Open: T-Sat 12-6 pm NR *to Prince St.*

Dumbbox
Dakota Jackson's new gallery derives its name from its nature: as a dumb box, it has no intrinsic meaning. Rather, it derives meaning from the party or function it's being used for at the moment. Whatever.
Soho, 43 Mercer St. (bet. Broome and Grand St.), NR *to Canal St.*

Exit Art — The First World
A huge upstairs loft space, complete with a café made for lingering when gallery hopping becomes tiresome, and a shop filled with art trinkets. Never stodgy, themed group shows are favored. Past innovations include having the artists move their studios into the gallery and an exhibit of art/paraphernalia from social protest movements. Openings here should not be missed.
SoHo, 548 Broadway, 2nd Fl. (bet. Prince and Spring Sts.), (212) 966-7745, www.exitart.com. Open T-F 10am-6Pm, Sa 11am-6pm. NR *to Prince Street.*

Jack Tilton Gallery (also Anna Kustera Gallery)
The space is taken up by a wide variety of paintings and drawings, including a large number of Asian artists. Good curators make for diverse exhibits with video and performance as well.
SoHo, 49 Greene St. (bet. Broome and Grand Sts.), (212) 941-1775, www.jacktiltongallery.com. Open T-Sa 10am-6pm. A C E to Canal St.

Jeffrey Deitch Projects
The small entryway here gives way to big-time modern art inside. Don't pass up the chance to experience anything from relatively tame non-traditional sculpture installations to a Russian performance artist living inside a doghouse within the gallery and getting confrontational with visitors.
SoHo, 76 Grand St. (bet. Wooster and Greene Sts.), (212) 343-7300. Open T-Sa 12pm-6pm. J M N R Z 6 to Canal St. ♿

New World Art Center
This "New Renaissance" gallery has an ambitious agenda, as it seeks to unite fine, graphic, literary, film, video, photographic, designing, and performing artists under one roof. The splintered focus keeps exhibits changing monthly.
SoHo, 250 Lafayette St. (bet. Prince and Spring Sts.), (212) 941-9296. Open T-Sa 1pm-6pm. 6 to Spring St. ♿

Pace Wildenstein Gallery, SoHo
A Manhattan art world standard with several outlets throughout the city, the SoHo branch is a testament to the quality that sustains its popularity. Housed in a large and accessible street level space, they offer solo shows by some fine established artists not yet past their prime, such as Elizabeth Murray.
SoHo, 142 Greene St. (bet. Houston and Prince Sts.), (212) 431-9224, www.pacewildenstein.com. Open T-Sa 10am-6pm. N R to Prince St. ♿

Peter Blum
Frequently swerving towards the odd and often obscure, this snazzy space — a former fire station — features paintings and sculpture by known artists, as well as architectural sketches, and non-Western archeological artifacts.
SoHo, 99 Wooster St. (bet. Prince and Spring Sts.), (212) 343-0441, www.artnet.com. Open T-F 10am-6pm, Sa 11am-6pm. N R to Prince St. ♿

Phyllis Kind
Since the work of established white male artists still constitutes the majority of what makes it into serious galleries, this deceptively large space often contains shows that challenge this order. Artists like Alison Saar regularly produce some of the most thought-provoking installations you're likely to see.
SoHo, 136 Greene St. (bet. Prince and Houston Sts.), (212) 925-1200, www.phylliskindgallery.com. Open T-Sa 10am-6pm. *N R to Prince St.* ♿

Staley-Wise
Love photography? Sorting through the array of different styles that get thrown together based on the fact that they all somehow involve using a camera and film as media can be daunting. This is the place for those who love the glamour aspect of photography, featuring work ranging from old classic *Life* magazine-style celeb photos to work by today's most prominent fashion photographers. The attitude that commercial success is validation rather than a sign of selling out is prominent here.
SoHo, 560 Broadway, Suite 305 (at Prince St.), (212) 966-6223. Open T-Sa 11am-5pm. N R to Prince St. ♿

Thread Waxing Space
Homage is paid to musicians and pop culture in this gallery, which has seen the likes of Beck Hansen and his grandfather's mixed-media work. Past exhibits include series on the art of comics. Space is devoted to music performances, as well as pieces of performance art featuring intensive audience interaction.
Soho, 476 Broadway (bet. Broome and Grand Sts.),

PPOW
Started in the '80s in the East Village by two women, this gallery moved here after developing an excellent reputation. The two rooms generally each contain work by a different artist. Female artists are well represented here, as are others with perspectives that don't fit into the old standards so well, like those of the late well-known AIDS-chronicler David Wojnarowicz, whose estate the gallery owns.

SoHo, 476 Broome St., 3rd Fl. (bet. Wooster and Greene Sts.), (212) 941-8642. Open T-Sa 10am-6pm. N R to Prince St., 6 to Spring St. ♿

♦ LEISURE

New York Open Center
A holistic learning center which offers lectures, workshops and weekend retreats on topics ranging from screenwriting to flamenco dancing; call for a catalog. The meditation room is open to the public free of charge, pillow provided, if you forgot to bring your own.
SoHo, 83 Spring St. (bet. Crosby and Lafayette Sts.), (212) 219-2527, ⑥ to Spring St. ♿

♦ PERFORMANCE

HERE
The western end of SoHo is as underdeveloped as TriBeCa but with a funkier feel, creating the perfect atmosphere for this unconventional arts venue. Attractions include gallery shows of fine art and theater productions of new plays by younger playwrights with great stories to tell.
SoHo, 145 Sixth Ave. (bet. Spring and Broome Sts.), (212) 647-0202, www. here.org. Open T-Sa 2pm-10pm. MC, V, AmEx, ©Ⓔ to Spring St. ♿

Joyce SoHo
All professional and aspiring dancers are familiar with this branch of the Joyce, the venue of choice for seeing all genres in a setting that's not stiflingly formal. Performances are Thursday-Sunday nights, with tickets available 30 minutes before curtain.
SoHo, 155 Mercer St. (bet. Houston and Prince Sts.), (212) 334-7479, www.joyce.org. Cash Only, ⓃⓇ to Prince St. ♿

Poets House
This free reading room and resource center houses the largest collection of poetry books in the country. Current poetry and literary periodicals are available for browsing, and Walkmans are provided for listening. Call for information about programs.
SoHo, 72 Spring St. (bet. Crosby and Lafayette Sts.), (212) 431-7920, ⑥ to Spring St. ♿

♦ PARKS

SoHo Square
Take a seat and feed the birds. The monument of General Jose Artigas leader of Uruguay's independence is one of six sculptures dedicated to Latin American leaders that overlook the Avenue of the Americas.
SoHo, Spring St. and Ave. of the Americas, www.nyc-parks.org. ©Ⓔ to Spring St. ♿

♦ MUSEUMS & CULTURAL CENTERS

The Drawing Center
This nonprofit organization has an extensive collection of works on paper, including lots of drawings by a variety of new and established artists. The operation has been so successful that a second space recently opened across the street.
SoHo, 35 Wooster St. (bet. Grand and Broome Sts.), (212) 219-2166. Open T-F 10am-6pm, Sa 11am-6pm. Admission: free, Ⓐ©Ⓔ to Canal St. ♿

FIRE Museum
If a field trip to the fire station is a favorite childhood memory, don't miss this chance to relive it. The collection, housed in a renovated Beaux-Arts style firehouse from 1904, is the country's largest; it's full of all the standard firehouse trappings, old engines and pump cars, and plenty of intriguing NYC fire history.
SoHo, 278 Spring St. (bet. Houston and Varick Sts.), (212) 691-1303. Open T-Su, 10am-4pm. MC, V, AmEx, Admission: $1-$4, ©Ⓔ to Spring St. ♿

Guggenheim SoHo
Opened in 1992, an ENEL virtual reality gallery and an electronic reading room with CD-ROMs are several of the ultramodern highlights of this downtown counterpart to the Museum Mile heavyweight. Though the architecture is hardly Frank Lloyd Wright, the SoHo building, designed by Arata Isozaki, is airy and conducive to the curators' ambitious programs, which reexamine 20th century innovators like Max Beckmann and showcase contemporary stars like media artist Bill Viola.
SoHo, 575 Broadway (at Prince St.), (212) 423-3500, www.guggenheim. org. Open Su, W-F 11am-6pm, M,R 11am-6pm, Sa 11am-8pm. Admission: free, ⓃⓇ to Prince St. ♿

The Museum for African Art
Exhibits facilitating a greater understanding of African art change twice a year at this two-floor showcase, one of two of its kind in the country. Complex exhibits often incorporate elements of folk art, sculpture, and more conventional media to examine pervasive concepts in the tradition. Film and video presentations, performance art, and interactive, hands-on workshops take place in the newly opened Educational Department.
SoHo, 593 Broadway (bet. Houston and Prince Sts.), (212) 966-1313. Open T-F 10:30am-5:30pm, Sa-Su 12pm-6pm. MC, V, AmEx, Admission: $2.50-$5, ⓃⓇ to Prince St. ♿

The New Museum of Contemporary Art
Founded by Maciaa Tucker in 1977, this unique museum takes contemporary art to a whole new level: Its semi-permanent collection contains works created in the past decade; once the age of a piece reaches double digits, it is exchanged for something new, which is in turn retained for ten years.
SoHo, 583 Broadway (bet. Houston and Prince Sts.), (212) 219-1222. Open W, Su 12pm-6pm, R-Sa 12pm-8pm. Admission: $3-$5 (under 18 free), B D F Q *to Broadway-Lafayette St.,* N R *to Prince St.*

Nightlife

♦ BARS

Bar 89
A stylish crowd and pricey drinks are nothing unusual in this neck of the words. What's special about Bar 89 is the fabulous unisex bathrooms whose technology boggles the noodle: the clear glass doors suddenly turn opaque upon closing.
SoHo, 89 Mercer St. (bet. Spring and Broome Sts.), (212) 274-0989. Open M-Su 12pm-1:45am. MC, V, AmEx, 1 9 *to Canal St.,* 6 *to Spring St.*

The Cub Room
"I've sworn off martinis, except at this place," remarks a patron of this lovely bar. Business attire is the unwritten dress code for the young and affluent who enjoy expensive cocktails and a serious pick-up scene, while lounging on the comfy furniture.
SoHo, 131 Sullivan St. (at Prince St.), (212) 677-4100, www.cub-room.com. Open M-Su 6pm-2am. MC, V, AmEx, C E *to Spring St.*

Sway
It's pretty difficult to get past the velvet ropes at the door, but if you do, the scene is cool, with awesome music and interesting people. It's so popular these days that it is even really busy during the week.

SoHo, 305 Spring St. (bet. Greenwich and Hudson Sts.), (212) 620-5220. Open M-Su 10pm-4am. MC, V, AmEx 1 9 to

Denial
The drinks and the hospitality are noteworthy at this sake bar. It's quiet during the week, and with its subtle décor and soft candlelight, it's good for romantic conversation. On Thursday nights the '80s and hip-hop parties are worth checking out.
SoHo, 46 Grand St. (bet. W. Broadway and Thompson St.), (212) 925-9449. Open T-R 7pm-3am, F-Sa 9pm-4am. MC, V, AmEx 1 9 *to Canal St.*

Double Happiness
Double Happiness is eclectic and funky, offering diverse entertainment. Come to Segue, the weekly poetry reading, or to Saturday night's Latin-inspired dj set. Double Happiness' Chinese influenced-décor, nightly dancing and bounty of cool folks and stiff drinks make it a worthwhile visit.
Soho, 173 Mott St. (at Broome St.), (212) 941-1282. Open F-Sa 6pm-4am, Su-R 6pm-3am. MC, V, AmEx 6 *to Spring St.*

Ear Inn
This place used to be a brothel! These days it's just a homey bar that attracts a sort of hip, sort of yuppie crowd. Ask about their seasonal poetry readings.
SoHo, 326 Spring St. (bet. Greenwich and Washington Sts.), (212) 226-9060, www.earinn.com. Open 12pm-4am. MC, V, AmEx, C E *to Spring St.*

ñ
Savor pitchers of sangría while admiring the Wednesday night flamenco dancers, and don't even try to resist the tapas. It's tiny, though, so stake out a place early and camp out all night.
SoHo, 33 Crosby St. (bet. Broome and Grand Sts.), (212) 219-8856. Open Su-R 5pm-2am, F-Sa 5pm-4am. Cash Only, J M N R Z 6 *to Canal St.*

Pravda
Pravda embodies neither post-Soviet mayhem nor hard-core proletariat boozing. Still, the eighty flavors of vodka (including the decidedly bourgeois mango and raspberry), caviar and rust-tinted decor almost justify the name. High-class SoHo-ites eschew communism for black market prices.
SoHo, 281 Lafayette (bet. Prince and Houston Sts.), (212) 226-4696. Open M, T, W 5pm-2am, R 5pm-2:30am. MC, V, AmEx, B D F Q *to Broadway-Lafayette St.,* N R *to Prince St.*

Recess
This cozily-furnished bar-lounge is the perfect place to escape the pretension of many of the bars in the neighborhood and to hang out with friends or meet new ones. The atmosphere is great, the bartenders are friendly and there is plenty of room in the back to dance.
SoHo, 310 Spring St. (bet. Greenwich and Renwick Sts.), (646)

613-8521. Open M-Su 6pm-4am. Cash Only. CE to Spring St., 19 to Houston St.

The SoHo Grand Bar
This hotel bar is growing ever more popular, for guests and drop-ins with their "martinis", to sophisticated neighborhooders and their "nightcaps".
SoHo, 310 W. Broadway (bet. Canal and Grand Sts.), (212) 965-3000. Open M-Su 12pm-2am. MC, V, AmEx, D, ACE to Canal St.

Spy
Wear the trendiest outfit you can find and approach the bouncers with all the arrogance you can muster. And internalize this: money and beauty aren't everything.
SoHo, 101 Greene St. (bet Prince and Spring Sts.), (212) 343-9000. Open M-Su 8pm-4am. MC, V, AmEx, DC, CE to Spring St., NR to Prince St.

Veruka
This is a hot spot for celebrities and the trendy SoHo crowd that loves them. It's noisy and busy every night of the week; in other words, more a place for dancing and mingling with hotshots than hanging out with friends. Every Tuesday the DJ spins progressive house and hip-hop.
SoHo, 525 Broome St. (bet. Thompson St. and Sixth Ave.), (212) 625-1717. Open M-Su 8pm-4am. MC, V, Amex 19 23 ACE to Canal St.

Void
A great free film series is the heart of this nightspot. Find out what the event is ahead of time and be prepared to appreciate it; there's no other social scene, just people lining the walls, mesmerized by the big screen.
SoHo, 16 Mercer St. (at Howard St.), (212) 941-6492, www.escape.com/~void. Open T-R 8pm-4am, F-Sa 8pm-3am. Cash only, 19 to Canal St.

♦ CLUBS

Culture Club
This is the place for the ultimate '80s escapade, with Reagan-era pop served up in this two-story club. It boasts a casual atmosphere, murals of your favorite '80s artists, and even a Delorean that Michael J. Fox would envy.
SoHo, 179 Varick (bet. King and Charlton Sts.), (212) 243-1999. MC, V, AmEx, D, Cover: $15-$20, 19 to Houston St.

Don Hill's
This clubhouse is consistently crowded with crazy college kids, especially on Wednesday nights for the Beauty party, when kids come out to groove '80s style, and Hot Fudge Sundays, which features soul and hip hop music, and the Famous Squeeze Box on Friday nights: a gay rock drag queen party.
SoHo, 511 Greenwich St. (at Spring St.), (212) 334-1390. Open M-Su 9pm-4am. MC, V, AmEx, D, CE to Spring St., 19 to Canal St.

NV
Fashion types pout, air-kiss, and lounge as only they can inside this SoHo kennel for the chi chi. Sneakers, naturally, are prohibited.
SoHo, 289 Spring St. (at Varick St.), 929-6969. MC, V, AmEx, Cover: $20, CE to Spring St.

Keeping it Reel

The best way to experience film in New York, next to being on set, is to catch one of the City's myriad of film festivals. There are festivals in New York to celebrate every type of film and filmmaker. In order to keep up with it all, it's important to keep an eye on *The New York Times*, and on what's going on at Lincoln Center and the Museum of Modern Art (MoMA), which host prestigious, big-name festivals.

The **New York Film Festival**, held annually in September and October, has been celebrating American and foreign films for several decades. Tickets for this event, particularly opening and closing night, are snapped up weeks in advance.

Another hot festival, particularly as the trend for indies continues to heat up, is the **New Directors/New Films** series produced by the Film Society of Lincoln Center and held at MoMA in March and April. Here, industry bigwigs and idealistic film students eye one another with wary hunger. (For both of these big festivals call the Film Society of Lincoln Center at 212-875-5610 for more information.)

Films looking for distribution are also featured at the **Independent Feature Film Market** in September at the Angelika Film Center, sponsored by the Independent Feature Project. The IFP has been a godsend to filmmakers in New York — but the tickets at the Film Market are priced to cater to serious filmmakers, and are expensive even with the membership discount. (Call the Angelika Film Center for info at 212-995-2000).

Once summer arrives, films are screened for free at The **HBO/Bryant Park Film Festival** (Sixth Ave. at 42nd St.) on Mondays at sunset. For an authentic New York City experience, bring a picnic dinner, a blanket, and a friend — sit back and watch *King Kong* or *Vertigo* under the stars. (Call the hotline at 212-512-5700 for more information, and be aware that Tuesdays serve as rain dates.)

During the first two weeks of every August, enjoy air-conditioned splendor and affordable ticket prices at the **Harlem Week Black Film Festival** at the Adam Clayton Powell Jr. State Office Building (212-749-5298). Also, keep an eye out for independent arts theaters like the Film Forum (212-727-8110), which has festivals of its own, year-round.

East Village

Rents are up, the cell-phone set lines sidewalks looking for a signal, most of the squatters and artists are long gone, and almost nobody remembers the 1988 riots in Tompkins Square Park. But while it takes more cash than it used to, the East Village is not quite over: it's a pathology that can be treated but not cured, still a hotbed of bars and street activity, even on cold winter nights. In the summer, it can be explosive.

If Tompkins Square Park is more genteel now than in the past, it still remains a stomping ground for Socialists, Reds, squatters, artists, and other left-wingers. Though it's since moved to the west side, Wigstock, the biggest drag fest of all time, began here — its camp, sass, and political overtones a perfect match for East Village sensibilities. You can still find drag queens on Sundays at Stingy Lulu's, every evening serving food at Lucky Cheng's, and on the street with girlfriends of both sexes.

A scene from *Die Harder* shot in the park a few years ago forced a clean-up of sorts, though city workers are said to have found a pot plant near one of the park buildings since then. Most people think it was spurious, like volunteer corn sprouting in a field of soybeans, but others think it was more than a freak occurrence. Not coincidentally, "NYPD Blue" is set in the East Village; meanwhile, film school kids have probably shot every lamppost and street corner ten times over.

This neighborhood is built on used-to's, and St. Marks used to be the hip street of the East Village. W.H. Auden lived here and, with Allen Ginsburg, a block South,Kerouac, Burroughs, et al. pass through. Not anymore. Now you can get tattoos, cheap jewelry, used CDs, and a few good meals, but the vein of the neighborhood is Avenue A and moving East. The Fillmore East used to be here and every band you've ever heard of, and forgotten, played there. Gone. So's the gay disco The Saint. And, though, it's still here, CBGB's—once host to Talking Heads, The Police, Blondie and the Ramones—has turned into a place where mediocre bands play for a $5 cover.

The realtors who dubbed it the East Village in the first place look for new hooks, subsections within the area have sprung up in recent years, all with snazzy nomenclature: Trendy NoHo fits between the Villages, bordered by Lafayette Street and Second Avenue to the west and east, and (go figure) Houston to the south. NoLita (North of Little Italy) describes the intersection of NoHo, the East Village, and the Lower East Side. While these acronymic derivatives still fit under the umbrella of East Village, they are growing too refined (not to mention pricey) to stay much longer under its auspices.

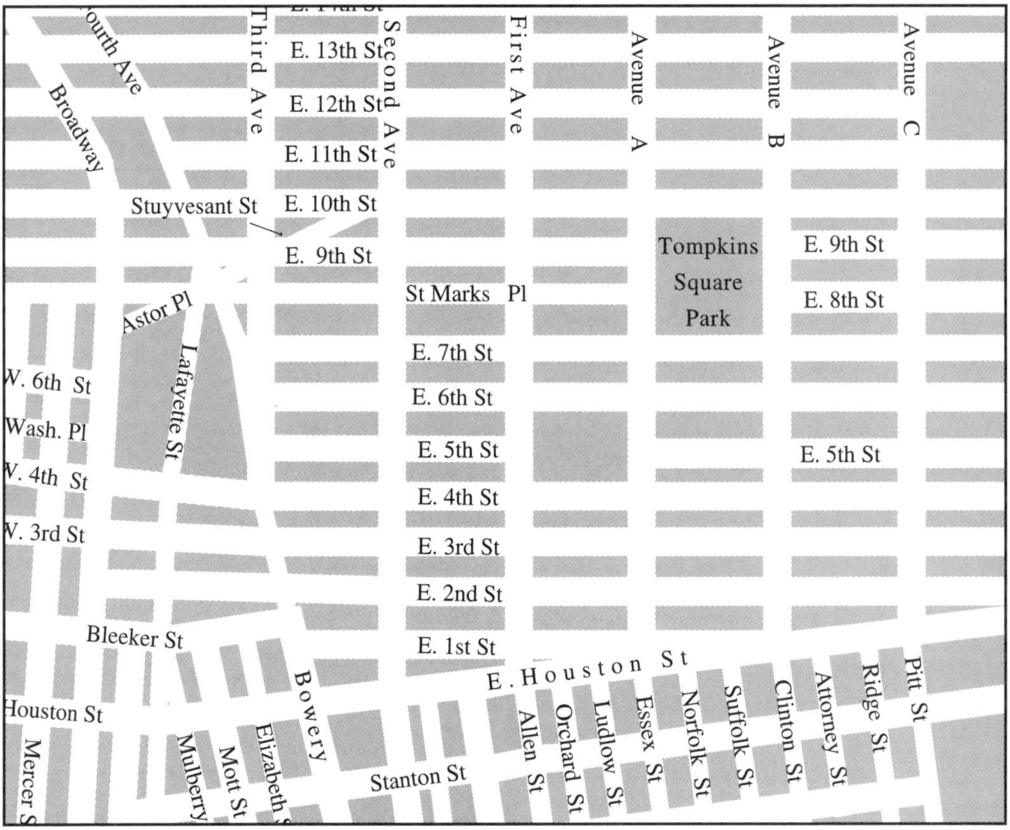

Dining

♦ RESTAURANTS

Angelica Kitchen

A vegetarian's paradise as well as an introductory course for vegan-phobic carnivores, offering tangy soups, tofu and pesto sandwiches, and tofu-lemon "cheesecake." Portions are generous and very moderately priced.

East Village, 300 E. 12th St. (bet. First and Second Aves.), (212) 228-2909. Open M-Su 11:30am-11:30pm. Cash Only, Entrées: $6-$12, L to First Ave., NR456 to Union Sq.-14th St.

Around the Clock

There's not much to recommend during the day, but the late-late-night crowd qualifies as a revealing cross-section of the East Village's maladjusted. Depending on how far the hands are past midnight when you swing by, either bleary-eyed club kids with the munchies are killing time or else the harried waitstaff is halfheartedly trying to oblige the grumpy, idiosyncratic, early-morning regulars.

East Village, 8 Stuyvesant St. (at Third Ave.), (212) 598-0402. Open M-Su 24hrs. MC, V, AmEx, DC, D, Entrées: $5-$10, 6 to Astor Pl.

Bendix Diner

Whether it's because of the restaurant's "get fat" or because of the subsequent surprise of a health-conscious menu, patrons have been congregating at this casual hot-spot in such numbers that owners have been forced to expand. Greasy spoon prices mean the American-Thai fusion dishes leave no room for guilt.

East Village, 167 First Ave. (bet. 10th and 11th Sts.), (212) 260-4220. Open Su-R 8am-11pm, F-Sa 8am-12am. MC, V, AmEx, Entrées: $6-$18, 6 to Astor Pl.

Bereket Turkish Kebab House

This 24-hour hot spot, right down the street form Orchard Street's cheap leather boutiques, provides greasy Middle Eastern food. The best time to go is drunk, sometime after midnight when it's packed and the only people louder than the patrons are the workers.

East Village, 187 E. Houston St. (at Orchard St.), (212) 475-7700. Open M-Su 24hrs., Cash only, Entrees $5-8, F to Second Ave,

PLACES TO GO:

Mamlouk
Middle Eastern food of the highest quality, with large, large hookas to boot.

Russian and Turkish Baths
Never was there a better place to recover from a hang over. A New York experience not to be missed.

Masterbakers
Pornographic cakes taken to an artistic level. Foot long penises never looked so approachable.

Joe's Pub at the Public Theater
Some of the best live music from former members of the JBs to other old and new soul, blues and rock sensations.

Boca Chica

Great for anyone who likes to have fun when paying to eat out. The atmosphere is decidedly festive and colorful, a perfect match for the South American and Caribbean food they serve. Best bets are the pork or seafood dishes, staples of the cuisine that you've probably never tasted before, which should definitely be accompanied by one of their exotic margaritas.

East Village, 13 First Ave. (at 1st St.), (212) 473-0108. Open M-R 5:30pm-11pm, F-Sa 5:30pm-12am, Su 12pm-11pm. MC, V, AmEx, D, Entrées: $8-$17, F *to Second Ave.*

Café Pick Me Up

With a view of bustling Tompkins Square park, Café Pick Me Up serves as a prime people-watching locale, particularly if you're fortunate enough to secure an outside table. In addition to its delicious beverages, Pick Me Up offers a wide array of tasty morsels to help refuel the weary traveler.

East Village 145 Avenue A (corner of 9th St), (212) 673-7231. Open Su-R 7am-1:30am, F-Sa 7-2:30, L *to 1sst Ave.*

Cafe Yola

On a warm night, step through the cozy asymmetrical dining room into the back garden. Tucked in between apartment buildings, the outdoor space has a European feel.

Candlelight, ivy, and good wine make this the ideal place for a romantic dinner and quiet conversation.

East Village, 337 E. 10th St. (bet. A and B Aves.), (212) 677-1913. Open T-Su 5:30pm-12am. Cash Only, Entrées: $8-$17, L to *First Ave.*

Cyclo

You can't miss this East Village eatery, what with the cyclo parked out front. Though the noise volume is high and the tables a bit cramped, the light, fresh Vietnamese cuisine more than compensates. The jellyfish and shrimp salad in a chili lime dressing is one of the more unusual appetizers, and the oxtail broth with noodles, sliced beef, scallions, and fresh herbs with fill you up without bogging you down.

East Village, 203 First Ave. (bet. 12th and 13th Sts.), (212) 673-3957. Open M-R 11:30am-10:30pm, F-Sa 11:30am-11:30pm, Su 5:30pm-11:30pm. MC, V, AmEx, Entrees: $9-$14, L *to First Ave.*

Dojo

The American and Japanese influenced dishes really only please fans of macrobiotic fare., but the dirt-cheap prices and a frisky social scene are enough to lure NYU undergrads away from their mealplans.

East Village, 24 St. Marks Pl. (bet. Second and Third Aves.), (212) 674-9821. Open Su-R 11am-1am, F-Sa 11am-2am. Cash Only, Entrées: $4-$8, 6 *to Astor Pl.*

First

Show a date you're hip by eating at this swanky, late night crowd pleaser. Martinis come in several sizes, shapes, and flavors while the seasonal menu offers an unusual mix of incredible dinners. The candle lit tables and low lighting

> "Living in New York is like being at some terrible late night party. You're tired, you've had a headache since you arrived, but you can't leave because then you'd miss the party."
>
> —Simon Hoggart

may make you feel like you have entered a black & white movie — put on your Humphrey Bogart accent and grab a cigar!

East Village, 87 First Ave. (bet. 5th and 6th Sts.), (212) 674-3823. Open M-R 6pm-2am, F-Sa 6pm-3am, Su 11am-4pm, 5pm-1am. MC, V, AmEx, Entrées: $18-$22, F to Second Ave.

Five Roses Pizza

We've met three of the Roses, and they are all lovely women who can make some of the best topping pizzas in NYC. They also make great lentil and garlic soups and standard Italian dishes at very reasonable prices. If you're lucky, some days you can see the oldest Rose peeling a mountain of garlic at one of the tables and chatting away to no one in particular.

East Village, 173 First Ave. (bet. 10th and 11th Sts.), (212) 228-2840. Open Su-W 12pm-10pm, R-Sa 12pm-12am. Cash only, Entrees: $2-$15, F train to Second Ave.

Global 33

This low-lit lounge/restaurant remains true to its name with a menu of international tapas-style dishes and an interior reminiscent of a 60s airport lounge. The petite dishes are artfully presented and delicious: Tart ceviche is heaped into a martini glass, cool roasted beets are served with warm goat cheese. Global also has a full menu of swanky cocktails, highlighted by some of the best Cosmopolitans around. Rotating DJs add to the festive feel (and the noise level).

East Village, 93 Second Ave. (bet. 5th and 6th Sts.), (212) 477-8427. Open Su-R 6pm-12am, F-Sa 6pm-2am. MC, V, AmEx, Entrées: $4-$12, F to Second Ave.

Kate's Joint

Kate's serves cheap vegan cuisine in a diner atmosphere, complete with fake bacon and tofu mayo. They serve some nice salads and veggie burgers that fill that greasy need the night after drinking.

East Village, 58 Ave. B (bet 4th and 5th Sts.) (212) 777-7059. Open Su-R 9am-12am, F-Sa 9am-1am. MC, V, AmEx, DC, D. Cover $4-$13, S to Second Ave, N R to 8th St., 6 to Astor Pl.

La Nouvelle Justine

Think of Nouvelle Justine as a theme restaurant like the Hard Rock Café where, in place of Marilyn Monroe's underwear encased on the wall, you can buy your dining companion a spanking or whipping instead. S&M has finally gone legit and La Nouvelle Justine is the first of what may hopefully be not too many restaurants that allow you to eat French and New American dishes while watching a Long Island girl beg to be spanked as her heavily made-up friends drunkenly cheer her on.

East Village, 101 E. 2nd St. (at First Ave.), (212) 673-8908. Open W-Sa 6pm-11pm, Su 7pm-4am. MC, V, AmEx, D, Entrees: $13-$21 F train to Second Ave.

Lanza's

Authentic Italian food *sans* gimmicks or fancy perversions. The clientele is large and loyal, filling the restaurant nightly for both the classy old-style ambiance and superior food at bargain prices. Thankfully it's neither trendy nor cutting-edge.

East Village, 168 First Ave. (bet. 10th and 11th Sts.), (212) 674-7014. Open M-Su 12pm-9pm. MC, V, AmEx, DC, Entrées: $11-$17, N R 4 5 6 to 14th St.-Union Sq., L to First Ave.

Le Tableau

An unusual reprieve from typical East Village flamboyance, this adorable French restaurant offers high quality food and wonderful service to a casual mix of clientele. The daily rotating specials menu should encourage you to make repeat visits, but be sure you make a reservation Friday or Saturday nights for parties of five and up to enjoy the live jazz band (and remember, a full band in a popular restaurant makes for cozy dining!).

East Village, 511 E. 5th St. (bet. A and B Aves.), (212) 260-1333. Open M-R 6pm-11pm, F-Sa 6pm-12pm. Cash Only, Entrées: $10-$18. F to Second Ave., 6 to Astor Pl.

Life Cafe

Featured in the Broadway play *Rent*, this eclectic source of nutritious Cal-Mex is an East Village landmark of laid-back creativity. Check out the rotating exhibits by local artists, preferably during the weekday happy hour (5pm-9pm).

East Village, 343 E. 10th St. (at Ave. B), (212) 477-8791, www.lifecafenyc.com. Open M-Sa 7am-7pm. MC, V, D, Entrées: $7-$12, L to First Ave.

Mamas Food-Shop

Mama is, in fact, a man who cooked so much food for his friends that his space evolved into a restaurant. All the food

is homestyle excellence, and the portions are huge. Try the grilled salmon and don't miss the awesome mac-and-cheese. Across the street, get soup and sandwiches at Stepmamas, a spin-off.
East Village, 200 E. 3rd St. (bet. Aves. A and B), (212) 777-4425. Open M-Sa 11:30am-10pm. Cash Only, Entrées: $6-$8, F to Second Ave.

Mamlouk
The prix-fixe menu changes monthly at this Middle Eastern, vegetarian-friendly restaurant, but you can always expect six delicious courses. After your meal, enjoy a hookah the size of a small child with rose or strawberry tobacco as you lounge on the couches and marvel at your content.
East Village, 211 E. 4th (bet. Aves A and B), (212) 529-3477. Open T-Su 6 pm to 12 am. MC, V, AmEx, Prix-fixe: $30, F to Second Ave.,

Mekka
People of all types are drawn to the excellent Southern and Caribbean food at this urban hip-hop restaurant. Difficult as it is to resist, don't devour too much of the complementary cornbread, or you may find yourself incapable of walking at the end of the night, or worse yet, you won't have room for the peach cobbler, which is a must.
East Village, 14 Ave. A (bet. Houston and 2nd Sts.), (212) 475-8500, www.mekkarestaurant.com. Open Su-W 5pm-11pm, R 5pm-12am, F-Sa 5pm-1:30am. MC, V, AmEx, D, Entrées: $14, F to Second Ave.

Mitali East
The stretch of 6th Street between 1st and 2nd Avenues is overrun with mediocre Indian food joints – Mitali isn't one of them. Most of the chicken dishes here are quite tasty and not too greasy, and they give you a lot of bang for your buck.
East Village, 334 E. 6th St. (bet. First and Second Aves.), (212) 533-2508. Open M-Su 12pm-12am. AmEx, MC, V, Entrees: $7-$10, F to Second Ave.

Nino's Pizza
There must be a thousand different slice joints in this city, but this is without a doubt one of the very best. In addition to making great pizza, the place looks out on Tompkins Square Park and keeps hours as late as any bar. A plain slice is always a safe bet, but the more adventuresome shouldn't miss the white pizza with fresh tomatoes. Mmmmmm.
East Village, 131 St. Marks Pl. (at A Av.), (212) 979-8688. Open M-Su 11am-4am. Cash Only, Entrées: $10, 6 to Astor Pl.

Odessa

The hippest of the East Village's Eastern European diners, open 24 hours. Everything from standard diner food to potato pancakes and other regional fare finds its way onto the menu. The location makes it perfect for a food break while cruising the Ave. A bar scene, and to continue drinking you need only walk next door to their lounge, where the cheapest gin and tonics in Manhattan are served by a surly, old Russian lady.

East Village, 119 Ave. A (bet. 7th and 8th Sts.), (212) 253-1470. Open M-Su 24hrs. MC, V, AmEx, Entrées: $6-$12, F to Second Ave.

Old Devil Moon

East Village restaurant specializing in southern food with a cool and funky atmosphere and big portions.

East Village, 511 E. 12th St. (bet. A and B Aves.), (212) 475-4357. Open M-F 5pm-11pm, Sa-Su 10am-4pm, 5pm-11pm. MC, V, AmEx, DC, Entrées: $12, L to First Ave.

Paquito's Restaurant

Think California taquerias – fast, cheap, and incredibly tasty Mexican food – transported to NYC. Paquito's has all the prerequisite items like burritos, enchiladas, and tacos, but is a step above most of the New York joints that dare to call themselves Mexican. It's a tiny place, but everyone devours their food so quickly that you can usually get a table without much of a problem.

East Village, 143 First Ave, (212) 674-2071. Open M-Su 11:30am-11:30pm. Cash only, Entrees: $2-$7, F train to Second Ave., 6 train to Astor Pl.

Pommes Frites

Nothing to expect at this cramped spot except for Belgian fries in a paper cone. There's only one type of fry to be had here, but several toppings, including mustard, ketchup, peanut sauce, and some spicier condiments. The service is quick, and you probably won't spend more than five bucks or five minutes as you grab your fries and go on your way.

East Village, 123 Second Ave. (at St. Marks Pl.), (212) 674-1234. Open M-F 11:30 am-1am, Sa-Su 11:30am-2 am. Cash only, 6 to Astor Pl.

Step Mama's

Right across the street from Mama's is this sandwich, soup, salads, and dessert shop. Step in and order one of their large, tasty chicken or meatloaf sandwiches, or maybe just one of the big cookies on your way home from work. It's cheap take-out food (you can eat in, too) that hits the spot.

East Village, 199 3rd St. (bet A and B Aves.), (212) 228-2663. Open M-Sa 11am-10pm. Cash only, Entrees: $5-$8, F to Second Ave.

Time Cafe

Around mealtimes there are rarely many free tables in this vast, lofty space, and it's no wonder, since this is one of the better places filling the niche between greasy coffee shop and fancy restaurant. Health-conscious organic food and an extensive menu with selections like fancy tuna sandwiches and pan roasted penne are sure to satisfy nearly any craving.

East Village, 380 Lafayette (bet. Great Jones and 4th Sts.), (212) 533-7000, www.timecafenyc.com. Open M-R 8am-12am, F-Sa 8am-1am, Su 10:30am-11pm. MC, V, AmEx, Entrées: $12-$22, 6 to Bleecker St.

Second Avenue Kosher Deli

Hit this legendary deli for the matzoh balls, blintzes, and other traditional dishes that kick your Grandma to the curb. Recent renovations have dispelled some of the old-country flair which made the Deli a kosher home away from home, but completely unmanageable sandwiches and the miniature museum honoring stars of the Yiddish theater with a "walk of fame" still remain.

East Village, 156 Second Ave. (at 10th St.), (212) 677-0606, www.2ndavedeli.com. Open Su-R 7:30am-12am, F-Sa 7:30am-3am. MC, V, AmEx, DC, D, Entrées: $6-$24, 6 to Astor Pl.

Two Boots Restaurant

Two Boots specializes in Cajun-Creole fare, creative pizzas with kitschy names like "The Divine" and "Mrs. Peel", and lots of vegan options. In other words, it's for the coolest kids in town. And as a bonus, the food's really good too.

East Village, 37 Ave. A (bet. 3rd and 4th Sts.), (212) 505-2276. Open M-Su 12pm-2am. MC, V, AmEx, D, Entrees $8-10, F to Second Ave,

♦ CAFES

Alt.coffee

The comfy couches are here because you'll be sitting awhile, checking the hotmail and figuring out where you'll go tonight. The staff is as handy with the latte maker as they are with any of your internet questions.

East Village, 139 Ave. A (bet. St. Marks Pl. and 9th St.), (212) 529-2233, www.altdotcoffee.com. Open M-R 9am-1:30am, F 9am-3:30am, Sa 10am-3:30am, Su 10am-1am. Cash Only, 6 to Astor Pl.

Atomic Passion

Choice vintage selections without the crowds: Atomic Passion is one of many that line East 9th yet it adds its own whimsical touch of trash and flash. Be sure to poke around

the back for some bright sundresses or fifties-style sunglasses.

East Village, 430 E. 9th St. (bet. First and A Aves.), (212) 533-0718. Open M-Su 1pm-9pm. MC, V, AmEx, L to First Ave.

Bistro Jules

This cozy, authentic French café provides impoverished romantics with candles, trendy mood music, and wine affordable enough for the cash-poor to get sufficiently buzzed, leaving them enough change to pick up some roses on the way home. Spring through fall, the seating out front on the tiny sunken patio is ideal for leisurely afternoons of nursing lemonade and chain smoking. Live jazz nightly.

East Village, 65 St. Marks Pl. (bet. First and Second Aves.), (212) 477-5560. Open Su-R 11am-1am, F-Sa 11am-2am. AmEx, 6 to Astor Pl.

Cafe Orlin

Blend in by ordering an espresso and whipping out some sort of portfolio. Leave it open on the table and enjoy a smoky omelet or a slice of chocolate cake. Most regulars are artsy East Village chain smokers, cum aspiring directors. The low-angle view allows a glimpse of the shoes passing by on St. Marks Place.

East Village, 41 St. Marks Pl. (bet. First and Second Aves.), (212) 777-1447. Open Su-R 9am-2am, F-Sa 24hrs. Cash Only, 6 to Astor Pl.

Internet Cafe

New York's first cybercafé offers weekly classes for between $25 and $200. Or pay the $5 cover to listen to striving artists unleash their souls in the cozy pub. Gourmet beers, including a large Belgian selection, go well with live jazz, heard every night.

East Village, 82 E. 3rd St. (bet. First and Second Aves.), (212) 614-0747, www.bigmagic.com. Open M-Sa 11am-2am, Su 12pm-12am. MC, V, F to Second Ave.

Masturbakers

The most popular item at this appropriately titled bakery, housed in the Old Devil Moon restaurant, is the penis cake. Their breast cake, bearing the words "Breast Wishes," runs a close second. With moist devil's food cake, rich frosting and naughty details, their bakery lives up to their motto: "tasty but tasteless."

East Village, 511 E. 12th St. (bet. Aves. A and B), (212) 475-0476. Open M-F 10am-5pm (M-Su 10am-10pm for pick-up only). MC, V, AmEx, L to First Ave.

Veniero's

What mood are you in? Contemplative? Maybe you just broke up with somone. That's what the lonely couter's for. Scribble in your journal and stare at your coffee. Loneliness not the case. Sit at one of the many tables and work on the dialogue for your big script. Either way try the scrumptious pastries and great drinks. One of the best in the city.

East Village, 342 E. 11th St. (bet. First and Second Aves.), (212) 674-7070, www.homedelivery.com. Open Su-R 8am-11:30pm, F-Sa 8am-12:30am. MC, V, AmEx, D, L N R 4 5 6 to 14th St.-Union Sq.

Yaffa Cafe

East Village funkadelic café with reasonably priced sandwiches, salads, pastas, omelets, and crepes, as well as a handsome selection of vegetarian items and unbelievable desserts. Enjoy the kitschy decor and sit outdoors when weather permits to observe the goings-on on St. Marks Pl. Open 24 hours.

East Village, 97 St. Marks Pl. (bet. 1st St. and Ave. A), (212) 677-9001. Open M-Su 24hrs. MC, V, AmEx, 6 to Astor Pl.

Shopping

◆ CLOTHING & SHOES

Air Market
This boutique represents much of the East Village; funky, rather expensive, colorful clothing with retro flair. Vinyl handbags, wallets and pastel-colored polyester tops in tiny sizes line the walls.
East Village, 97 Third Ave. (bet. 12th and 13th Sts.), (212) 995-5888, www.airmarket.com. Open M-Sa 12pm-7:30pm, Su 12pm-7pm. MC, V, AmEx, D, L *to Third Ave.*

Blue
Gowns and dresses of every style and color and be found here; search in this boutique for puffy taffeta or sleek satin depending on your mood. These are made-to-fit dresses for special occasions, and the prices are rightfully expensive.
East Village, 125 St. Mark's Pl. (bet. First and A Aves.), (212) 228-7744. Open M-Su 12pm-7:30pm. MC, V, AmEx. 6 *to Astor Pl.*

Filth Mart
The epitome of "white trash rock and roll", this funky store would win the award for best place to buy old rock concert t-shirts. In general, there's a great turn-over of groovy tees which all seem to fall in the $8-$25 range. Also has a great selection of used jeans and coats, and other items affectionatly termed "trashy chic".
East Village, 531 E. 13th St. (between A and B Aves.), (212) 387-0650. Open Su-T 12:30pm-7pm, W-Sa 12pm-8pm. MC, V, D, L N R 4 5 6 *to Union Sq.-14th St.* ♿

The Good, The Bad and The Ugly
Excellent selection of vintage clothing, suits, purses and shoes for men and women; customers are treated with a smile. You won't be afraid to try on those crazy plaid pants with that western style jacket, as you might in other downtown thrift stores. Don't let the thrift category fool you; prices at The Good, The Bad and The Ugly are just plain ugly.
East Village, 437 E. 9th St. (bet. First and A Aves.), (212) 473-3769. Open M-Su 1pm-9pm. MC, V, AmEx, D, L *to First Ave.*

INA (Men)
If you can't afford designer menswear on Fifth Avenue, come to INA (Men) and try on some more gently worn (read: vintage/consignment). Here you'll find suits, shirts and accessories from famous makers such as Prada. Prices are still expensive but not as unaffordable as INA's retail counterparts.
East Village, 262 Mott St. (bet. Houston and Prince Sts.), (212) 334-2210. Open Su-R 12pm-7pm, F-Sa 12pm-8pm. MC, V, AmEx. 6 *to Bleecker St.*

Lord of the Fleas
So popular that they're currently operating several outlets within spitting distance of each other. This is the place to go to add a few trendy pieces to your existing wardrobe or to find something appropriate for a night of club-hopping. The prices and quality are both generally pretty low which is ideal for stuff that's in now but probably won't be next year.
East Village, 305 E. 9th St. (bet. First and Second Aves.), (212) 260-9130. Open M-Su 12pm-8:30pm. MC, V, AmEx, D, 6 *to Astor Pl.* ♿

Also at:
East Village, 437 E. 12th St. (bet. First and A Aves.), (212) 533-3554. Open M-Sa 10am-6pm. MC, V, AmEx, D, L *to First Ave.* ♿

Meg
Designer Meg Kinney gives you futuristic fabrics and designs in this boutique; here you won't find froufrou dresses with bows. Look for sexy, slimming ensembles and skirts in stretchy materials with minimalist styling. The prices are expensive, but the look is tasteful and trendy.
East Village, 312 E. 9th St. (bet. First and Second Aves.), (212) 260-6329, www.megshop.com. Open M-Su 12pm-6pm. MC, V, AmEx. 6 *to Astor Pl.*

99X
This boutique sells some of the hippest threads in the city, with the usual high prices. The look is that oh-so-trendy "60's mod", featuring a large selection of (what else?) British imports, from labels like Fred Perry, Lonsdale, and Ben Sherman.
East Village, 84 E. 10th St. (bet. Third and Fourth Aves.), (212) 460-8599, www.99xny.com. Open M-Sa 12pm-8pm, Su 12pm-7pm. MC, V, AmEx, D, N R *to 8th St.,* 6 *to Astor Pl.*

Screaming Mimi's
You might pass Screaming Mimi's by if not for the window display, which shows off its kooky wares. You'll find some of the most outrageous vintage clothing in the city here, including Elvis suits, pink leisure outfits, leather pants and neon colored patched shirts. The excellent condition of the clothing marks up the prices a bit, but well worth it if you dare to wear.
East Village, 382 Lafayette St. (4th and Great Jones Sts.), (212) 677-6464. Open M-Sa 12pm-8pm, Su 12pm-6pm. MC, V, AmEx, DC, D. 6 *to Astor Pl.*

Tokio 7

A stylish New York City vintage stop that's affordable – most items are $20-$100. A good selection of male and female clothes from the seventies through the present, including designer names such as Moschino, DKNY and Comme Des Garcons.

East Village, 64 E. 7th St. (bet. First and Second Aves.), (212) 353-8443. Open M-Su 12pm-8:30. MC, V, AmEx, 6 to Astor Pl.

Trash and Vaudeville

Once this split-level store defined a look that made New York famous. Now merchandise appears trashy and punk-ish, but the shoe and boot selection in the back is still one of the best in town.

East Village, 4 St. Marks Pl. (bet. Second and Third Aves.), (212) 982-3590. Open M-Su 12pm-8pm. MC, V, AmEx, D, 6 to Astor Pl.

Urban Outfitters

This hipster playground for urban youth packs its industrial interior with racks of multicolored, funky kid fashion, suitable for an array of day or evening urban outings. Weave through aisles of vintage clothing, sassy sundresses, and trendy housewares while swaying to the smooth rhythms of ambient music played in the background.

East Village, 628 Broadway (bet. Bleeker and Houston Sts.), (212) 475-0009, www.urbanoutfitters. com. Open M-Sa 10am-10pm, Su 12pm-8pm. MC, V, AmEx, D, B D F Q to Broadway-Lafayette, 6 to Bleeker St.

Also at:

East Village, 162 Second Ave. (bet. 10th and 11th Sts.), (212) 375-1277, www.urbanoutfitters.com. Open M-W 11am-10pm, R-Sa 11am-11pm, Su 11am-9pm. MC, V, AmEx, 6 to Astor Pl.

♦ BOOKS, MAGAZINES & RECORDS

Accidental Records

A 24-hour used book and CD store carries everything from the hottest new releases to the obscure Latin music you've been searching for. Their extensive catalog selection of music is sure to please.

East Village, 140 Delancy St. (bet. Norfolk and Suffolk Sts.), (212) 677-3180. Open M-Su 10am-7pm. MC, V, AmEx. F to Delancy St.

Blackout Books

The radical writings available here are required reading for any potential East Village resident. Browsers can educate themselves on political uprisings, sexual liberation, or just have a good laugh with the books, newspapers, magazines, and alternative comic books. For the civic-minded, there's a board in back noting local meetings.

The Squatters of East 13th Street

Squatters had been as much a fact of the East Village as drugs or punk music when in the mid 90s they found themselves on their own. By then the clean up of the neighborhood had started and a string of buildings on East 13th Street, that had been occupied by sqatters for as much as twelve years, were raided and closed by the city.

The squatters of the East Village were different than most squatters. They'd converted their empty buildings into livable apartments made up of not just artists and anarchists but anyone who was willing to pitch in and make a decent home. Everyone knew of the squatters, they were the people that kept drugs off the block and organized community events. But, they lived in the East Village illegally.

On August 8, 1996 an Appellate Court reversed a State Supreme Court decision barring eviction, months away from the date that would pass ownership over to the squatters. Early in the morning on August 13 the New York Police Department arrived in riot gear with the Fire Department behind to confiscate everything in the buildings. Eighty people were quickly evicted and the block was sealed off while the police gutted all the buildings in order to make them uninhabitable.

Tompkins Square Park was packed the next day and a procession of 350 people headed up to 10th Street and unsealed another closed, squatted building. More police arrived with shields, tear gas, smoke bombs and everything else usually reserved for third world uprisings. There were 29 arrests and little support for the squatters. Editorials railed against their unwillingness to be part of the system and like that the last symbols of what the East Village was, were, for better or worse, swept away and replaced by bars.

East Village, 50 Ave. B (bet. 3rd and 4th Sts.), (212) 777-1967, www.panic.com/~blackout. Open M-Su 11am-10pm. Cash Only, F to Second Ave. ♿

Dance Tracks

If you're disappointed in the dance/electronica selection of your neighborhood megastore, look no further. At Dance Tracks you'll discover a wide selection of eurodance, club imports, your favorite DJ's remixes and house, house and more house music. The knowledgeable staff also gives fine recommendations catering to your particular taste, be it techno or trance.

East Village, 91 E. 3rd St. (at First Ave.), (212) 260-8729. Open M-F 12pm-9pm, Sa 12pm-8pm, Su 1:30pm-6pm. MC, V, AmEx, D. F to Second Ave.

Footlight Records

You probably won't find a more comprehensive vinyl shop dedicated to balladeers and crooners. Don't look for electronica or indie rock, this is more your grandma's kind of music: show tunes are big, and so is big band and international music. Prices are standard; used vinyl is under twenty bucks.

East Village, 113 E. 12th St. (bet. Third and Fourth Aves.), (212) 533-1572. Open M-F 11am-7pm, Sa 10am-6pm, Su 11am-5pm. MC, V, AmEx L to Third Ave.

Mondo Kim's

The sheer size and breadth of the selection, that goes far beyond the world of big name pop stars, is namely what recommends this alternative and indie megastore. The used selection is equally good, and their used CD policy a steal — they'll exchange your old stuff, as long as it's not damaged, straight across for any other used CD.

East Village, 6 St. Marks Pl. (at Third Ave.), (212) 505-0311, www.kimsvideo.com. Open M-Su 10am-12am. MC, V, AmEx, 6 to Astor Pl. ♿

Norman's Sound and Vision

Super friendly and knowledgeable Norman claims his store has the "best selection of jazz in New York." Also browse the vast assortment of rock, punk, indie, Latin and world music. Downstairs features used videos, CDs, vinyl and laserdiscs plus T-shirts and even leather jackets. The eager and unpretentious staff won't make you feel ashamed for buying that No Doubt CD.

East Village, 67 Cooper Sq. (bet. 7th and 8th Sts.), (212) 473-6599. Open M-Su 10am-10pm. MC, V, AmEx, DC, D, N R to 8th St.

St. Marks Books

Why go to a chain when everything you'd ever want can be found in the tall racks of this favorite excursion? Literature, sci-fi, and mystery are all strong suits. Plus, it's just cooler to shop here.

East Village, 31 Third Ave. (at 9th St.), (212) 260-7853. Open M-Sa 10am-12am, Su 11am-12am. MC, V, AmEx, D, 6 to

See Hear

Want to buy a 'zine without getting stared down and scoffed at by the ultra-cool record store guy? Check out the largest array of homemade publications around, with lots of stuff for hardcore and indie-rock fans as well as those who just appreciate irreverent writing that doesn't answer to advertisers.

East Village, 59 E. 7th St. (bet. First and Second Aves.), (212) 505-9781, www.zinemart.com. Open M-Su 12pm-8pm. MC, V, 6 to Astor Pl.

Shrine Records

Get your record players out; then get yourself to Shrine records, where you can find almost all of the music genres represented in their small but dense collection of vinyl and CDs. For three years, Shrine has catered to the more off-beat musical enthusiasts. An endless parade of "new" tunes goose steps through daily.

East Village, 9th St. (bet. First and A Aves.), (212) 529-6646. Open M-Su 12pm-10pm. Cash only, 6 to Astor Pl.

The Sound Library

Don't expect anything except quality vinyl at The Sound Library, where you'll find downtown Manhattan's best collection of soul, hip-hop, disco, jazz, reggae and blues. Other perks include flexible hours and the listening stations dedicated to the serious music connoisseur and DJ. Prices range from 10 bucks a vinyl; beware: the more rare the vinyl, the more pricey it gets.

East Village, 214 Ave. A (at E. 13th St.), (212) 598-9302. Open M-Su 12pm-9pm. MC, V, AmEx, D, L to First Ave.

St. Mark's Comics

From "The X-Men" to less conventional titles like "Sexy Sushi," there's enough here for any comic book connoisseur. Sales people, very deprived of sun, and nurtured on comics, help the eager and scoff at the stupid questions.

East Village, 11 St. Marks Pl. (bet. Second and Third Aves.), (212) 598-9439. Open T-Sa 10am-1am, Su-M 10am-11pm. MC, V, AmEx, 6 to Astor Pl.

St. Mark's Sounds

Split between two similar stores, rock, punk and indie, cheap new releases and a vast used CD selection make Sounds an unbeatable bargain for the non-top 40 set. An impoverished classical and jazz section is crammed in the back corner, while R&B, world music and other genres are

squeezed to the side. An eccentric shopper may find something in the 88 cent CD bin.
East Village, 20 St. Marks Pl. (bet. Second and Third Aves.), (212) 677-3444. Open Su-R 12pm-10:30pm, F-Sa 12pm-11:30pm. Cash only, ❻ to Astor Pl.

♦ GROCERY, GOURMET & SPECIALTY

Astor Wines and Spirits
Looking to get the most expensive wine around? Or maybe the cheapest one you can find? They have it all here. This store is famous for its huge selection, so for everything from hard liquor to the best champagne, it's the place to go.
East Village, 12 Astor Pl. (at Lafayette St.), (212) 674-7500, www.astoruncorked.com. Open M-Sa 9am-9pm. MC, V, AmEx, D, ❻ to Astor Place. ♿

East Village Meat Market
So they don't speak great English, the food's still remarkable at this Polish meat market. They have a dozen varieties of sausage alone. Struggling with the language barrier is well worth it.
East Village, 139 Second Ave. (bet. St. Marks Pl. and 9th St.), (212) 228-5590. Open M-Sa 8am-6pm. Cash Only. ❻ to Astor Pl.

Healthy Pleasures
Healthy Pleasures offers a wide selection of organic produce and meats, a range of vitamins and dietary supplements that would appease even the biggest hypochondriacs among us, plus prepared foods, health and beauty products, and healthy versions of every grocery item imaginable. With prices comparable to regular supermarkets (and sizable student discounts), Healthy Pleasures will help your body get into shape without trimming too much from your wallet.
East Village, 93 University Pl. (bet. 11th and 12th Sts.), (212) 353-3663, www.healthypleasures.com. Open M-Su 7:30am-11:30pm. MC, V, AmEx, D, ⓁⓃⓇ❹❺❻ to Union Sq.-14th St.

Veniero Pasticceria
This legendary Italian bakery is murder on the waistline — spectacular desserts, sensational pastries by the pound, and legendary wedding cakes.
East Village, 342 E. 11th St. (between First and Second Aves.), (212) 674-7264. Open M-Su 8am-12am. MC, V, AmEx, D, Ⓛ to 1st Ave. ♿

♦ MISCELLANEOUS

Alphabets
This place is pretty much a toy store for grown-ups. They carry all sorts of cards, postcards, t-shirts, and other goodies, so have fun and act like a kid again.
East Village, 115 Ave. A (bet. 7th and 8th Sts.), (212) 475-7250. Open M-F 12pm-10pm, Sa 11am-10pm, Su 12pm-8pm. MC, V, AmEx. ❻ to Astor Place. ♿

The Art Store
Okay, the name says it. This brand relatively new retailer with a downtown vibe has all of the supplies you need as well as some extras.
East Village, 15 Bond St (bet. Broadway and Lafayette St.), (212) 533-2444, www.artstores.com. Open M-F 9am-8pm, Sa 10am-7pm, Su 11am-6pm. MC, V, AmEx, ❻ to Bleecker St. ♿

Cinema Classics
A café/restaurant, video store and mini-movie theatre rolled into one, Cinema Classics provides a soothing atmosphere from which to view its eclectic film selections. Here you'll grab a cup of espresso and watch a silent film, or you may chance upon another offbeat cinematic delight. They're all classics here.
East Village, 332 E. 11th Street (bet. First and Second Aves.), (212) 971-1015, www.cinemaclassics.com. Open M-F 11:30-7:30 pm, Sa 12pm-6pm. Admission: $5-$5.50, Ⓛ to First Ave.

Kiehl's
A must for the famous lip balm, this landmark pharmacy has been in the same location since 1851. Stands out for its friendly service and best of all, it offers generous samples of fabulous skincare products.
East Village, 109 Third Ave. (bet. 13th and 14th Sts.), (212) 677-3171. Open M-W, F 10am-6pm, R 10am-7:30pm, Sa 10am-6pm. MC, V, AmEx, DC, ⓁⓃⓇ❹❺❻ to Union Sq.-14th St. ♿

Utrecht
Supply closet for many Parsons School of Design students, Utrecht has all of the basic art supplies. Unlike other art stores in the area, however it carries its own line of products, usually less expensive than equivalent brand names.
East Village, 111 Fourth Ave. (bet. 11th and 12th Sts.), (212) 777-5353, www.utrechtart.com. Open M-Sa 9am-7pm, Su 11am-5pm. MC, V, AmEx, D, ⓁⓃⓇ❹❺❻ to Union Sq. -14th St. ♿

White Trash
From shiny silver toasters to impressively tacky glassware sets, your own grandmother probably got rid of '50s and '60s junk like this twenty years ago. Nevertheless, it's all hip again and the prices aren't too inflated to be a reasonable and interesting alternative to outfitting your home in Lechters standards.
East Village, 304 E. 5th St. (bet. First and Second Aves.), (212) 598-5956. Open T-Sa 2pm-9pm, Su 1pm-8pm. MC, V, Ⓕ to Second Ave., ❻ to Astor Pl.

Arts & Recreation

♦ LEISURE

Anthology Film Archives

Started in 1970 as a museum devoted to avant garde cinema, this institution has since become a mecca for established and aspiring artists seeking inspiration and hardened film buffs seeking things even they've never heard of. With a vast library and programming designed to showcase it, an excellent opportunity is provided to see rare foreign films, early works by now-established directors, and legendary but rarely seen Warhol flicks, etc.

East Village, 32 Second Ave. (at 2nd St.), (212)505-5181, www.anthology-filmarchives.org. F *to Second Ave.*

City Cinemas Village East

By all indications this seems to be just another many-screened showplace for big-budget Hollywood productions, but within the nondescript exterior lies the preserved interior of the old Yiddish Theater complete with its original adornments and multitiered theater-style seating. So for a real treat, buy a ticket for whatever is showing in Theater Number One and get there early to check out this historical landmark.

East Village, 181-189 Second Ave. (at 12th St.), (212) 529-6799. L N R 4 5 6 *to Union Sq.-14th St.* ♿

The Tenth Street Baths and Heath Club

The Russian Room: All stone, dark, real big space, maybe 180 degrees, steam. Turkish Room: wood paneling, little smaller but plenty big, same temperature, dry heat. In between: shower, conversation with locals, ice-cold pool. Whether it's for you, who knows – that it feels great is enough. You go from hot to cold as many times as you can while your body, once in shock, numbs into a sort of bliss.

East Village, 268 E.10th St. (bet. First and A Aves.) (212) 473-8806, www.russianturkishbaths.com. Open M-F 9am-10pm, Sa-Su 7:30am-9pm. Men only Su 9am-2pm; Women only Wed. 9am-2pm. MC, V, AmEx, D 6 *to Astor Pl.*

♦ PERFORMANCE

Amato Opera Theatre

Head downtown to see the divas of tomorrow paying their dues in this intimate setting. An alternative for opera lovers who lack the funds for nosebleed seats at the Met. One of Amato's goals is to foster opera appreciation by making it more accessible, so many performances are English translations of Italian operas.

East Village, 319 Bowery St. (at 2nd St.), (212) 228-8200, www.amato. org. Cash Only, 6 *to Bleecker St.*

Public Theater

Founded by the legendary Joseph Papp, "A Chorus Line" started here. The beautiful red brick Italian Renaissance style building was once the Astor Library and became the permanent home of the New York Shakespeare Festival in 1967. Along with the Bard and other classics, the five stages here also host an eclectic mix of European imports, established and up-and-coming American playwrights. New York's most venerable avant-garde theater, now featuring Joe's Pub, a performance space/bar has live music, dance and spoken word.

East Village, 425 Lafayette St., (bet. Astor Pl. and 4th St.), (212) 539-8500, MC, V, AmEx, D, 6 *to Astor Pl.*

Context

"Like a kitchen with lots of different vegetation," is the somewhat convoluted definition for this multi-media performing arts space, showing dance theater, experimental musical performances, and opera regularly. Shows can go on for up to two weeks by popular demand.

East Village, 28 Ave. A (bet. 2nd and 3rd Sts.), (212) 505-2702. MC, V, AmEx, F *to Second Ave.*

La MaMa etc.

Four small theaters offer new and experimental dance and theater, as well as off-beat performance. The avant-garde nature of the place means shows are hit or miss, but cheap tickets make it worthwhile to test the odds.

East Village, 74A E. 4th St. (bet. Second Ave. and Bowery St.), (212) 475-7710, www.lamama.org. MC, V, AmEx, F *to Second Ave.*

New York Theatre Workshop

This downtown theater staple caters to a hip crowd and often presents work from the farther corners of the mainstream. It's the original home of Broadway sensation *Rent*, as well as the rock musical *Bright Lights, Big City* and *The Most Fabulous Story Ever Told*. Annual "Just Add Water" festival presents work in development for future seasons. Rush tickets are available for most performances.

East Village, 79 E. 4th St. (bet. Second Ave. and The Bowery), (212) 460-5475. MC, V, AmEx, DC. F *to Second Ave.* ♿

P.S. 122

This small performance space in a converted school serves as a showplace for cutting-edge dance, theater and performance art. Artists range from obscure but talented newcomers to established members of the downtown scene.

East Village, 150 First Ave. (at 9th St.), (212) 770-5288. MC, V, AmEx, 6 *to Astor Pl.* ♿

Pearl Theatre

This classic repertory/resident company sticks to a strict pre-WWI itinerary, with productions of Shakespeare, Moliere, Sophocles, and others of their ilk, as well as revived relics. Shows generally run seven weeks.

East Village, 80 St. Marks Pl. (at First Ave.), (212) 598-9802, www.pearltheatre.org. MC, V, D, 6 *to Astor Pl.* ♿

St. Mark's Church-in-the-Bowery

A quiet and beautiful cultural oasis in the bustling East Village, this century-old church is home to three excellent arts "projects," including Danspace and the Ontological Theater. Most notable is the Poetry Project, one of the only programs of its kind, offering special literary events and workshops for budding poets, a forum for both well-known and up-and-coming poets to read their work.

East Village, 131 E. 10th St. (at Second Ave.), (212) 533-4650. Cash Only, 6 *to Astor Pl.*

Variety Arts Theater

Campy theater and a distorted dose of pop culture. Recent productions have included a new work by writer/drag queen Charles Busch and a musical based on the life of Patsy Cline. Proof that theater doesn't have to be dull or squeaky-clean.

East Village, 110 Third Ave. (bet. 13th and 14th Sts.), (212) 239-6200. MC, V, AmEx, D, L N R 4 5 6 *to Union Sq.-14th St.* ♿

♦ MUSEUMS & CULTURAL CENTERS

Ukrainian Museum

This small museum features exhibits of contemporary Ukrainian culture and history. Recent exhibitions have included folk art and Easter eggs.

East Village, 203 Second Ave. (bet. 12th and 13th Sts.), (212) 228-0110, www.brama.com/ukranian_ museum. Open W-Su 1pm-5pm. Cash Only, Admission: $2-$3, L N R 4 5 6 *to Union Sq.-14th St.* ♿

♦ PARKS

Tompkins Square Park

Notorious for the 1988 riots, Tompkins Square Park has tamed a bit since the 1992 renovations. East Village mothers can be seen toting around their babies in prams, walking right past the ever-present homeless population. Impromptu jam sessions, chalk designs supporting the "no heroin" campaign and chess marathons remind us that the gentries still share this public space with the East Village's namesake.

East Village, bet. Aves. A and B (bet. E. 10th and E. 7th Sts.), 6 *to Astor Pl.*

♦ GALLERIES & LIBARIES

Bullet Space

This "Urban Artist Collaborative" in a deteriorating building showcases city artists known for political and challenging works. The stark gallery also has a musical space, community center, and residence for artists. Open weekends 2pm-5pm, by appointment only.

East Village, 292 E. 3rd St. (bet. Aves. C and D), (212) 982-3580. F *to Second Ave.*

Cooper Union

An all expense paid college specializing in art, architecture and engineering education, Cooper Union's standards are some of the highest in the country. The school houses the Houghton Art Gallery and the Great Hall, the site of an 1860 speech by Abraham Lincoln.

East Village, 7 E. 7th St. (at Third Ave.), (212) 353-4100, 6 *to Astor Place.,*♿

Gracie Mansion Gallery

This gallery has long been the housing site of many prestigious contemporary artists from its birth in the East Village to its present incarnation in Chelsea. Warhol, Basquiat, Haring and Lewitt are just a few famous names in their collection. Today Gracie Mansion Gallery retains its potency in presenting and curating exhibits that cover the spectrum of striped neon sculptures to muted earth-toned paintings.

East Village, 54 Saint Marks Pl. (bet. First and Second Aves.), (212) 505-7055. Open by appointment. 6 *to Astor Place, *L to First Ave. Temporary exhibition location in: Chelsea, 504 W. 22nd St. (at Tenth Ave.), (212)645-7656, Open T-Sa 11am-6pm and by appointment* A C E *to 23rd St.*

Nightlife

♦ BARS

2A
A duplex of debauch. Yes, two levels of libation and liberation. Go where the rest of Avenue A goes to throw aside the ridged framework of what is deemed socially respectable out on the street of the East Village. An hour of merriment inside these walls and the volume and crowd don't seem so bad.
East Village, 27 Ave. A (at 2nd St.), no phone. Open M-Su 4pm-4am. Cash Only, F to Second Ave.

Ace Bar
You can have a beer and play darts or pool in this neighborhood bar and never be pushed around, because it's such a cavernous place. Take a gander at the array of old lunchboxes you owned or wanted to own when you were in grade school. It's never too loud or too crowded and that in itself makes it a good place to go.
East Village, 531 E. 5th St. (bet. Aves. A and B), (212) 979-8476. Open M-Su 2pm-4am. MC, V, AmEx, D, F to Second Ave.

Angel's Share
House rules border on the Draconian: no loud conversation, no parties bigger than four, and no standing. But the trouble is worth it. The ambience is consequently intimate, the drinks professionally mixed and the floor-to-ceiling windows offer an excellent view of Stuyvesant Street. Bring a date.
East Village, 8 Stuyvesant St. (at Third Ave.), (212) 777-5415. Open M-Su 7pm-2am. MC, V, AmEx, DC, 6 to Astor Pl.

B Bar
Models still pose beneath the globular lights of this NoHo scene staple, though it's not the fashion mecca it once was. The spacious, enclosed outdoor seating is popular.
East Village, 40 E. 4th St. (at Bowery St.), (212) 475-2220. Open T-Su 11pm-4am, M 11pm-2am. MC, V, AmEx, DC, 6 to Bleecker St.

Barmacy
Owner Deb Parker (of Beauty Bar fame) welcomes private functions, film shoots, photo shoots, and "anything else you'd like to shoot except drugs" at her establishment. It's not reserved most nights, however, when stylish downtowners crowd the place for generously-poured drinks.
East Village, 538 E. 14th St. (bet. A and B Aves.), (212) 228-2240. Open M-F 5:30pm-4am, Sa-Su 7:30pm-4am. MC, V, L to First Ave.

Beauty Bar
Sparkling walls glitter and vintage hair dryers function as lounge chairs at this beauty salon-turnedbar. The owner's own collection of 40s hairpins and pomade ads add to the deliciously kitschy mood. Wednesday afternoon manicure and drink specials are a must.
East Village, 231 E. 14th St. (bet. Second and Third Aves.), (212) 539-1389. Open M-F 5pm-4am, Sa-Su 7pm-4am. MC, V, L N R 4 5 6 to Union Sq.-14th St.

The Boiler Room
This is more lounge than bar; the pool table, for example, is used only as seating. Classic disco sets the stage for light cruising. Frugal lushes indulge in one-dollar beers and shots on Mondays. There's a mixed crowd in the early evening, but around nine the boys take over.
East Village, 86 E. 4th St. (bet. First and Second Aves.), (212) 254-7536. Open M-Su 4pm-4am. Cash Only, F to Second Ave.

Botanica
Botanica's Santerìa-inspired decor and snappy but friendly bartenders make this one of the neighborhood's most comfortable places to get sloppy. There's a full bar and a decent selection of draft beers, but don't ask for anything too complicated or silly unless you're prepared to take the heat.
East Village, 47 E. Houston St. (bet. Mulberry and Mott Sts.), (212) 343-7251. Open M-Su 5pm-4am. Cash Only, N R to Prince St., 6 to Spring St.

Box Car Lounge
They have a cool glass and metal bar area at the front and a lounge area at the back-nice setup. What they don't have is a liquor license, so you can't get the hard stuff, but Box Car Lounge makes up for it with sake martinis and other adventurous drinks. It also has an airy garden and good happy hour bargains.

East Village, 168 Ave. B (bet. 10th and 11th Sts.), (212) 473-2830. Open M-F 4:30pm-4am, Sa-Su 6pm-4am. MC, V, AmEx, DC, (L) to First Ave.

Cherry Tavern

It's small. It's cheap. It's got a pool table and a good jukebox but on weekends it can be suffocatingly packed and smoky. So it's a good place to go to kick back a few beers after work or whatever and a place to avoid on a Saturday night.

East Village, 441 E. 6th St. (bet. First and A Aves.), (212) 777-1448. Open M-Su 6pm-3:45am. Cash Only (6) to Astor Pl.

The Cock

The name says it all? Bring your earplugs and surgical masks, because it's not for the faint of lungs or ears. On Saturday nights the party is called Foxy, where anything can and usually does go; and on Sundays it's Sperm, where, obviously, only boys dare to tread.

East Village, 188 Ave. A (at 11th St.), (212) 777-6254. Open M-Su 9.30-4am. Cash Only (L) to First Ave.

Coyote Ugly

For all those not in the know, a coyote ugly is when you get so loaded that you wind up going home with someone and waking up to find that they are singularly unattractive and you would rather cut off your own arm than wake them up so that you can slip out. It's not pretty and neither is this East Village standard.

East Village, 153 First Ave. (bet. 9th and 10th Sts.), (212) 477-4431. Open M-R 2pm-4am, F-Su 12:30pm- 4am. MC, V, (6) to Astor Pl.

Decibel

Go early and with a small group, because this small, beautiful sake bar gets packed fast. Hipsters descend on it because it's ultimately cave like and mellow, great for dates. If you want something more fast-paced, check out its spawn Megadecibel.

East Village, 240 E. 9th St (bet. Second and Third Aves.), (212) 979-2733. Open M-Sa 8pm-3am, Su 8pm-1am. MC, V, AmEx. (6) to Astor Place.

Doc Holiday's

"I'm trapped in here with the convicts who love me," moans bartender Tari — and she's just talking about the regulars. On weekends, this rollicking country-western joint swarms with hell-raisers who come to admire the wild animal pelts on the walls and the even wilder staff who can often be found dancing on the bar. Try the homestyle BBQ food.

East Village, 141 Ave. A (bet. 8th and 9th Sts.), (212) 979-0312. Open M-Su 12am-4am. Cash Only, (L) to First Ave.

CBGB

Owner and founder Hilly Kristal came up with the name as an acronym of what he thought was then the most popular music: Country, Bluegrass, Blues. A bunch of these bands played but without much success.

A couple months after the December 1973 opening Kristal was fixing an awning when three young men, in tattered jeans, asked what was going on inside then walked away. A few days later the three men's manager came by and booked CBGB's first punk act, Television. Television, brought along another band The Ramones.

The Stilletos were next but they quickly broke up and Debbie Harry took over as the head of Blondie. Television front man Tom Verlaine showed up with new friend, a poet, Patti Smith. That's when Allen Ginsburg and Andy Warhol became regulars alongside the crowds of kids.

Monday nights were when new bands auditioned and when the Talking Heads auditioned in 1975. Other bands included Mink Deville, Suicide, The Miami's, The Shirts, Orchestra Luna and Tom Petty and the Heartbreakers. It wasn't punk then, it was street rock, and an escape from disco and the drawn out solos of rock bands. It's spirit lives on in phases, some times latent, sometimes in your face, at CBGBs, in the East Village.

Drinkland
This hip spot has three separate drinking areas, all decorated in '60s kitsch. Most notable is the White Room, whose walls are completely covered with white padded vinyl. This kind of atmosphere more than makes up for the inconsistent drinks.
East Village, 339 East 10th Street (bet. Aves. A and B), (212) 228-2453, www.drinkland.com. Open M-Sa 6pm-4am, Su 8pm-3am. Cash Only, 6 *to Astor Pl.*

11th Street Bar
Locals fleeing the influx of Avenue A tavern tourists find asylum in this newcomer. Narrow in front at the crowded bar, it opens up in the back with a handful of tables large enough to fit all your roommates or new friends.
East Village, 510 E. 11th St. (bet. Aves. A and B), (212) 982-3929. Open M-F 4pm-4am, Sa-Su 3pm-4am. MC, V, AmEx, L *to First Ave.*

Holiday Cocktail Lounge
Steven Lutak's bar hasn't changed much since he bought it in the '50s, although the crowd has. A small working-class Eastern European contingent still hangs out during the early hours, but at nights a younger clientele, who "like to wear used clothing," as Lutak puts it, move in to take advantage of the cheap drinks and excellent jukebox.
East Village, 75 E. 8th St. (bet. First and Second Aves.). Open M-Su 3pm-1am. Cash Only, N R *to 8th St.,* 6 *to Astor Pl.*

International Bar
Cheap drinks can make you dizzy and claustrophobic at this small dive. You'll have to squeeze past the long bar to the small back part where, if you're lucky, you can get a seat. It's got a mixed crowd and a decent jukebox-and did we mention the cheap drinks yet?
East Village, 120 First Ave. (bet. 7th and 8th Sts.), (212) 777-9244. Open M 12pm-4am, T-W 7pm-4am, F-Su 2pm-4am. Cash Only, 6 *to Astor Pl.*

KGB
Old Soviet paraphernalia give this small upstairs barroom an illicit feel, which is reinforced by the regular poetry readings and theater downstairs. It's perfect for bringing out your inner subversive artist with a good stiff drink.
East Village, 85 E. 4th St. (bet. The Bowery and Second Ave.), (212) 505-3360. Open M-Su 7pm-4am. Cash Only, F *to Second Ave.*

Lakeside Lounge
Come prepared to wait for your drinks since this hipster haunt is packed even on nights the bartender calls "real slow." Lots of live bands, too.

East Village, 162 Ave. B (at 10th St.), (212) 529-8463, www.lakesidelounge.com. Open M-Su 4pm-4am. MC, V, AmEx, D, L *to First Ave.*

Manitoba's
Owned and operated by "Handsome" Dick Manitoba, frontman for NYC's legendary punkers the Dictators, Manitoba's pours some of the East Village's strongest drinks. Dick books live music ranging anywhere from country to rock 7 nights a week.
East Village, 99 Ave. B (bet. 6th and 7th Sts.), (212) 982-2511. Open M-Su 4pm-4am. MC, V, AmEx, N R *to 8th St.,* 6 *to Astor Pl.*

Mars Bar
A rowdy and boozy bunch fill this tattered shoebox of a bar at all hours. Possibly the dumpiest, most dishevelled bar on the planet but, for some inexplicable reason, charming nevertheless. There's a less than five-percent chance you'll get on favorable terms with the bartender, but if you succeed you'll never pay for a drink again. Ever.
East Village, 25 E. 1st St. (at Second Ave.), No Phone. Open M-Su 12pm-4am. Cash Only, F *to Second Ave.*

Milano's Bar
Milano's has graced this site for over 100 years and it looks like it. Yet there's a kind of charm to this neighborhood bar, due to its air of timelessness. Faded photos of Sinatra and the Yankees grace the walls, and a jukebox plays standards and classic rock.
East Village, 51 E. Houston St. (bet. Mulberry and Mott Sts.), (212) 226-8632. Open M-Su 8am-4am. Cash Only, N R *to Prince St.,* 6 *to Spring St.*

Mona's
Punk rock lives! In the jukebox at Mona's! It's a favorite place for your East Village squatter "homeless" kids who come here complete with their mangy dogs and multiple tattoos and piercings (which cost a lot more that the dollar they ask from you on Ave A) and families back in Connecticut who just want their little baby to come back home.
East Village, 224 Ave. B (bet. 13th and 14th Sts.), (212) 353-3780. Open M-Su 3pm-4am. Cash Only, L *to First Ave.*

M & R Bar
A simple combination of good drinks and classic American food have kept the M & R in style, despite increased competition from Orchard and Ludlow Streets. Open for brunch on Saturdays.
East Village, 264 Elizabeth St. (bet. Houston and Spring Sts.), (212) 226-0559. Open M-Su 5:30pm-2am. MC, V, AmEx, Ⓝ Ⓡ *to Prince St.* ♿ 🚬

Niagara
Niagara puts a hip spin on nostalgia. From the bartenders in their silk, hand-painted ties to the bamboo-walled tiki lounge downstairs, Niagara pays homage to America's pre-Vietnam years. The tiki lounge features a full range of tropical drinks guaranteed to turn any East Village hipster into a zombie for the night.
East Village, 112 Ave. A (bet. 7th and 8th Sts.), (212) 420-9517. Open M-Su 4pm-4am. MC, V, AmEx, Ⓝ Ⓡ *to 8th St.,* ⑥ *to Astor Pl.* 🚬

No Malice Palace
Be careful; you might walk right past this signless black hole in the wall. But if you don't, inside you will find a comfortable dark hideaway to lounge your body and lubricate your tonsils. The drinks tend to be on the pricey side.
East Village, 197 E. 3rd St. (bet. A and B Aves.), (212) 254-9184. Open M-Su 7:30pm-4am. Cash Only Ⓕ *to Second Ave.*

9C
Formerly the Red Bar, 9C's a tiny space that packs in a down-to-earth crowd for the Sunday Blue Grass Jam and Alphabet City Opry on Monday nights.
East Village, 700 E. 9th St. (at Ave. C), (212) 358-0048. Open M-Su 5pm-4am. Cash Only, Ⓛ *to First Ave.*

The Opium Den
Find shockingly clean downtown kids at this gothic lock-in. Saints and votive candles filling the room lend it a creepiness that would prompt anyone to reach for another drink.
East Village, 29 E. 3rd St. (bet. The Bowery and Second Ave.), (212) 505-7344. Open M-Su 8pm-4am. Cash Only, Ⓕ *to Second Ave.* 🚬

Starlight
A long, dark bar with an open couch-filled area in the back, Starlight is a usually crowded gay bar that caters to the lesbian population on its massively popular Sunday night party. Other than that, it's mostly a boy place.
East Village, 167 Ave. A (bet. 10th and 11th Sts.), (212) 475-2172. Open W-Su 8pm-4am. Cash only ⑥ *to Astor Pl.*

Temple Bar
It's the epitome of understated elegance; the dark wood interior is quietly beautiful, rather than forcibly chic. The perfect place to impress a date if money is no object.
East Village, 332 Lafayette St. (bet. Bleecker and Houston Sts.), (212) 925-4242. Open M-R 5pm-1am, F-Sa 5pm-2am, Su 7pm-12am. MC, V, AmEx, DC, ⑥ *to Bleecker St.,* Ⓑ Ⓓ Ⓕ Ⓠ *to Broadway-Lafayette St.* ♿ 🚬

Wonder Bar
Unwind after work at this mellow dive. The decor recalls a circus, with the DJ peeking through a hole in the wall while a blue polka-dot strobe lights up zebra-striped walls.

Best and Worst Bars on Avenue A

Worst Bar

No Malice Palace
This place is hard to find and that's good. If you do you'll be greeted by the sort of lounge furniture you can find at much better lounges for the same prices.

Best Bar

Drinkland
If you're going to make it as a bar in New York, you don't just serve drinks. There has to be something special about you and there's something special about the James Bond-bad-guy, retro decor of this bar, which is like no other.

East Village, 505 E. 6th St. (bet. A and B Aves.), (212) 777-9105. Open M-Su 6pm-4am. Cash Only, F *to Second Ave.*

XVI

A hip-hop vibe moves the crowd in the downstairs lounge while upstairs the mood mellows. Sophisticates gather in the front hallway and goths congregate in the back. A friskier-than-usual, tourist-free pick-up scene is a plus here.
East Village, 16 First Ave. (bet. 1st and 2nd Sts.), (212) 260-1549. Open M-Su 8pm-4am. AmEx, F *to Second Ave.*

♦ CLUBS

Flamingo

It's striving to overcome its reputation as a snooty Euro bar, by booking cutting edge techno and house DJs that wouldn't be caught dead spinning bubblegum dance for the bridge and tunnel crowd.
East Village, 219 Second Ave. (bet. 13th and 14th Sts.), (212) 533-2860. MC, V, AmEx, D, Cover: $5-$10, 6 *to Astor Pl.,* L *to Third Ave.*

Guernica

Occupying the space of the now-defunct after-hours club Save the Robots, Guernica has a hard act to follow. Although hardly as decadent as its predecessor, Guernica makes up for its tameness with a gourmet late night menu and some top house and drum and bass DJs.
East Village, 25 Ave. B (bet. 2nd and 3rd Sts.), (212) 674-0984, www.guernicanyc.com. MC, V, AmEx, Cover: free-$5, F *to Second Ave.*

Joe's Pub at the Public Theater

This elegant but cozy lounge hosts some of the city's best live music, from hip-hop to cabaret, and acts are nearly always followed by a DJ. The drinks may be expensive but the waitstaff makes up for the prices by being so genial you want to hug them. Live acts are consistently good, so come by even if you have never heard of the musicians.
East Village, 425 Lafayette St. (bet. East 4th and Astor Pl.), (212) 539-8777, www.joespub.com. MC, V, AmEx, Cover: $5-$20, 6 *to Astor Pl.*

Webster Hall

This is one of the city's biggest nightclubs, were the sophisticated to the zany come to bump and grind. Four spacious floors spin disco, reggai and techno. You can even shoot a game of pool. Don't miss out on the flying trapeze show in the wee hours.
East Village, 125 E. 11th St. (bet. Third and Fourth Aves.), (212) 353-1600. MC, V, AmEx, D, Cover: $20-$25, L N R 4 5 6 *Union Sq.-14th St.*

♦ MUSIC

Bowery Ballroom

The Bowery Ballroom is one of the premiere venues in the city- it consistently gets good acts, the space is simultaneously cavernous and cozy, and for God's sake, the coat check line moves.
acoustic, country, eclectic, hip-hop, latin, pop
East Village, 6 Delancey St. (bet. The Bowery and Chrystie St.), (212) 533-2111, www.boweryballroom. Open F-Sa 8pm-4am. MC, V, Cover: $10-$20, B D Q *to Grand St.*

Brownies

One of the best places to catch bands not quite on the commercial radio scene. Sunday shows are all ages.
blues, rock
East Village, 169 Ave. A (bet. 10th and 11th Sts.), (212) 420-8392, www.browniesnyc.com. Open 7pm-3am. MC, V, AmEx, Cover: $6-$10, 6 *to Astor Pl.,* L *to First Ave.*

CBGB

A legend, CB's has been a mecca for artists and punks since the 70s, helping to launch acts like Blondie, the Ramones and Patti Smith. You can still catch local and national acts every night of the week.
alternative, pop, rock
East Village, 315 Bowery (at Bleecker St.), (212) 982-4052, www.cbgb.com. Open 7pm-4am. Cash Only, Cover: $3-$12, 6 *to Bleecker St.*

CB's 313 Gallery

The kinder, gentler sibling of CB's. It boasts a superior sound system and staff, and some of the best acoustic based music in town. A downstairs lounge, with DJ, serves brick oven pizza.
acoustic, electronica, folk, rock
East Village, 313 Bowery St. (at Bleecker St.), (212) 677-0455, www.cbgb.com, Open M-Su 12pm-4am. MC, V, AmEx, DC, D, Cover: $5-$8, F *to Second Ave.,* 6 *to Bleecker St.*

Continental

Everybody from Patti Smith to The Ramones have played this famous club. Even Guns n' Roses could be seen here before they hit it big. There's an indoor ATM for the cash-strapped.
hard rock, ska
East Village, 25 Third Ave. (at St. Marks Pl.), (212) 529-6924, www. nytrash.com/continental. Open 4pm-4am. Cash Only, Cover: Free-$10, 6 *to Bleecker St.*

Den of Cin

One of the East Village's newest clubs is a small listening room underneath the famous Two Boots Video. It's a comfortable space to hear up-and-coming artists. Many performers play solo here because of the small space, which only adds to the intimacy of the show. Beer and wine available.

acoustic, pop, solo artists

East Village, 44 Ave. A (at 3rd St.), (212) 613-1670. Open M-Su 8pm-1am. Cash Only, No cover, F *to Second Ave.*

Fez under Time Cafe

Originally the site of Sticky Mike's, a Warhol hangout, now housing hip singer-songwriters like Ellis Paul, Peter Mulvey, and Jennifer Kimball. This unique room has mirrored columns and sparkly vinyl booths, and every so often the room vibrates from the subway train passing by underneath. Hidden treasure: the Mingus Big Band every Thursday night. Full menu, full bar.

acoustic, comedy, jazz, rock, singer-songwritter

East Village, 380 Lafayette St. (at Great Jones St.), (212) 533-3000, www.timecafenyc.com. Open Su-R 6pm-2am, F-Sa 6pm-4am. Cash only, Cover: $8-$20, 6 *to Bleecker St.,* \

The Fort at Sidewalk Cafe

Before moving to the backroom of the Sidewalk Cafe, the Fort was an after-hours club on the Lower East Side. It still retains its underground appeal, centered around manager Lach's Anti-Folk Anti-Hoot on Mondays, which is an open mic unlike others in the Bleecker St. folk scene. Sidewalk Cafe features one of the cheapest breakfast specials in NYC, as well as a full menu and bar.

folk, anti-folk, rock

East Village, 94 Ave. A (at 6th St.), (212) 473-7373. Open Su-R 8pm-5am, F-Sa 24hrs. MC, V, AmEx, Cover: $3, F *to Second Ave.*

Irving Plaza

Mostly a venue for national touring acts with major record label backing and a fair amount of radio play. It's a place to come for the music, not the atmosphere; a long, narrow design causes the crowd to crush at the front.

most genres of music (radio-friendly)

East Village, 17 Irving Pl. (at 15th St.), (212) 777-6800, www.irvingplaza. com. Open M-F 12pm-6:30am, Sa 1pm-4am. AmEx, call for cover charges for individual shows, L N R 4 5 6 *to Union Sq.-14th St.*

The Living Room

Currently reigning as one of the hippest songwriter venues in New York, even though (or maybe because) it's been around for years. A small room with a relaxed atmosphere and some of the top names in innovative music playing for tips only, like local faves Trina Hamlin and Dayna Kurtz. Not a place to sit and chat, but your silence will be well-rewarded. Food is excellent and cheap, and there is a full bar.

acoustic, experimental, folk, jazz

East Village, 84 Stanton St. (at Allen St.), (212) 533-7237, www.living roomny.com. Open 6:30 pm-2am. Cash Only, Cover: $5 (suggested), F *to Second Ave.*

Mercury Lounge

Once a headstone shop, the Mercury Lounge has established itself as a premiere venues for "just-breaking" bands. High stage, excellent sound system, and standing room only for three to five acts per night.

acoustic, alternative, rock

East Village, 217 East Houston St. (bet. Essex and Norfolk Sts.), (212) 260-1214, www.mercuryloungenyc. com. Open 8pm-12am. MC, V, Cover: $7-$12, F *to Second Ave.*

Nightingale Bar

The Nightingale has a reputation for being the favorite late night jam spot for many now-famous acts. Chris Barrow from the Spin Doctors can still be seen solo on Wednesday nights. You can see local acts here seven nights a week. Happy hour from 1pm-8pm daily!

pop and rock bands with the occasional soloist

East Village, 213 Second Ave. (at 13th St.), (212) 473-9398. Open M-Su 1pm-4am. Cash Only, Cover: free-$5, L N R 4 5 6 *to Union Sq.-14th St.*

Nuyorican Poets Cafe

The Nuyorican has made a name for itself as a center for experimental music and spoken word art in New York City. Besides its performances, visitors can see visual art exhibits and film retrospectives. Best value: Friday night poetry slam, from which is fielded NYC's nationally competitive team. No food, but wine & beer available.

acoustic, experimental, hip-hop, latin, jazz, salsa, spoken word

East Village, 236 East 3rd St. (bet. Aves. B and C), (212) 505-8183, www.nuyorican.org. Call for schedule and showtimes. Cash Only, Cover: $6-$25, F to 2nd Ave.

Greenwich Village

Greenwich Village has earned its reputation as the elder statesman of hip, having housed generations of artists, revolutionaries, and writers like Dylan Thomas and Edna St. Vincent Millay. In addition to countless clusters of coffee houses, jazz and cabaret clubs, and taverns, the Village is home to New York University, perhaps the area's greatest cultural influence nowadays.

Bordered by two major downtown thoroughfares to the north and south (14th and Houston Streets, respectively), the Village is a limitless resource in a city of limitless resources. Its epicenter, flanked by Seventh Avenue South and Broadway, is constantly abuzz, though perhaps softcore for some grittier urbanites. Shoe shops line 8th Street east of Sixth Avenue, while record stores are ubiquitous along Bleecker and MacDougal Streets.

Meanwhile, Washington Square Park is an open playground for residential and visiting masses alike, replete with live street shows, sun bathing, and chess. To the south and the east of the park, the shops which crowd the NYU area foist their schlocky wares upon the newcomers 365 days per year, be they tourists or the fresh crop of gawking freshman. After dark, hip nightcrawlers ascend from the subway station at Sheridan Square, thrust into the big city atmosphere of the Village's busiest and most confusing intersection before dispersing into the various cafés, clubs, and theaters which fan out along the nearby streets.

However, Greenwich Village is not simply a commercial center and tourist destination. It's also one of the city's few neighborhoods which has artfully blended its past and present, supporting an ever more radical and diversified gay and artistic community while still accommodating the many families who quietly thread through the sea of tourists on their way to Balducci's to pick up bagels and lox. Just when nostalgic critics begin to arm themselves with accusations of the neighborhood having sold out, the Village reveals its authenticity.

The area west of Seventh Avenue South, known appropriately as the West Village, is one of the most quiet and beautiful sections of the city. This cloistered neighborhood shelters a nest of tangled, tranquil streets, among which it's easy to lose oneself. Lined with slender trees and fussy federal style doorways with fluted columns on either side, residential streets like Barrow, Commerce, Jane, and Perry have held true to their roots as a genteel enclave, remaining remarkably settled and serene. These routes, architecturally reminiscent of the narrow nooks of Amsterdam, are peppered with some of the most romantic restaurants the city has to offer.

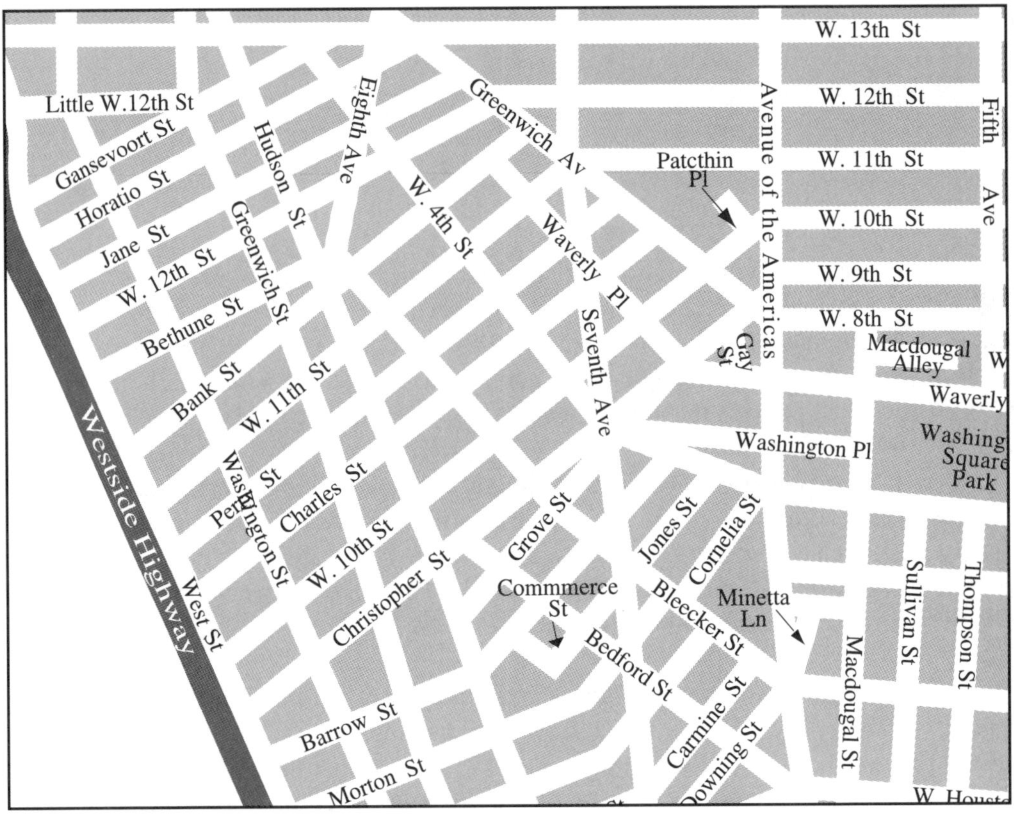

Dining

♦ RESTAURANTS

Anglers and Writers

No longer home to the *Paris Review* crowd, but the soups and stews are probably better now than they were in the good old days. There will often be a wait for Sunday brunch.

Greenwich Village, 420 Hudson St. (at St. Luke's Pl.), (212) 675-0810. Open M-Su 10am-11pm. Cash Only, Entrées: $8-$14, 1 9 *to Christopher St.-Sheridan Sq.* ♿

Chi-Chi Steak

Featuring a 4pm-8pm happy hour with extensive cocktail menu, this trendy spot serves American fare to a largely gay clientele.

Greenwich Village, 135 Christopher St. (bet. Hudson and Greenwich Sts.), (212) 462-0027. Cash Only, Entrées: $5-$10, 1 9 *to Christopher St.-Sheridan Sq.*

Cornelia Street Cafe

The leisurely ambiance of soothing lights coupled with a background jazz and blues blend complements the similarly unforced take on simple New American cuisine. Venture downstairs after dinner to catch nightly theater, jazz, and poetry performances in the cabaret.

Greenwich Village, 29 Cornelia St. (bet. Bleecker and W. 4th Sts.), (212) 989-9318, www.corneliast cafe.com. Open M-Su 10am-12am. MC, V, AmEx, DC, Entrées: $12-$15, A B C D E F Q *to West 4th St.-Washington Sq.* ♿

Corner Bistro

Locals lament the marathon waits at this immensely popular burger-and-beer joint, but they still throng despite the slow service. It's the prime territory to see and be seen: the basic, effortlessly funky version of the neighborhood haunt made palatable to yuppie Villagers by virtue of its enduring cachet and steady stream of televised college basketball games. Tables long ago marked by penknives crowd the middle, though intimate space may be free in back.

Greenwich Village, 331 W. 4th St. (bet. 12th and Jane Sts.), (212) 242-9502. Open M-Su 11:30am-4am. Cash Only, Entrées: $4-$6, A C E *to 14th St.,* L *to Eighth Ave.* ♿

PLACES TO GO:

One if by Land Two if by Sea
Very, very romantic dining. "I've been thinking about you, Liz." "I've been thinking about you too, Rob." "I love you." "I love you." This sort of thing is overheard.

Lectorum Bookstore
The place to go for all of your Spanish literary needs.

Film Forum
Always a combination of a new movie you should see and a retrospective of a movie you've always meant to see.

Spa
The hottest club in New York, while it lasts.

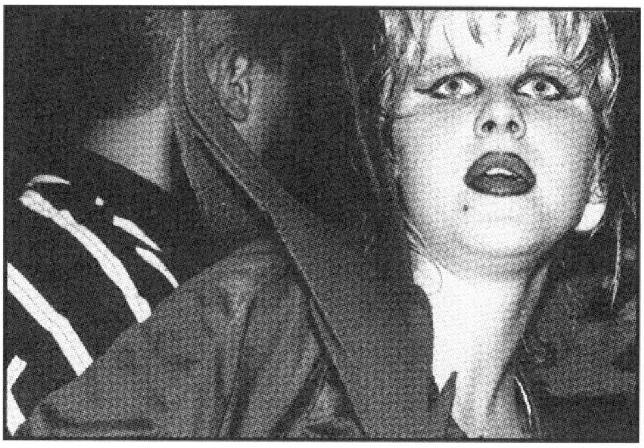

Cowgirl Hall of Fame
Before riot-girls there were cowgirls, and at this Greenwich Village fave, owner Sherry Delamarter won't let gringos forget. Come for the history lesson and eclectic Chuckwagon dishes like eggplant fritters and Frito pie. Yeehaw!
Greenwich Village, 519 Hudson St. (at 10th St.), (212) 633-1133. Open Su-R 11am-11pm, F-Sa 11am-12am. MC, V, AmEx, Entrées: $8-$15, 1 9 to Christo-pher St.-Sheridan Sq.

Dojo
The American and Japanese influenced dishes really only please fans of macrobiotic fare. The dirt-cheap prices and a frisky social scene are enough to lure NYU undergrads away from their meal-plan fare.
Greenwich Village, 14 W. 4th St. (bet. Mercer St. and Broadway), (212) 505-8934. Open Su-R 11am-1am, F-Sa 11am-2am. Cash Only, Entrées:$4-$8, NR to 8th St.-NYU, 6 to Bleecker St.

Florent
Fanciful bistro fare is available at all hours on weekends for a sophisticated and slightly affected mixed gay and straight crowd in the hip Meat-Packing District. Housed in an old diner, the space is cool and understated; dishes are a mix of French and American classics.
Greenwich Village, 69 Gansevoort St. (bet. Greenwich and Washington Sts.), (212) 989-5779. Open Su-R 9am-5am, F-Sa 24hrs. Cash Only, Entrées: $6-$16, A C E to 14th St., L to Eighth Ave.

Garage Restaurant & Café
Suburban steak house meets Greenwich Village panache at this sprawling multi-leveled village favorite. Its famous weekend jazz brunch offers both top-notch music and a mean eggs benedict. During the week, come for the music but stay for the unforgettable mussels, or their hearty sandwiches and raw bar.
Greenwich Village, 99 Seventh Ave. S. (at Grove St.), (212) 645-0600. Open M-F 12pm-2am, Su 12pm-1am. MC, V, AmEx, Entrées: $8-$25, 1 9 to Christopher St.-Sheridan Sq.

Gotham Bar and Grill
Architecturally brilliant entrées like Atlantic salmon with ramps, morels, sweet peas, and chervil, betray the hand of one of the city's finest gourmets, Alfred Portale, and his kitchen team of all-star chefs, who've made Gotham's New American cuisine a staple for New York connoisseurs. Entrées bypass typical meats for rabbit, pheasant, and a couple so rare they're probably endangered. Sample it all with a $19.99 prix fixe lunch in the spacious, angular dining room. Don't pass up the most divine warm chocolate cake in all of NYC.
Greenwich Village, 12 E. 12th St. (bet. Fifth Ave. and University Pl.), (212) 620-4020. Open M-R 12pm-2:30pm,

5pm-10:30pm, F-Su 5pm-11:30pm. MC, V, AmEx, DC, Entrées: $25-$40, L N R 4 5 6 to-Union Sq.-14th St.

The Grange Hall

The coziest corner in the Village is home to one of its very finest restaurants. One of Uma Thur-man's known haunts, this classy outpost of European refinement and American-style roasts and chicken dishes displays excellent taste without being ostentatious. Great for cocktails, the Hall is also famed for brunch.

Greenwich Village, 50 Commerce St. (bet. Bedford and Hudson Sts.), (212) 924-5246. Open M-R 12pm-3pm, 5:30pm-11:30pm, F 12pm-3pm, 5:30pm-12am, Sa 11am-3pm, 6pm-12am, Su 10:30am-4pm, 6pm-11pm. MC, V, AmEx, Entrées: $12-$25, 1 9 to Christopher St.-Sheridan Sq.

Greenwich Cafe

Skip the entrées for the stylish array of appetizers at this spacious 24-hour cafe, staffed by waitpeople with the best cheekbones and most chic wardrobes in the West Village. Weekend night-hawks might encounter a chic party for slinky models and their agents; brunch guests are serenaded with soothing jazz. Outdoor seating is available in the summer.

Greenwich Village, 75 Greenwich Ave. (at Seventh Ave. S.), (212) 255-5450, www.food.com. Open M-Su 24hrs. MC, V, AmEx, D, Entrées: $10-$15, 1 2 3 9 to Union Sq.-14th St.

Home

The name conjures up the American iconography of mom and apple pie, but despite the low pretension and familiar line-up of pork chops and chocolate pudding, this refined Village eatery is a bit too urbane to qualify as a suburban transplant. Chefs may not infuse the catfish with mom's love, but they are committed to resisting the strong French trends in New American cuisine, instead steering culinary attention toward hometown faves. Home's homemade ketchup proves again why classics never go out of style.

Greenwich Village, 20 Cornelia St. (bet. Bleecker and W. 4th Sts.), (212) 243-9579. Open M-F 9am-3pm, 6pm-11pm, Sa-Su 11pm-4pm, 6pm-11pm. AmEx, Entrées: $13-$19, A B C D E F Q to West 4th St.-Washington Sq.

BBQ

An eden for budget-constrained carnivores. The decor is trite and the breadth of the menu is confined to the obvious, but where do fall-off-the-bone tender meat with satisfyingly greasy fries sell for less than the price of a couple of Happy Meals? The only things missing from the Southern cookout ambience are the horseflies.

Greenwich Village, 21 University Pl. (at 8th St.), (212) 674-4450. Open M-R 11am-12:30am, F-Sa 11:30am-1:30am. MC, V, AmEx, Entrées: $5-$10, N R to 8th St.-NYU.

Indigo

Creative cuisine and impeccable presentation make this tucked-away gem a find. With chef Scott Bryan from Siena (the restaurant, not the city), this excellent but unpretentious French-American bistro also has reasonable prices. Votive candles set a subtle indigo mood and the coat check gives everyone a little more room. Try the sorbet for dessert and understand why the next table called it 'orgasmic.'

Greenwich Village, 142 W. 10th St. (bet. Greenwich Ave. and Waverly Pl.), (212) 691-7757, www.indigo jazz.com. Open M-R 6pm-11pm, F-Sa 6pm-11:30pm, Su 5:30pm-10:30pm. AmEx, Entrées: $14-$16, 1 9 to Christopher St.-Sheridan Sq.

Ithaka

The authentic Greek fare and unpretentious atmosphere attracts locals interested in food, not hype. Preparing the food before you in an open kitchen, the portly chef expertly unfolds filo dough as he greets the regulars and offers recommendations. You may be tempted to stuff yourself on the abundant entrées, such as the striped bass baked with feta cheese, but leave room for the baklava and other homemade desserts.

Greenwich Village, 48 Barrow St. (bet. Bedford St. and Seventh Ave. S.), (212) 727-8886. Open M-F 5pm-11:30pm, Sa-Su 12pm-12am. MC, V, AmEx, DC, Entrées: $15-$22, 1 9 to Christopher St.-Sheridan Sq, A B C D E F Q to West 4th St.-Washington Sq.

John's of Bleecker Street

This thin, coal oven baked pizza is preceded by its well-deserved reputation. A good place for groups to hang out. No slices, only whole pies, the mark of an excellent pizzeria.

Greenwich Village, 278 Bleecker St. (bet. Sixth and Seventh Aves.), (212) 243-1680. Open M-Sa 11:30am-12am, Su 12pm-12am. Cash Only, Entrées: $12, A B C D E F Q to West 4th St.-Washington Sq.

Le Café Bruxelles

One of a number of Belgian joints now open on the West Side, this is perhaps the most consistent. The staff is authentically ethnic, the setting cozy, and the food — mussels, fabulous frites, and beers brewed at monasteries — is très, très bon.

Greenwich Village, 118 Greenwich Ave. (at 13th St.), (212) 206-1830. Open M-Su 12pm-11:00. MC, V, AmEx, DC, Entrées: $12-$18, A C E to 14th St., L to Eighth Ave.

Gay Pride Parade

The Stonewall Riots, June 27, 1969, sparked the gay rights movement. It's legacy lives on through out the year, but is celebrated for a week towards the end of June during Gay and Lesbian Pride Week. The events of the week culminate in the Gay Pride Parade which goes from 52nd and Seventh Avenue and ends on Waverly Place. A lesbian motorcycle gang "Dykes on Bikes" starts things off and what follows is a procession of gay rights organizations and a circus of endless show and bravado.

Les Deux Gamins

French-inspired omelets, salads, and rich entrées consistently attract crowds at this endearing, perennially popular bistro. Brunch goes down perfectly with cafe au lait or cocoa in warmed bowls on a lazy Sunday morning. Service can be harried, though the crowd of low-key locals in their late 20s is tolerant.

Greenwich Village, 170 Waverly Pl. (at Grove St.), (212) 807-7357. Open M-Su 8am-12pm. AmEx, Entrées: $14-$23, 1 9 to Christopher St.

Marylou's

Elegant restaurant and bar sunken into the basement level of a fashionable townhouse. Entrées tend towards expensive seafood, but the bar is cozy and the crowd mostly regulars.

Greenwich Village, 21 W. 9th St. (bet. Fifth and Sixth Aves.), (212) 533-0012. Open M-R 5:30pm-12am, F-Sa 5:30pm-1am, Su 12pm-4pm, 5:30pm-10pm MC, V, AmEx, Entrées: $14-$22, A B C D E F Q to W. 4th St.-Washington Sq.

Mi Cocina

Mexican cuisine, West Village-style: haute, pricey, and with a generous supply of liquor. The most savory south-of-the-border dishes here may not be authentic, but the place is chic.

Greenwich Village, 57 Jane St. (at Hudson St.), (212) 627-8273. Open M-R 5:30pm-10:45pm, F 5:30pm-11:45pm, Sa 4:30pm-11:45pm, Su 4:30pm-10pm. MC, V, AmEx, DC, Entrées: $13-$22, A C E to 14th St., L to Eighth Ave.

Monte's

Extant since 1918, the charm of this amicable basement trattoria will remain long after the taste has slipped away. The menu spares no calorie, so go all the way and try the zabaglione served cold with strawberries.

Greenwich Village, 97 MacDougal St. (at 3rd St.), (212) 228-9194, www.594.com. Open Su-M, W-R 12pm-11pm, F-Sa 12pm-11:30pm. MC, V, AmEx, DC, D, Entrées: $7-$13, A B C D E F Q to West 4th Street-Washing-ton Sq.

Moustache

Nestled on a peaceful backstreet in the West Village, Moustache transports you to a more pleasant time and place, a feeling intensified by the delicious food, from traditional fare such as the merguez sandwich to their innovative "pitzas." Also try Moustache's East Village location at 265 E 10th St, famed for its garden.

Greenwich Village, 90 Bedford St. (bet. Grove and Barrow Sts.), (212) 229-2220. Open M-Su 12pm-12am. Cash only, Entrees: $5-$12, 1 9 to Christopher St.

One if by Land, Two if by Sea

Don't be fooled by the unassuming exterior of this converted 200-year-old carriage house once owned by Aaron Burr. With an extensive wine list and an exquisite tasting menu, this gem of colonial history provides for the ultimate in romantic dining experiences. The Bluefin Tartare is incredible and the superb Beef Wellington is rightfully called the house specialty. The friendly and knowledgeable wait staff is more than happy to talk about the restaurant's history or unassumingly help you choose which utensil is appropriate for the next course.

Greenwich Village, 17 Barrow St. (bet. Seventh Ave. and W. 4th St.), (212) 228-0822. Open Su-R 5:30pm-10:30pm, F-Sa 5:30pm-11:30pm. MC, V, AmEx, DC, Entrees: $41-$60. 1 9 to Christopher Street-Sheridan Sq.

Pão!

When dinning at Pão! watch motorcycles zoom by and taxis clatter up the street. Huge framed menus feature delicious Port-uguese seafood dishes, but the steak, topped with garlic and spicy cream sauce is their specialty. A small bar

inside.

Greenwich Village, 322 Spring St. (at Greenwich St.), (212) 334-5464. Open M-F 12pm-2:30pm, 6pm-11pm, Sa-Su 6pm-11pm. MC, V, AmEx, Entrées: $14-$17, C E to Spring St. ♿

Peanut Butter & Co.

As the name suggests, this cozy little take-out café serves peanut butter in all forms, ranging from classic Fluffernutters and peanut butter pie to unorthodox PB&J shakes. Prices are high ($6.50 for most sandwiches), but that doesn't keep NYU students and local businessmen from packing the place at lunchtime.

Greenwich Village, 240 Sullivan St. (bet. Bleecker & W. 3rd Sts.), (212) 677-3995. Open Su-R 11am-9pm, F-Sa 11am-10pm. MC, V, AmEx, DC, D, Entrees: $5-7, A C B D F Q to 4th or 1 9 to Houston St.

Petite Abeille

Scads of Tintin paraphernalia and tasty Belgian bites make this a popular feature of Little Belgium. Absolutely divine fries and *moules* (mussels)!

Greenwich Village, 400 W. 14th St. (bet. Ninth and Tenth Aves.), (212) 727-1505. Open M-R 7am-11:30pm, F-Sa 9am-12am, Su 9am-10pm. Cash Only, Entrées: $10-$12, A C E to 14th St., L to Eighth Ave. ♿

Also at:

Greenwich Village, 466 Hudson St. (bet. Barrow and Grove Sts.), (212) 741-6479. Open 7am-3:45pm, 5pm-11pm. MC, V, Entrées: $10-$12, 1 9 to Christopher St.-Sheridan Sq.

Pó

So popular that it is not uncommon to require reservations a month in advance, this charming little West Village Italian draws in customers with its warm atmosphere, reasonable prices, and generous portions. Whether the quality of the food lives up to the restaurant's reputation is debatable, it nonetheless makes for a trendy evening out.

Greenwich Village, 31 Cornelia St. (bet. Bleecker and W. 4th Sts.), (212) 645-2189. Open T 5:30pm-11pm, W-R 11:30am-2:15pm, 5:30pm-11pm, F-Sa 11:30am-2:15pm, 5:30pm-11:30pm, Su 11:30am-2:15pm, 5pm-10pm. AmEx, Entrées: $15, A B C D E F Q to West 4th St.-Washington Sq.

Quantum Leap

Handpicking the best in natural dishes that Mexico, Japan, and the Middle East have to offer, this healthy kitchen excels at weekend breakfasts which include whole grain, buckwheat, or blue corn waffles and/or pancakes smothered with organic maple syrup. Not exactly the ascetic way, but better than bacon.

Greenwich Village, 88 W. 3rd St. (bet. Thompson and Sullivan Sts.), (212) 677-8050. Open M-F 11:30am-11pm, Sa 11am-11pm, Su 11am-10pm. MC, V, AmEx, Entrées: $5-$10, A B C D E F Q to West 4th St.-Washington Sq. ♿

Sammy's Noodle Shop and Grill

Hurried urbanites took their time in warming up to this noodle shop's flavorful fare, though now it's an indispensable lunch fixture, with an annexed bakery serving fresh desserts. Try the roast meat soups and dumplings.

Greenwich Village, 453 Sixth Ave. (bet. 10th and 11th Sts.), (212) 924-6688. Open Su-R 11:30am-12am, F-Sa 11:30am-1am. MC, V, AmEx, D, Entrées: $10-$12, F to 14th St., L to Sixth Ave. ♿ 🚲

Souen

Downtown New Yorkers may delight in their manufactured indulgences, but this unassuming, primarily macrobiotic restaurant has been helping them get in touch with their earthier side for twenty years. The Japanese influenced menu specializes in dishes featuring tempeh, seitan, and organic vegetables, and the sugar-free futomaki and tempeh croquettes are noteworthy.

Greenwich Village, 28 E. 13th St. (bet. University Pl. and Fifth Ave.), (212) 627-7150. Open M-Su 10am-11pm, Su 10am-10pm. MC, V, AmEx, DC, D, Entrées: $8-$16, L N R 4 5 6 to Union Sq.-14th St. 🚲

Sud

The red bare brick, limited space, and French speaking staff make you feel like you're in a real French bistro. A casual, unpretentious dining spot, Sud offers authentic, homemade French-Mediterranean cuisine that evokes Paris, though the service is quite an improvement: Don't be surprised if co-owner Danielle joins you for a brief chat at your table; her friendly personal service helps to give the tiny restaurant its charm.

Greenwich Village, 210 W. 10th St. (bet. Bleecker and 4th Sts.), (212) 255-3805. Open T-Su 11am-4pm, 6pm-12am. MC, V, AmEx, D, Entrées: $15-$20, 1 9 *to Christopher St.-Sheridan Sq.*

Surya

This chic West Village Indian offers a unique array of tastes several notches above its counterparts in the East Village: fresh seafood glazed with a subtle date sauce, perfectly spiced basmati, and creamy deserts with a hint of cardamon. Wash it down with a "Tajamopolitan" or other unique specialty drinks.

Greenwich Village, 302 Bleecker St., (bet. Seventh Ave. S. and Grove St.), (212) 807-7770, www.suryanyc.com. Open M-F 5pm-11:30pm, Sa-Su 5pm-12pm. MC, V, AmEx, DC, D, Entrées: $16-$24, 1 9 *to Christopher St.-Sheridan Sq.*

Tartine

There's nothing more pleasant on a Sunday morning than brunch at Tartine with the sun shining through the floor-to-ceiling windows and birds chirping. The menu is standard and portions are hardly generous, but the staff has orange juice on the table by the time patrons sit down. Alas, by noon the wait outside is 45 minutes, but here's a tip: They actually open at 9am for coffee, not the posted 10:30.

Greenwich Village, 253 W. 11th St. (at W. 4th St.), (212) 229-2611. Open T-F 9am-4pm, 5:30pm-10:30pm, Sa-Su 9am-4pm, 5:30pm-10:30pm. Cash Only, Entrées: $8-$14, A C E *to W. 14th St.,* L *to Eighth Ave.*

Tavern on Jane

This tavern serves much more than pub food, but at pub food prices. While the fish and chips is a reliable delight, customers go crazy for the grilled leg-of-lamb with sour cherry sauce, potatoes au gratin and garlic spinach, and the Moroccan tuna, served with saffron, lemon and garlic couscous, and wilted watercress get rave review. The atmosphere is cozy and inviting— regulars are bound to strike up a friendly conversation over a pint of beer. Simply put, you know a place is great when the staff hangs out there on their nights off.

Greenwich Village, 31 Eighth Ave. (at Jane St.), (212) 675-2526. Open M-F 12pm-4am, Sa-Su 11:30am-4am. MC, V, AmEx, Entrées: $7-$15, A C E *to 14th St.,* L *to Eighth Ave.*

Wok 'n Roll

They don't kick you out till 3am on weekends, and you'll never significantly alter the level of your water glass at this airy dumpling house, where the polished wood decor and predictable noodle and dumpling fare feels like a friend's mom's dinner you can always count on. Fair prices keep it packed with NYU kids.

Greenwich Village, 169 Bleecker St. (at Sullivan St.), (212) 260-6666. Open Su-R 11:30am-1am, F-Sa 11:30am-3am. MC, V, AmEx, D, Entrées: $7-$13, A B C D E F Q *to W. 4th St.-Washington Sq.*

Ye Waverly Inn

One of the vestiges of 19th century Village life, this former carriage house exudes a quaint, Colonial feel with wooden ceiling beams and old fashioned offerings from both north and south, like Yankee pot roast and southern fried chicken, with excellent puddings and muffins. Occasionally, local celebs drop by.

Greenwich Village, 16 Bank St. (at Waverly Pl.), (212) 929-4377. Open Su-R 11:30am-3:30pm, 5pm-10:30pm, F-Sa 11:30am-3:30pm, 5pm-11:30pm. MC, V, AmEx, DC, Entrées: $12-$17, 1 2 3 9 to 14th St.

♦ CAFES

Café Milou

Named after Tintin's dog, this bistro is a breath of fresh air in the midst of trendy theme-oriented eateries on Seventh Ave. Opened by Abraham Merchant, of Merchant's, with a menu created by an ex-Windows on the World chef.

Greenwich Village, 92 Seventh Ave. S. (bet. Bleecker and Grove Sts.), (212) 414-9824. Open M-T 12pm-12am, W-R 12pm-1am, F-Sa 11am-2am, Su 11am-12am. MC, V, AmEx, DC, 1 9 *to Christopher St.-Sheridan Sq.*

Caffe Danté

Famous both for its Buffalo mozzarella and espresso, this space may be small but it is well arranged. If your stomach is craving a larger meal, check out the trattoria next door, which is under the same management.

Greenwich Village, 79-81 Macdougal St. (bet. Bleecker and Houston Sts.), (212) 982-5275. Open M-R 10am-2am, F-Sa 10am-3am. Cash Only, 1 9 *to Houston St.*

Caffe Reggio

The standard by which Village cafés are measured, Caffe Reggio's charm makes it popular among students, hipsters, and aging Bohemians. The dark interior is suitable for curling up with a book or your significant other. Prices respect the starving artist's pocketbook.

Greenwich Village, 119 MacDougal St. (bet. Bleecker and 3rd Sts.), (212) 475-9557. Open Su-R 10am-2am, F-Sa 10am-4am. Cash Only, A B C D E F Q *to West 4th St.-Washington Sq.*

Caffé Sha Sha

The summertime patio is a refuge amidst the midday mayhem. Get your hands on some java and commit yourself to the entire Sunday Times.

Greenwich Village, 510 Hudson St. (bet. Christopher and 10th Sts.), (212) 242-3021. Open Su-R 11am-12am, F 11am-1am, Sa 11am-2am. Cash Only, 1 9 *to Christopher St.*

French Roast

Art Nouveau dominates the decor at this airy, bustling café. Brunch and lunch available; try the consistently delicious soups.

Greenwich Village, 458 Sixth Ave. (at 11th St.), (212) 533-2233. Open M-Su 24hrs. MC, V, AmEx, A B C D E F Q *to W. 4th St.-Washington Sq.*

Go Sushi

Pop culture's turning Japanese. This newcomer capitalizes on both the sushi trend and the still burgeoning coffee bar culture: sleek stools and tattered copies of *Paper* meet sushi samples of fatty tuna and salmon prepared fresh around-the-clock by an in-house chef. Wash it all down with Go's own freshly brewed ginger ale.

Greenwich Village, 3 Greenwich Ave. (bet. Sixth Ave. and 8th St.), (212) 366-9272. Open M-Su 11:30am-11:30pm. Cash Only, A B C D E F Q *to West 4th St.-Washington Sq.*

The Grey Dog's Coffee

Bring a novel, your laptop, or your friends to this warm rustic café where sunlight pours in through the open French windows and casts shadows on the pressed tin ceilings above. Order a big chunk of fresh-baked bread, a terrific cup of coffee, and amble back to one of the artsy tables with apples, fish, or chili peppers painted on top. At night the lights dim and the place becomes a casual wine bar.

Greenwich Village, 33 Carmine St. (bet. Bleeker and Bedford

Sts.), (212) 462-0041. Open M-Su 7am-11:30pm. Cash Only, A B C D E F Q *to West 4th St., Washington Sq.,* 1 9 *to Houston St.*

Taylor's

One of the best things about culinary life in the West Village is this bakery, which has several other locations in downtown Manhattan. A fabulous selection of pastries, cakes, and other decadent desserts, as well as soups, sandwiches, and typical beverages. The scones can be amazing, but you should get there early or your choices will be limited.

Greenwich Village, 523 Hudson St. (bet. 10th and Charles Sts.), (212) 378-2890. Open M-Su 7am-10pm. Cash Only, 1 9 *to Christopher St.-Sheridan Sq.*

Shopping

♦ CLOTHING & SHOES

Andees Cheapees

Though on the expensive side, Andee's houses a large selection of mostly polyester-influenced vintage men's and women's clothing, plus a more reasonably priced collection of used jeans. Always in stock: your grandpa's cabana wear – but he'd roll over in his grave if he saw what they're charging for it.

Greenwich Village, 691 Broadway (bet. 3rd and 4th Sts.), (212) 420-5980. MC, V, AmEx, B D F Q *to Broadway-Lafayette St.,* 6 *to Bleecker St.*

Fat Beats

Indispensable for hip-hop fans, witness row after row of vinyls as the music coming from the speakers forces on you that this thing, hip-hop, started here in New York. Doesn't do too badly in the reggae department either.

Greenwich Village, 406 Sixth Ave. (bet. 8th and 9th Sts.), (212) 673-3883, www.fatbeats.com. Open M-R 12pm-9pm, F-Sa 12pm-10pm, Su 12pm-6pm. MC, V, A B C D E F Q *to West 4th St.-Washington Sq.*

Antique Boutique

This trendy and lively Broadway institution shouts New York at very high prices. Newer, modern, edgy sportswear takes up most of the upstairs, while downstairs is devoted to top-notch vintage coats, shirts, and jeans.

Greenwich Village, 712 Broadway (at Washington Pl.), (212) 460-8830. Open M-R 11am-9pm, F-Sa 11am-10pm, Su 12pm-8pm. MC, V, AmEx, DC, D, N R *to 8th St.-NYU.*

Cheap Jack's

Don't be fooled by the name of this groovy vintage store; the place is anything but cheap. Browse through the vast selection of plain and Hawaiian shirts, one-of-a-kind coats, and '40s-, '50s-, '60s- and '70s-style dresses on the first floor; head downstairs where a myriad of jeans hang. Patience and a keen eye may lead to a heavenly bargain.

Greenwich Village, 841 Broadway (bet. 13th and 14th Sts.), (212) 777-9564, www.cheapjacks.com. Open M-Sa 11am-8pm, Su 12pm-7pm. MC, V, AmEx, D, L N R 4 5 6 *to Union Sq.-14th St.*

Luichiny

What you buy here depends on how condescending you want to be when you're wearing their shoes. Luichiny's has everything from six inch spiked heels to five inch flat platforms to cure any Napolean complex.

Greenwich Village, 21 W. 8th St. (bet. Fifth and Sixth Aves.), (212) 477-3445, www.luichiny.com. Open M-Sa 11am-9pm, Su 12pm-8pm. MC, V, AmEx, A B C D E F Q *to W. 4th St.-Washington Sq.*

Patricia Field

From the woman who brings you fresh, fun fashion on HBO's Sex and the City, beloved downtown designer Patricia Field keeps her own store stocked with all the creations you love to see on Carrie, Miranda, Samantha and Charlotte. The perfect place if you want something really "funky," Patricia Field has men's and women's clothing, accessories, lingerie, suits, make-up, shoes, toys and a hair and wig salon! Work, it, girl!

Greenwich Village, 10 E. 8th St. (bet, University Pl. and Fifth Ave.), (212) 254-1699, www.patriciafield.com. Open Su-F 12pm-8pm, Sa 12pm-9pm. MC, V, AmEx, D N R *to 8th St.-NYU*

♦ BOOKS, MAGAZINES & RECORDS

Biography Bookshop

Muckrakers, voyeurs, and fan club presidents come to this high-ceilinged and brick-walled store for the latest on their respective idols. Boasts an impressive gay & lesbian section.

Greenwich Village, 400 Bleecker St. (at 11th St.), (212) 807-8655. Open M-R 11am-10pm, F-Sa 11am-11pm, Su 11am-7pm. MC, V, AmEx, D, 1 9 *to Christopher St.-Sheridan Sq.*

Bleecker Bob's

Packed with a huge vinyl selection, including rare albums, Bob's is a hub for DJ's and music collectors alike. Their rock, metal, indie, emo, punk and hardcore CD selection draws everyone else. Other bonuses include the posters, bongs ("for tobacco only") and body piercing/tattoo shop in the back.

Greenwich Village, 118 W. 3rd St. (bet. MacDougal St. and First Ave.), (212) 475-9677. Open M-Su 12pm-1am. MC, V, AmEx, D, A C E B D F Q *to 4th St.*

East-West Books

A crash course for Western readers in the literature of the East. Specializing in religious and philosophical traditions from Mahayana Buddhism to neo-Confucianism. The staff will make special orders.

Greenwich Village, 78 Fifth Ave. (bet.13th and 14th Sts.),(212) 243-5994, Open M-Sa 10am-7:30pm, Su 11am-6:30pm. MC, V, AmEx, L N R 4 5 6 *to Union Sq.-14th St.* ♿

Off-Broadway

Off-Broadway originally meant theaters in Greenwich Village, the majority of which have a seating capacity of 500 or less. Lately, however this term has come to refer to smaller theaters anywhere in the city. Off-Broadway shows tend to have a greater literary and social importance, a wider variety in the quality of productions and cheaper ticket prices (up to $40). Resident theaters like the **Manhattan Theater Club**, **Roundabout Theater**, **Playwrights Horizons** and **Vineyard Theater** are all examples.

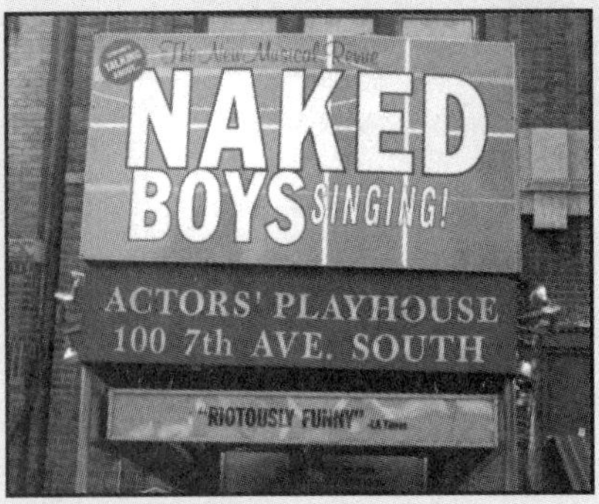

Forbidden Planet

Comics fans seeking everything from superheroes to the latest Eightball cruise the racks to weed out the best of the new and used selection.

Greenwich Village, 840 Broadway (at 13th St.), (212) 473-1576. Open M-Sa 10am-10pm. MC, V, AmEx, D, L N R 4 5 6 to *Union Sq.-14th St.* ♿

Generation Records

The best selection of punk, hardcore and underground music in the city. Cheap movie and music posters, T-shirts, used CDs and an extensive vinyl stock soothe the emotional scars inflicted by the glaring staff.

Greenwich Village, 210 Thompson St. (bet. Bleeker and 3rd Sts.), (212) 254-1100. Open M-R 11am-10pm, F-Sa 11am-1am, Su 12pm-10pm. MC, V, AmEx, A C E B D F Q *to 4th St.*

Lectorum Book Store

Spanish and Latin American authors whose native-language tomes are dispersed throughout the store comprise the bulk of the selection. Translations of popular titles by the likes of Stephen King and James Cavell, Bibles, dictionaries, and a host of other reference books round out the offerings. Check at the desk for information on lectures and readings.

Chelsea, 137 W. 14th St. (bet. Sixth and Seventh Aves.), (212) 741-0220. Open M-Su 9:30am-6:15pm. MC, V, AmEx, 1 2 3 9 *to 14th St.,* F L *to Sixth Ave.* ♿

Macondo Books, Inc.

Pick up an import from either Spain or South America here. The store caters to native speakers with an excellent selection of literature, plays, and poetry.

Chelsea, 221 W. 14th St. (bet. Seventh and Eighth Aves.), (212) 741-3108. Open M-Su 10am-7pm. MC, V, AmEx, 1 2 3 9 *to 14th St.* ♿

Oscar Wilde Memorial Bookstore

For over twenty-five years, New York City's flagship gay bookstore has been offering books for and by gays and lesbians, as well as videotapes, music, T-shirts, and jewelry. Occasional readings by established authors are scheduled.

Greenwich Village, 15 Christopher St. (at Sixth Ave.), (212) 255-8097, www.oscarwildebooks.com. Open M-Sa 11am-8pm, Su 12pm-7pm. MC, V, AmEx, D, 1 9 *to Christopher St.-Sheridan Sq.*

Other Music

Well-deserved haven for indie-rock lovers which also offers a full selection of ambient, rock, psychedelia, and noise. Keep an eye out for special in-store performances which have already featured Yo La Tengo and Jowe Head.

Greenwich Village, 15 E. 4th St. (bet. Broadway and Lafayette St.), (212) 477-8150, www.othermusic.com. Open M-R 12pm-8pm, F-Sa 12pm-10pm, Su 12pm-7pm. MC, V, AmEx, N R *to 8th St.-NYU,* 6 *to Astor Pl.* ♿

Partners & Crime

Serving West Village mystery aficionados, P&C carries a lot of current mysteries and a shelf of out-of-print books; the staff will special order books not in stock. Call for a schedule of readings and radio plays.

Greenwich Village, 44 Greenwich Ave. (bet. Sixth and Seventh Aves.), (212) 243-0440, www.crimepays. com. Open M-R 12pm-8pm, F-Sa 12pm-10pm, Su 12pm-7pm. MC, V, AmEx, A B C D E F Q to West 4th St.-Washington Sq.

Posman's

Avoid coming during the beginning-of-the-semester madness in January or September, as the lines to buy school books are endless. Off-season, browse through new and used academic titles at your leisure.

Greenwich Village, 1 University Pl. (bet. Waverly Pl. and 8th St.), (212) 533-2665. Open M-F 10am-8pm, Sa-Su 12pm-6pm. MC, V, AmEx, D, N R to 8th St.-NYU. ♿

Also at:

Greenwich Village, 70 Fifth Ave (at 13th St.), (212) 633-2525. Open M-F 9am-7pm, Sa-Su 12pm-6pm. MC, V, AmEx, D, L N R 4 5 6 to 14th St.-Union Sq. ♿

Shakespeare & Co.

One of four locations left after the recent demise of the Upper West Side store, offering a diverse selection of books, and the soul of a real bookstore.

Greenwich Village, 716 Broadway (at Washington Pl.), (212) 529-1330, www.shakespeare-nyc.com. Open Su-R 10am-11pm, F-Sa 10am-12am. MC, V, AmEx, N R to 8th St.-NYU.

The Strand Bookstore

Advertising "eight miles of books," The Strand is a heavenly sight for New York's many bibliophiles: three cavernous floors of bookshelves, stuffed solid, and tables crammed into the few remaining spaces in between. The right strategy is key — browse slowly, and, with the proper investment of time, you'll turn up books you never even dreamed existed.

Greenwich Village, 828 Broadway (at 12th St.), (212) 473-1452, www.abebooks.com. Open M-Sa 9:30am-10:30pm, Su 11am-10:30pm. MC, V, AmEx, D, L N R 4 5 6 to 14th St.-Union Sq.

Vinylmania

Specializing in house music and imports. You can listen before you buy.

Greenwich Village, 60 Carmine St. (bet. Seventh Ave. and Bedford St.), (212) 924-7223, www.vinylmania. com. Open M-Sa 11am-9pm, Su 11am-7pm. MC, V, AmEx, 1 9 to Houston St.

♦ GROCERY, GOURMET & SPECIALTY

Aphrodisia

Herbs, spices, and a variety of teas intended to rejuvenate mind and body.

Greenwich Village, 264 Bleecker St. (bet. Cornelia and Jones Sts.), (212) 989-6440. Open M-Sa 11am-7pm, Su 12pm-5pm. MC, V, AmEx, A B C D E F Q to West 4th St.-Washington Sq. ♿

Balducci's

Heaven for the downtown gourmet. From the appetizers to the desserts, Balducci's has everything you'll need to mix up a delicious meal and impress your friends and family. Wander in just to admire the pastries or salivate over the gourmet delicacies. The best cinnamon raison bread in the history of Western Civilization.

Greenwich Village, 424 Sixth Ave. (at 9th St.), (212) 673-2600. Open M-Su 7am-8:30pm. MC, V, AmEx, A B C D E F Q to West 4th St.

White Columns

With the air of the future and a giant showcase space, this gallery beats all other galleries of its genre. Dedicated to promoting innovative artists of all mediums, including drawing, sculpting, painting and performance art, the curators here have an eye for the colorful and the bizarre. The crowd is similar in its dynamic with the gallery.

Greenwich Village, 320 West 13th St. (bet. W 4th and Hudson.), (212)924-4212. www.whitecolumns.org Open: W- Sun 12-6, A C E L to 14th St.

Ecce Panis

A bread store with an extra (and expensive!) flair, they most definitely have bragging rights to the best chocolate bread in NYC. Go for the generous selection of free samples.

Greenwich Village, 434 Sixth Ave. (at 10th St.) , (212) 460-5616. Open M-Sa 8am-8pm, Su 8am-7pm. MC, V, AmEx, D, 1 9 to Christopher St.

♦ MISCELLANEOUS

Bigelow Chemists

This is the oldest apothecary in the nation, but don't let the fact that it's a registered landmark make you think that

they're not up-to-date in the products they sell. This pharmacy is on the cutting edge; they have everything you need, including an incredible inventory of natural healing products.
Greenwich Village, 414 Sixth Ave., (bet. West 8th and West 9th Sts.), (212) 473-7325. Open M-F 7:30am-9pm, Sa 8:30am-7pm, Su 8:30am-5:30pm. MC, V, AmEx, D. A B C B D F Q to West 4th St. ♿

Matt Umanov Guitars
Anyone in a band knows this long-time Village institution. Acoustic and electric instruments at reasonable prices; knowledgeable staff to boot.
Greenwich Village, 273 Bleecker St. (at Morton St.), (212) 675-2157. Open M-Sa 11am-7pm, Su 12pm-6pm. MC, V, AmEx, D, A B C D E F Q to West 4th St.-Washington Sq., 1 9 to Christopher St.-Sheridan Sq. ♿

Arts & Recreation

♦ LEISURE

Angelika Film Center
Recently taken over by City Cinemas, this film multiplex remains largely unchanged from its independent days. The films aren't as great as they used to be and they come and go a lot quicker, but enjoying cappuccino and gelato from the well-stocked café in the lobby is still an option as is the possibility of running into celebrities like Bono or Brad Pitt. Just be careful not to mess with the sassy staff.
Greenwich Village, 18 West Houston St. (at Mercer St.), (212) 995-2000. B D F Q to Broadway-Lafayette St. ♿

Bicycle Habitat
If the quality of a bike store can be determined by counting the number of customers' bikes that are chained outside, then this is one of the best in the city. Customers here are serious about their bikes and the same people can be found day after day checking out new models,
picking up parts or just discussing their obsession.
Greenwich Village, 244 Lafayette St. (bet. Prince and Spring Sts.), (212) 431-3315, www.bicyclehabi tat.com. Open M-R 10am-7pm, F 10am-6:30pm, Sa-Su 10am-6pm. MC, V, AmEx, N R to Prince St. ♿

Blades Boards & Skates
The helpful staff would readily join their patrons on Astor Pl. at one of the wheels-only lunch break congregations. Slick new styles of in-line skates, roller skates, and skater gear also available at the standard, not-so-unconventional

prices.
Greenwich Village, 659 Broadway (bet. Bleecker and Bond Sts.), (212) 477-7350, www.blades.com. Open 10am-9pm, Su 11am-6pm. MC, V, AmEx, D, B F D Q to Broadway-Lafayette St., 6 to Bleecker St.

Cinema Village
This duplex has a reputation for hosting questionable flicks of the adult persuasion, but it actually accommodates a far wider array of independent films, with themes ranging from homosexuality to kung-fu action to African Diaspora.
Greenwich Village, 22 East 12th St. (bet. University Pl. and Fifth Ave.), (212) 924-3363. L N R 4 5 6 to 14th St.-Union Sq.

Film Forum
Two programs run in this classic setting. Program One has first-run independent and foreign feature films as well as some excellent documentaries. Program Two screens revivals including reissues of individual classics as well as film series featuring everything from the complete works of great, if sometimes obscure, directors to genre films.
Greenwich Village, 209 West Houston St. (bet. Sixth Ave. and Varick St.), (212) 727-8110, www.filmforum.com. 1 9 to Hou-ston St. ♿

NYU's Program Board
By the students, for the students, and offered at the oh-so-student-friendly rate of $2 a pop. The theater's screen spans a minimal width and metallic fold-up chairs do little to keep viewers comfortable, but the cash saved can readily be shoved into a back pocket for extra padding.
Greenwich Village, 36 East 8th St. (at University Pl.), (212) 998-4111, www.nyu.edu/programoffice. N R to 8th St.-NYU.

Quad Cinema
So the screens are a little samll, who cares? The films, a lot of foreign and a bunch of revival series, are so choice that screen size is the last thing considered. Tucked away from heavy street traffic on 13th St., and with only 4 screens hosting its wares, there's little chance the intimate, neighborhood

appeal of this movie house will be mainstreamed anytime soon.
Greenwich Village, 34 West 13th St. (bet. Fifth and Sixth Aves.), (212) 255-8800, www.quadcinema.com. LNR456 *to 14th St.-Union Sq.* ♿

Village Chess Shop
Play chess from noon to midnight with fellow experts, or indulge by purchasing sets made from materials ranging from nuts and bolts to ivory (is that legal?) and onyx.
Greenwich Village, 230 Thompson St. (bet. Bleecker and 3rd Sts.), (212) 475-9580, www.chess-shop.com. Open M-Su 12pm-12am. MC, V, AmEx, ABCDEFQ *to 4th St.-Washington Sq.* ♿

♦ PERFORMANCE

Actor's Playhouse
Gay-and-lesbian-themed shows oft-en command the stage at this Off-Broadway space. Though the seats may be dingy and worn, and the floor may retain a stickiness from a soda that was spilled long ago, it's still the best cutting-edge queer theater.
Greenwich Village, 100 Seventh Ave. South (bet. Grove and Bleecker Sts.), (212) 463-0060. MC, V, AmEx, D, 19 *to Christopher St.-Sheridan Sq.*

Bouwerie Lane Theatre
Founded in 1973 by Eve Adamson, this old-fashioned, European-style, one-stage theater is home to the Jean Cocteau Repertory which performs modern updates of theatrical classics.
Greenwich Village, 330 Bowery (at Bond St.), (212) 677-0060, www. jeancocteaurep.org. MC, V, AmEx, D. BDFQ *to Broadway-Lafayette St.,* 6 *to Bleecker St.*

Castillo Theater
For the last decade, this space has served as a "cultural laboratory" for Artistic Director Fred Newman to practice Developmental Theater, a genre which is predicated on a number of post-modern philosophies but boils down to the idea of psychotherapy for performer and audience members alike. The focus is on black, Latino, gay, and the international avant-garde — which means you can expect anything.
Greenwich Village, 500 Greenwich St. (bet. Spring and Canal Sts.), (212) 941-1234, www.castillo.org. MC, V, AmEx, D, ACE19 *to Canal St.* ♿

Cherry Lane Theatre
Founded in the 1920s by a literary circle headed by the poet Edna St. Vincent Millay, Cherry Lane's productions are led by the best of the century's avant-garde and adventurous new pieces.
Greenwich Village, 38 Commerce St. (bet. Seventh Ave. South and Barrow St.), (212) 989-2020, www.cherrylanetheatre.com. MC, V, AmEx, 19 *to Christopher St-Sheridan Sq.* ♿

Lucille Lortel Theater
Cramped between the music-pumping, glittered, merchandise-selling shops of Christopher St. is this premiere Off-Broadway space, site of the first American production of Brecht and Weill's *Threepenny Opera*. Other successes include *Collected Stories* and *As Bees in Honey Drown*.
Greenwich Village, 121 Christopher St. (bet. Bleecker and Hudson Sts.), (212) 924-2817. MC, V, AmEx, 19 *to Christopher St.-Sheridan Sq.* ♿

Literary Addresses

More than any other neighborhood, Greenwich Village has been most famous for attracting people who would become really big time writers. This is where they hung out.

♦ **Louisa May Alcott** wrote *Little Women* at 130 MacDougal Street.

♦ **O. Henry** got his inspiration for the story *The Last Leaf* at the gate at 10 Grove Street.

♦ **Thomas Paine** allegedly wrote *Common Sense* at 59 Grove Street.

♦ **Edgar Allen Poe** wrote *The Raven* at a club at 83 West 3rd St. while living at 49 East 9th Street.

♦ **Edna St. Vincent Millay** lived at 75 1/2 Bedford Street

♦ One Washington Square North housed **Edith Wharton** and **Henry James**.

♦ And, **Dylan Thomas** had 18 scotches at the White Horse Tavern, 567 Hudson, before going home to the Chelsea Hotel and passing away.

Minetta Lane Theater

Revues and new plays in a notably comfortable setting. One big show was the acclaimed docudrama *Gross Indecency — The Three Trials of Oscar Wilde*, recounting the legal ordeals that made the artist one of homosexuality's most prominent martyrs.

Greenwich Village, 18 Minetta Lane (bet. MacDougal St. and Sixth Ave.), (212) 420-8000. MC, V, AmEx, A B C D E F Q *to West 4th St.-Washington Sq.* ♿

Sullivan St. Playhouse

Home since 1960 to *The Fanta-sticks*, the longest running show in U.S. history. Don't miss the art gallery upstairs, which boasts a varied collection of *Fantasticks* memorabilia from around the world so extensive that it shares space with the ladies' room.

Greenwich Village, 181 Sullivan St. (bet. Houston and Bleecker Sts.), (212) 674-3838. AmEx, 1 9 *to Houston St.* ♿

Theatre for a New Audience

Some of the most innovative, provocative, and thoughtful productions of Shakespeare and other classics. Call for venue locations.

Greenwich Village, 154 Christopher St., Suite 3D (bet. Greenwich and Washington Sts.) (212) 229-2819, www.tfana.org. MC, V, AmEx, D, 1 9 *to Christopher St.-Sheridan Sq.* ♿

Hogs & Heifers

Appropriately named for the less-than-fragrant part of town in which it resides, this

rowdy biker bar attracts the stars despite its meat-packing district address. The decorative highlight is a bra-clad moosehead.

Greenwich Village, 859 Washington St. (at 13th St.), (212) 929-0655. Open M-Su 1am-4am. Cash Only, A C E to 14th St., L to Eighth Ave. ♿

♦ MUSEUMS & CULTURAL CENTERS

Bronfman Center for Jewish Student Life

In a townhouse built for Lockwood De Forest, a wealthy exporter, the Center presents free lectures focusing on Jewish religious concerns and Israeli politics for an almost exclusively NYU audience. De Forest founded workshops in India to revive the art of woodworking, so the center is replete with the fruits of his labor — intricately-carved teak wood imported from India.

Greenwich Village, 7 East 10th St. (bet. University Pl. & Fifth Ave.), (212) 998-4114, www.nyu.edu/ bronfman. N R *to 8th St.-NYU.* ♿

Casa Italiana Zerilli-Marimò

The former home of General Winfield Scott, hero of the Mexican-American War and Chief-of-Staff of the U.S. Army in the 1850s. Call for information about free lectures, films, and art exhibits that focus on Italian culture.

Greenwich Village, 24 West 12th St. (bet. Fifth and Sixth Aves.), (212) 998-8730, www.nyu.edu/pages/casaital iana. Open M-F 9am-5pm. Admission: free, F to 14th St., L to Sixth Ave.

Congregation Beth Simchat Torah

This congregation serves the lesbian, gay, bisexual and transgender Jewish community. The focus is on social justice, prayer and study. There are also singles events and group trips to Israel.

Greenwich Village, 57 Bethune Street (bet. Washington and West), (212) 929-9498. A *to 14th St.*

Deutsches Haus

Lecture series by scholars and cultural emissaries, readings by visiting German language authors, and a beautiful gallery space and library with an extensive periodical section are all open to the public. The NYU community enjoys a free film series showcasing everything from Weimar cinema to the contemporary work of artists like Wim Wenders. A ten week German language program costs $430.

Greenwich Village, 42 Washington Mews (bet. University Pl. and Fifth Ave.), (212) 998-8660, www.nyu.edu/deutschehaus. Open: M-F 11am-9pm, Sa 10am-4pm. Admis-sion: free, N R *to 8th St. NYU.* ♿

King Juan Carlos I of Spain Center

King Juan Carlos I himself showed up along with Queen Sophia and Hillary Clinton to inaugurate the new hub of Spanish culture in the city. Housed in architect Stanford White's historic 19th Century Renaissance-style Judson Hall, the center encourages the study of Spain and the rest of the Spanish-speaking world via lectures, colloquia, and conferences with scholars and dignitaries.

Greenwich Village, 53 Washington Square South (bet. Thompson and Sullivan Sts.). (212) 998-3650, www.nyu.edu/pages/kjc. Call for schedule. Admission: free, A B C D E F Q *to West 4th St.-Washington Sq.* ♿

La Maison Française

The epicenter of Francophone and Francophilic life at New York University. Call for information about free lectures, usually in French, along with conferences and exhibitions which are presented in the center's historic 19th century car-

The Freshman, 1990

Mathew Broderick costars with Marlon Brando in this Godfather spoof set in and around the NYU campus. If you ever wanted to know what a part-time job working for gangsters would be like, this is the movie to watch.

riage house.
Greenwich Village, 16 Washington Mews (at University Pl.), (212) 998-8750, www.nyu.edu/gsas/dept/french/mbase. N R to 8th *St.-NYU.* ♿

Lesbian and Gay Community Services Center
The place for all of your gay/lesbian/bisexual/trangender needs all in one. For years, the Center has served the gay community with everything from support groups and health services to social events. It's a great resource for everything homosexual in New York.
Greenwich Village, 208 W. 13th Street (at 7th Ave.), (212) 620-7130, www.gaycenter.or. M-Su 9am-11pm. 1 2 3 9 *to 14th St.*

♦ GALLERIES & LIBRARIES

Grey Art Gallery
Both foreign and domestic contemporary artists display their work at this offbeat gallery on New York University's main campus.
Greenwich Village, 100 Washington Sq. East (bet. Waverly Pl. and Washington Sq.), (212) 998-6780, www.nyu.edu\/greyart. Open T, R-F 11am-6pm, W 11am-8pm, Sa 11am-5pm. N R to *8th St.-NYU.* ♿

Nightlife

♦ BARS

Absolutely 4th Street
This small, snazzy little lounge is valiantly holding out against the incipient NYU menace. A slightly older, slightly calmer crowd relaxes at the jewel-toned bar, oblivious to the underage debauchery outside.
Greenwich Village, 228 W. 4th St. (at Seventh Ave.), (212) 989-9444. Open M-Su 5pm-3am. MC, V, AmEx, D, 1 9 to Christopher St. ♿ 🚬

Automatic Slim's
When it gets late — very, very late — dancing on the bar is allowed, one might even say encouraged.
Greenwich Village , 733 Washington St. (at Bank St.), (323) 645-8660. Open T-Sa 6pm-4am. MC, V, AmEx. ACE to 14th St., L *to Eighth Ave.,* 1 9 *to Chistopher St.-Sheridan Sq.* ♿ 🚬

Bar d'O
Arguably the place that initiated the lounge craze. On Tuesdays, Saturdays, and Sundays Joey Arias and Raven-O host the all-night festivities.
Greenwich Village, 29 Bedford St. (bet. Sixth Ave. and Hudson St.), 627-1580. Open: 7pm-??. Cash Only, 1 9 *to Christopher St.-Sheridan Sq.* 🚬

Blind Tiger Ale House
With 24 micro-brews on tap and bottled beers from 12 countries, this haunt satisfies just about anyone's palate for brew. The crowd is strictly white-collar, after-work, and non-Budweiser.
Greenwich Village, 518 Hudson St. (at 10th St.), (212) 675-3848, www.blindtigeralehouse.com. Open M-Su 12pm-4am. MC, V, AmEx, D, 1 9 *to Christopher St.-Sheridan Sq.* 🚬

Boots and Saddle
Urban and rural cowboys flock to this Western-style veteran, proving that denim is the friendlier gay male counterpoint to leather. Features happy hour M-F. 3-9pm and Saturday and Sunday Beer Blasts that boast $1.50 drafts and $2.50 bottles.
Greenwich Village, 76 Christopher St. (at Seventh Ave.), (212) 929-9684. Open M-Sa 8am-4am, Su 12pm-4am. Cash Only, 1 9 *to Christopher St.* 🚬

Cedar Tavern
Pay tribute to Willem de Kooning with a visit to this spacious tavern that the famous abstract expressionist frequented. The patrons are no longer the counterculture scenesters of the '60s, but the Tiffany lighting and the monumental 19th century bar remain.
Geenwich Village, 82 University Pl. (bet. 11th & 12th Sts.), (212) 929-9089. Open M-Su 12pm-4am. MC, V, AmEx, DC, D, L N R 4 5 6 *to 14th St.-Union Sq.* ♿ 🚬

Chumley's
Go here to catch up. It's an old speakeasy with a hard-to-find entrance that opens into a large bar with their own beers on tap and pictures of famous writers on every wall. Chumley's is cozy-fire places, wooden everything, and not too bright. No matter the season, you walk in and feel sud-

denly warmer and ready to stay a while.
Greenwich Village, 86 Bedford St. (bet. Barrow and Grove Sts.), (212) 675-4449. Open M-R 4pm-12am, F-Sa 3pm-2am, Su 1pm-12am. Cash Only, 1 9 to Christopher St.

Crazy Nanny's
Go to this lesbian bar on the weekends for a fun, racially mixed crowd of trucker-types and femmes.
Greenwich Village, 21 Seventh Ave. South (at Leroy St.), (212) 366-6312. Open M-F 4pm-4am, Sa-Su 3pm-4am. MC. V, AmEx, 1 9 to Christopher St.-Sheridan Sq.

Cubbyhole
Favored by friendly college-aged women of various sexual persuasions, this small, dark, dyke rendezvous spot lives up to the double entendre in its name. The bar has a $5 cover on Saturday nights from 8:30pm to 10pm.
Greenwich Village, 281 West 12th St. (at Fourth Ave.), (212) 243-9041. Open M-R 4pm-3am, F 4pm-4am, Sa 2pm-4am, Su 2pm-3am. Cash Only, L N R 4 5 6 to 14th St.-Union Sq.

Down the Hatch
Down the Hatch is pretty straightforward about its essential nature: it's a dingy, cheap, and rowdy college bar with foosball tables and christmas lights. It attracts mostly NYU kids, and a few older passerbys who are sometimes outraged by the sometimes tepid beer.
Greenwich Village,179 W. 4th St. (bet. Jones and Barrow Sts.), (212) 627-9747. M-Su 4pm-3am. MC, V N R to W. 4th St.

Hell
At Hell one finds an interesting mix of straight and gay pretty people in their mid-twenties to late thirties. Some are on their way to nearby fetish clubs; others are content sipping a fiery martini in Hell's comfy lounge. The drinks are stiff (but stay away from the nightly specials)
Greenwich Village, 59 Gansevoort St. (bet. Washington and Greene Sts.), (212) 727-1666. Open Su-Sa 7pm-4am. MC, V, AmEx, A C E 1 2 3 9 to 14th St.-Union Sq.

Henrietta Hudson
This internationally-renowned, number-one women's bar in NYC. The scene is mostly women, although the bar claims to be "male-friendly."
Greenwich Village, 438 Hudson St. (at Morton St.), (212) 924-3347. Open M-F 4pm-4am, Sa-Su 1pm-4am. MC, V, AmEx, 1 9 to Christopher St.-Sheridan Sq.

Mega Decibel
The sequel to everyone's favorite hideaway, Decibel, makes up for in energy what it lacks in intimacy. It also features over 90 varieties of sake.
Greenwich Village, 71 University Place (between 10th and 11th Sts), (212) 260-6407. Su-T 6pm-2am, F-S 6pm-3am. MC, V, AmEx, D, DC. 6 to 14th St.

Nowbar
Intimate without being cramped, the downstairs dance floor is complemented by an upstairs lounge. Creative, indirect lighting renders the festive poly-sexual crowd surprisingly visible.
Greenwich Village, 22 Seventh Ave. South (at Leroy St.), (212) 293-0323. Call for hours. MC, V, AmEx, 1 9 to Houston St.

Off the Wagon
While most of the bars on or near Bleeker strive towards trendy or some quirk that sets them apart, Off the Wagon insists that just being a bar where people get smashed is enough. The name pretty much says it and if obliteration and top forty hits are your thing, well then you should go.
Greenwich Village, 109 Mac Dougal St. (bet. Bleeker and 3rd Sts.), (212) 533-4487. M-R 2pm-4am, F-Su 12pm-4am. MC, V, Amex, D A C E D F Q B to W. 4th St.

Polly Esther's
Kitsch by the truckload here; psychedelia, beaded curtains and the requisite Brady Bunch and Sonny and Cher homages will satisfy every Gen-Xer's fantasy of Flower Power and free love. The prices aren't retro, but at least they're reasonable.
Greenwich Village, 186 West 4th St. (bet. Sixth and Seventh Aves.), (212) 924-5707, www.pollyesthers.com. Open W-Sa 8pm-4am. MC, V, AmEx, DC, D, Cover: $8, A B C D E F Q to W. 4th St.-Washington Sq.

The Slaughtered Lamb
This is one of the Village's best-known pubs. Tourists flock to this horror-film theme bar for the shocker movies and overpriced drinks.
Greenwich Vill-age, 182 West 4th St. (bet. Sixth and Seventh Aves.), (212) 727-3350. Open Su-R 6pm-2am, F-Sa 6pm-4am. MC, V, AmEx, DC, D, A B C D E F Q to West 4th St.-Washington Sq.

Stonewall
On the night that Judy Garland died in 1969, cops raided the

gay bar Stonewall for the umteenth time, and this time the boys and girls fought back, starting a riot that started the gay rights movement. Now you can swing your hips to loud dance music and maybe even find that Mr. Right for the night too.
Greenwich Village, 53 Christopher St. (at Seventh Ave.), (212) 463-0950. Open M-Su 2:30pm-4am. Cash Only, 1 9 to Christopher St.

The White Horse Tavern
A Village landmark, reputed to be the place where Dylan Thomas drank himself to death. But the poets are long gone, supplanted by a pedestrian twenty-something crowd. Dinner essentials are served, including good burgers.
Greenwich Village, 567 Hudson St. (at West 11th St.), (212) 243-9260. Open Su-R 11am-2am, F-Sa 11am-4am. Cash Only, 1 9 to Christopher St.-Sheridan Sq.

The Village Idiot
You go to the Idiot and you get drunk. This is why the Idiot exists and their mission is made clear the moment you walk in. It's loud-no-conversation-loud, trashy-country-music loud. The bartenders dance on the bar periodically and force shots on anyone naive enough to ask for a glass of water. The beer is the cheapest in Manhattan.
Greenwich Village, 355 W. 14th St. (at Ninth Ave.), (212) 989-7334. Open M-Su 12pm-4am. Cash Only, A C E to 14th St.

♦ CLUBS

Bowlmor Lanes
Mondays herald the Night Strike: How much do heavy house, drum and bass and disco improve your bowling technique? With glow-in-the-dark pins and shoes, a strike or two are ought to happen.
Greenwich Village, 110 University Place (bet. 12th and 13th), 255-8188. MC, V, AmEx, Cover: $14 for "Night Strike", L N R 4 5 6 to 14th St.-Union Sq.

The Lure
Leather-bound S&M boys manifest their darkest fantasies. Not exactly for the faint at heart.
Greenwich Village, 409 West 13th St. (bet. Ninth Ave. and Washington St.), 741-3919. Cash Only, Cover: $0-$5, A C E to 14th St., L to Eighth Ave.

Spa
If you can get into this club, you are obviously elite. The security is tight and temperamental, and thus the patrons (many who are celebs) are a lucky bunch. Décor is bright and clean, drinks are exceptional, and DJs are of the highest caliber.
Greenwich Village, 76 E. 13th St. (bet. Broadway and Fourth Ave.), (212) 388-1060. Open T-Sa 10pm-4am. MC, V, Amex N R L 4 5 6 to 14th St.

♦ MUSIC

Acme Underground
All cleaned up and ready to get dirty: this low-frills basement stage got a makeover and a brand new sound system for its spruced-up lineups. Have legitimate ID ready; the doorman is not taking any sorry excuses.
alternative rock
Greenwich Village, 9 Great Jones St. (bet. Broadway and Lafayette St.), (212) 677-6963, Open 7pm-4am. Cash Only, Cover: $5-$10. N R to 8th St.-NYU, 6 to Astor Pl.

The Baggot Inn
A darkly-lit venue in the heart of the Village. It's a great place to see some of your acoustic singer/songwriters, with plenty of table seating and dollar draft happy hours.
acoustic, pop, rock
Greenwich Village, 82 West 3rd St. (bet. Thompson and Sullivan Sts.), (212) 477-0622. www.thebaggotinn. com. Open 11am-3am. MC, V, AmEx, Cover: free-$5, A B C D E F Q to West 4th St.-Washington Sq.

The Bitter End
Opened 40 years ago, The Bitter End has seen countless performers rise from its stage to stardom, including Bob Dylan, Joni Mitchell, Tracy Chapman, and Jackson Browne.
blues, folk, funk, R&B, rock
Greenwich Village, 147 Bleecker St. (bet. Thompson St. and LaGuardia Pl.), (212) 673-7030, www.bitter end.com. Open Su-R 7pm-2am, F-Sa 8pm-4am. MC, V, AmEx, DC, D. Cover: $5-$10, A B C D E F Q West 4th St.-Washington Sq.

Blue Note
Though the regular features are a bit of an assault on the pocketbook, the five dollar after-hours shows on Fridays and Saturdays are a real bargain. Don't miss B.B. King's annual visit, and if you have the money to spend, see some of the national jazz acts that come through that you won't see anywhere else. Full continental menu, full bar.

jazz
Greenwich Village, 131 West 3rd St. (bet. MacDougal St. and 6th Ave.), (212) 475-8592, www.bluenote.net. Open Su noon-6pm and 7pm-2am, M-Th 7pm-2am, F-Sa 7pm-4am. MC, V, AmEx, Cover: $25 and up, A B C D E F Q *to West 4th St.-Washington Sq.*

Bottom Line
One of New York's oldest and most celebrated venues, beloved by performers and audiences alike. Welcomes local and national acts ranging from '70s artists Jimmy Webb, John Hiatt, and Paul Simon to contemporary faves Dan Bern, Jill Sobule, and David Wilcox. Full kitchen, full bar.
all genres and periods
Greenwich Village, 15 West 4th St.(at Mercer St.), (212) 228-7880. Call for schedule and showtimes. Cash Only, Cover: $15-$25, N R *to 8th St.-NYU,* 6 *to Bleecker St.*

The Cooler
Once a cavernous refrigerator in the Meat-Packing district, this spot is aptly named. Dangling carcasses used to slide on overhead rails still surrounding the chic bar, and a massive meat scale still squats in the back. With music so good and an ambience so groovy, though, you'll soon forget the Cooler's grisly past.
Indie and experimental rock, electronic, avant-jazz
Greenwich Village, 416 W. 14th St. (bet. 9th and Washington Aves.), (212) 229-0785. Open M-Sa 8pm-4am. MC, V, AmEx, D, Cover: $5-$10, A C E L *to 14th St.*

The Duplex
This piano bar right off Sheridan Square has been providing live show tunes for years. A mature contingent lingers here, so tweed is more prevalent than muscle-tees. Large and elegantly decorated, the legendary space offers cabaret upstairs; shows are varied and frequent, so make reservations.
cabaret
Greenwich Village, 61 Christopher St. (at Seventh Ave. South), (212) 255-5438, www.geocites.com/ ~duplexnyc. Open M-Su 4pm-4am. Cash Only, no cover, 1 9 *to Christopher St.-Sheridan Sq.*

Elbow Room
A long, spacious room with comfy couches along the wall. It's got a hip vibe, but it's rapidly becoming a tourist trap thanks to a rash of celebrity sightings.
pop, rock
Greenwich Village, 144 Bleecker St. (bet. Thompson St. and La-Guardia Pl.), (212) 979-8434. Open 6pm-4am. MC, V, AmEx, Cover: $5-$15, A B C D E F Q *to West 4th St.-Washington Sq.*

Kenny's Castaways
One of the landmark bars in the West Village. It's a good place to have a beer and see some up-and-coming local bands. You can listen to the music from the cozy upper level if you want to get away from the crowd.
blues, rock
Greenwich Village, 157 Bleecker St. (bet. Thopson and Sullivan Sts.), (212) 473-9870. Open 12pm-4am. MC, V, AmEx, Cover: $5-$10, A B C D E F Q *to West 4th St.-Washington Sq.*

SOB's
Though the name stands for "Sounds Of Brazil," that doesn't even begin to cover the scope of the first world beat club in New York. A bastion of world rhythm, groove and hip-hop, it's like stepping into a different country every night as African, Middle Eastern, Celtic, Caribbean and Latin American artists use this club as a home base for national tours.
world beat
Greenwich Village, 204 Varick St. (at Houston St.), (212) 243-4940, www.sobs.com. Open M-Sa 6:30pm-4am. MC, V, AmEx, Cover: $10-$25, 1 9 *to Houston St.*

Sweet Basil
This homey jazz restaurant feautres a Saturday and Sunday brunch with Chuck Folds & Friends; other days, Cho the bartender is reason enough to stop by.
jazz
Greenwich Village, 88 Seventh Avenue South (bet. Grove and Bleecker Sts.), (212) 242-1785, www.sweetbasil.com. Open Su-R 8:30pm-1am, F-Sa 12pm-3am. MC, V, AmEx, Cover: $17.50-$20, 1 9 *to Christopher St.-Sheridan Sq.*

The Village Vanguard
With regulars like Woody Guthrie and Pete Seeger, this 64-year-old club was renowned as a center for folk before it became a legend as a jazz club in the fifties. Some of the most important jazz recordings in the world, from Coltrane to Davis to Rollins to Evans, were created within these hallowed walls. You can still catch the top quality mainstream and avant-garde jazz acts each night.
jazz
Greenwich Village, 178 Seventh Ave. South (bet. 11th St. and Waverly Pl.), (212) 255-4037, www.villagevan guard.net. Open Su-R 8:30pm-1am, F-Sa 8:30pm-2am. Cash Only, Cover: $15-$20, 1 2 3 9 *to 14th St.*

So You're Broke

Your first week in New York drained your brand new checking account, and then you meant to stay in but your friends were going to this really great club and there goes the savings account you've had for five years, or maybe you're just cheap. Contrary to what most people tell you New York isn't expensive at all, it's free, you just have to know where to go.

For year-round free fun try the **Staten Island ferry**. Docking near the South Ferry subway station (the last stop on the 1/9 line) on Manhattan's southern tip, this massive vessel is a 25-minute ride by Manhattan's greatest hits: The Statue of Liberty, Ellis Island and the skyline. Call 718-815-BOAT for scheduling info.

Once on Staten Island, make it a fully free day and visit the **Staten Island Zoo** (free on Wednesdays) or the **Snug Harbor Cultural Center**, an 80-acre ode to greenery, Greek Revival architecture, and garden art that offers frequent free concerts and cultural exhibits. Call 718-815-SNUG for concert and exhibit info.

Speaking of scenery, **Central Park**, all 843 sprawling acres of it, offers stunning year-round views that will almost make you forget you're in the middle of a major metropolis. Central Park also frequently hosts great free cultural events and outdoor concerts like Shakespeare in the Park, the New York Opera, the New York Philharmonic, SummerStage and the Metropolitan Opera. Visit the park's Web site at www.centralpark.org for information.

Located along Central Park's eastern border is Fifth Avenue, a colossal thoroughfare lined with world-class art and history museums, historic apartment towers and **St. Patrick's Cathedral**, the Gothic edifice that serves as spiritual home to the city's Roman Catholics. St. Patrick's doors (50th and 51st Streets) rarely close, letting passers-by in to be awed by the vaulted ceilings, majestic altars, and brilliant tapestries inside. Many of the museums, meanwhile, open themselves up free-of-charge at specific times.

On Tuesday evenings, the **Guggenheim** (89th St. and Fifth Ave.), the **Cooper-Hewitt** (91st St. and Fifth Ave.), the **Whitney** (75th St. and Madison Ave.), the **American Craft Museum** (53rd St. bet. Fifth and Sixth Aves.), and the **National Academy of Design** (89th St. and Fifth Ave.) are all free.

On Thursday evenings, meanwhile, the **Museum of Modern Art**, or MoMA (53rd St. and Fifth Ave., opens its doors free of charge. Finally, on Thursday and Friday evenings, the **American Museum of Natural History** (79th St. and Central Park West) offers free admission. Visit www.ny.com/museums and consult the Visual Arts section for more info about all of these museums.

For indoor amusement, take a free, guided tour of the **New York Stock Exchange** floor (20 Broad St., bet. Exchange and Wall Sts.) or the **Federal Reserve Bank's vaults** (33 Liberty St., bet. William and Nassau Sts.). Make reservations a week in advance, and take pity on the money-obsessed, stressed-out brokers. Suckers.

Gramercy

Although originally a swamp, the area surrounding Gramercy Park has long been one of the most fashionable addresses in New York. Thanks to its turn-of-the-century intellectual residents, the historical Gramercy has been called an "American Bloomsbury." Past residents include James Harper (founder of the Harper Collins publishing house), Edith Wharton, Herman Melville and Eugene O'Neill. O. Henry wrote *The Gift of the Magi* in a local restaurant.

In 1831, Samuel Ruggles, longtime trustee of Columbia College, drained the swamp and laid out 66 English-style lots around a private park, still standing as the neighborhood's famed Gramercy Park. By the late 1920s, the development of high-rise apartment buildings, the extension of the Third Avenue L, and the onset of the Depression meant that an address around Gramercy Park was no longer as desirable as it once was.

The neighborhood's majestic mansions crumbled a bit, and the early 1900s elite shopping Mecca, "Ladies' Mile", became the "temple of love" after an influx of brothels. On the heels of capital flight came a vibrant population of leftists and artists, including Andy Warhol who opened his legendary Factory in Gramercy. The neighborhood became an enclave of rebels ranging in identity from communists to junkie divas.

Today, Gramercy is a hub for fashion models and photographers as well as an eyeful of young celebs; at the right moment, you might catch an informally dressed Winona Ryder on her way to one of the spacious, pricey restaurants that fill up for Sunday brunch. Still, Gramercy stays true to its literary roots: the National Arts Club and the Poetry Society of America are both housed in the stately building at 15 Gramercy Park South.

With its clean, residential side-streets crossing elegantly commercial avenues Gramercy may feel to some more like a fantasy land. It's impossible not to admire its beauty. If you have the time take the subway to Union Square and, instead of walking South to hip East Village, walk North where charming houses (alas, no key included) sit alongside prim restaurants and markets. This is Oz and even if you can't stay, there's no reason to go home.

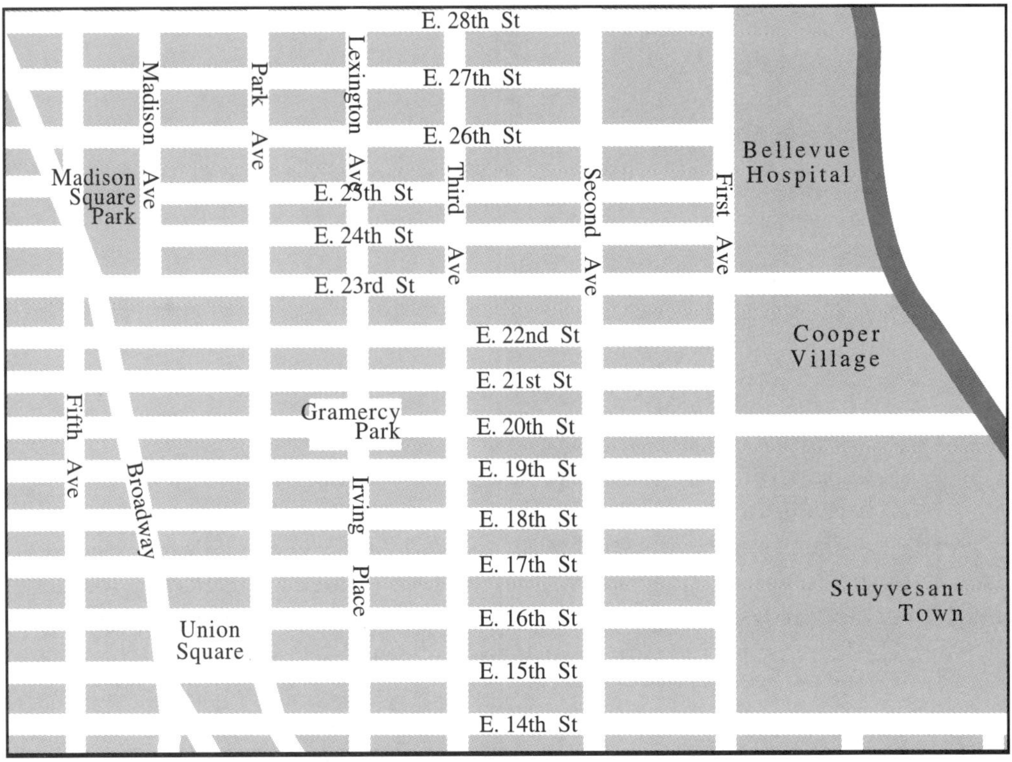

Dining

◆ RESTAURANTS

Bachue

Vegan breakfast, lunch, and dinner is a rare treat: just picture in your head delicious (egg-less) pancakes and waffles, as well as a fine selection of bean, pasta, seitan, tempeh, tofu, and vegetable dishes.

Gramercy, 36 W. 21st St. (bet. Fifth and Sixth Aves.), (212) 229-0870. Open M-F 8am-10pm, Sa 10am-11pm, Su 11am-7pm. MC, V, AmEx, D, Entrées: $5-$13, F to 23rd St., N R to 23rd St.

Blue Water Grill

With everything from live jazz to an oyster bar, this delightful seafood café will keep you happy whether you're looking to eat or simply people-watch.

Gramercy, 31 Union Square W. (at 16th St.), (212) 675-9500, www.beourguestrestaurants.com. Open M-F 11:30am-12am, Sa-Su 11:30am-1am. MC, V, AmEx, Entrées: $15-$25, L N R 4 5 6 to 14th St.-Union Sq.

Bolo

Food Network favorite Bobby Flay's version of "Fantasy Spanish" cuisine doesn't miss a beat at this relaxed Flatiron restaurant. Sangria, rabbit on roasted pea risotto, and sautéed wild mushrooms with chile oil are only a few of Mr. Flay's playful gastronomic creations. A comprehensive selection of fine wines and ports are perfect complements to a meal that is the stuff dreams are made of.

Gramercy, 23 E. 22nd St. (bet. Broadway and Park Ave. S.), (212) 228-2200. Open M-F 12pm-2pm, 5:30pm-10pm, Sa-Su 5:30pm-10pm. MC, V, AmEx, DC, D. Entrées: $25-$30, N R to 23rd St.

Cal's

A striking open loft space gives you ample elbow room and surprising privacy while dining, yielding an unusually relaxed atmosphere for this trendy neighborhood. The food is good, the risotto is standout and the waitstaff is stand up.

Gramercy, 55 W. 21st St. (bet. Fifth and Sixth Aves.), (212) 929-0740, www.calsrestaurant. com. Open M-F 11:30am-5pm, 5pm-12am, Su 5pm-10:30pm. MC, V, AmEx, DC, Entrées: $16-$22, F to 23rd St., N R to 23rd St.

City Crab and Seafood Co.

Big, brash, and bustling, this urbane seafood house just

steps from Union Square is a mainstay for the area's white-collar crowd. The giant oyster bar is quite a scene after work; it's trendy and gimmicky, but it works.
Gramercy, 235 Park Ave. S. (at 19th St.), (212) 529-3800, www.citycrab.com. Open M-R 12pm-11:30pm, F 11:30am-1am, Sa 12pm-1am, Su 12pm-11pm. MC, V, AmEx, DC, Entrées: $15-$28, L N R 4 5 6 *to 14th St.-Union Sq.*

Eleven Madison Park
This upscale hotspot serves New York seasonal cuisine with a French influence. Along with the regular menu they have a fine à la carte. Go just for the grandeur of the space, which it shares with another creation by the same restauranteur — Tabla.
Gramercy, 11 Madison Ave. (at 24th St.), (212) 889-0905, www.eleven madisonpark.com. Open Su-R 11:30am-2pm, 5:30pm-10:30pm, F-Sa 12pm-2pm, 5:30pm-11pm. MC, V, AmEx, DC, D, Entrées: $21-$32, 6 *to 23rd St.*

Friend of a Farmer
Only in Gramercy could you find a Vermont snugness more convincing than anything in the Green Mountain State itself. While dinner is hearty and well-prepared, featuring stick-to-your-ribs specialties like shepherd's and chicken pot pies, the crowded brunch is the best feature. Another plus is that you've possibly seen similar prices in Montpelier.
Gramercy, 77 Irving Pl. (bet. 17th and 18th Sts.), (212) 477-2188. Open M-Su 8am-10pm. MC, V, AmEx, DC, D, Entrées: $8-$22, L N R 4 5 6 *to 14th St.-Union Sq.*

Galaxy
This dark, cozy, Irving Plaza neighbor has a ceiling spattered with twinkling stars and swirling blue planets. After sampling hemp-infused dishes like soba noodles, tiger shrimp, and garden burger, you might feel like you're dining on cloud nine. For your non-culinary needs, they also sell a complete line of hemp products, from lip balm to textiles.
Gramercy, 15 Irving Pl. (at 15th St.), (212) 777-3631, www.galaxyglobaleatery.com. MC, V, Entrées: $8-10, L N R 4 5 6 *to 14th St.-Union Sq.*

Gramercy Tavern
Don't be fooled by the rustic decor: Prices reflect the all-star clientele at this hot-spot for hobnobbing and networking. Stargazers may be willing to pay the price for a chance at sharing lunch with Johnny Depp.
Gramercy, 42 E. 20th St. (bet. Broadway and Park Ave. S.), (212) 477-0777, www.gramercy tavern.com. Open Su-R 12pm-11pm, F-Sa 12pm-12am. MC, V, AmEx, DC, D, Entrées: $18-$25, N R *to 23rd St.*

PLACES TO GO:

Gramercy Tavern
It sounds like an Irish bar, but really it's the restaurant critics say, again and again, is the best in New York.

Pongal
Not enough people make it up to the block of amazing Indian restaurants on Lexington Avenue, in the 20s. This is the best of them.

Around Union Square

Union Square is a meeting place of all the cultures of the neighborhoods surrounding it: skateboarding teenagers from below, families from above and rich young people from the west. The mixture makes for a truely unique blend that no other area can claim.

♦ **Blue Water Grill**
One of a string of high price playhouses for up-and-coming young professionals.

♦ **Union Square Café**
Competes with the Gramercy Tavern as New York's best restaurant.

♦ **Virgin Megastore**
Waterworld on DVD, the *Waterworld* soundtrack, maybe even a copy of the script of *Waterworld*, and basically anything to satisfy your listening/viewing needs.

♦ **Union Square Greenmarket**
Fresh produce from jams to peaches to watermelon's the size of Robert De Niro's ego.

♦ **Luna Park Café**
Open from mid-April to mid-October, here's the chance to drink and talk outside and maybe, maybe see a star.

♦ **De La Guarda**
Performance art taken to new levels, literally. They dance up walls, fall from the ceiling, sometimes take audience members with them, and give a show that compares to nothing else.

Les Halles
Authentically Parisian, down to the boucherie by the front door, this bustling brasserie is well known for its memorable steak frites and onion soup. Cramped tables mean people-watching and eavesdropping are favored diversions.
Gramercy, 411 Park Ave. S. (bet. 28th and 29th Sts.), (212) 679-4111. Open M-Su 12pm-12am. MC, V, AmEx, Entrées: $14-$22, 6 to 28th St. ♿

Madras Mahal
Vegetarian Kosher Indian food attracts an eclectic crowd, ranging from vegetarian Indians to Orthodox Jews. The atmosphere is friendly and service staff is dedicated.
Gramercy, 104 Lexington Ave. (bet. 27th and 28th Sts.), (212) 684-4010. Open M-F 11:30am-3pm, 5pm-10pm, Sa-Su 12pm-10pm. MC, V, AmEx, D, Entrées: $7-$12, 6 to 28th St. ♿ 🚲

Mesa Grill
Bobby Flay's limitless imagination has bestowed upon the city a masterful array of Southwestern flavors served in a light, airy space that pulses with festivity. A New York favorite, this restaurant is an eye-opener for those yet unacquainted with the exuberance of Flay's cuisine.
Gramercy, 102 Fifth Ave. (bet. 15th and 16th Sts.), (212) 807-7400, www.mesagrill.com. Open M-R 12pm-2:30pm, 5:30pm-10:30pm, F 12pm-2:30pm, 5:30pm-11pm, Sa 11:30am-3pm, 5:30pm-11pm, Su 11:30am-3pm, 5:30pm-10:30pm. MC, V, AmEx, D, Entrées: $18-$39, L N R 4 5 6 to 14th St-Union Sq. ♿

Park Avalon
Sink back and soak up the high self-esteem of this crowded, gothic hot spot, where the pleasure's in the seeing as much as in the eating. In spite of its popularity, claustrophobia is unlikely due to the spacious interior. The Mediterranean-American food, by the way, isn't shabby either.
Gramercy, 225 Park Ave. S. (bet. 18th and 19th Sts.), (212) 533-2500, www.beourguestrestarants.com. Open M-R 11:30am-12:30am, F-Sa 11:30am-1am, Su 11am-4pm, 5:30pm-12:30am. MC, V, AmEx, DC, Entrées: $14-$20, L N R 4 5 6 to Union Sq.-14th St. ♿

Patria
Professionals give way to cover girls as the sky darkens and the scene heats up in the multi-tiered dining area, lights streaming through the huge windows. The menu includes Latin American cuisine from countries ranging from Brazil to Mexico and comes out meticulously styled, like tamales cradled in corn husks; there's a prix fixe dinner every night for $54 a person.
Gramercy, 250 Park Avenue S. (at 20th St.), (212) 777-6211. Open M-R 12pm-2:30pm, 6pm-11pm, F-Sa 12pm-2:30pm,

5pm-12am, Su 5:30pm-10:30pm. MC, V, AmEx, DC, Entrées: $19-$29, ❻ *to 23rd St.* ♿

Pongal

The best Indian restaurant on the strip of the best Indian restaurants in New York. Pongal's South Indian vegetarian dishes have made it a time and review tested institution that shows no sign of closing or changing.

Gramercy, 110 Lexington Ave. (bet 27th and 28th Sts.), (212) 696-9458. Open M-F 12pm-3pm, 5pm-10pm, Sa-Su 12pm-10pm. MC, V, D, Entrees: $15-25, ❻ *to 28th St.*

Tabla

One of the few restaurants where you can get American food infused with Indian spices. Be aware that your choices are prix fixe, à la carte, or a tasting menu; all are delicious.

Gramercy, 11 Madison Ave. (at 25th St.), (212) 889-0667, www.tablanyc.com. Open M-F 12pm-2pm, 5:30pm-10:30pm, Sa-Su 5:30pm-10:30pm. MC, V, AmEx, DC, D, Entrées: $52, ❻ *to 23rd St.* ♿

Tamarind

Memphis-based Raji Jallepalli rocks the house with some of the best Indian food in NYC. The focus is on regional Indian dishes at this spacious restaurant, where waiters are numerous and attentive and the food is delicious. It's quite pricey, but well worth it.

Gramercy, 41-43 E. 22nd St. (bet. Broadway and Park Ave. S.), (212) 674-7400. Open M-Su 11:30am-3pm, Su-R 5:30pm-11:30 pm, F-Sa 5pm-12am. MC, V, AmEx, Entrees: $31-40, ❻ *to 23rd St.*

Union Square Cafe

Five times this restaurant has been voted most popualr restaurant by critics. The food's gourmet, but not the intimidating kind that makes you think your holding your fork wrong. Union Square Cafe is a landmark, whose great food and friendly sevice are here to stay.

Gramercy, 21 E. 16th St. (bet. Fifth Ave. and Union Sq. W.), (212) 243-4020. Open M-R 12pm-2:30pm, 6pm-10:30pm, F-Sa 12pm-3:30pm, 6pm-11:30pm, Su 5:30pm-10pm. MC, V, AmEx, DC, D, Entrées: $25-$35, Ⓛ Ⓝ Ⓡ ❹ ❺ ❻ *to Union Sq.-14th St.* ♿

Zen Palate

This mostly-vegan, mostly-Asian restaurant serves up mostly excellent food at moderate prices, ensuring its continuing popularity with the coveted 18-34 demographic. No alcohol, unfortunatly.

Gramercy, 34 Union Sq. E. (at 16th St.), (212) 614-9291. Open M-F 11:30am-11pm, Sa 12pm-12am, Su 12pm-10:30pm. MC, V, AmEx, DC, Entrees: $12-20, Ⓛ Ⓝ Ⓡ ❹ ❺ ❻ *to Union Sq.,* ♿

♦ CAFES

Java N Jazz

Java N Jazz is working hard to prove that they can do the coffee bar thing better than their mega chain counterparts, and it shows. Though they claim to be a relaxing place, so much is going on in and around this tiny café that you feel like everyone there has exceeded their daily caffeine limit. The walls are decked with art exhibits from neighborhood artists, they have live jazz on Friday and Saturday nights. You can even grab a box lunch to take back to work, or to bring over for a picnic in nearby Union Square Park.

Gramercy, 868 Broadway (bet. 16th and 17th Sts.), (212) 473-4200, www.java-n-jazz.com. Open M-R 7am-11pm, F-Sa 7am-12:30am, Su 9am-10:30pm. MC, V, AmEx, D, Ⓛ Ⓝ Ⓡ ❹ ❺ ❻ *to Union Sq.-14th St.* ♿ 🚲

Shopping

♦ CLOTHING & SHOES

Club Monaco

This Canadian Company has transformed New York. They have basics with a Trendy kick. Check out their CMX sports line.

Gramercy, 160 Fifth Ave, (at 21st St.), (212) 352-0936, www.clubmonaco.com. Open M-Sa 10am-8pm, Su 11am-6pm. MC, V, AmEx, DC, Ⓝ Ⓡ *to 23rd St.* ♿

Moe Ginsburg

Over 50,000 square feet of suits, overcoats, sportswear, accessories, and shoes, with suppliers from Italy, Canada, and the States. A good option if you just got that internship at Goldman Sachs.

Gramercy, 162 Fifth Ave. (at 21st St.), (212) 242-3482. Open M-W, F 9:30am-7pm, R 9:30am-8pm, Sa-Su 9:30am-6pm. MC, V, AmEx, D, Ⓝ Ⓡ *to 23rd St.* ♿

♦ BOOKS, MAGAZINES & RECORDS

Disc-O-Rama

This small chain was serving downtown New York's audio/visual needs before the words “DVD” and “CD” entered our vocabulary. Though they've updated their inventory since then, offering an extensive collection of current music and video releases, Disc-O-Rama still keeps it old school with a vinyl department, and album prices that are always cheaper than a movie ticket. Try finding either of those features in a megastore!

Gramercy, 40 Union Sq. E. (bet. 16th and 17th Sts.), (212) 260-8616, www.discorama.com. Open M-T 8:30am-6:15pm, W-F 8:30am-6:45pm, Sa 10am-6pm, Su 11am-5:30pm. MC, V, AmEx, LNR456 *to Union Sq.-14th St.* ♿

Shakespeare & Co.

One of four locations left after the recent demise of the Upper West Side store, offering a diverse selection of books, and the soul of an actual bookstore, too.

Gramercy, 137 E. 23rd St. (at Lexington Ave.), (212) 505-2021, www.shakespeare-nyc.com. MC, V, AmEx, D, 6 *to 23rd St.*

Virgin Megastore

Megastore is right! One of two in the city, the Union Square store is the place to be for everything in books, magazines, movies, and especially music. Giggle over the Virgin brand condoms by the register as you pay for your goodies.

Gramercy, 52 E. 14th St. (at Broadway), (212) 598-4666, www.virginmega.com. Open M-Sa 9am-1am, Su 10am-12am. MC, V, AmEx, D, 456 *to Union Sq.-14th St.* ♿

♦ GROCERY, GOURMET& SPECIALTY

Sal Anthony's Mio Pane Mio Dolce

For the same price as chips and a soda at a nearby deli, treat yourself to a panini on fresh semolina bread, some freshly baked cookies, or some homemade pastries. For special occasions, be sure not to miss the Black and White cake, a Sal Anthony's specialty, or a chocolate covered strawberry for a quick bite of bliss.

Gramercy, 77 Irving Pl. (bet. 18th and 19th Sts.), (212) 677-1627. Open M-F 7am-11pm, Sa 8am-11pm, Su 9am-11pm. Cash Only, 456LNR *to Union Sq.-14th St.* ♿

Union Square Greenmarket

Year round, farmers bring their fresh produce, meats, breads, and other delectables to sell at this outdoor market. Offering mostly seasonal goods, and quality that far surpasses any D'agostinos, the Greenmarket is the ideal place to do your weekly shopping. Get a fresh snack on the way home, or a have a leisurely lunch in the park.

Gramercy, Union Sq. Park, 15-17th Sts. (at Broadway), (Office: 130 E. 16th St.), (212) 477-3220. Open M, W, F, Sa (times vary). Cash Only. 456LNR *to Union Sq.-14th St.*

♦ MISCELLANEOUS

ABC Carpet and Home

Expect to find ample mother-daughter pairs oohing and aahing their way through six floors of housewares, antiques, and knickknacks. Although fairly expensive, the store is worth a visit for its creative window displays and extraordinary finds such as a ten foot tall gilded bird cage. The Parlour Cafe on the ground floor allows weary shoppers to lounge and lunch on the furniture that they can't afford to buy.

Gramercy, 881 and 888 Broadway (at 19th St.), (212) 473-3000, www.abchome.com. Open M-F 10am-8pm, Sa 10am-7pm, Su 11am-6:30pm. MC, V, AmEx, D, LNR 456 *to Union Sq.-14th St.* ♿

Fishes Eddy

Mix and match from overstocks of commercial dishes and glasses to set a dinner table that no one else will have. Watch the price tags, though– many of the plates and detailed glasses cost more than you'd think. Don't leave without checking out the bins in the back for $1 saucers and the shelves around the sides for $2 wine glasses. Fishes Eddy will leave anyone feeling like a homebody who can set a unique discounted table – that will definitely get your family and guests talking.

Gramercy, 889 Broadway (at 19th St.), (212) 420-9020, www.fisheseddy.com. Open M-Sa 10am-9pm, Su 11am-8pm. MC, V, AmEx, LNR456 *to 14th St.-Union Sq.*

Also at:

Upper West Side, 2176 Broadway (at 77th St.), (212) 873-8819. 19 *to 79th St.*

SoHo, 60 Mercer St. (at Broome St.), (212) 226-4711. NR *to Prince St.*

Just Bulbs

The name really says it all. Find every variety of light bulb imaginable, including those for decoration, gifts, and spe-

"A hundred times I have thought 'New York is a catastrophe' and fifty times: 'It is a beautiful catastrophe'."

—Le Courbusier

Manhattan Murder Mystery, 1993

Diane Keaton and Alan Alda sip wine in the National Arts Club overlooking Gramercy Park. This delightful Woody Allen comedy follows unlikely detectives as they search for the truth about a neighbor's death.

cific holidays.
Gramercy, 936 Broadway (bet. 21st and 22nd Sts.), (212) 228-7820, www.justbulbs.com. Open M-W, F 9am-6pm, R 9am-7pm, Sa 10am-6pm, Su 12pm-6pm. MC, V, AmEx, D, N R *to 23rd St.* ♿

Oasis Day Spa
This aptly-named refugee from the bustle of Union Square offers a variety of body and skin therapies. You can get your skin polished and your life force energy spiritually guided– all before lunch. The highlight is the Lava Stone massage, which involves hot rocks being dragged all over you, but is somehow sublime.
Gramercy, 108 E. 16th St. (bet. Park Ave. and Astor Pl.), (212) 254-7722, www.nydayspa.com. Open M-F 10am-10pm, Sa-Su 9am-9pm. MC, V, AmEx, D. L N R 4 5 6 *to 14th St.-Union Sq.*

Paragon
Whether the game is badminton, snowboarding, or basketball, this sports superstore is sure to have the right gear. The shoe department often has better deals than the chains.
Chelsea, 867 Broadway (at 18th St.), (212) 255-8036, www.paragonsports.com. Open M-Sa 10am-8pm, Su 11am-6:30pm. MC, V, AmEx, 1 9 *to 18th St.*

Sam Flax
Whether in search of gouache, canvas, or some stylish wrapping paper, shoppers will find it all at this well-staffed store. Check out the sale section in back for some good furniture bargains as well.
Gramercy, 12 W. 20th St. (bet. Fifth and Sixth Aves.), (212) 620-3038. Open M-F 9am-6:30pm, Sa 10am-6pm, Su 12pm-5pm. MC, V, AmEx, D, F *to 23rd Street,* N R *to 23rd St.*

Arts & Recreation

♦ LEISURE

American Ballet Theatre
Drop-in classes to the tune of $12 a pop ($110 buys ten classes) for aspiring prima donnas at one of the country's premiere studios. Alaine Haubert and Diana Cartier teach regularly, though guest instructors from the ABT Artistic Staff occasionally fill in. Advanced dancers should stop by at 10am Monday, Wednesday, or Friday, while intermediates will be best served by the 6pm weekday classes.
Gramercy, 890 Broadway (at 19th St.), 3rd fl., (212) 477-3030, www.abt.org. L N R 4 5 6 *to Union Sq.-14th St.* ♿

♦ PERFORMANCE

Vineyard Theatre
In recent years this Union Square favorite has emerged as a major source of excellent new plays and musicals. The Vineyard's 120-seat theater was the site of the New York premieres of Pulitzer Prize winners "Three Tall Women" and "How I Learned To Drive." Special discount passes available for students.
Gramercy, 108 E. 15th St. (bet. Union Sq. and Irving Pl.), (212) 353-3366, www.vineyardtheatre.org. MC, V, AmEx, L N R 4 5 6 *to 14th St.-Union Sq.* ♿

♦ SITES

Flatiron Building
While 21 stories barely constitutes a skyscraper in modern parlance, this triangular office building at the intersection of Fifth Avenue and Broadway, erected in 1902 by Daniel H. Burnham, certainly impressed turn-of-the-century tourists; the men were especially eager to see if the unusual flow of air created by the building's angle really did lift ladies' skirts above their ankles. For many, its rusticated limestone façade and steel frame symbolized the dawn of the skyscraper era.
Gramercy., 175 Fifth Ave. (bet. 23rd St. and Broadway), N R *to 23rd St.*

School of Visual Arts
Founded in 1847 as a school for cartoonists and illustrators, this private arts college has become one of the country's most prestigious producers of artsy-fartsy types – you can almost inhale the creative energy just hanging around the school's environs. In addition to operating a professional gallery in SoHo, the school operates six student galleries at this main campus; check them out and jot down names, so

that in ten years you can say you saw so and so when he or she was just starting out.
Gramercy, 209 E. 23rd St. (bet. Second and Third Aves.), (212) 592-2000, 6 to 23rd St.

Theodore Roosevelt's Birthplace
Saturday afternoons are the best time to visit the birthplace of out 26th President for a spin around his childhood home, a couple of museum galleries and admission to a chamber music concert. Ask about Roosevelt's playboy uncle Robert, who lived in the brownstone next door.
Gramercy., 28 E. 20th St. (bet. Park Ave. S. and Broadway), (212) 260-1616. Open: W-Su 9am-5pm. Cash Only, Admission: $2, 6 to 23rd St.

♦ GALLERIES AND LIBRARIES

Dixon Place
A gallery and performance showcase, Dixon Place specializes in providing an intimate setting for dynamic dance, art, literary and musical works. With an audience capacity of 60 and an ever-changing eclectic program devoted to pioneering performance art and poetry reading, the space is both memorable and versatile. You won't forget a night at Dixon Place: you can even discuss and critique the performances with the artists themselves.
Gramercy, 309 E. 26th St. (at Second Ave.), (212) 532-1546, www.dixonplace.org. Call for showtimes, Admission: free-$12. N R to 28th St. 6 to 28th St.

Nightlife

♦ BARS

119 Bar
This unassuming little dive is known for its stiff drinks and the dark booths where you can pretty much get away with anything. It's a great place to, say, cheat on your significant other.
Gramercy, 119 E. 15th St. (bet. Irving Pl. and Park Ave. S.), (212) 995-5904. Open M-Su 4pm-4am. Cash Only, L N R 4 5 6 to Union Sq.-14th St.

Belmont Lounge
The Belmont Lounge is a dark and comfy spot to enjoy a cigar and drinks with friends after a concert at Irving Plaza. Weekends tend to get a bit crazy, as the Lounge hosts DJs that pack 'em in on Fridays and Saturdays to the tune of a $5 cover.
Gramercy, 117 E. 15th St. (bet. Irving Pl. and Lexington Ave.), (212) 533-0009. Open M-Su 4pm-4am. MC, V, AmEx, L N R 4 5 6 to Union Sq-14th St.

Heartland Brewery
Take the pulse of the after work crowd at this hip Union Square bar; patrons move fast, talk fast, and drink fast, enjoying the award winning house brews while communing with cell phones, PDAs, and sometimes even each other. For the more leisurely diner, plenty of seating is available.
Gramercy, 35 Union Square West (at 17th St.) (212) 645-3400. Open M-R 12pm-1am, F-Sa 12pm-3am, Su 1q2pm-12am. MC, V, AmEx, DC, L N R 4 5 6 to Union Sq.

Located right on Madison Square Park, curious passerby and neighborhood locals find it hard to resist this urban rendition of the Louisiana bayou. Force your way past the boisterous happy hour crowd to the tables in back in order to sample the Cajun shrimp or the mesquite BBQ.
Gramercy, 14 East 23rd St. (bet. Broadway and Madison Ave.), (212) 353-2400. Open M-Sa 11am-2am. MC, V, AmEx, N R to 23rd St.

Metronome
Slightly more polished and pricey than the other Gramercy bars, Metronome draws an older, professional crowd. There's dancing on Saturday nights and live jazz Wednesday through Saturday.
Gramercy, 915 Broadway (at 21st St.), (212) 505-7400. Call for schedule. MC, V, AmEx, DC, N R to 23rd St.

Paddy Reilly's Music Bar
The world's first and only all-draught Guiness bar. That's pretty much their deal. They have traditional Irish music seven days a week. Subtle though, a bunch of old guys in a

corner with instruments in their hands, jamming away. Celebrities love the bar, maybe because it's quiet and you can get a seat.
Gramercy, 519 Second Ave. (at 29th St.), (212) 686-1210. Open M-Su 4pm-4am. MC, V, AmEx, 6 to 28th St.

Pete's Tavern
Pete's has been a local hangout for ages. Although it's mostly a bar, the Italian menu is more than adequate.
Gramercy, 129 East 18th St. (at Irving Pl.), (212) 473-7676. Open M-Su 12pm-2am. MC, V, AmEx, L N R 4 5 6 to Union Sq.-14th St.

Red Room at the Gershwin Hotel
The newly renovated Gershwin Hotel's Red Room bar isfast becoming one of the Flatiron District's hottest hangouts. The bar serves only beer and wine, but that doesn't seem to stop the young and pretty mid-twenties crowd from packing the place on weekends. Tuesday nights feature stand-up comedy.
Gramercy, 7 East 27th St. (bet. Fifth and Madison Aves.), (212) 252-1005. Open Su-Sa 6pm-3am. Cash Only, N R 6 to 23rd St.

Rodeo Bar & Grill
Don't expect cowboy hats and big belt buckles at this cozy wild west watering hole, but then again, don't let the giant stuffed buffalo above the bar surprise you. The menu is limited, but live free rockabilly bands keep the place swingin'.
Gramercy, 375 Third Ave. (at 27th St.), (212) 683-6500, www.rodeo bar.com. Open M-Su 11:30am-4am. MC, V, AmEx, DC, D, 6 to 28th St.

♦ MUSIC

OHM Nightclub
Latin music and live bands on Wednesdays as well as savory Spanish cooking draws a crowd that is young, mixed and attractive. Free admission for ladies before 9pm.
dance, hip hop, house, funk, R&B
Gramercy, 16 West 22nd St. (at Fifth Ave.), (212) 229-2000, www.ohmnyc.com. Open: R-Sa 8pm-4am. MC, V, Am Ex, Cover: $5-$15, N R to 23rd St.

The Gargoyles of Gramercy

A walk through Gramercy promises beautiful buildings, people and monsters everywhere. Start your walk on Irving Place and 19th Street and instead of looking ahead, look up.

The biggest cluster of imps can be found wrapping around, at eye level, **81 Irving Place**. Staring at you, smirking, is devil after ghostbuster-like devil. If their stares make you uncomfortable, walk around the corner to the alley between 81 Irving and **119 East 19th**. The gargoyles here are frozen in a stone carnival; hobos and carny types look down, mouths open, almost beckoning you to join.

The actual gargoyles on 119 aren't as impressive—a bunch of winged gargoyles and a row of carved heads—and while the ones on **34 Gramercy** are better, they are higher up. This doesn't really matter though, built before the Dakota and other buildings like it, 34 Gramercy is as Gothic and Gotham as New York gets. It's almost as if putting the rows of cherubs and heads high up was done on purpose because it forces you to take all of this beautiful building.

Amble next door to **36 Gramercy** and enter a medieval world of fat angels and knights, warning you that while you can enjoy them as much as you want, unless you have a key, you can't go inside.

Chelsea

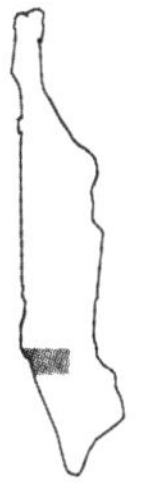

Uprooted by high rent and close quarters, New York's art galleries have quietly resettled not just north of Houston but north of 14th Street near the Hudson River. The new art scene and the social scene on Eighth Avenue (Mom, why are there no women in that bar?) nicely complement the already established-shops on Sixth Avenue and regal townhouses between Ninth and Tenth Avenues. This mixture of old and new makes for one of the most interesting neighborhoods in New York. Plus, it's one of the friendliest places; its eateries spilling into the streets, creating a sense of common space and community.

The architecture of Chelsea is amazing: London Terrace, the glorious block-long expanse of London Terrace on 23rd Street between Ninth and Tenth Avenues; the McKim, Mead and White designed Post Office; and, of course, the Chelsea Hotel, site of thespian myth and mischief. Nancy died at Sid's hand here and Leonard Cohen, Dylan Thomas and Norman Mailer, among others, have made the hotel their one time home.

The 80s ushered in a renaissance of commercial prosperity. Superstores arrived, and entrepreneurs capitalized on Chelsea's bevy of vacated warehouses to create monster dance clubs, attracting sex-and-drug trades to the area. Depreciated land values by the Hudson River led to low rents, attracting the galleries as SoHo prices began to soar. The city's premier sports and recreation center, aptly named Chelsea Piers, was built over abandoned docks no one thought would ever be used again.

Parts of Chelsea may be too "exuberant" for some, but by and large this section of town has found its niche. Between an ethnic pocket right out of bygone Spain, the flower district on 28th Street, an enormous movie multiplex, and enough restaurants to challenge the flattening effect of its plentiful gyms, Chelsea has muscled its way into being an integral part of New York City life.

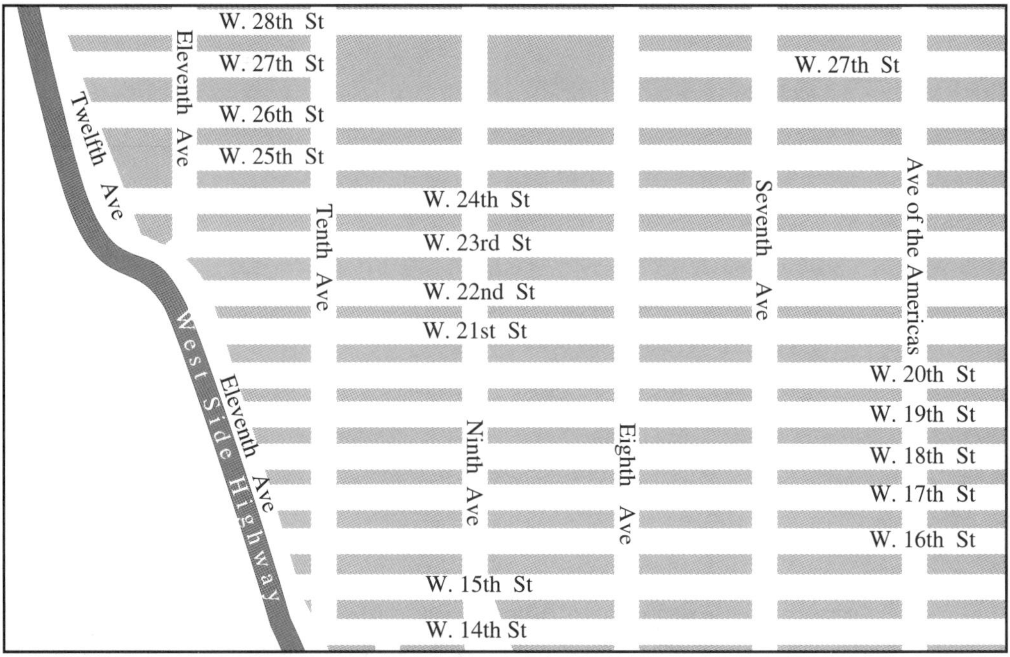

Dining

♦ RESTAURANTS

147

Known as much for its fashionable clientele as for its delicious menu, the decor here is subtle yet elegant, the food simple yet scrumptious. You can't go wrong ordering, but we especially recommend the chilled vegetable rolls as an appetizer. After your meal, hang out until the wee hours at the stylish bar.

Chelsea, 147 W. 15th St. (bet. Sixth and Seventh Aves.), (212) 929-5000. Open Su-R 6am-12am, F-Sa 6am-4am. MC, V, AmEx, Entrées: $15-$25, 1 2 3 9 *to 14th St.*

Alley's End

Literally at the end of an alley on a vaguely unsavory block of Chelsea, finding this restaurant is half the fun. But only half. Prim and relaxed, this hide-away is a hidden jewel, with an interior garden and a banquet room, complete with fireplace, for larger parties. No longer undiscovered, there tends to be a crowd weekend nights, but the cute quarters and quality food make it worthwhile.

Chelsea, 311 W. 17th St. (bet. Eighth and Ninth Aves.), (212) 627-8899, www.alleysend.com. Open M-Su 6pm-11pm. MC, V, D, Entrées: $16-$24, A C E *to 14th St.,* L *to Eighth Ave.,* 1 9 *to 18th St.*

Amin Indian Cuisine

Dinner here avoids the circus-like pitfalls of Sixth Street's outfits. Curries, kebabs, and kormas are spicy enough to satisfy natives, and will only set you back about $10. Combo platters allow for both gluttony and variety.

Chelsea, 155 Eighth Ave. (bet. 17th and 18th Sts.), (212) 929-7020. Open M-R 11:30am-11pm, F-Sa 11:30am-11:30pm. MC, V, AmEx, Entrées: $7-$19, A C E *to 14th St.*

Bendix Diner

Whether it's because of the motto's invitation to "get fat" or because of the subsequent surprise of a health-conscious menu, patrons have been congregating at this casual hot-spot in such numbers that owners have been forced to expand. Greasy spoon prices mean the American-Thai fusion dishes leave no room for guilt.

Chelsea, 219 Eighth Ave. (at 21st St.), (212) 366-0560. Open M-F 8am-12am, Sa-Su 8am-1am. MC, V, AmEx, D, Entrées: $6-$9, C E *to 23rd St.*

Empire Diner

Featured in the opening montage of Woody Allen's *Manhattan*, this almost-24-hour eatery (it's closed 4am-8:30am) boasts an upscale dinner menu, complemented by a jazz pianist. It's a great club-hopping pit stop; staying up for prix-fixe brunch is well worth the sleep deprivation. Don't go à la carte, as the prices soar.

Chelsea, 210 Tenth Ave. (at 22nd St.), (212) 243-2736. Open M-Su 8:30am-4am. MC, V, AmEx, Entrées: $5-$18, C E *to 23rd St.*

Gascogne

Feast on sumptuously prepared food, sip cognac, and surreptitiously loosen your belt a notch. Creative fare like quail, wild boar, and rabbit all grace the menu. If the weather proves as good as the food, take a seat in the exquisite back garden, though indoors is atmospheric as well. As close to royalty as the bourgeoisie can get.

Chelsea, 158 Eighth Ave. (bet. 17th and 18th Sts.), (212) 675-6564. Open M-Su 12pm-3pm, 6pm-12am. MC, V, AmEx, Entrées: $18-$23, A C E to 14th St., L to Eighth Ave.

PLACES TO GO:

Cheetah

Jay-Z mentioned it in his song "Give it to Me" as one of the clubs you could find him at.

Joyce Theater

It's off beat but it is not wierd. The caliber of the Joyce's dancers are no different from the Met's.

Chelsea Piers

The one place in New York where you can play ice hockey, baseball and golf.

Le Gamin

A more successful stab than most at replicating a Parisian café, this neighborhood joint serves crepes, croque monsieur, quiche, and salads to a laid-back, lingering crowd. Family types mix with the downtown chic; the lack of a liquor license encourages people to bring their own beer or wine. A great stopover for a cappuccino while club-hopping or a good setting for more lengthy leisure and a latte. The French menu has English subtitles.

Chelsea, 183 Ninth Ave. (at 21st St.), (212) 243-8864, www.legamin.com. Open M-Su 8am-12am. Cash Only, Entrées: $7-$10, C E to 23rd St.

Le Madri

Le Madri blends homey and chic in a spacious restaurant featuring modern dishes rooted in Italian tradition. Conventional creations, like French fries and fried calamari, come off surprisingly well, but best are the house-made pastas, anything from the wood-burning oven, the seafood, and the popular osso buco. Desserts deserve special mention, truly Italian in their subtlety and simplicity. (Try a *real* tiramisu.) There's also the extra perk of a possible celebrity spotting, and valet parking.

Chelsea, 168 W. 18th St. (at Seventh Ave.), (212) 727-8022. Open M-Su 12pm-3pm, 5:30pm-11:30pm. MC, V, AmEx, DC, D, Entrées: $13-$32, 1 9 to 18th St.

Merchants, NY

At this downtown branch of a trio of sleek establishments of the same name, some actually order food here to go with their martini or cosmopolitan; check out the downstairs sofa scene for ultimate cushiness. The appetizer and dessert menus are excellent.

Chelsea, 112 Seventh Ave. (bet. 16th and 17th Sts.), (212) 366-7267. Open M-Su 11:30am-4am. MC, V, AmEx, D, Entrées: $10-$18, 1 9 to 18th St.

O Padeiro

This Portuguese bakery-cum-restaurant-cum- bar accomplishes noteworthy feats with egg and garlic, but its most tasteful feature is the decor: elevated breads, baked on the premises, and stylish fans accent the lofty ceilings. A café by day, it successfully converts itself into a casual dinner spot. Try the wine tasting menu to sample delicious, but underappreciated, Portuguese wines.

Chelsea, 641 Sixth Ave. (bet. 19th and 20th Sts.), (212) 414-9661. Open M-R 7am-10pm, F 7am-11pm, Sa 9am-11pm, Su 10am-7pm. MC, V, AmEx, Entrées: $16, F to 23rd St., 1 9 to 18th St.

Petite Abeille

Scads of Tintin paraphernalia and tasty Belgian bites make this a popular feature of Little Belgium. Absolutely divine fries and *moules* (mussels)!

Chelsea, 107 W. 18th St. (bet. Sixth and Seventh Aves.), (212) 604-9350. Open M-F 7am-7pm, Sa-Su 9am-6pm. Cash Only, Entrées: $10-$12, 1 9 to 18th St.

Rocking Horse Cafe Mexicano

One of a string of Mexican restaurants along Eighth Ave., this is the most upscale, with fresh food, a perky waitstaff, and a popular brunch. Interesting twists on traditional fare include variations with crab and lobster, but the old standards are excellent as well — burritos, enchiladas, and margaritas.

Chelsea, 182 Eighth Ave. (bet. 19th and 20th Sts.), (212) 463-

9511, www.rockinghorse.com. Open Su-R 11:30am-11pm, F-Sa 11:30am-12am. MC, V, AmEx, Entrées: $14-$20, C E to 23rd St., 1 9 to 18th St.

Tonic
The glamourous sister of the famous downtown Tonic. Authentic bar in front, beautiful dining room in back, and attractive French waiters make it well-worth the steep prices.
Chelsea, 108 W. 18th St. (bet. Sixth and Seventh Aves.), (212) 929-9755. Open M-R 12pm-3pm, 5pm-10:30pm, F-Sa 12pm-3pm, 5pm-11pm. MC, V, D, AmEx, Entrees: $20-$25, 1 9 to 18th St.

Viceroy
Come to this trendy spot for "see-food" — Chelsea's bold and beautiful are on display from the inside or out, with floor to ceiling windows providing a free peek. Viceroy features some great dishes (and the food's not half-bad either). This cool, comfortable place makes for a glam time. Plus, given who's biting, you never know what you'll catch.
Chelsea, 160 Eighth Ave. (at 18th St.), (212) 633-8484, www.the viceroy.com. Open M-W 11:30am-12am, R-F 11:30am-1am, Sa 9am-1am, Su 9am-12am. MC, V, AmEx, DC, D, Entrées: $10-$20, 1 9 to 18th St.

♦ CAFES

Big Cup
Day-glo colors and paisley patterns recall the '60s, but the very buff, short-coiffed gay male clientele is pure '90s. Lounge all day in comfy chairs, sip a mocha, and watch the cityscape tumble by. A major singles scene.
Chelsea, 228 Eighth Ave. (bet. 21st and 22nd Sts.), (212) 206-0059, Open Su-R 7am-1am, F,Sa 7am-2am. Cash Only, C E to 23rd St.

El Cid Tapas
Fit for Picasso, this tiny secret features the most authentic tapas this side of Barcelona. Go with a group and split a pitcher of white or red sangria, and fight over the last bite of marinated quail, seafood salad, or, their specialty, braised sweetbreads in garlic sauce. Come early on weekends.

Chelsea, 322 W. 15th St (at Eighth Ave.)., (212) 929-9332. Open T-Su 12pm-3pm, 5pm-11pm. AmEx, DC, Entrées: $10-$18, A C E to 14th St., L to

Emack and Bolios
Looking for something sweet and delicious? Look no further. For delicious gourmet ice cream, yogurt, and smoothies, Emack and Bolios cannot be beat. There are three locations throughout the city, so you're never too far from your sweet-tooth-fix.
Chelsea, 56 Seventh Ave. (bet. 13th and 14th Sts.), (212) 727-1198. Open M-Su 12:30pm-12pm. Cash Only, Entrees: $2-$3, 1 9 to 14th St.

Shopping

♦ CLOTHING & SHOES

Burlington Coat Factory
Why pay more? With six floors of discount coats, suits, shirts and casual sportswear, you're sure to find what you need at the right price.
Chelsea, 707 W. 23rd St. (at Sixth Ave.), (212) 229-1300, www.coat.com. Open M-Sa 10am-9pm, Su 10am-6pm. MC, V, AmEx, DC, D, F to 23rd St.

Emporio Armani
Cleanly cut casual suits that are a bit more accessible price-wise than Armani's main line. Just about everything looks classy in the renovated Stanford White building.
Chelsea, 110 Fifth Ave. (at 16th St.), (212) 727-3240, Open M-F 11am-8pm, Sa 11am-7pm, Su 12pm-6pm. MC, V, AmEx, L N R 4 5 6 to 14th St.-Union Sq.

Filene's Basement
This bargain staple superstore carries Calvin Klein, Perry Ellis, Kenar, and other designer names, and is worth a look for shoes, lingerie, coats, suits, and evening wear. Check out the occasional clearance sales where many prices are slashed to below $5.
Chelsea, 620 Sixth Ave. (bet. 18th and 19th Sts.), (212) 620-3100, www.filenesbasement.com. Open M-Sa 9:30am-9pm, Su 11am-7pm. MC, V, AmEx, D, 1 9 to 18th St.

Loehmann's
As legendary as Century 21 in designer junkie circles, this 5-floor Chelsea outpost rewards the shopper who makes the trek: lots of big-name labels and high stock turnover justify frequent trips.
Chelsea, 101 Seventh Ave. (bet. 16th and 17th Sts.), (212) 352-0856, www.loehmanns.com. Open M-Sa 9am-9pm, Su 11am-7pm. MC, V, D, 1 9 to 18th St.

Parke and Ronen
This store features clothing by two local designers: appropriately enough, Parke and Ronen. The store carries predominantly sportswear, and at moderate prices - moderate,

that is, relative to other New York designers.
Chelsea, 176 Ninth Ave. (bet. 20th and 21st Sts.), (212) 989-4245, www.parkandronen.com. Open T-Sa 12pm-8pm, Su 1pm-6pm. MC, V, AmEx, D. CE to 23rd St. ♿

♦ BOOKS, MAGAZINES & RECORDS

A Different Light
The East Coast branch of the largest gay and lesbian specialty book vendor in the country. A mellow crowd browses through great selections from kitsch to academia and partakes of the small cafe's coffee and sandwiches. The store regularly hosts lectures, musicians, and poets, and offers free movies (with popcorn!) on Sundays.
Chelsea, 151 W. 19th St. (bet. Sixth and Seventh Aves.), (212) 989-4850, www.adlbooks.com. Open M-Su 11am-10pm. MC, V, AmEx, 19 to 18th St. ♿

Fashion Design Books
Located at the heart of FIT's urban campus, this unique take on the university bookstore stocks a plethora of fashion mags, from the popular to the obscure, and art and design books. In lieu of office accessories, you'll find art and sewing supplies.
Chelsea, 234 W. 27th St. (bet. Seventh and Eighth Aves.), (212) 633-9646, www.fashiondesign books.com. Open M-Su 9am-5pm. MC, V, AmEx, D, 19 to 28rd St. ♿

Manhattan Comics and Cards
Action figures gaze down at customers navigating the stacks of comic books; mags run the gamut of old, new, latest, and greatest. Scavenge through the half-price bins.
Chelsea, 228 W. 23rd St. (bet. Seventh and Eighth Aves.), (212) 243-9349. Open M-T 10am-8pm, W-Sa 10am-9pm, Su 12pm-8pm. MC, V, AmEx, D, 19 to 23rd St., CE to 23rd St.

Midnight Records
Calling all spinners, DJs, and jazz heads. Remember those large round disks with deep grooves in them? This dealer of vinyl, with both old and new collectibles, is living proof that albums have not completely gone the way of the dinosaur. *Chelsea, 263 West 23rd St. (bet. Seventh and Eighth Aves.), (212) 675-2768. Open T, R-Sa 12pm-6pm. MC, V, AmEx, D, 19 to 23rd St., CE to 23rd St.*

Unity Book Store
"You say you want a revolution?" If reading about one suffices, this smallish shop, chock-full of radical leftist writings, is the place to go. Check out the great Marxist, African-American, and women authors who most likely didn't make your high school government class reading list.
Chelsea, 237 W. 23rd St. (bet. Seventh and Eighth Aves.), (212) 242-2934. Open M, R, F 11:30am-5pm . Cash Only, CE to 23rd St., 19 to 23rd St.

♦ GROCERY, GOURMET & SPECIALTY

New York Cake and Baking Distributors, Inc.
Attempting to make a cake without the aid of the local bakery? You'll need the stuff they sell here. They have all sorts of baking supplies, from pans to those little flowers you'll be adorning your creation with.
Chelsea, 56 W. 22nd St. (bet. Fifth and Sixth Aves.), (212) 675-2253, www.nycakesupply.com. Open M-F 9:30am-6pm, Sa 10am-6pm, Su 11am-5:30pm. MC, V, AmEx, F to 22nd St.

♦ MISCELLANEOUS

Azure Day Spa and Laser Center
As soon as you smell the incense wafting onto the street, you can expect to soon find yourself naked and wrapped up in a plush white robe ready to get the sugar rub down and hot stone massage. Before that you can get your ears candled (which drains your ears of all that wax), a facial, body wrap or laser off unwanted body hair. At Azure, you can have a luxurious day-long event or just an hour of bliss – but all for substantial amounts of cash. But hey, you're worth it.
Chelsea, 29th St. (bet. Seventh and Eighth Aves.), (212) 563-5364, azuredayspa.com/index.cgi. Open M-F 9:30am-8pm, Sa 9am-6pm. MC, V, AmEx, D, 19 to 28th St.

Chelsea Second Hand Guitars
Just window shopping is enough to make Eddie Van Halen bust a nut. "Anything you're looking for, we can find through our network," boasts the dude at the counter. Go in and try

> God, gallery after gallery, with pristine white walls of Culture, the black wooden floors, and the Culture buds, a little Renoirish softness in the autumn faces.
>
> —Tom Wolfe

one on for size: Strats, Les Pauls, Fenders, etc. Vintage guitars for the finger-picking connoisseur.
Chelsea, 220 W. 23rd St. (bet. Seventh and Eighth Aves.), (212) 675-4993. Open M-Su 11am-7pm. MC ,V, AmEx, 1 9 to 23rd St., C E to 23rd. St. ♿

Dish Is
For lovely hand-painted Italian ceramics, don't miss this Chelsea treasure. They also feature a large variety of home furnishings. The store isn't as large as some, but the items make up for it.
Chelsea, 228 Seventh Ave., (bet. 23rd and 24th Sts.), (212) 352-9051, www.dishis. com. Open M-F 11am-8pm, Sa-Su 11am-7pm. MC, V, AmEx, 1 9 to 23rd St. ♿

Materials for the Arts
Starve no more, artists! Located above the new chi-chi shopping center in an old warehouse, MFA offers furniture and props, a full selection of fabrics, paints, and other materials free of charge. The City of New York, through the Department of Cultural Affairs and the Department of Sanitation, saves material that would otherwise go to waste and donates it to nonprofit cultural, educational organizations, and individual artists to use for specific projects. Once you get through the paperwork, you get tags with which to mark your new acquisitions. Materials change according to availability, but the selection is usually pretty good.
Chelsea, 75 Ninth Ave. (bet. 15th and 16th Sts.), (212) 255-5924. A C E to 14th St. ♿

Arts & Recreation

♦ LEISURE

Capitol Fishing Tackle Co.
Rounding out an eclectic mix of stores on this block, this emporium specializes in everything an angler would ever want or need: rods, hooks, tackle, etc. No chance of blending in with the loyal clientele of piscine nimrods unless you're one of them.
Chelsea, 218 W. 23rd St. (bet. Seventh and Eighth Aves.), (212) 929-6132. Open M-W 9am-6pm, R 9am-7:30pm, F 9am-6pm, Sa 9:30am-5pm. MC, V, AmEx, D, 1 9 to 23rd St.

Chelsea Piers
Price gouging at its finest, Chelsea Piers is a cavernous series of indoor recreational facilities on the Hudson that makes up for what it lacks in charm with an impressively eye-pleasing clientele. It may cost more money that your first car, but where else in Manhattan can you play golf, go bowling, ice skating and rock climbing in the same place?
Chelsea, Piers 59-62, Twelfth Ave. (at 23rd St.), (212) 336-6800. C E to 23rd St.

Little Spain
Though the population of Spanish sailors that burgeoned after the Civil War has since waned, snatches of Spanish still drift out of restaurants onto the streets and a few bookstores tell of a Spanish past now gone.
Chelsea, 14th St. (W. of Sixth Ave.), F to 14th St.

♦ PERFORMANCE

Bessie Schonberg Theater
Home to the Dance Theater Workshop, a non-profit organization dedicated to assisting and promoting independent artists in the community, this intimate space seats 100 people and stages cutting-edge dance and musical performances.
Chelsea, 219 W. 19th St. (bet. Seventh and Eighth Aves.), (212) 924-0077, www.dt.org. MC, V, 1 9 to 18th St.

The Irish Repertory Theatre
An intimate performance space for a variety of Irish and Irish-American plays.
Chelsea, 132 W. 22nd St. (bet. Sixth and Seventh Aves.), (212) 727-2737, www.irishrepertorytheatre.com. MC, V, AmEx, F to 23rd St., 1 9 to 23rd St. ♿

Joyce Theater
The unlikely successor to a former porno palace, this hotbed of talent inherited a large stage and virtually clear sightlines, which create an ideal setting for performances by top touring companies from around the world. The "Altogether Different" series promotes promising up-and-coming companies yearly.
Chelsea, 175 Eighth Ave. (at 19th St.), (212) 242-0800, www.joyce. org. MC, V, AmEx, 1 9 to 18th St. ♿

The Kitchen
Located among dismal warehouses, this raw space thrives on experimental music and dance performed in a black box theater with bleachers seating about 150 and a multi-media lab with visual arts exhibitions. Past performers include

Laurie Anderson, David Byrnes, and
Eric Bogosian. Check out the café theater on the second floor.
Chelsea, 512 W. 19th St. (bet. Tenth and Eleventh Aves.), (212) 255-5793. MC, V, AmEx, ❶❾ to 18th St. ⒸⒺ to 23rd St. ♿

♦ SITES

General Post Office
A beautiful example of McKim, Mead and White architecture, circa 1913, this imposing, columned structure on the cusp of Chelsea and Clinton bears the famous postal slogan ("Neither snow nor rain…"). Open to the public 24 hours a day.
Chelsea, 421 Eighth Ave. (at 30th St.), (212) 967-8585, ⒶⒸⒺ to *34th St.-Penn Station ♿*

♦ MUSEUMS & CULTURAL CENTERS

Fashion Institute of Technology and Shirley Goodman Resource Center
Exhibits feature famously fabulous designers, as well as work by talented FIT students.
Chelsea, 227 W. 27th St. (at Seventh Ave.), (212) 217-5848, www.fitnyc.suny.edu. Open Tu-F 12pm-8pm, Sa 10am-5pm. Admission free, ❶❾ to 28th St. ♿

Feigen Contemporary
This newly opened gallery is one of many that crops up on the streets of Chelsea hoping their artists (and their rental space) will have some longevity. Past exhibits include digitally tweaked color photo prints of stark interiors and human and bodily oddities.
Chelsea, 535 W. 20th St. (bet. Tenth and Eleventh Avenue), (212) 929-0500. Open T-Sa 11am-6pm ⒶⒸⒺ to 23rd St.

♦ GALLERIES & LIBRARIES

Aninna Nosei Gallery
No video or performance here. Artist, Nosei does a brillaint job of featuring the best paintings, drawings, sculpture and photography from all over the world. Be ready for her taste to get you thinking.
Chelsea, 530 W. 22nd St., 2nd Fl. (bet. Tenth and Eleventh Aves.), (212) 741-8695, Open T-F 11am-6pm, Sa 10am-6pm. ⒸⒺ to 23rd St. ♿

Barbara Gladstone
This enormous space has tall ceilings and two levels displaying contemporary and modern art in various media, including rotating painting, sculpture, video installations, and photography.
Chelsea, 515 W. 24th St. (bet. Tenth and Eleventh Aves.), (212) 206-9300, www.gladstonegallery.com. Open T-Sa 10am-6pm. ⒸⒺ to 23rd St. ♿

Dia Center for the Arts
Dia opened its main exhibition facility in a four-story renovated warehouse in 1987, dedicating it to large-scale, long-term exhibitions, offering artists the opportunity to develop new work or a focused presentation of work on a full floor.
Chelsea, 548 W. 22nd St. (bet. Tenth and Eleventh Aves.), (212) 989-5566, www.diacenter.org. Open W-Su 12pm-6pm. ⒸⒺ to 23rd St. ♿

Best and Worst Gallery in Chelsea

Worst Gallery

Paul Morris Gallery
Sadly, the people who started a lot of Chelsea's trends end up being the same one's that finish it for themselves. Nothing you haven't seen before.

Best Gallery

Feigen Contemporary
A new gallery with some of the newest art. They don't always hit the mark, but always hit something interesting.

Fredericks Freiser Gallery
Housed in a brownstone building, this smallish space consists of one main viewing room showcasing established and emerging artists.
Chelsea, 504 West 22nd St. (bet. Tenth and Eleventh Aves.), (212) 633-6555, Open T-Sa 11am-6pm. Ⓒⓔ *to 23rd St.*

Gagosian
A vast gallery filled by established artists who are often eager to take advantage of the space. As such, large paintings, three-dimensional pieces, and sculpture often come into play, and the results can be more absorbing than a similar show executed in a smaller area. Even when this physical potential isn't realized, the art is usually worth checking out.
Chelsea, 555 W. 24th St. (bet. Tenth and Eleventh Aves.), (212) 228-2828, www.gagosian.com. Open T-Sa 10am-10pm. Ⓒⓔ *to 23rd St.* ♿

Gavin Brown's Enterprise
Join Chelsea's trendiest crowds at this ultra-hip if somewhat pretentious gallery. Nestled in a trendy new spot among old warehouses, Gavin Brown and his "family" of artists have gotten great press coverage. Stop in at the adjoining bar, complete with disco-light floor, after the gallery closes.
Chelsea, 436 W. 15th St. (bet. Ninth and Tenth Aves.), (212) 627-5258. Open T-Sa 10am-6pm. ⒶⒸⓔ *to 14th St.* ♿

Greene Naftali Gallery
A western exposure bathes the space in natural light. Works are contemporary and tend to be ex-perimental; genres range from sculpture and painting to multimedia exhibits.
Chelsea, 526 W. 26th St., 8th Fl. (bet. Tenth and Eleventh Aves.), (212) 463-7770. Open T-Sa 10am-6pm. Ⓒⓔ *to 23rd St.* ♿

Linda Kirkland Gallery
Modest in size, but not in vision, the gallery's focus is to "exhibit art that combines a conceptual bent with a sensual visual form." Past exhibits include finger-painted word smears and large burlap bag sculptures.
Chelsea, 504 W. 22nd St., 2nd Fl. (bet. Tenth and Eleventh Aves.), (212) 627-3930, www.lindakirk land.com. Open by appointment. Ⓒⓔ *to 23rd St.*

Matthew Marks
Marks fills his two downtown spaces, both outposts of his extinct Madison Avenue gallery, with contemporary big names, including Nan Goldin, Brice Marden and Willem de Kooning.
Chelsea, 523 W. 24th St. (bet. Tenth and Eleventh Aves.), (212) 243-0200. Open T-Sa 10am-6pm. Ⓒⓔ *to 23rd St.* ♿

Also at:
Chelsea, 522 W. 22nd St. (bet. Tenth and Eleventh Aves.), (212) 243-0200. Open T-Sa 10am-5:30pm. Ⓒⓔ *to 23rd St.* ♿

Metro Pictures
A slick 3-room gallery featuring up to three artists at a time, Metro represents hot U.S. talent, and notable imports, such as the German Martin Kippenberger.
Chelsea, 519 West 24th St. (bet. Tenth and Eleventh Aves.), (212) 206-7100, www.metropictures gallery.com. Open T-Sa 10am-6pm. Ⓒⓔ *to 23rd St.* ♿

Pat Hearn
Formerly part of the East Village and SoHo scenes, Hearn's Chelsea gallery presents offbeat work by emerging to mid-career Contemp-orary American and European artists. A veteran of the art scene, she has propelled numerous artists' careers, among them George Condo, Philip Taaffe, and Peter Schuyff.
Chelsea, 530 W. 22nd St. (bet. Tenth and Eleventh Aves.), (212) 727-7366. Open T-Sa 11am-6pm. Ⓒⓔ *to 23rd St.* ♿

Paul Morris Gallery
Formerly Morris Healy, Chelsea pioneers Paul Morris and Thomas Healy have gone their separate ways. Healy's space displays contemporary art.
Chelsea, 465 W. 23rd St. (bet. Ninth and Tenth Aves.), (212) 727-2752. Open T-Sa 11am-6pm. Ⓒⓔ *to 23rd St.* ♿

Paula Cooper Gallery
Hard to find but not to miss, this gallery's collections have included Sol Le Witt and Joel Shapiro, to name a few. A beautiful facade, fogged windows and high ceilings make for an impressive exhibition space.
Chelsea, 534 W. 21st St., (bet. Tenth and Eleventh Aves.), (212) 255-1105. Open T-Sa 10am-6pm. Ⓒⓔ *to 23rd St.* ♿

Also at:
Chelsea, 521 W. 21st St., 2nd Fl. (bet. Tenth and Eleventh Aves.), (212) 255-1105. Open T-Sa 11am-6pm. Ⓒⓔ *to 23rd St.*

303 Gallery
An intimate gallery on a single floor exhibits contemporary work in many different media.
Chelsea, 525 W. 22nd St. (bet. Tenth and Eleventh Aves.), (212) 255-1121, www.303gallery.com. Open T-Sa 10am-6pm. C E *to 23rd St.*

Nightlife

♦ BARS

Barracuda
Dark and cruisy in front, with a funky lounge complete with lava lamps, this offering attracts a young crowd of good-looking men and a smaller crowd of equally hip and attractive women more interested in chatting and having a good time than proving how beautiful they are.
Chelsea, 275 W. 22nd St. (bet. Seventh and Eighth Aves.), (212) 645-8613. Open 4pm-4am. Cash Only, C E *to 23rd St.,* 1 9 *to 23rd St.*

Bongo
According to co-owner Andrea, this 2-year-old bar/seafood lounge "pioneered the area" of Chelsea, clearing out the riffraff that didn'tknow to mix oysters with cocktails. Famed for their New England-stylelobster rolls, and authentic 50's furniture, this comfortable lounge encourages a low-key atmosphere.
Chelsea, 299 Tenth Ave. (bet. 27th and 28th Sts.), (212) 947-3654. Open M-W 5pm-2am, R-Sa 5pm-3am. MC, V, AmEx, DC, D, C E *to 23rd St.*

The Break
Trendy clubgoers, gym boys and locals make this low-key space the place to begin or end a night on the town. Recent renovations have made the small locale a little roomier, but be prepared to stand crowded shoulder-to-shoulder with all sorts of attractive men.
Chelsea, 232 Eighth Ave. (bet. 21st and 22nd Sts.), (212) 627-0072, Open M-Su 2pm-4am. Cash Only, C E *to 23rd St.*

Ciel Rouge
Gaze into your date's eyes while reveling in the anonymity and intimacy of this hip hideaway. Sexy and swanky, with all the illicit glamour of a Prohibition-era speakeasy, this retreat offers drinks for a sophisticated palate. Hide in the scarlet lounge complete with plush chairs and a baby grand piano, the ultimate in retro chic.
Chelsea, 176 Seventh Ave. (bet. 20th and 21st Sts.), (212) 929-5542, www.germannews.com/mikeb/cielrouge. Open Su-R 7pm-2am, F-Sa 7pm-4am. Cash Only, 1 9 *to 23rd St.*

Dusk
With cracked mirror walls and a bathroom so dark you can't check yourmake-up, this bar makes it clear that appearances are not the point, sorelax and have a drink. The pool table in the front is always busy and thebar further back serves the mostly local crowd "killer cosmopolitans and margaritas," according to the usual patrons.
Chelsea, 147 W. 24th St. (bet. Sixth and Seventh Aves.), (212) 924-4490. Open M-W 6pm-2am, R-Sa 6pm-4am. MC, V, AmEx, DC, D, 1 2 3 9 *to 23rd St.*

"g"
This hotspot is a refreshing alternative to the gym-obsessed Chelsea scene. Casual elegance is the key here.

Where the Boys Are

♦ The Spike NYC
Tensions run high at this haven of testosterone. Girls beware, this treehouse is boys only.

♦ Barracuda
Really good looking men swarm, swim and attack occasionally. Great place to go on a cruise.

♦ Twilo
Gay men and teenagers on ecstasy, or a combination of both, dance until around 10.30 am.

♦ Jocko
"A line of contemporary men's sportswear, gym wear and swim wear, aimed at in shape sophisticated guys."

♦ Fire Island
It's summer and the prettiest boys have left for Fire Island, Long Island. Beautiful beaches and one of the best nightlife's outside of the city.

The subtly-lit bar is surrounded by lounges galore, and the back features coffee and gourmet juices.
Chelsea, 223 W. 19th St. (bet. Seventh and Eighth Aves.), (212) 929-1085. Open M-Su 4pm-4am. Cash Only, 1 9 to 18th St.

Her/She Bar
There's a popular Friday night party sponsored in part by the infamous and ubiquitous WOW promoters, where women dance, cruise, and strut their stuff. Sports bras and bare midriffs abound, and there's hot lesbian porn shown on the televisions above the bar.
Chelsea, 301 W. 39th St. (at Eighth Ave.), (212) 631-1093. Open M-Su 10pm-5am Cash Only, A C E to 42nd St.

King
Libido rules this three-tiered yet cramped dance bar. Monday nights promise boys $1 drinks if they take off their shirts, so it's a perfect venue for gym rats to flaunt their hard work. Cover varies from $5 to $10. Wednesdays offer an Amateur Strip Contest worth $200.
Chelsea, 579 Sixth Ave. (bet. 16th and 17th Sts.), (212) 366-5464. Open M-Su 5pm-indefinite. Cash Only, 1 9 to 18th St.

Lava
Lava is known for its sweet vodka drinks like the Lava Flow, Blue Lagoon and Purple Haze, all served in gigantic tiki bowls designed to get six of you trashed. If you'd like, the bartenders will set them afire. Faux lava flows down the walls and trees dot the place.
Chelsea, 28 W. 20th St. (bet. Fifth and Sixth Aves.), (212) 627-7867, www.lavanyc.com. Open W-Sa 5pm-4am. MC, V, AmEx, F to 23rd St. ♿

Passerby
The signless door front and flashing red, yellow, and blue checkered floor suggest another trendy bar. But with nary a martini glass in sight, this low-key watering hole favors locals over supermodels any day. Stick to beer and chat with the ever-changing crowd of gallery employees, yuppies, geeks, artists, loners, and the ambiguously gay.
Chelsea, 436 W. 15th St. (bet. Ninth and Tenth Aves.), (212) 206-7321. Open M-Su 6pm-4am. MC, V, AmEx, A C E to 14th St.

The Park
The Park is yet another skanky playhouse for young, rich and successful squares. Their big claim right now is that soon they'll have an indoor pool to compliment the rest of the ridiculousness. But don't people like this melt in water?
Chelsea, 118 Tenth Ave. (bet. 17th and 18th Sts.), (212) 352-3313. Open M-Su 11:30am-2am. MC, V, AmEx, D, 1 9 to 18th St. ♿

The Spike
The name, both a weapon and a charming wink at male genitalia, sums up the awkward experience of trying to gain entrance into this gay men's bar. It's located inside what appears to be an apartment complex. The buzzer on the door says simply "The Spike" and an intercom system is used to weed out any girls. So take the hint, this tree-house is boys only.
Chelsea, 120 Eleventh Ave. (at W. 20th St.), (212) 243-9688. Open M-Su 5pm-4am. MC, V, AmEx, C E to 23rd St.

Slate
The former Chelsea Billiards has been revamped as New York's swankest pool hall. Low blue lighting lends the place a vaguely amniotic effect. There's surprisingly little attitude for this part of town, and the new restaurant, featuring Mediterranean fusion cuisine, is fantastic.
Chelsea, 54 W. 21st St. (bet. Fifth and Sixth Aves.), (212) 989-0096. Open M-Su 3pm-3am. MC, V, AmEx, DC, D, 1 9 to 18th St.

♦ CLUBS

Centro-fly
This hot spot is filled with all kinds of folks, from club kids to slickster industry types to seriously beautiful people. Complaints have been growing about the attitude factor, but, at least for the time being, Centro-fly is enjoying its time in the…limelight.
Chelsea, 45 W. 21st St. (bet. Fifth and Sixth Aves.), (212) 627-7770. Open M-Su 10pm-indefinite. MC, V, Amex, D N R F to 23rd St.

Cheetah
Maybe most clubs get involved in some Faustian pact: you can get real popular for a few months, but then you have to suck. Cheetah avoided this fate; it's never been white-hot, but it's always been respected for its plush interior, beautiful crowd and great hip-hop.

Chelsea, 12 W. 21st St. (bet. Fifth and Sixth Aves.), (212) 206-7770. Open M-Su 9:30pm-4:30am. MC, V, AmEx, D, F N R *to 23rd St.*

Joy
From the knot of burly, black-sheathed doormen up front to the pouting, aspirant models flouncing about behind the bar, Joy proclaims attitude and chic. Very glitzy and expensive-looking interior decorating and an excellent sound system. Go if you think your money impresses people; it will.
Chelsea, 263 W. 28th St. (bet. Seventh and Eighth Aves.), (212) 244-3005. MC, V, AmEx, Cover: $15-$25, 1 9 *to 28th St.*

Limelight
One of the most notorious clubs of the last decade in its heyday, Limelight has toned down some. But the catwalks, multiple floors, and ominous-looking H.R. Giger room still keep the place amusing. before coming.
Chelsea, 47 W. 20th St. (at Sixth Ave.), (212) 807-7059. MC, V, AmEx, D, Cover: $10-$20, F *to 23rd St.*

GYMS

If you're in Chelsea you probably want to know where the gyms are, so here's whom you call to find which is nearest to you.

♦ **Bally Total Fitness**
14 Locations in Manhattan
800-230-0606

♦ **Crunch**
7 Locations in Manhattan
212-758-3434

♦ **New York Health and Racquet Club**
7 Locations in Manhattan
212-269-9800

♦ **New York Sports Club**
70 Locations in Manhattan
212-868-0820

♦ **Reebok Sports Club**
Upper West Side, 160 Columbus Ave.
212-362-6800

Nell's
Three rooms on two floors offer an eclectic mix of music ranging from reggae, hip-hop, and jazz to Latin, funk, and disco. The elegance of the spacious upstairs room calls for a sophisticated drink from the well-stocked bar. Downstairs, relax in a more intimate lounge or move to house, R&B, or classics aimed at a stylish crowd described by the bouncer as a mix of "tourists, regulars, and DJs."
Chelsea, 246 W. 14th St. (bet. Seventh and Eighth Aves.), (212) 675-1567. MC, V, AmEx, Cover: $5-$10, A C E *to 14th St.,* L *to Eighth Ave.*

Rebar
Not the largest site in the area, but dubbed hip by the club crowd, which forms the lines snaking out onto Eighth Ave.
Chelsea 127 Eighth Ave. (at 16th St.), (212) 627-1680. MC, V, AmEx, Cover: $5-$15, A C E *to 14th St.,* L *to Eighth Ave.*

Roxy
Almost always crowded, the place plays host to track performers, AIDS benefits and nonstop dancing. The crowd is different every night; Saturday packs in the Chelsea boys.
Chelsea, 515 W. 18th St. (bet. Tenth and Eleventh Aves.), (212) 645-5156. Cash Only, Cover: $20, C E *to 23rd St.*

Serena
A low ceiling, red walls, and curious tin chandeliers lend a cozy atmosphere to this basement lounge under the Chelsea Hotel. Perch yourself atop one of the seats surrounding the gargantuan U-shaped bar or sink, drink in hand, deep in a couch lining one of the adjacent rooms and dig the foxy clientele.
Chelsea, 222 W. 23rd Street (bet. Seventh and Eighth Aves.), (212) 255-4646. MC, V, AmEx, Cover: None, 1 9 *to 23rd St.*

Tunnel
Its popularity is somewhat flagging since Junior Vasquez moved to Twilo, but the Tunnel's labyrinthine corridors and multiple rooms render the place still interesting enough to get yourself lost in, and there's still lots of cute club kids to take home with you.
Chelsea, 220 Twelfth Ave. (at 27th St.), (212) 695-4682. MC, V, AmEx, Cover: $20-$25, A C E *to 23rd St.*

Twilo
Definitely the most populated club in New York City, Twilo attracts crowds by the thousands to hear turntable heavies such as Junior Vasquez and Sasha & Digweed.
Chelsea, 530 W. 27th St. (bet. Tenth and Eleventh Aves.), (212) 268-1600, www.twiloclub.com. MC, V, AmEx, Cover: $7-$30, 1 9 *to 28th St.* C E *to 23rd St.*

Sports in the City

Pro Sports

The last ten years saw much success for professional sports in New York. The Yankees won four World Series, the Rangers won a cup, the Giants won and lost a Super Bowl, and the Knicks seem to just miss a championship every season. New York, though not a town bred on Friday night High School Football or Saturday morning college games, is the Mecca of pro sports. New York is where baseball was invented and basketball was reinvented, and still has some of the best pro sports around.

Baseball

In the 50s, New York owned baseball. Of the 14 teams that went to the World Series from 1951-1957, 12 of them were the Yankees, Dodgers, and Giants. But when Walter O'Malley and Horace Stoneham took the Dodgers and Giants West, the prospect of a subway series ever happening again looked bleak, if that good. When the Mets came to town in 1962 and lost 120 games, the idea faded even more. But with the dream finally coming true last year, New York is baseball crazy again. But where is the best baseball in New York? Well, you've got a few choices.

Yankee Stadium
161st St. and River Avenue
The Bombers won four of the last five World Championships and are perennial contenders. The D B and 4 trains all go to the House that Ruth Built, and so should you. Get there early enough to see a little batting practice – it gives time to settle in and hit the food court before game time, as well as see guys like Williams and Posada crank a few home runs before the game.
The best seats to see the game are anywhere between first and third base and home plate, but you'll have more fun in the bleachers. Truly, one of the greatest things about the stadium is the role call – as the "bleacher creatures" chant for each Yankee until they turn around and wave. And a tip: if you'd like to get on the scoreboard, sit in the Lodge seats just past first base. The camera hits that section roughly ten times per game.

Shea Stadium
Willets Point, Flushing
It may be tacky, it may be ugly, but damn, it's a good time. You'll find a lot of friendly ball fans at Shea, regardless of what John Rocker said about the seven train. Try to sit half way between first and home plate in order to get the best view of the infield's highlight film at second, third, and shortstop. The best dollar value at the concession stand is the Pizza Hut booth, and soda gets cheaper as the game goes on.

If you want to move down as people leave their seats, your best bet is to actually ask the ushers instead of trying to sneak by them. Half will expect a tip, but half are nice guys and will gladly let you advance a few rows. If you're looking for autographs, you're allowed to hang out on field level until an hour before the first pitch. Most times, if you just extend your hand, say excuse me, and call to a player, you'll get your ball signed.

Cheap Answer: St. John's
The Queens school is New York City's solution for NCAA sports fans. The Red Storm even play at Shea Stadium a few times a year. The Storm's pitching improved last season, featuring seven hurlers with winning records, and the hitting was great as usual – with four regulars batting over .300.

Free Answer: George Washington High School, Inwood
What? Watch high school baseball in New York? Well, GW is different. The powerhouse that produced MLBers like Alex Arias and Manny Ramirez, George Washington routinely has a player or two drafted every year. Coach Steve Mandl leads a strong program every season, and sometimes even ranks tops in the nation. If you're looking for some sports and not in the mood to spend a dime, take in a few games – you might be watching the next all star.

Basketball and Hockey

Madison Square Garden
34th and 7th Avenue
The world's most famous arena, MSG is home to the Knicks and Rangers, and they split time drawing huge crowds to every game. If you want your tickets, get them early because they go quickly. Though nothing used to sell out quicker than Knicks/Bulls games, there are still a few great rivalries – the Rangers and Islanders and the Knicks and Heat.
When it comes to basketball and hockey, don't bother with the cheap seats – you may as well watch the game from home. Try something middle range – not too expensive, but not so cheap that you can't see the action. The Knicks have been contenders for the past decade, and the Rangers fade in and out. If you're looking for a win, you can wait until a bad team comes to town, but the tougher games are always more fun.

Cheap Answer: St. John's
Again, the Red Storm is the college team to watch, but the basketball team stands out much more than their baseball program. A two seed in the NCAA tournament two years ago, the Storm routinely play atop one of the toughest divisions in the country. A Red Storm game is almost as exciting as a Knicks game, and much much cheaper.

Free Answer: Street Ball
If you want real basketball New York style, and want to save some money, head up to Rucker Park, 155th Street and Eight Avenue, or down to the cage on West Fourth. Rucker is where playground legends like Richard "Pee Wee" Kirkland played before he was drafted to the Bulls, went to jail for ten years and now coaches Manhattan's Dwight School. Rucker is also where the Entertainer's Basketball Classic is played each summer, and a good chance to catch NBA and NCAA players in the off season. NBA players like Anthony Mason, also show up at the cage, but it tends to be swamped in tourists.

Football

New York has no football team, though it still lays claim to the both the Jets and the Giants. Tickets are very hard to come by, and if you do, you still have to trek out to New Jersey. If you're looking for football, there isn't a decent alternative for college or high school football either. But if you're willing to watch from the comfort of an armchair, then seek out the most comfortable armchairs in town, at the viewing room in ESPN Zone. The Zone is in Times Square on 42nd Street, and has twice the atmosphere that the now defunct All-Star Café ever had.

Tennis

Arthur Ashe Tennis Center
Every year in late August, the US Open comes to town. And in case you forget when it is, just wait for the traffic on the Grand Central Parkway to be thicker than Martina Navratilova's hair. Tickets are not that hard to come by, since the event goes on sale in early June, but it will be tough to score tickets to see the players you want to see. Though the price might be a little higher, get tickets for the later rounds so you see players that you've heard of. And though it's tempting (i.e. cheaper) to buy a ticket just to get onto the grounds, but it's a hell of a lot more fun to see an actual match. Take the 7 Train as if you were going to Shea Stadium, but when you get off, follow the sign that says "Tennis."

Midtown

This is the New York of Times Square. The New York locals will tell you isn't New York at all, but the New York the city would be at a loss of character without. Not too many people live in Midtown; people work here and tourists play and get ripped off here.

Two hundred years ago Midtown was dusty roads. All that changed in 1811, when, under the Commissioner's Plan, the city bought out estates, subdivided them into blocks, and resold the lots. The New York and Harlem Railroads pushed north. When Cornelius Vanderbilt, who ran the company, was warned he was staking money on a losing game, he replied "Put the road there and people will go there to live."

He was right and in 1904 the *New York Times* relocated to a dull area known as Long Acre Square; the move was announced on December 31st with a fireworks show at midnight. A New Year's Eve tradition was born and the square was renamed. Meanwhile, Tin Pan Alley was the heart of the country's music publishing industry throughout the early 1900s, supporting songwriters like Cole Porter, the Gershwins and Irving Berlin.

The city's retail trade advanced from Union Square, marking first Sixth Avenue and then Herald Square as mercantile districts. During the 1930s the business district saw the rise of the great modernist edifices that still draw tourists today.

The rough traditions of Hell's Kitchen died hard. Though the Irish gang the Westies were still running things up until the 70s, gentrification proved more resilient than the local toughs. The attitude still lingers today, Hell's Kitchen, now Clinton, is arguably the last true New York Neighborhood in Manhattan — just ask the late night bar crowd at Rudy's or the Blarney Stone. In the meantime, on First Avenue, the United Nations General Assembly opens to the many nationalities of its members. A perfect match for the many nationalities of tourists cross town, mixing with each other for completely different reasons.

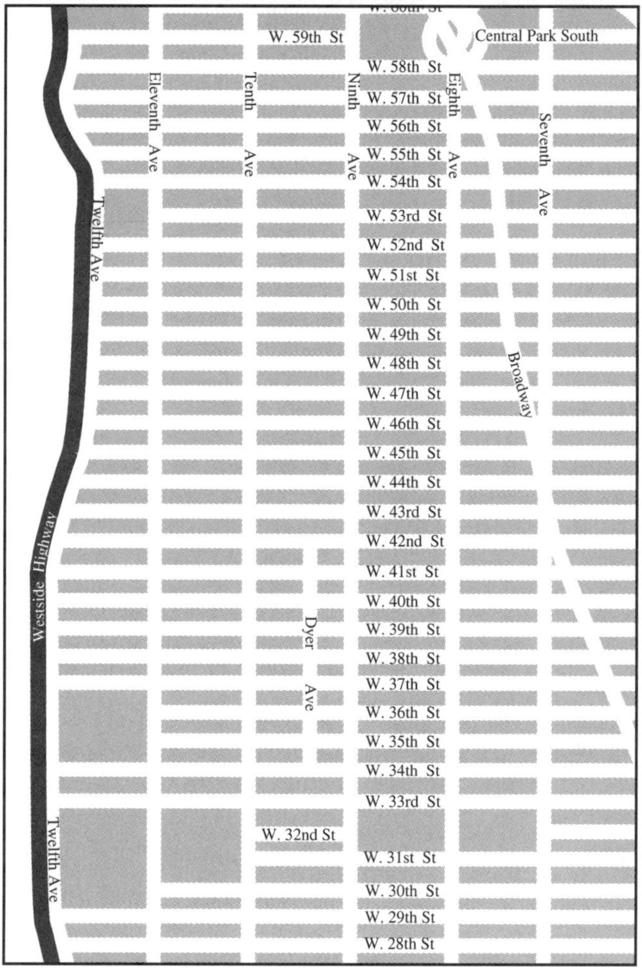

Dining

♦ RESTAURANTS

44 Restaurant at the Royalton Hotel

Dining at this restaurant is a special treat. Its ultra-trendy ambience and Phillip Starck-designed interior make its European-American food seem even better than it is. The customers are a glamorous, black-clad crowd, often admiring themselves in the restaurant's giant mirrors. It's quite expensive (ask your date or parents to pay the tab) but worth it if you like classic steak and fish dishes in a fancy spot.

Midtown, 44 W. 44th St. (bet. Fifth and Sixth Aves.), (212) 944-8844. Open M-R 7am-11pm, F 7am-3pm, Sa 8am-3pm, Su 8am-11pm. MC, V, AmEx, Entrees: $22-36, ❶❾ *to 42nd St.* ♿

Asia de Cuba

If only all of NYC were as good looking and stylishly-dressed as this crowd. You might have to wait upwards of an hour for a table at prime-time even if you have a reservation, but the delicious food and sophisticated atmosphere make it worth the wait. Enjoy one of their excellent mixed drinks to help fan out the burning hole in your wallet.

Midtown, 237 Madison Ave. (bet. 37th and 38th Sts.), (212) 726-7755. Open M-W 12pm-11:30pm, R-F 12pm-12am, Sa 5:30pm-12am, Su 5:30pm-11pm. MC, V, AmEx, DC. Entrees: $17-$30. ❹❺❻❼Ⓢ *to Grand Central Station.*

Broadway's Jerusalem II Kosher Pizza

The most popular Kosher pizza joint in Manhattan. Lots of students from the nearby Stern College for Women drop by for a slice, as do Jewish office workers or tourists heading out to a Broadway show. Delivery is available to almost anyone, anywhere in the world.

Midtown, 1375 Broadway (bet. 37th and 38th Sts.), (212) 398-1475, www.flyingpizzas.com. Open M-R 7am-12am, F 7am-sundown, Su 11am-12am. Cash Only, Entrées: $5-$15, ❶❷❸❾ *to 34th St.* ♿ 🚲

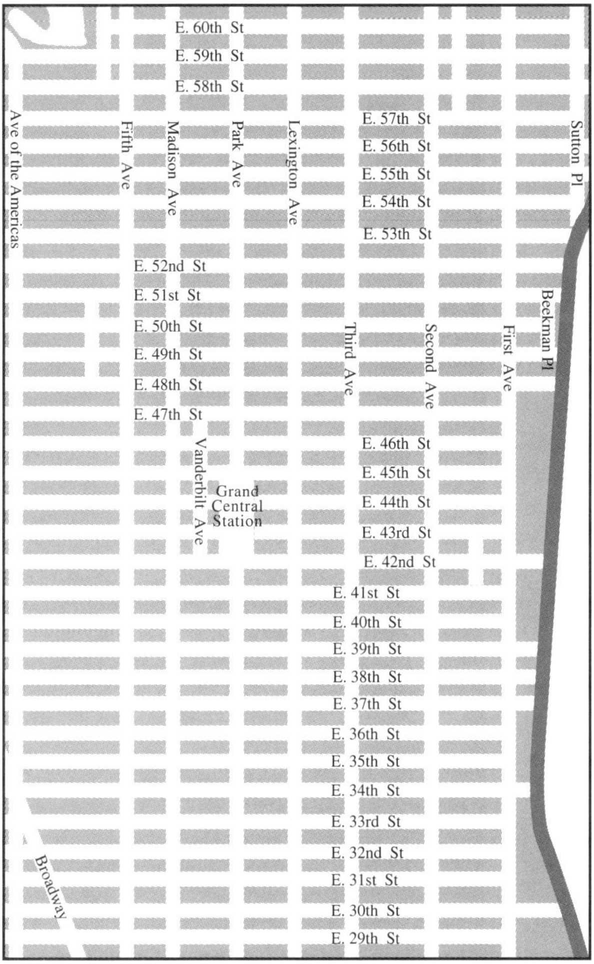

PLACES TO GO:

Hangawi
All vegan Korean food seems like a pretty specific niche, but it's good enough that all vegan Korean is all it needs to be.

Away Spa
This isn't where you go to relax a little; it's where you go to completely spoil yourself.

The Drama Bookshop
Everyone is serious at this all drama bookstore that has anything from the score of *The Producers* to the script of *Springtime for Hitler.*

Siberia
The best place to meet someone for a drink in Manhattan, with the best jukebox.

M i d t o w n

Bryant Park Grill

Nestled up against the backside of the main branch of the Public Library, a restaurant would be hard-pressed to be more pic-turesque, especially in spring, when Bryant Park assumes its full majesty. The American-Continental food is tasty, if pricey, and the after-work bar and dinner scene at the Grill and its outdoor cafe buzzes with "suits" letting loose. Brunch is excellent.

Midtown, 25 W. 40th St. (bet. Fifth and Sixth Aves.), (212) 840-6500, www.arkrestaurants.com. Open M-Su 11:30am-3:30pm, 5pm-10pm. MC, V, AmEx, Entrées: $14-$24, B D F Q *to 42nd St.,* 7 *to Fifth Ave.* ♿

Café Un Deux Trois

Though a little strenuous on the wallet, this busy, touristy spot is perfect for a bowl of savory French onion soup or a delectable dish of crème brulée. Avoid the high prices by sitting at the bar. If you're up for a full meal, sit table-side for a plate of steak and pomme frittes and let your imagination run wild as you design your own table cloth with a cup full of crayons.

Midtown, 123 W. 44th St. (bet. Sixth Ave. and Broadway), (212) 354-4148. Open M-F 12pm-12am, Sa-Su 11am-12am. MC, V, AmEx, DC, Entrees: $15-24, N R S 1 2 3 7 9 S *to 42nd St.-Times Sq.* ♿

Carmine's

Come with a group of friends and order up a storm of family-style Italian. Seating is slow, so a visit to this enormous darkwood institution happily mandates a stop at the lovely bar.

Midtown, 200 W. 44th St. (bet. Broadway and Eighth Ave.), (212) 221-3800. Open M-R 11:30am-3pm, 5pm-11pm, F 11:30am-3pm, 5pm-12am, Sa 11am-12am, Su 2pm-10pm. MC, V, AmEx, Entrées: $15-$25, N R S 1 2 3 7 9 *to 42nd St.-Times Sq.*

Churrascaria Plataforma

Meat, meat, meat, meat, meat. A carnivore's paradise the size of an airport hangar, Plataforma offers round after round of teasingly salted, moist meats, the oft overlooked fish-of-the-day, and a salad bar bigger than most New York apartments. All you can eat.

Midtown, 316 W. 49th St. (bet. Eighth and Ninth Aves.), (212) 245-0505. Open M-Su 12pm-12am. MC, V, AmEx, D, Entrees: $40-60, B C 1 9 *to 50th St.,* ♿

Dish of Salt

Giant wooden parrots and colorful banners cater to the exotica stereotype, but the greasy and decidedly Americanized Chinese food is safe enough for the after work and pre-theater crowds.

Midtown, 133 W. 47th St. (bet. Sixth and Seventh Aves.), (212) 921-4242, www.dishofsalt.com. Open M-F 12pm-11pm, Sa 4pm-11pm. MC, V, AmEx, Entrées: $18-$27, N R *to 49th St.*

Don Giovanni

For a slice of the neighborhood, sit outside at a table and enjoy a pie at Don Giovanni. Made in a brick oven, with thin crust, fresh mozzarella, and a sweet tomato sauce, this pizza is bound to please. Be forewarned: delivery takes at least an hour.

Midtown, 358 W. 44th St. (bet. Eighth and Ninth Aves.), (212) 581-4939, www.dongiovanni-ny.com. Open Su-R 12pm-12am, F-Sa 12pm-2am. MC, V, AmEx, Entrées: $7 - $22, A C E *to 42nd St.* ♿

The Flame

Better known as a neighborhood icon than for its food, The Flame nonetheless ably serves up the expected diner menu, from omelets to burgers to gyros. The business crowd converges around 1pm for lunch, but otherwise there is ample seating and rarely (if ever) a wait. A good place to chat without having to fork over lots of dough.

Midtown, 893 Ninth Ave. (at 58th St.), (212) 765-7962. Open M-Su 6am-12am. MC, V, AmEx, D, Entrées: $4-$12, A B C D 1 9 *to 59th St.-Columbus Circle.* ♿

Fresco Tortilla Grill

Times Square's best – or arguably, only – secret is this tiny Mexican hole-in-the-wall. A great place to satisfy your hunger for good food and New Yorker credibility for less than five bones.

Midtown, 125 W. 42nd St. (bet. Broadway and Sixth Ave.), (212) 221-5849. Open M-Su 10am-9pm. Cash only, Entrees: $3-5, N R 1 2 3 9 7 A C E S *to Times Square.*

Hangawi

Just for fun, bring someone really square and uptight to this sublime, all-vegan Korean restaurant. By the third course,

he'll be so seduced by the otherworldly calm that he won't even notice he's eating a lemon stuffed with mushrooms.
Midtown, 12 E. 32nd St. (bet. Fifth and Madison Aves) (212) 213-0077. Open M-F 12pm-11pm, Sa 1pm-11pm, Su 1pm-10pm. MC, V, AmEx, DC, Entrees: $15-20, N R to 28th St.

Joe Allen
Upscale thespians, including bonafide Broadway celebs in search of some post-performance relaxation, come to this dark and elegant but unpretentious eatery to fill up on gourmet meatloaf and hot fudge pudding cake. On Sunday nights 8pm to closing, fifteen percent of every check goes to Broadway Cares/Equity Fights AIDS.
Midtown, 326 W. 46th St. (bet. Eighth and Ninth Aves.), (212) 581-6464, www.joeallen-orso.com. Open M-T, R-F 12pm-11:45pm, W 11:30am-11:30pm, F-Sa 11:30am-12am, Su 11:30am-11:45pm. MC, V, Entrées: $10-$21, A C E to 42nd St.

La Bonne Soupe
An authentic French bistro, right down to the waiters' thick accents and the creamy chocolate mousse. Red-checkered tablecloths and colorful paintings add to the homey, rural atmosphere. Start with a glass of wine and some fondue or the Paysanne soup, then try the duck platters, and end the meal with crème caramel. It'll be one "bonne" meal under $25…tres bien!
Midtown, 48 W. 55th St. (bet. Fifth and Sixth Aves.), (212) 586-7650, www.labonnesoupe.com. Open M-Su 11:30am-12am. MC, V, AmEx, D, Entrées: $10-20, N R to 57th, E F to 53rd.

Le Cirque 2000
Set in the historic Villard Houses and attached to the New York Palace Hotel, Le Cirque combines the refinement of the past with giddy designs of the future. Longtime chef Sottha Khunn's classic French creations add civility to Adam Tihany's pleasantly outrageous decor, and Jacques Torres' perfect desserts will leave you reeling.
Midtown, 455 Madison Ave. (bet. 50th and 51st Sts.), (212) 303-7788, www.lecirque.com. Open M-Sa 11:30am-2:30pm, 5:30pm-10:30pm, Su 5:30pm-10:30pm. MC, V, AmEx, DC, Entrées: $28-$38, 6 to 51st St., E F to Lexington Ave.

Mangia
Gourmet Mediterranean cuisine and friendly waitstaff at this lunch restaurant make it a culinary hot-spot for the surrounding working worlds of businesses, galleries and museums. Mangia's diverse array of pastas, sandwiches, and entrées — including an "antipasto table," with a wonderful selection of foods ranging from paella to rare tuna — is sure to quench anyone's desire for a gastronomic thrill. In a rush? Stop at the café downstairs for equally delicious take out dining.
Midtown, 50 W. 57th St. (bet. Fifth and Sixth Aves.), (212) 582-5554. Open M-F 7am-8pm, Sa 8:30am-6pm. MC, V, AmEx, DC, D, Entrées: $11-15, N R B Q to 57th St.

The Buildings of Midtown

♦ Citicorp Center
The slanted roof on this all black, glass structure was originally a gigantic solar panel that would provide extra energy for the bank, but it never worked.

♦ Chrysler Building
For one year, 1930, the tallest building on earth and undoubtedly New York's most beautiful. An Art Deco ideal whose gargoyles are really oversized hood ornaments.

♦ Empire State Building
When people think of the tallest building in the world they think of this, even though they know it's not, and it's because nothing embodies the skyscraper like the Empire State.

♦ Ford Foundation Building
Built in 1967, it houses the first of the atriums that are now common place in many buildings, though this one is the most lush and green of them.

♦ Met Life Building
Formerly the Pan Am building, it rises way up over Grand Central in what it's former owners hoped would look like the wing of a plane.

♦ G.E. Building
Seventy stories and the Jewel of Rockefeller Center. This is where NBC is if you're planning on going to the Today Show or Saturday Night Live.

Also At:
Midtown, 16 E. 48th St. (bet Fifth and Madison Aves.), (212) 754-0637. Open M-F 11:30am-4pm. MC, V, AmEx, DC, D, Entrées: $11-15, 6 to 51st St.

Michael Jordan's Steakhouse
This upscale steakhouse is part of Grand Central's make-over. Stop by for dinner before grabbing the Metro North upstate, or make the trip to this gorgeous station to enjoy a martini at the end of the day.
Grand Central Station (on the W. balcony), 23 Vanderbilt Ave. (bet. Park and Lexington Aves.), (212) 655-2300. Open M-Sa 12pm-3pm, 5pm-11pm, Su 1pm-10pm. MC, V, AmEx, Entrées: $17-$32, S 4 5 6 7 to 42nd St.-Grand Central Station.

The 1863 Draft Riots

During the Civil War a newly passed Conscription Act made it so that rich men could buy a substitute to serve in their place. The names of the replacements were chosen by lottery and posted in the local newspaper. In New York the first man on the list was a resident of 46th Street and Tenth Avenue who went home enraged and ignited the riot's flame.

Over a period of four days draft offices were burnt, railroads were stopped, policeman and soldiers were hunted down and beaten up. Worst of all the mobs turned on the black community, killing three and leaving 70 missing. To date no one's sure exactly how many people were killed. Hell's Kitchen was the crowded home of 350,000 immigrants and anywhere from 2,000 to 20,000 people may have died.

Milos
By-the-pound pricing. A Greek piscatory/restaurant where the fish are laid out for you to pick. Fresh fish too, cooked for you in Mediterranean sauces. Nothing compares to the seafood at Milos, it floats somewhere above, an ideal not to be touched.
Midtown, 125 W. 55th St. (bet. Sixth and Seventh Aves.), (212) 245-7400. Open M-R 11:30am-2:45pm, 5:30pm-11pm. F-Sa 5:30pm-11:45pm, Su 5pm-11pm. MC, V, AmEx, DC, Entrées: $40-$60, N R to 57th St.

Orso
With an un-impressive Italian menu, the post theater crowds and sometimes star-studded clientele make Orso more exciting for its atmosphere than cuisine. The service is stuffy and the meals are oily or just "okay". If you're a people watcher, you've come to the right place. If you like food, leave now.
Midtown, 322 W. 46th St. (bet. Eighth and Ninth Aves.), (212) 489-7212. www.orsorestaurant.com. Open M, T, R, F 12pm-11:45 pm, W, Sa, Su 11:30am-11:45pm. MC, V, 1 2 3 9 N R A C E *to 42nd St.*

Osteria del Circo
Everyone should be able to find something at this Midtown Northern Italian restaurant, with staples of fish, pasta, pizza, and meat so tried and true it's near impossible to do them wrong.
Midtown, 120 W. 55th St. (bet. Sixth and Seventh Aves.), (212) 265-3636, www.osteriadelcircio.com. Open M-Sa 11:30am-2:30pm, 5:30pm-11pm, Su 5:30pm-11pm. MC, V, AmEx, DC, Entrées: $30-$40, N R to 57th St.

Pamir
Savory pilaf complements the well-executed lamb and chicken dishes, from kebabs to quabilli palaw, at this cozy uptown enclave of Afghan cuisine adorned with hand-tooled metalwork and bright Afghan rugs. Denim-clad patrons will feel self-conscious in the upscale atmosphere.
Midtown, 1065 Second Ave. (at 58th St.), (212) 644-9258. Open M-F 12pm-2:30pm, 5pm-10:30pm, Sa-Su 5pm-10:30pm. MC, V, AmEx, Entrées: $11-$16, 6 to 77th St.

Pietrasanta
A Hell's Kitchen neighborhood secret where the chef actually comes out of the kitchen to ask how customers are enjoying their meals. For an appetizer, try the succulent scallops in a rich pesto sauce, and order the pumpkin ravioli in sweet pepper sauce as an entrée. Delish!
Midtown, 683 Ninth Ave. (at 47th St.), (212) 265-9471. Open M-T 12pm-11pm, W-F 12pm-12am, Sa 11am-12am, Su 11:30am-11pm. MC, V, AmEx, Entrées: $8-$16, C E to 50th St.

Ruby Foo's

Fun, cool, hip pan-Asian with everything from dim sum to sushi and a popular Sunday brunch.

Midtown, 1626 Broadway (at 49th St.), (212) 489-5600. Open M-Su 11:30am-4am. MC, V, AmEx, Entrées: $25, C E to 50th St.

Soup Kitchen

While Seinfeld fanatics are bemoaning the end of an era, one remnant lives on: The lines at this pop-culture landmark are unreal at lunch time, but have you noticed how smoothly it moves along? Patrons have made up their minds what to order by the time they reach the counter of this famous take-out. Otherwise it's "No soup for you!"

Midtown, 259-A W. 55th St. (bet. Eighth Ave. and Broadway), (212) 757-7730. Open M-F 12pm-6pm. Cash Only, Entrées: $6-$8, N R to 57th St.

Sparks Steak House

One of the best steakhouses in New York City. Come with a full wallet and an empty stomach for incredible meat and seafood.

Midtown, 210 E. 46th St. (bet. Second and Third Aves.), (212) 687-4855. Open M-R 12pm-3pm, 5pm-11pm, F-Sa 5pm-11:30pm. MC, V, AmEx, DC, Entrées: $22-$35, 4 5 6 7 to 42nd St.-Grand Central.

Toledo

The cherry wood, archways, and courtly dining hall of this midtown Spanish restaurant evoke the elegance of a bygone century. Ask, and the retinue of waiters will proudly point you to the best dishes. Or try the authentic paella prized for its fresh seafood and savory saffron rice. The sangria is almost too delicious for your own good, and after a few glasses you'll sing its praises like a troubadour.

Midtown, 6 E. 36th St. (bet. Fifth and Madison Aves.), (212) 696-5036. Open M-Sa 12pm-3pm, 5pm-10:30pm. MC, V, AmEx, DC, Entrées: $22-$26, B D F N Q R to 34th St.

Topaz Thai Restaurant

This spot may be cramped and a bit hard to find, but the food's tasty and, judging by the constant flux of diners, happy on the budget. Upon your arrival, a smiling, speedy waiter will seat you at a table three inches from your neighbors on all sides. However, the delicious curried entrees and Thai iced tea will make you forget the cramped quarters.

Midtown, 127 W. 56th (bet. Sixth and Seventh Aves.), (212) 957-8020. Open M-F 12pm-11pm, Sa-Su 4pm-11pm. MC, V, AmEx, D, 1 9 B D Q to Columbus Circle.

Trattoria Dell'Arte

Tons of well-heeled Manhattanites dine here on their way to a show, but the decor is the biggest celebrity at this huge modern Italian restaurant opposite Carnegie Hall: Busts of famous noses, enormous paintings of close-up body parts, and electric-colored walls make the space happening. This chic spot also boasts polished service and the tastiest bread in New York City.

Midtown, 900 Seventh Ave. (at 57th St.), (212) 245-9800. Open M-F 11:45am-3pm, 5pm-11:30pm, Sa-Su 11am-3pm, 5pm-11:30pm. MC, V, AmEx, D, Entrées: $17-$38, N R to 57th St.

Turkish Kitchen

Turkish music brings to mind the minarets of Istanbul silhouetted across the Golden Horn, and shockingly red wallpaper coupled with a laundry list of kebabs strives to maintain exotic authenticity. Don't be afraid to experiment; just about anything with lamb is sure to be good.

Midtown, 386 Third Ave. (bet. 27th and 28th Sts.), (212) 679-1810, www.turkishkitchen.com. Open M-F 12pm-3pm, 5:30pm-11pm, Sa 5pm-11:30pm, Su 5pm-10:30pm. MC, V, AmEx, DC, D, Entrées: $10-$18, 6 to 28th St.

Uncle Nick's Greek Cuisine

Serving enormous kebobs, salads brimming with stuffed grape leaves and olives, and huge wedges of flaming saganaki cheese, Uncle Nick's Greek Cuisine won't leave you hungry. The bustling atmosphere, attentive waitstaff, and speedy service make this restaurant great for pre-theater dining.

Midtown, 747 Ninth Ave. (bet. 50th and 51st Sts.), (212) 245-7992. Open M-Su 12pm-10:30pm. MC, V, AmEx, D, Entrées: $9-$15, A C E to 50th St.

Uncle Vanya

Delicious, inexpensive, authentic — what more could you possibly want? To top it off, the vodka flows freely, the food is hardy (the Russian dumplings are out of this world!), and there's often live music, a pleasant folk singer, incomprehensible to non-russophones. In fact this place is so authentic the whole staff is hard to understand they are so Russian. Dasdarovya.

Midtown, 315 W. 54th St. (bet. Eighth and Ninth Aves.), (212) 262-0542. Open M-Sa 12pm-11pm, Su 2pm-11pm. Cash Only, Entrées: $8-$12, CE to 50th St.

◆ CAFES

Columbus Bakery

For everything from yummy breakfast pastries to salads and sandwiches, this midtown spot can provide you with a variety of delicious treats. You can sit inside for a break from the streets, or, when it's warm enough, sit outside to watch the passersby s you snack.

Midtown, 957 First Ave. (bet. 52nd and 53rd Sts.), (212) 421-0334, www.arkrestaurants.com. Open M-F 7:30am-9pm, Sa-Su 8am-9pm. MC, V, AmEx, D, Entrees: $3-$7, 6 to 51st St.

Cupcake Cafe

A quaint bakery with pink walls and tin ceilings on the raunchiest stretch in Hell's Kitchen. Great donuts, waffles, and (duh!) cupcakes, with a few tables for immediate consumption. The location is unfashionable for a food pilgrimage, but come for old-fashioned sweets.

Midtown, 522 Ninth Ave. (at 39th St.), (212) 465-1530. Open M-F 7am-7pm, Sa 8am-7pm, Su 9am-5pm. Cash Only, NRS123479 to 42nd St.-Times Sq.

Emack and Bolios

By the time you get to the fourth floor of Macy's, you'll need a break. Look no further than Emack and Bolios for sanwiches and sweeter goodies. Then pick up your bags and start again, rejuvenated by your sweet tooth fix.

Midtown, Macy's, 151 W. 34th St., 4th Floor, (212) 494-5853. Open M-Su 10am-7:30pm. MC, V, AmEx, Entrees: $4-$6, 19 to Herald Square.

Ferrara Bakery and Café

America's oldest espresso bar has been a Little Italy staple since 1892. If you can't make the trip all the way downtown, visit this midtown location to satiate yourself until your next visit. Everything is homemade!!!

Midtown, 363 Madison Ave (bet. 45th and 46th Sts.), (212) 226-6150, www.ferrarra-cafe.com. Open M-F 7am-10pm. Sa 8am-10pm, Su 8am-9pm. MC, V, AmEx, NRS4567 to Grand Central-42nd St.

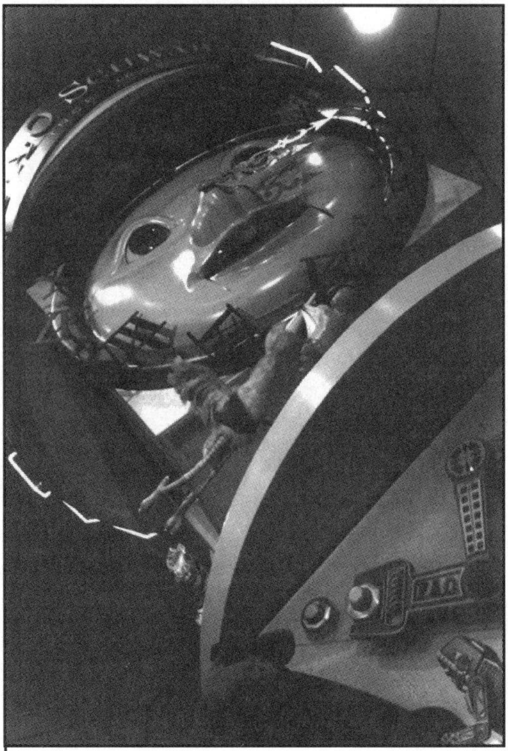

Krispy Kreme

A southern import, these donuts melt in your mouth so fast and taste so good that it's impossible to eat fewer than three.

Midtown, 2 Penn Plaza, Amtrak Level (bet.. 32nd and 33rd Sts.), (212) 947-7175, www.krispykreme.com. Open M-Su 6am-10pm. Cash Only, BDFQNR19 to 34th St.-Herald Sq.

Also at:

Midtown, Port Authority Bus Terminal, Eighth Avenue (bet.. 40th and 41st. Sts.), (212) 290-8644, www.krispykreme.com. Open M-F 6am-9pm. Cash Only, ACENRS123479 to Times Square-42nd St.

The Palm Court

Lovely, if overpriced, for desserts and tea in the Plaza Hotel. You can sit back and sip your tea while you watch the privileged but touristy walk in and out of the hotel. Then browse through The Plaza yourself; there's logic behind its fame.

Midtown, The Plaza Hotel, 768 Fifth Ave. (at Central Park S.), (212) 759-3000. Open M-Su 6:30am-12am. MC, V, AmEx, D, Entrees: $19-$30, NR to Fifth Ave.

Shopping

♦ CLOTHING & SHOES

Alberene Cashmere
Offers high-quality cashmere goods at prices lower than you'll find for comparable goods in department stores. Browse through their more than 2000 styles for both men and women, including capes, pullovers,
v-necks, and twin-sets in a variety of vibrant colors.
Midtown, 435 Fifth Ave, 3rd Fl. (bet.. 38th and 39th Sts.), (212)689-0151 or (800)566-681, www.scottishcashmere.com. Open M-F 10am-6pm, Sa 11am-5pm. MC, V, D, AmEx. 4 5 6 7 to Grand Central, B D Q R N to 34th St. ♿

Chanel
Coco would be proud. Complete with uniformed doorman, this sparkling shrine to simple elegance with a flair sells clothing, cosmetics, jewelry, shoes, accessories, and, of course, perfume.
Midtown, 15 E. 57th St. (bet.. Fifth and Madison Aves.), (212) 355-5050, www.chanel.com. Open M-W, F-Sa 10am-6:30pm, R 10am-7pm. MC, V, AmEx, DC, Q to 57th St. ♿

Emporio Armani
Cleanly cut casual suits that are a bit more accessible price-wise than Armani's main line.
Midtown, 601 Madison Ave. (bet. 57th and 58th Sts.), (212) 317-0800. Open M-F 10am-8pm, Sa 10am-7pm, Su 12pm-6pm. MC, V, AmEx, D, N R 4 5 6 to 59th St.-Lexington Ave. ♿

Ermenegildo Zegna
Although less well-known than Armani, his suits are certainly among the finest.
Midtown, 743 Fifth Ave. (bet.. 57th and 58th), (212) 421-4488, www.zegna.com. Open M-W, R 10am-8pm, F 10am-7pm, Sa 10am-6pm, Su 12pm-5pm. MC, V, AmEx, DC, F N R to Fifth Ave. ♿

H & M
Crowded to the point of suffocating, Euro import H & M draws hordes of fashion-hungry New Yorkers to its two Manhattan outlets with its chic clothes at ludicrously cheap prices. Of course, no one ever accused H & M of making their clothes well. But if you want to look like a million bucks and only pay ten, follow the Scandinavian lead.
Midtown, 34th St. at Herald Square (at Broadway), (646) 473-1164. Open M-Sa 9am-9pm, Su 11am-8pm

Also at:
Midtown, 6405 Fifth Ave. (at 57th St.), (212) 489-0390. Open M-Sa 10am-8pm, Su 11am-7pm. MC, V, AmEx, D, E F to Fifth Ave.

Manolo Blahnik
Just slipping one of these shoes on will make you feel like a princess. From the moment the doorman ushers you into the orchid-scented showroom, lined with plush carpets and flower arrangements, you'll find yourself surrounded by a cornucopia of some of the most elegant shoes imaginable. Though they have a mail order department, forgoing the shopping experience would be missing half the fun. Be warned; if glass slippers had cost this much, Cinderella may have missed the ball.
Midtown, 31 W. 54th St. (bet. Fifth and Sixth Aves.), (212) 582-3007, Open M-F 10:30am-6pm, Sa 10:30am-5pm. MC, V, AmEx, B D F Q to Rockefeller Center, NR to Fifth Ave. ♿

Original Levi's Store
A quirky, funky interior shows off Levi's complete clothing line. The selection and prices offered here are good, but not supercheap – the women's floor especially will leave you wondering if it was worth the four-flight climb. Expect to pay about $40 for a shirt and $60 for a pair of jeans. The Original Levi's Store definitely deserves a visit if you're in the area, but don't make a special trip.
Midtown, 3 E. 57th St. (bet.. Fifth and Madison Aves.) (212) 838-2188, 1-800-LEVI-USA, www.levis.com. Open M-Sa 10am-8pm, Su 11am-6pm. MC, V, AmEx, N R to 57th St. ♿

Also at:
Upper East Side, 750 Lexington Ave. (bet. 59th and 60th Sts.) (212) 826-5957, 1-800-LEVI-USA, www.levis.com. M-S 10am-7pm, Su 12am-6pm. MC, V, AmEx, N R 4 5 6 to 59th St.-Lexington Ave. ♿

♦ BOOKS, MAGAZINES & RECORDS

Argosy Bookstore
Rare books, old maps, and lithographs fill this time warp of towering bookshelves and cluttered desks. The bargains here are on the outside table.
Upper East Side, 116 E. 59th St. (bet. Park and Lexington Aves.), (212) 753-4455, www. argosybooks. com. Open M-F 10am-6pm. MC, V, AmEx, NR456 to 59th St.-Lexington Ave.

Coliseum Books
In a warehouse-like atmosphere, Coliseum Books is light years away from the ambiance at Barnes and Noble. Still, they stock everything for all tastes and interests, and often have the books that the B&N superstores run out of. With friendly staff and great hold policies, it seems almost silly to even stop up the street.
Midtown, 1775 Broadway (at 57th St.), (212) 757-8381. Open M-Su 8am-11:30pm. MC, V, AmEx, D, 19 to 59th St.

Complete Traveller
The best store for new and out-of-print books providing information for real trips and fuel for the imagination; the prices reflect the quality and the selection. The staff is amiable, versed and willing to discuss anything from city politics to traveling in the sub-Sahara.
Midtown, 199 Madison Ave. (at 35th St.), (212) 685-9007. Open M-F 9am-7pm, Sa 10am-6pm, Su 11am-5pm. MC, V, AmEx, D, DC, 6 to 33rd St. ♿

The Drama Bookshop
Plays, biographies, acting/directing and writing manuals, and much more. You might even spot a broadway star or two picking out a script for their next role!
Midtown, 723 Seventh Ave. (bet. 48th and 49th Sts.), 2nd fl., *(212) 944-0595, www.dramabookshop.com. Open M-F 9:30am-7pm, Sa 10:30am-5:30pm, Su 12pm-5pm. MC, V, AmEx, D, 19 to 50th St., NR to 49th St.* ♿

Gotham Book Mart
This average-sized bookstore may not be the greatest place to pick up the latest best seller, but with a generous selection of new and used books and with helpful salespeople, this is an ideal place to find some great literature.
Midtown, 41 W. 47th St. (bet. Fifth and Sixth Aves.), (212) 719-4448. Open M-F 9:30am-6:30pm, Sa 9:30am-6pm. MC, V, AmEx, BDFQ to 47-50 Sts.-Rockefeller Center.

Hacker Art Books, Inc.
An eager, knowledgeable staff headed by Pierre, the Parisian manager and conversationalist extraordinaire, can help browsers wade through the initially intimidating selection. The clientele are true art-lovers, not just casual collectors.
Midtown, 45 W. 57th St. (bet. Fifth and Sixth Aves.), (212) 688-7600, www.hackerartbooks.com. Open M-Sa 9:30am-6pm. MC, V, NR to Fifth Avenue, EF to 5th Ave. ♿

Hotalings
Walls of magazines, including one of the city's finest selections of foreign-language periodicals.
Midtown, 1660 Seventh Ave. (bet. 46th and 47th Sts.), (212) 840-1868. Open M-Su 8am-8pm. MC, V, AmEx, NRS12379 to 42nd St.-Times Sq. ♿

Kinokuniya Bookstore
Japanese books, some in English translation, with a diverse selection of stationery and gifts.
Midtown, 10 W. 49th St. (bet. Fifth and Sixth Aves.), (212) 765-7766, www.kinokuniya.com. Open M-Su 10am-7:30pm. MC, V, AmEx, BDFQ to 47th-50th Sts.-Rockefeller Center. ♿

Librairie de France
One-stop shopping for French émigrés and Francophiles. New York's largest French-language bookstore sells magazines upstairs and a vast assortment of literature, history, and biographies available downstairs. Spanish language materials also available.
Midtown, 610 Fifth Ave. on the Rockefeller Center Promenade (bet. 49th and 50th Sts.), (212) 581-8810, www.frencheuropean.com. Open M-Sa 10am-6pm. MC, V, AmEx, BDFQ to 47th-50th Sts.-Rockefeller Center. ♿

The Mysterious Bookshop

Serving the city's voracious mystery readers, this store stocks both current and out-of-print books as well as a healthy number of imports from Britain.

Midtown, 129 W. 56th St. (bet. Sixth and Seventh Aves.), *(212) 765-0900, www.mysteriousbookshop. com. Open M-Sa 11am-7pm. MC, V, AmEx, A B C D 1 9 to 59th St.-Columbus Circle*

Rizzoli

Pop in to escape the chaos of Midtown and get lost in this dark, warm store which, like its downtown counterpart, specializes in beautiful architecture, art, design, and coffee table books. Literature and non-fiction selections are not inspiring.

Midtown, 31 W. 57th St. (bet. Fifth and Sixth Aves.), (212) 759-2424. Open M-Sa 10am-7:30pm, Su 11am-7pm. MC, V, AmEx, D, N R to 57th St. ♿

Urban Center Books

Books on every architectural topic, from urban design to Freudian interpretations of city planning, line the walls of this cozy nook, complete with a fireplace and library ladders. Enjoy your purchase in the courtyard outside.

Midtown, 457 Madison Ave. (at 51st St.), (212) 935-3592, www.urbancenterbooks.com. Open M-R 10am-7pm, F 10am-6pm, Sa 10am-5:30pm. MC, V, E F to Fifth Ave. ♿

♦ GROCERY, GOURMET & SPECIALTY

Ecce Panis

A bread store with an extra (and expensive!) flair, they most definitely have bragging rights to the best chocolate bread in NYC. Go for the generous selection of free samples.

Midtown, 30 Rockefeller Plaza (bet. 49th and 50th Sts.), (212) 315-0099. Open M-Su 7am-6pm. MC, V, AmEx, D, B D F Q to Rockefeller Center. ♿

Fifth Avenue Chocolatiere

A family owned and operated business, Fifth Avenue Chocolatiere takes care in creating fine chocolates in fun shapes. With over 6,000 different molds, they are believed to have the largest selection of chocolate molds in the country. Ask about gift deliveries within Manhattan or order by mail across the US.

Midtown, 510 Madison Ave. (at 53rd St.), (212) 935-5454. Open M-F 9am-6:30pm, Sa 9:30am-6pm, Su 11am-6pm. MC, V, AmEx, D. 6 E F to 51st St.-Lexington Ave. ♿

Richart Design et Chocolat

With the store's minimalist décor, it's no surprise that these French imported chocolates are minimal in size. But what they lose in mass, they gain in taste with exotic fillings like

pure malt scotch, curry, and bergamot. Each chocolate is a tiny edible masterpiece with designs stenciled in red or gold-stained cocoa butter and packaged in square white cardboard drawers. Packaged selections range from a miniature $10 drawer to a pricey five-drawer chest for $250.

Midtown, 7 E. 55th Street (bet. Fifth and Madison Ave), (212) 371-9369. Open M-F 10am-7pm, Sa 10am-6pm. MC, V, AmEx. E F to Fifth Ave. ♿

♦ MISCELLANEOUS

Away Spa at the W New York Hotel

If you're looking to pamper yourself and splurge, the Away Spa is the perfect spot. Here you can schedule massages, hot oil therapy, facials, manicures and other such luxuries. Estheticians specialize in treatments from the Far E.. If you can't afford the $175 Bali Spice acupressure massage and spice mask, go for the 30-minute Swedish massage. Finish off your trip with a refreshing cup of tea in the Tea Room and shower yourself down in the private locker room.

Midtown, 541 Lexington Ave. (at 49th St.), Fourth Fl. (212) 407-2970. www.TheAwaySpa.com. Open M-F 9am-9:30pm, Sa-Su 8:30am-6:30pm. MC, V, AmEx, D, E F to Lexington Ave. 6 to 51st St.

Bergdorf Goodman

Tour the museum-quality merchandise worthy of its chandelier and marble surroundings in this home of high fashion. To actually purchase something, leave the clientele of wealthy Upper East Siders behind and travel to the fifth floor where less expensive (though still somewhat pricey) sportswear abounds. All monetary transactions occur in a "back room" whose doors blend with the walls. Window displays here are among Fifth Avenue's finest.

Midtown, 754 Fifth Ave. (at 58th St.), (212) 753-7300. Open M-Sa 10am-7pm, R 10am-8pm. MC, V, AmEx, DC, D, N R to Fifth Ave. ♿

B and H Photo

It's no wonder B and H has been around for over 25 years.

This photography, audio and video Mecca calls itself "the professional's source" and "the world's largest dealer." The knowledgeable staff is comprised of working professionals who are eager to assist you, especially after you wait in one of their notoriously immense lines.
Midtown, 420 Ninth Ave. (bet. 33rd and 34th Sts.), (212) 444-6615, www.bhphotovideo.com. Open M-R 9am-7pm, F 9am-1pm (winter) 2pm (summer), Su 10am-5pm. A C E to 34th St. ♿

Counter Spy Shop
The perfect store for the paranoid, the Counter Spy Shop sells everything you need to keep the government/stalkers/aliens/KGB off your back, including bullet proof vests, video cameras concealed in teddy bears and books entitled "How to Disappear Completely and Never Be Found."
Midtown, 444 Madison Ave. (bet. 49th St.), (212) 688-8500, www.counterspyshop.com. 6 to 51st St.

FAO Schwarz
Long before Tom Hanks and "Big," F.A.O. has drawn crowds of wide-eyed youngsters and their equally impressed parents during the holiday season, and it's hard not to get pulled in – the store puts on a helluva show. That said, unless you enjoy triple digit markups, leave the purchases for Toys 'R' Us.
Midtown, Fifth Ave. (at 58th St.), (212) 644-9400, www.fao.com. Open M-W 10am-7pm, R-Sa 10am-8pm, Su 11am-7pm. MC, V, AmEx, D, N R to 59th St.-Fifth Ave.

Henri Bendel
One of the plushest shopping experiences around. An elegant staircase winds its way up through the many-storied townhouse, maintaining the splendor of Bendel's original boutiques while incorporating modern accents. Same type of clothing as Bergdorf Goodman or Saks, but somehow classier.
Midtown, 712 Fifth Ave. (bet. 55th and 56th Sts.), (212) 247-1100. Open M-W, F-Sa 10am-7pm, R 10am-8pm, Su 12pm-6pm. MC, V, AmEx, D, N R to Fifth Ave. ♿

Jack's 99¢ Stores
Good for the bargain conscious shopper, including items like housewares, groceries, school supplies, toys and shampoo. You know, everything. Upstairs there's Jack's World, featuring more upscale merchandise.
Midtown, 110 W. 32nd St. (bet. Sixth and Seventh Aves.), (212) 268-9962. Open M-F 7:30am-7:45pm, Sa-Su 10am-6pm. MC, V, D, 1 2 3 9 to 34th St.-Penn Station X

Also at:
Midtown, 16 E. 40th St. (bet. Fifth and Sixth Aves.), (212) 696-5767. Open M-F 7:30am-7:45pm, Sa-Su 10am-6pm. Cash only, B D F Q to 42nd St., 7 to Fifth Ave.

Lee's Art Shop
Paints and brushes are just the beginning at this valuable resource for artists who work in all media. Drafting supplies, silk screens, a good selection of pens and stationery, and a framing service.
Midtown, 220 W. 57th St. (bet. Seventh Ave. and Broadway), (212) 247-0110. Open M-F 9am-7pm, Sa 9:30am-6pm, Su 12:30am-5:30pm. MC, V, AmEx, N R to 57th St.

Macy's
"The Largest Store in the World" often resembles the chaos of the Thanksgiving Day parade they sponsor, especially after work and around Christmas. Most items are lower priced than other department stores, but the service and bathrooms reflect this reduction.
Midtown, 34th St. (at Broadway), (212) 695-4400, www.macys.com. Open M-Sa 10am-8:30pm, Su 11am-7pm. MC, V, AmEx, B D F N Q R to 34th St. ♿

Metamorphosis Day Spa
The spa services only four clients at a time, so you are sure to get a personal, friendly experience. Although the atmosphere is overshadowed by the bet.ter-known storefront spas, their prices, in comparison, make the massages, aromatherapies, facials and other rejuvenating treatments equally as amazing. Buy a package and treat yourself.
Midtown, 30 E. 60th St. Suite 808 (bet. Park and Madison Aves.), (212) 751-6051, www.metspa.com. Open by appointment. MC, V, AmEx, N R 4 5 6 to Fifth Ave.

Saks Fifth Avenue
This classy store makes for great, if somewhat dizzying, browsing. Window displays make the Fifth Ave. promenade a bit more exciting; Salvador Dali reputedly crashed his car into one of them after artists didn't execute his design well enough.
Midtown, 611 Fifth Ave. (bet. 49th and 50th Sts.), (212) 753-4000, www.saksfifthaveneue.com. Open M-W, F-Sa 10am-7pm, R 10am-8pm, Su 12pm-6pm. MC, V, AmEx, DC, D, B D F Q to 47th-50th Sts.-Rockefeller Center. ♿

Sam Ash

Sprawling along 48th St., these four music shops fulfill almost every music-making need, selling acoustic instruments, recording equipment, MIDI systems, computers and software, DJ equipment, lighting, sheet music, and other items. The staff knows its stuff, and most locations rent and repair instruments and equipment.

Midtown, 160 W. 48th St. (bet. Sixth and Seventh Aves.), (212) 719-2299, www.samashmusic.com. Open M-F 10am-8pm, Sa 10am-7pm, Su 12pm-5pm. MC, V, AmEx, D, N R *to 49th St.,* B D F Q to 47-50 St.-Rockefeller Center. ♿

Sephora

Customize your face. Experienced sales people help customers weed through an inventory deeper than Santa Claus' sack. The idea is you shouldn't be focusing on brands but what colors work best for you. If a brand doesn't have your color they make colors for you and, hours later, you leave, your face covered in the person you always knew you could be.

Midtown 636 Fifth Ave (at 51st. St.), (212) 245-1633, www.sephora.com. Open M-Sa, 10am-8pm, Su 11am-7pm. MC, V, AmEx, D, B D F Q *to Rockefeller Center.* ♿

Also at:

Midtown, 1500 Broadway (bet. 43rd and 44th Sts.), (212) 944-6789, www.sephora.com. Open M-R, 10am-10pm, F-Sa 10am-12am, Su 10am-8pm. MC, V, AmEx, D, N R S 1 2 3 7 9 to *Times Sq-42nd St.* ♿

Arts & Recreation

♦ SITES

Empire State Building

A semi-obligatory tourist stop, the 86th floor observation deck offers panoramic views of Manhattan, New Jersey and Long Island. Open 365 days a year, summer months and after-it's-dark visiting times are the busiest. Don't be intimidated by the lovers, young and old; this stop is for all ages, nationalities and giant gorillas alike.

Midtown, 350 Fifth Ave. (at 34th St.), (212) 736-3100, www.esbnyc.com. Open M-Su 9:30am-12am. MC, V, AmEx, D, Admission: $9 adults, $7 military and seniors, $4 children 5-11, 5 and under are free, 1 2 3 9 *to 34th.*

Rockefeller Center

Midtown's primary tourist attraction is, paradoxically, an oasis of serenity -- except when its famed Christmas Tree is on display. Intriguing spaces, breathtaking urban vistas, and, yes, the fabled ice rink make Rockefeller Center a classic New York institution straight out of a Truman Capote piece. The sign-waving tourists in front of the "Today Show" window, however, do not.

Midtown, 49th to 52nd Sts. (bet. Fifth and Seventh Aves.) B D F Q *to 47th-50th Sts..-Rockefeller Center.* ♿

TKTS

This booth sells same day tickets to Broadway shows and Off-Broadway dance and opera at 25-50% discounts. Even the best seats are available, but come early or you'll wind up with a "partial view" seat. The wait can be long—over an hour, but is usually enlivened by the constant chaos of your Times Square surroundings.

West 47th (at Broadway), (212) 221-0013, Cash Only, Open: W-Sa (for matinees) 10am-2pm, M-Sa (for evening shows) 3pm-8pm, Su 11am-closing.

Also at:

2 World Trade Center (at mezzanine), (212) 221-0013, Cash Only, Open: M-F 11am-5.30pm, S 11am-3.30pm.

♦ LEISURE

Circle Line Cruises

Don't be put off by the thought of another "three hour tour." Land is always in site – and that's the best part of the Circle Line Cruise. Some of the greatest vistas of the Manhattan skyline, the tours highlight the seven bridges, three rivers and the Statue of Liberty. You can hop on at Pier 83 in Midtown or at the Seaport location at South Street Seaport. For the less sea-worthy, Circle Line offers shorter cruises from 30 minutes to two hours. There's no rush hour when you're on the water.

Midtown, 42nd St. (at Twelfth Ave.), (212) 563-3200. Open M-Su 8:30am-7pm. MC, V, AmEx. $24/person; $19 seniors; $12 children 12 and under. A C E *to 42nd St.*

Javits Center

Manhattan's primary convention space appears to be an alien spacecraft from the other side of the Hudson, a covert national security device from the W. Side Highway, and a soul-crushing scourge on humanity from Eleventh Avenue. It's none of those though, the building's monstrous shroud of black glass and steel simply lends it the chameleon-like identity that makes it a perfect meeting space for everyone from the New York Auto Show to the Greater New York Dental Meeting.

Midtown, Eleventh Ave. (bet. 34th and 39th Sts.), (212) 216-2000. www.javitscenter.com. N R S 1 2 3 7 9 to 42nd St.-Times Sq. ♿

Madison Square Garden

As "The World's Most Famous Arena," the Garden is home to the Knicks, Rangers, college basketball and the Paramount Theater. The complex underwent massive renovations in 1991, including the addition of 89 corporate box suites. The original arena was on 26th Street and Madison Avenue, where turn-of-the-century New Yorkers packed themselves like sardines to watch boxing, horse racing and live cabaret.

Midtown, 4 Penn Plaza (bet. Seventh Ave. and 32nd St.), (212) 465-6000, 1 2 3 9 *to 34th St.-Penn Station* ♿

NBC Today Show

Get your chance to say "Minnesota is number 1!" on like TV! Rain or shine, crowds gather in Rockefeller Center to peer behind the glass walls of the studio, where Katie Couric and Matt Lauer entertain millions of viewers each morning. Be prepared for huge crowds on summer days and big musical guest appearances. Even though you have to get up early (the show airs from 7am-9am), it's worth the price – free!

Midtown, 49th St. at Rockefeller Pl. (bet. Fifth and Sixth Aves.), (212) 664-4249. B D F Q *to 47th-50th Sts.-Rockefeller Center* ♿

The Paris

Possibly the most upscale movie theater in Manhattan, the Paris is a great place to go on a date after a fancy dinner, and watch foreign films in elegance and old-world splendor.

Midtown, 4 W. 58th St. (bet. Fifth and Sixth Aves.), (212) 688-3800. MC, V, AmEx N R to Fifth Ave. ♿

Worldwide Cinemas

Inflation recently pushed the price per movie from two bucks to three, but it's still a great deal for slightly older films. Groups of teenagers sometimes talk back to the screen.

Midtown, 340 W. 50th St. (bet. Eighth and Ninth Aves.), (212) 246-1583. C E *to 50th St.* ♿

The Ziegfeld Theater

This namesake of the old show palace that housed the Ziegfeld Follies restores some of the glamour and sense of occasion to the typical movie-dinner date. The biggest and best screen in town on which to see blockbuster new releases and re-mastered old ones like *Vertigo*, *Lawrence of Arabia*, and the *Star Wars* Trilogy.

Midtown, 141 W. 54th St. (bet. Sixth and Seventh Aves.), (212) 765-7600. B D E *to Seventh Ave.*

♦ PERFORMANCE

Alvin Ailey American Dance Theater

"The dance came from the people. It should be given back to the people," said the choreographer for whom this theatre, located in City Center, was named. Ailey developed the repertoire here with the uniqueness of black cultural

expression in mind. Pieces are often set to music by jazz greats such as Duke Ellington and Wynton Marsalis. Works performed include both those choreographed by the late Ailey himself and choreographers who shared his vision.
Midtown, 131 W. 55th St. (bet. Sixth and Seventh Aves.), (212) 581-1212. MC, V, AmEx, NR *to 57th St.* ♿

Carnegie Hall
A century has passed since Tchaikovsky conducted at the inauguration, but this stage keeps abreast of musical trends in their many variations: The Beastie Boys and the Tibet.an Freedom Fighters have appeared on the same stage as today's classical giants like Emanuel Ax. Jazz performers are also frequent guests.
Midtown, 881 Seventh Ave. (at 57th St.), (212) 247-7800, www.carnegie hall.org. MC, V, AmEx, DC, D. NR *to 57th St.* ♿

City Center
The façade of this theater, a mosque-like panoply of gold and colorful mosaic, is a show in itself, with an equally decadent lobby in marble and gold. Once you get past this fanfare, however, the performance space itself is fairly modest. Two stages, each of which seats less than 300 people, display American dramas and comedies, popular revivals, and ballets.
Midtown, 131 W. 55th St. (bet. Sixth and Seventh Aves.), (212) 581-1212. MC, V, NRS *to 57th St.* BQ *to 57th St.* ♿

Manhattan Theatre Club
Terence McNally, A.R. Gurney, and Richard Greenberg are just a few of the playwrights whose work has been featured at MTC, one of the oldest subscription-based theater companies in the City. The company presents a broad range of work, mixing audience-pleasers and more challenging pieces on its two stages. MTC received a great deal of media attention in 1998 as the site of McNally's controversial *Corpus Christi.*
Midtown, 131 W. 55th St. (bet. Sixth and Seventh Aves.), (212) 399-3000, www.mtc-nyc.org. MC, V, AmEx, NR *to 57th St.* ♿

Merkin Concert Hall
This modest performance space and new music venue is home to the Festival Chamber Music Society, which strives to provide quality music in a "warm, beginner-friendly environment." Each performance begins with a short lecture about the piece and ends with a champagne reception where audience members can meet the artists.
Midtown, 129 W. 67th Street (bet. Broadway and Amsterdam Ave.), (212) 501-3330. Cash Only 1239 *to 66th St.* ♿

New Amsterdam Theater
Once you get past the blinding yellow lights, cheesy souvenir stand, and suffocating crowd (all a result of The Lion King's popularity), the interior of the theater is an oasis of art deco elegance with marble friezes, lilac chandeliers, and an enormous, ornate concert hall. Blockbusters like The Lion King, Aida, and Beauty and the Beast have shown here.
Midtown, 214 W. 42nd St., (bet. Seventh and Eighth Aves.), (212) 282-2900. Open M-Sa 10am-8pm, Su 10am-7pm ACE12397S *to Times Square* ♿

Playwrights Horizons
Long the anchor of Theater Row, this theater company has been premiering innovative and new American plays for the past twenty-five years. The work of Christopher Durang and Wendy Wasserstein was first presented here, as was Stephen Sondheim and James Lapine's Pulitzer Prize-winning musical *Sunday In The Park With George*. The upstairs Studio Theater presents work by up-and-coming writers.
Midtown, 416 W. 42nd St. (bet. Ninth and Tenth Aves.), (212) 564-1235, www.playwrightshorizons.org. MC, V, AmEx, ACE *to 42nd St.*

Roundabout Theatre
The most consistently intelligent indigenous productions and Euro-pean imports on Broadway proper, including the recent Tony-winning hit, *Cabaret.*
Midtown, 231 W. 39th St. (bet. Seventh and Eighth Aves.), (212) 719-9393, www.roundabouttheatre.org. MC, V, AmEx, NRS12379 to 42nd St.-Times Sq. ♿

St. Clement's Theatre
A working theater for thirty-five years, this charming little church has hosted some of the best Off-Broadway theater in the city. Epis-copal services are still held regularly. Conveniently located on Restaurant Row and around the corner from the greatest concentration of ethnic restaurants in the city.
Midtown, 423 W. 46th St. (bet. Ninth and Tenth Aves.), (212) 246-7277, MC, V, AmEx, NRS12379 *to 42nd St.-Times Sq.* ♿

M i d t o w n

Second Stage

Dedicated to reinventing plays that "didn't get a fair shot the first time around," this unassuming theater of second chances has produced the works of Stephen Sondheim, Edward Albee, August Wilson, Athol Fugard, Mary Zimmerman and Wallace Shawn, to name a few.

Midtown, 307 W. 43rd St. (at Eighth Ave.), (212) 246-4422, www.secondstagetheater.com, MC, V, A C E to 42nd Street ♿

Signature Theatre Company

Under the leadership of visionary artistic director James Houghton, the Signature has carved out a unique mission: highlighting the work of one major playwright each season. Past seasons have included retrospectives and world premieres from Arthur Miller, John Guare, Adrienne Kennedy, and Sam Shepard.

Midtown, 555 W. 42nd St. (bet. Tenth and Eleventh Aves.), (212) 244-7529. MC, V, AmEx, A C E to 42nd St. ♿

♦ MUSEUMS & CULTURAL CENTERS

American Craft Museum

Utilitarian 20th century American art, from chairs to teapots, finds a home in this magnificent space. Exhibits in the past have included textiles and intricate weavings.

Midtown, 40 W. 53rd St. (bet. Fifth and Sixth Aves.), (212) 956-3535, www.americancraftmuseum.org. Open T-W, F-Su 10am-6pm, R 10am-8pm. Cash Only, Admission: $2.50-$5, E F to Fifth Ave. ♿

The International Center for Photography

Founded in 1974, one of the youngest members of Museum Mile showcases over 45,000 photographs and serves as a learning center for budding photographers of all levels of expertise.

Midtown, 1133 Sixth Ave. (at 43rd St.), (212) 768-4682, www.icp.org. Open T-R 10am-5pm, F 10am-8pm, Sa-Su 10am-6pm. Cash Only, Admission: $4-$6, B D F Q to 42nd St. ♿

Intrepid Sea Air Space Museum

The former aircraft carrier USS Intrepid, commissioned in 1943, served 31 years in the US Navy. It survived numerous attacks including seven bombings, five kamikaze assaults and a torpedo. The carrier retired in 1974; it now exhibits naval destroyers, guided-missile submarines, aircrafts and Felix DeWeldon's original Iwo Jima Memorial Statue.

Midtown, Pier 86 (bet. Twelfth Ave. and 46th St.), (212) 245-0072. www.intrepidmuseum.org. Call for hours. Admission: $12; $9 for seniors, veterans and students; $2-$6 for children. A C E 1 2 3 9 N R S 7 to 42nd St.-Times Sq.

Japan Society

An all-purpose center of Japanese art and culture, located appropriately enough in Japan House, with exhibitions on the second floor and a stone-lined pool garden on the first floor, complete with bamboo shafts.

Midtown, 333 E. 47th St. (bet. First and Second Aves.), (212) 832-1155, www.japansociety.org. 6 to 51st St., E F to Lexington Ave. ♿

The Morgan Library

The country's largest collection of Mesopotamian cylinder seals now rests where J.P. Morgan used to pad about in slippers, though the appeal of this library and museum is much broader. The library's renowned collection of rare books, manuscripts, and drawings have, as their principal focus, the history, art, and literature of Western civilization.

Midtown, 29 E. 36th St. (bet. Madison and Park Aves.), (212) 685-0610, www.morganlibrary.org. Open T-R 10:30am-5pm, F 10:30am-8pm, Sa 10:30am-6pm, Su 12pm-6pm. Cash Only, Admission: $5-7, 6 to 33rd St. ♿

The Russian Vodka Room

Professionals and pony-tailed mobsters come to this bar and drink expensive vodka. Expensive vodka like no vodka you've ever had before, in flavors kept secret for years by the Soviet Union. Now free in America, the Vodka Room's 51 flavors come in big heart- shaped carafes, so go with a group.

Midtown, 265 W. 52nd St. (bet. Broadway and Eigth Ave.), (212) 307-5835. Open T-Sa 4pm-4am, Su-M 4pm-2pm. MC, V, AmEx, D, B C to 50th St. ♿

Museum of Modern Art

Toeing a precarious line bet.ween avant-garde and establishment, this New York institution holds the world's most comprehensive collection of 19th and 20th century art, ranging from paintings to sculpture to photographs and beyond. Take a break amidst the Rodin sculptures in the outdoor garden. Admission is free on Friday 5:30pm-8pm, along with free jazz in the café.

Midtown, 11 W. 53rd St. (bet. Fifth and Sixth Aves.), (212) 708-9400, www.moma.org. Open M-T, R, Sa, Su 10:30am-5:45pm, F 10:30am-8:15pm. MC, V, AmEx, Admission: $5.50-$9.50, E F to Fifth Ave. ♿

Museum of Television and Radio

Watch TV all day and still feel cultured. Computer consoles and viewing cubicles access tens of thousands of programs (and you thought cable was overwhelming), though if your tastes are way obscure, you should order ahead of time. A nostalgic display of Kermit the Frog and friends alone is worth the trip.

Midtown, 25 W. 52nd St. (bet. Fifth and Sixth Aves.), (212) 621-6800. Open T-W, F-Su 12pm-6pm, R 12pm-8pm. MC, V, AmEx, Admission: $3-$6 (students), E F *to Fifth Ave.* ♿

The Rose Museum
Located on the second floor of Carnegie Hall, the Rose Museum usually features an exhibit about the historic music hall. Occasionally special exhibits are mounted on composers and musicians such as Leonard Bernstein or Tchaikovsky. Simple and to the point, The Rose is best appreciated by classical music lovers and musicians.
Midtown, 154 W. 57th St. (at Seventh Ave.), (212) 903-9600, Open M-T, R-Su 11am-4:30pm. A B C D E 1 9 *to 59th St.,* N R *to 57th St.* ♿

Scandinavian House
You don't have to be Swedish to appreciate this clean-lined, modern museum, which represents all aspects of modern Nordic culture through temporary art and design exhibits (photography, sculpture, installation), film screenings, concerts, lectures, and language classes. Children will delight in the cozy playroom and learning center and weary visitors of all ages will appreciate a bite at the Café Aquavit and a peek at the avant-garde gift shop.
Midtown, 58 Park Ave. (bet. 37th and 38th Sts.), (212)779-3587. Open T-Su 11am-5pm. Admission: Free, charge for special exhibits: $2 for students and seniors, $3 general 4 5 6 *to 33rd St.* ♿

St. Patrick's Cathedral
St. Patrick's Cathedral is the largest Catholic cathedral in the United States. Although in French Gothic style, most of the work is by American artists; Tiffany and Co. designed the altar, and the rose window is a must-see for any stained glass admirer. The Cathedral holds the seat of the archdiocese, and can accommodate over 2000 worshipers.
Midtown, Fifth Avenue (bet. 50 and 51st Sts.), (212) 753-2261. www.ny-archdiocese.org. Open M-Su 7am-9pm. E F *to Fifth Ave.*

♦ GALLERIES & LIBRARIES

Christie's New York
Scope out the goods at the free public viewing five days before an auction at this New York branch of the London legend; 19th and 20th century European art, traditionally favored here, is still a strong suit.
Midtown, 20 Rockefeller Pl. (bet. Fifth and Sixth Aves.), (212) 636-2300, www.christies.com. Open M-F 9:30am-5:30pm. B D Q E F *to Rockefeller Center.*

Mary Boone Gallery
This longtime SoHo staple recently headed for greener grass up north — an elegant address on Fifth Ave. Many artists, among them Ross Bleckner (who had a \show at the Guggenheim a few years back), came along for the ride.
Midtown, 745 Fifth Ave., 4th Fl. (bet. 57th and 58th Sts.), (212) 752-2929. Open T-F 10am-6pm, Sa 10am-5pm. N R *to Fifth Ave.* ♿

New York Public Library
The main facility of the city's extensive library system sits at 42nd St. and Fifth Ave. It was designed by Carrere and Hastings, and is considered one of the five greatest libraries in the world. The library issues borrowers' cards to anyone who lives, works, or attends school in New York State, so make sure to drop by any local branch and get yourself one.
Midtown, 455 Fifth Ave. (at 40th St.), (212) 930-0830, www.nypl.org. Open M, R-Sa 10am-6pm, T-W 11am-7:30pm. B D F Q *to 42nd St.,* 7 *to Fifth Ave.* ♿

Pace Wildenstein Gallery, Midtown
An old hand at this art thing, this multilevel space hosts somewhat famous names, like Alexander Calder and Chuck Close.
Midtown, 32 E. 57th St. (bet. Madison and Park Aves.), (212) 421-3292, www.pacewildenstein.com. Open T-Sa 10am-6pm. N R 4 5 6 *to 59th St.* ♿

Nightlife

♦ BARS

Campbell Apartments
With lush oriental carpeting, comfy lounge chairs, and an arabesque ceiling, Campbell Apartments is more than just a spot for Wall-Streeters to throw back a few before hitting the Metro-North. Be forewarned, drinks are pricey and the place closes around midnight. But when they kick you out you will promptly discover what a swell place Grand Central can be for drunken shenanigans.
Midtown, 5 Vanderbilt Ave. (at Grand Central), (212) 953-0409. Open M-Sa 3pm-1am, Su 3pm-11pm. MC, V, AmEx, S 4 5 6 7 *to 42nd St.-Grand Central.*

Carnegie Club
This two-floor cigar kingdom attracts the usual white-collar crowd. No smoking jackets spotted here, but patrons do enjoy feeling literary among the bookshelves while sipping fabulous martinis. Live jazz rounds out the ambience on weekends.
Midtown, 156 W. 56th St. (bet. Sixth and Seventh Aves.), (212) 957-9676. Open M-Sa 4:30pm-1am. MC, V, AmEx, B D E *to Seventh Ave.* ♿

Danny's Skylight Room at the Grand Sea Palace
While it claims to have one of the best sound and lighting

systems in the city, most people go to this reasonably priced bar for — surprise, surprise — the skylight.
Midtown, 346 W. 46th St. (bet. Eighth and Ninth Aves.), (212) 265-8130, www.danysgrandpalace.com. Open M-Su 12pm-12am. MC, V, AmEx, DC, D, N R S 1 2 3 7 9 *to 42nd St.*

The Ginger Man
The suits turn out in sassy little three-piece numbers to mix networking with cruising over cigars and rather anonymous-looking drinks in oh-so-stylish cocktail glasses.
Midtown, 11 E. 36th St. (bet. Fifth and Madison Aves.), (212) 532-3740, www.gingerman.com. Open M-W 11:30am-2am, R-F 11:30am-4am, Sa 12:30pm-4am, Su 3pm-12am. MC, V, AmEx, DC, B D F N R Q *to 34th St.*

Hudson Bar
Take a fluorescent green escalator to reach this trendy bar with shiny floors, bright lights, translucent gel cushions on Louis XV chairs and a main bar that glows from within. But this hip place also has overpriced drinks and an extremely pretentious crowd and staff. Guys coming alone will have a difficult time making it past the velvet rope.
Midtown, 356 W. 58th St. (bet. Eighth and Ninth Aves.), (212) 554-6343. Open M-Su 12pm-4am. MC, V, AmEx A B C D 1 9 2 3 *to 59th St.*

Jimmy Armstrong's Saloon
According to the menu, "tasty vittles, good grog, and sweet music" draw the many professional musicians, composers, and Julliard students to this jovial neighborhood pub bursting with bonhomie. The top-rate jazz guitarists playing Tuesday through Sunday are good enough to please even the pickiest music aficionados. Sate a hearty appetite with some of the savory offerings on the eclectic but moderately priced menu.
Midtown, 875 Tenth Ave. (at 57th St.), (212) 581-0606. Open M-Su 11:30am-1am. AmEx, A B C D 1 9 *to 59th St.-Columbus Circle.*

Jimmy's Corner
Escape the giddiness of the Theater District at this easy-going local dive, the site of some scenes in Raging Bull. Owner Jimmy Glen subsidizes his career as a boxing trainer and manager with the revenues from his hopping bar. An eclectic crowd of boxing fanatics, literateurs, grad students, and the occasional movie star gathers here.
Midtown, 140 W. 44th St. (bet. Sixth and Seventh Aves.), (212) 221-9510. Open M-Su 11am-4am. MC, V, AmEx, N R S 1 2 3 7 9 *to 42 St.-Times Sq.*

Julie's
Offering the mature elegance of The Townhouse Bar, but for women, Julie's fills nightly with thirty-something lesbians of professional employment. Wednesday nights sizzle with salsa and Sundays offer sexy afternoon tea dances.
Midtown, 204 E. 58th St. (bet. Second and Third Aves.), (212) 688-1294, Open F-Sa 5pm-4am, W 5pm-3am, R 5pm-2am. Cash Only, N R 4 5 6 *to 59th St.-Lexington Ave.*

La Nueva Escuelita
One of those rare places that manages to be popular without pretension, LaNueva Escuelita is a pseudo-salsa, heavily gay club that opts for mayhem over slickness. Best known for sheer fabulosity.
Midtown, 301 W. 39th St. (at Eigth Ave.), (212) 631-0588. Open T-Sa 10pm-indefinite, Su 7pm-indefinite. MC, V, AmEx, D, A C E *to 42nd St.*

Le Bar Bat
Three floors of mediocrity. Once a famous recording studio, Le Bar Bat has been remodeled into the kind of bar people go to when they either know nothing about music or nothing about New York. If there's a plus it's that you can go downstairs and be bored on the dance floor when you get bored of the live music, and when that fails amble upstairs to one of the boring backroom bars.
Midtown, 311 W. 57th St. (bet. Eighth and Ninth Aves.), (212) 307-7228. Open M-Su 5pm-4am. MC, V, AmEx, D, 1 9 A B C D *to 59th St.*

Monkey Bar
"It's hip, it's hopping, and it's hot," said a fifty-ish, dolled-up patron of this Art Deco masterpiece where a glamorous older crowd sips cocktails and flaunts Chanel. The epitome of swank.
Midtown, Hotel Elysée, 60 E. 54th St. (bet. Madison and Park Aves.), (212) 838-2600. Open M-R 12pm-2am, F 12pm-3am, Sa 5:30pm-3am, Su 5:30pm-12am. MC, V, AmEx, DC, 6 *to 53rd St.*

The Oak Room
One of two lounges at the Algonquin Hotel where Dorothy Parker's mordant wit presided over a legendary circle of writers and critics in the 20s. Dress up to fit in with the stylish crowd soaking up late-night cabaret performances in this stylish English tearoom.
Midtown, 59 W. 44th St. (bet. Fifth and Sixth Aves.), (212) 840-6800. Call for showtimes. MC, V, AmEx, B D F Q *to 42nd St.,* 7 *to Fifth Ave.*

O'flaherty's Ale House
The scene's crowded and eclectic; here, you'll also find the only pub with a tree growing right through the middle of the bar. In the back, discover a private garden away from the Midtown bustle. Live music, great beer and plenty of dancing keep everyone busy.
Midtown, 334 W. 46th St. (bet. Eighth and Ninth Aves.), (212)

581-9366. Open M-Su 12pm-4am. MC, V, AmEx, Entrees: $21-$30. DC, D, 1 9 to 50th St., N R to 49th St.

O'Lunney's Times Square Pub

This late night spot with a bit of a cult following serves food until 3 am. Expect Irish and American cuisine, and a rowdy post-theatre crowd. The selection of food is basic, but the beers are exceptional. Service can be lacking, but the ambiance is generally fun and the moderate prices on the menu will keep you in your seat.
Midtown, 151 W. 46th St. (bet. Broadway and Sixth Ave.), (212) 840-6688, www.olunneys.com. Open M-Su 11am-4am. MC, V, AmEx, DC, D, 1 2 3 9 N R 7 S to 42nd St.

Parnell's Pub

"It'll kill ya' or cure ya'," explains the redheaded waitress in her lilting brogue to customers inquiring about Guinness. Outfitted with a dark wood bar and plenty of Irish pride, this bar/restaurant serves traditional dishes along with the famous dark brew.
Midtown, 350 E. 53rd St. (at First Ave.), (212) 753-1761. Open M-Su 11am-4am. MC, V, AmEx, E F to Lexington. 6 to 51st St. ♿

Don't Tell Mama

Wrest control of the microphone away from fellow exhibitionists at this extrovert's paradise where patrons are invited to sing along with the waitstaff, the pianist, and the mixed gay/straight clientele.

piano bar, pop
Midtown, 343 W. 46th St. (bet. Eighth and Ninth Aves.), (212) 757-0788, www.donttellmama.com. Open M-Su 4pm-4am. MC, V, AmEx, DC, no cover for piano bar, call for individual cabaret covers, C E to

Revolution

Yuppies gather around the fireplace, smoke long cigarettes, and toss their heads back in laughter at this watering hole which is unusually hip and upscale for Hell's Kitchen.
Midtown, 611 Ninth Ave. (bet. 43rd and 44th Sts.), (212) 489-8451. Open M-F 5pm-4am. MC, V, AmEx, DC, D, A C E to 42nd St. ♿

Rudy's Bar and Grill

This venerable Hell's Kitchen dump is always crowded with theater types, both the starry-eyed and the occasional weary has-been. They come for the dirt-cheap pints, jazz on the juke, and free hot dogs. Although Rudy's is, technically speaking, a dive, such a vivacious crowd keeps the atmosphere upbeat.
Midtown, 627 Ninth Avenue (bet. 44th and 45th Sts.), (212) 974-9169. Open M-Su 8am-4am. Cash Only, A C E to 42nd St. ♿

The Townhouse Bar

An extremely professional gay bar catering to well-dressed men with big bank accounts and the fellows who love them. A piano bar in back augments the somewhat pretentious ambience.
Midtown, 236 E. 58th St. (bet. Second and Third Aves.), (212) 754-4649. Open Su-W 4pm-3am, R-Sa 4pm-4am. Cash Only, 4 5 6 to 59th St., N R to Lexington Ave.

Siberia

Literally a hole in the wall, Siberia is NYC's only bar actually inside a subway station. Small, dark, and reveling in its trashiness, Siberia attracts a diverse crowd, including actor/waiters to yuppies. Their jukebox is among the best in town, and they host DJs and film screenings weekly.
Midtown, 1627 Broadway (inside the 1, 9 subway station at 50th St.), (212) 333-4141. Open M-Su 3pm-4am. Cash Only, 1 9 to 50th St. .

♦ CLUBS

Exit

Massive and uninteresting, Exit's kind of the Wal-Mart of the New York club scene. The scene is mostly really young people, people on ecstasy or both. On the plus side, while it's not as hip as Spa or Saci, it has much less attitude.
Midtown, 610 W. 56th St. (bet. Tenth and Eleventh Aves.), (212) 582-8282. Open F-Sa 10pm-indefinite. MC, V, AmEx, D, C E to 50th St.

Float

Float is one of those clubs where all the boys are pretty good-looking and have their hair rumpled in a supposedly accidental way. It gets flak for having a sometimes-cheesy crowd, but it's still a comfortable, spacious and reasonably friendly club.
Midtown, 240 W. 52nd St. (bet. Eighth Ave. and Broadway), (212) 581-0055. Open T-Sa 10:30pm-4am. MC, V, AmEx, D, C E to 50th St.

Saci

Saci is an extremely pretentious warehouse with less decor than most raves. The crowd is generally attractive and well-dressed but guys without ladies will have to wait a long time to get in and enjoy. The staff is rude, the dance music is not the latest, and a good drink is extremely expensive (and comes in a plastic cup no less.)

Midtown, 135 W. 41st St. (bet. Sixth Ave. and Broadway), (212) 278-0988. Open R-Sa10pm-4am. MC, V, AmEx, DC, 1 2 3 9 7 N R S *to 42nd St.*

♦ MUSIC

Carnegie Hall

Still the reigning champ of bourgeois nightlife, this legendary institution is the artist's Valhalla. Concerts usually take place every night of the week except July- August, when the Hall is closed for the season. The majority of acts are classical, but you still may catch the occasional Joan Baez or David Bowie if you're lucky. Adjoining restaurant and bar serves American cuisine.

classical, pop, special events

Midtown, 881 Seventh Ave. (at 57th St.), (212) 247-7800, www.carnegie hall.org. Call for schedule and showtimes. MC, V, AmEx, Cover: $16-$150, N R *to 57th St.* ♿

Connolly's

You can't be Irish in New York if you haven't heard of Black 47, the Dublin rock band, a musical hero to the local Irish community. Black 47 plays at Connolly's every Saturday, with other acts occasionally playing the odd night. Connolly's is one of the few venues in New York centered around a single band. Full menu, full bar (of course).

Irish rock

Midtown, 14 E. 47th St. (bet. Fifth and Madison Aves.), (212) 867-3767, www.connollys-nyc. com. Open M-Su 11am-4am. MC, V, AmEx, Cover: $10, B D F Q *to 47-50th Sts.-Rockefeller Cen-ter.* ♿

Downtime

Plenty of seating at the bar and at tables makes this a comfortable room to listen to emergent New York bands. One of the best open mic nights in town (Thurs.). No food, full bar.

hip-hop, pop, rock

Midtown, 251 W. 30th St. (bet. Seventh and Eighth Aves.), (212) 695-2747. Open W-Sa 5pm-4am. MC, V, Cover $5-$10, 1 9 *to 28th St.* ♿

Hammerstein Ballroom

Opened in 1906 by Oscar Hammer-stein, the ballroom is the setting for a number of national touring acts as well as television broadcasts and corporate events. Music may be seen anywhere from zero to five nights a week, an eclectic roster ranging from Hanson to Manson. No food, several bars. ethnic, hip-hop, metal, pop, punk, rhythm, rock

Midtown, 311 W. 34th St. (bet. Eighth and Ninth Aves.), (212) 279-7740, www.mcstudios.com. Call for schedule and showtimes. Cash Only, Cover: $20-$60, A C E *to 34th St.-Penn Station.* ♿

Roseland

It started as a popular ballroom in the 1930s, and the newly renovated Roseland is still one of the more frequented venues in town. Large enough to draw a sizable crowd but small enough to retain some of that club charm, these days expect to find the bigger names in alternative acts like Radiohead and Beck stopping by for a gig. No food, full bar.

alternative rock, dance, pop

Midtown, 239 W. 52nd St. (bet. Broadway and Eighth Ave.), (212) 777-6800, www.roselandballroom.com. Call for schedule and showtimes. Cash Only, Cover: $15-$20. 1 9 *to 50th St.* ♿

The Supper Club

As one of New York's more elegant venues, be prepared to dress up for a night of dinner and dancing on the town. Historically a ballroom, The Supper Club is at the center of the swing scene every Friday and Saturday night. During the rest of the week, catch a live band under the sparkling chandelier and painted gold stars. French and American Continental served from 5:30pm-12:30am.

1940s lindyhop, jump, swing, occasional private rock/pop concerts

Midtown, 240 W. 47th St. (bet. Broadway and Eighth Ave.), (212) 921-1940, www.supperclub.com. Open F-Sa 5:30pm-4am. MC, V, AmEx, Cover: $20-$25, 1 9 *to 50th St.,* N R *to 49th St.* ♿

Swing 46 Jazz and Supper Club

Swing 46 is located amidst a row of restaurants aimed at a predominantly out-of-town, after-theater crowd. At Swing 46, this element mingles with a mixed and lively group of swing enthusiasts. Nightly, there is a complimentary swing lesson at 9:15pm, followed

by a live band around 10pm.

Midtown, 349 W. 46th St. (bet. Eighth and Ninth Aves.), (212) 262-9554. Open M-R 5pm-12am, F-Su 5pm-1am, band begins M-R 10pm, F-Su 10:30pm. MC, V, AmEx, S N R A C E 2 3 1 9 7 *to Times Square.*

W. Bank Café's Laurie Beachman Theatre

W. Bank Café's cabaret room is just below the restaurant and bar. It's a place for a nice dinner followed by a relaxing evening downstairs. Great for entertaining out-of-town business clients.

cabaret

Midtown, 407 W. 42nd St. (bet. Ninth and Tenth Aves.), (212) 695-6909. Open M-Sa 12pm-1am, Su 11:30am-3pm, 4pm-12am. MC, V, AmEx, call for cover charges for individual shows, A C E *to 42nd St.* ♿

Disabilities Access in New York City

There are few cities where disability will receive a higher profile than New York City. When the 10th anniversary of the Americans with Disabilities Act passed in 2000, the anniversary was celebrated with a cross-national Spirit of the ADA torch relay that culminated at the United Nations. Multiple organizations and agencies are able to aid people with disabilities in a complex, fast-paced city.

In a city with crowded sidewalks, streets, and subways, New York City's transportation system is remarkably disability-friendly. Most public buses have working wheelchair lifts and drivers who know how to use them, and there are now 40 accessible subway stations. For people with disabilities who are unable to use public bus or subway service for some or all of their trips, **Access-A-Ride** (1-877-337-2017) is a shared ride, door-to-door paratransit service. While the waits are notoriously long (plan to wait up to 30 minutes), like the rest of New York City transportation, service and availability has improved measurably over previous years.

Organizations that specialize in particular disabilities are conspicuously present in Manhattan. **YAI** assists people with developmental and learning disabilities and their families and **Lighthouse** (1-800-821-9200 or 212-821-9723 TTY) specializes in assisting and advocating for the visually impaired. However, **Independent Living Centers** are probably the best resource for general information on disability. In the spirit of the independent living movement, which states that people with disabilities are best able to help other disabled people, the majority of staff and board of directors are themselves people with disabilities. The **Center for Independence of the Disabled in New York** (212-674-2300 or 212-674-5619) provides advocacy and information, along with support groups and peer counseling. It is an excellent starting point for information, along with being a continual community resource.

For health, the **Initiative for Women with Disabilities Center** (IWD) (212-598-6429) at the **Hospital for Joint Diseases** is notable for being the only facility in New York City that provides total accessibility for women with physical disabilities who need gynecological as well as other comprehensive medical care.

The Achilles Club (www.achilles.org) is the running club for people with disabilities that made it possible for people with disabilities to run in mainstream events like the New York City marathon. For those with thespian ambitions, the **National Theatre Workshop of the Handicapped** (www.ntwh.org) advocates for persons with disabilities in the theatre and offers a forum of dramatic literature on themes of disability.

Able News (www.ablenews.com) is the New-York-based newspaper "Positively for, by, and about the Disabled." Aside from comprehensive news and editorials on important disability issues, personal ads in the classified section are a resource for meeting companions, friends, or spouses.
What should people do when they run into discrimination or inaccessibility? The **New York City Commission on Human Rights** (212-306-7500) is the government agency with which to register complaints.

Upper East Side

This is where the wealth is. Fifth Avenue, Madison Avenue, Park Avenue—all here. Before Central Park opened in 1873 the Upper East Side resembled what could have been farmland. The construction of the Second and Third Avenue elevated train lines, completed in 1859, changed all that and a wave of Eastern European and German immigration settled into the area east of Lexington Avenue.

Names like Tiffany, Astor, Rockefeller, Frick and so on didn't arrive until closer to the end of the century, setting up mansions the size of airport hangars along Central Park. Park Avenue's glamorous reputation came about after the New York Central Railway buried its above-ground tracks. Elegant apartment buildings lined the newly cleared blocks, while Madison Avenue's wealthy residents attracted upscale boutiques to the ground floors of the street's row houses.

A division developed between the working class neighborhood east of Lexington and the rich one to the west of it. However, this relationship has never been a hostile one. The mansions are gone, save castles turned museums like Carnegie's Cooper-Hewitt Museum and the Frick's aptly named Frick collection, but the aristocratic air lives on; to the uninitiated the Upper East Side can be an intimidating place. Gloved doormen still hail cabs, nannies still take the kids out strolling, adolescents in blue suits are groomed for inheritance, and some restaurants don't bother listing something as crass as prices.

But it's a neighborhood of many minds and East of Lexington everything is decidedly middle class. The area called Yorkville boasts a strong Hungarian population whose old-world delis, and moderately priced ethnic foods mix with bar after Irish bar. And it seems this is how things will stay. A teenager in a blue suit comes home from private school, has dinner with the family and around 10pm walks East with a fake ID in hand.

Dining

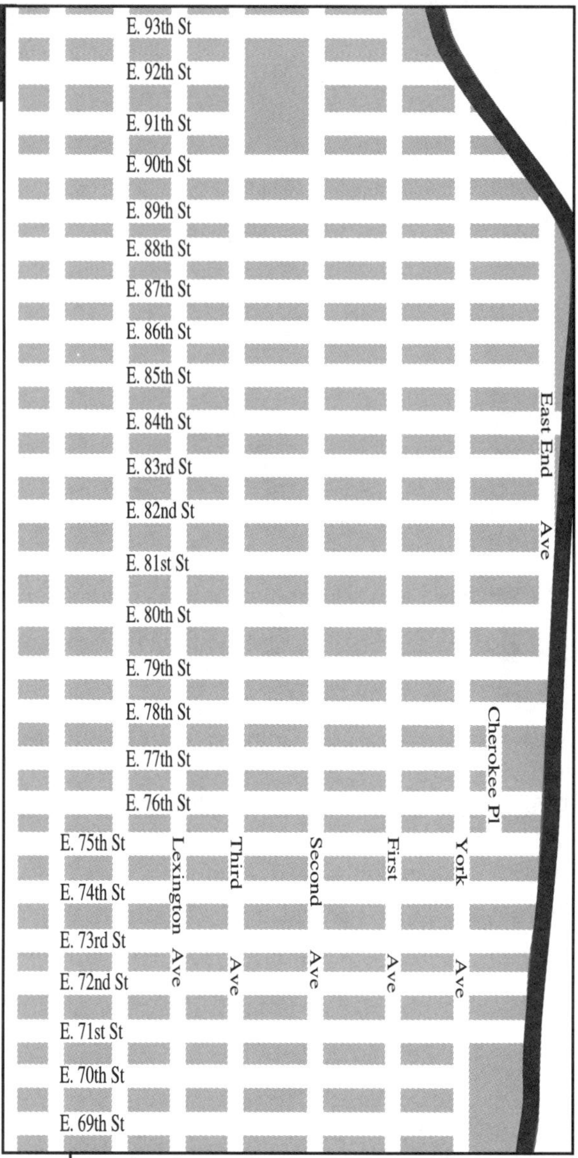

♦ RESTAURANTS

Arizona 206

Walk through the door and it's practically Sedona, by way of Third Avenue. The rustic floors, cozy tables, and stucco alcoves all make for nice atmosphere, though dining can get cramped. Prices are fine for retired condo denizens, but students may want to wait until the parents come to town.

Upper East Side, 206 E. 60th St. (at Third Ave.), (212) 838-0440. Open M-Su 12pm-4pm, 5:30pm-11pm. MC, V, AmEx, DC, Entrées: $15-$55, N R 4 5 6 59th St.-Lexing-ton Ave.

The Comfort Diner

This retro-hip diner takes itself pretty seriously, if the slightly bitter menu offers any clues - "Sorry, Mom, but we don't remember yours tasting this good," reads the meatloaf description. To their cred-it, it really is pretty good meatloaf.

Upper East Side, 142 E. 86th St. (bet. Third and Lexington Aves.), (212) 426-8600. Open Su-W 8am-11pm, R 8am-12am, F-Sa 8am-2am. MC, V, D, Entrees $8-10, 4 5 6 to 86th St.

Daniel

Another one of New York's finest: amazing food, beautiful setting, and, of course, prices to match.

Upper East Side, 60 E. 65th St. (bet Park and Madison Aves.), (212) 288-0033, www.danielnyc.com. Open T-Sa 12pm-2am, M-Sa 5:45-11pm. MC, V, AmEx, DC, Entrées: $40-$60, 4 5 6 to 68th St.-Hunter College.

El Pollo

All hail Peru's favorite bird — the chicken — at one of the city's very few Peruvian kitchens. Order the "pollo" in whole, half, or quarter portions and expect it to be spicy and succulent. Don't pass up the Andean peasant staples — the "mote" (Peruvian corn) and the "papas rellenas" (stuffed potatoes) are two of the country's crowning culinary achievements.

Upper East Side, 1746 First Ave. (bet. 90th and 91st Sts.), (212) 996-7810. Open M-Su 11am-11pm. MC, V, AmEx, DC, D. Entrées: $5-$10, 4 5 6 to 86th St.

Elaine's

A magnet for A-list hometown celebs often featured in gossip columns. This popular hangout serves up standard American fare; quality blows hot and cold (mostly cold), but coming here for the food is like living in New York for the weather: it just shouldn't be a priority. Regulars include Woody Allen, Barbara Walters, and George Plimpton.

Upper East Side, 1703 Second Ave. (bet. 88th and 89th Sts.), (212) 534-8103. Open M-Su 6pm-2am. MC, V, AmEx, DC, D, Entrées: $15-$35, 4 5 6 to 86th St.

Harry Cipriani

Throw on the channel suit and relax because your trust fund's paying for this meal, like it does everything else. If you can stand the attitude, come to look for celebrities and feel like one yourself.

Upper East Side, 781 Fifth Ave. (bet. 59th and 60th Sts.), (212)

PLACES TO GO:

92nd St. Y
A genuine intellectual experience without the coffee shop feel. Catch lectures, performances and star-studded poetry readings.

El Pollo
Chicken, usually that thing you order because you don't know what else to get, finally gets the respect it deserves.

Amsterdam Billiard Club
While most bars offer small pool tables with shaky cues, this Paul Sorvino owned gem, delivers on up-to-date pool eqipment and great ambience.

753-5566. Open M-Su 7am-10:30am, 12pm-3:30pm, 6pm-11:45pm. MC,V, AmEx, DC, D, Entrées: $40, N R 4 5 6 *to 59th St.-Lexington Ave.*

La Gouloue

Sure the food's great but this is a snobby place. If you don't fit into the snobby mold you will be treated like second rate cheese. However, if the snob thing is your thing, go to La Gouloue, try the skate fish, and guffaw, guffaw at all the people being told there's a two hour wait on all of the empty tables.

Upper East Side. 746 Madison Ave. (bet. 64th and 65th Sts.), (212) 988-8169. Open M-Sa 12pm-3:30 pm, 6pm-11:30pm, Su 12pm-4pm, 6pm-10:30pm. MC, V, AmEx, D, Entrees:$20-$35 6 *to 68th St.*

The Lobster Club

Chef/owner Anne Rosenzweig made headlines years ago when she stormed the citadel of all-male chefs at the city's top rated restaurants. Indulge in one of her signature dishes like corn cakes with crème fraîche and caviar, or chocolate-bread pudding swimming in brandy-custard sauce; in all her cooking, Rosenzweig expertly combines French technique and American heartiness.

Upper East Side, 24 E. 80th St. (bet. Madison and Fifth Aves.), (212) 249-6500. Open M-Sa 11:30am-3pm, 5:30pm-10pm. MC, V, AmEx, DC, Entrées: $18-$29, 6 *to 77th St.*

Sant Ambreous

Famous for the cakes you'll see displayed in the windows, this Upper East Side café is infamously overpriced. Rumor has it the cakes are prettier than they are tasty anyway. Still, there's no shortage of patrons at this Northern Italian cafe, where the cappuccinos and gelati are to die for. Think of it as a taste of Italy on the Upper East Side.

Upper East Side, 1000 Madison Ave. (bet. 77th and 78th Sts.), (212) 570-2211. Open M-Sa 9am-10pm, Su 10:30am-6pm. MC, V, AmEx, D, Entrees: $20-$30, 6 *to 77th St.*

Le Bilboquet

Chain-smoking Eurotrash trail crowds of beautiful people into this diminutive French bistro, currently boasting some of the hippest new lounging turf. Models can't appreciate the menu, but don't let that stop you from taking advantage of the well-executed bistro fare.

Upper East Side, 25 E. 63rd St. (bet. Madison and Park Aves.), (212) 751-3036. Open M-Su 12pm-11pm. MC, V, AmEx, Entrées: $17-$24, N R 4 5 6 *to 59th St.-Lexington Ave.*

Le Pain Quotidien

The smell of freshly baked bread welcomes you to this cozy Belgian bakery/café featuring a giant communal wooden table and some of the flakiest croissants this side of the Atlantic. Everything from rustic baguettes to country loaves, for which European flour is specially imported, is masterfully prepared and baked on the premises in batches

throughout the day. A delicious array of breakfast and lunch dishes are also served.
Upper East Side, 1311 Madison Ave. (bet. 84th and 85th Sts.), (212) 327-4900, www.painquotidien.com. Open M-F 7am-7pm, Sa-Su 8am-7pm. Cash Only, Entrées: $8-$12, 4 5 6 to 86th St.

Where the Rich People are Eating

The rich people of the Upper East Side might as well be an ethnic enclave. They have their own customs, dress, way of speaking and yes, food. Here's where you can go to experience one of America's oldest cultures.

♦ Elaine's

An institution that will be here longer than you, reading this now; even if the food were horrible the same crowd of celebs and wealthy would come.

♦ La Gouloue

The most obnoxious of the five places listed here. La Gouloue is full of the arrogance of a spoiled young man who's never had a job and never worried about money.

♦ Lobster Club

Bring a bib, the title says it all. If lobster isn't your thing there's plenty of other amazing choices to choose from.

♦ Payard Patisserie and Bistro

As good for a meal as it is for dessert. Stop in for five minutes or bring that special someone and finally pop the question.

♦ Rosa Mexicana

The Upper East Side's idea of Mexican food is actually better than Mexican food. If you can stomach that, which you will if you try the food, you'll have great time.

Match Uptown

A dose of uptown swank and sophistication with a dash of pretension flavor this hip New American menu with its own in-house sushi bar, sit-in bar, and caviar service. Mood lighting, an older crowd, and comfortable seating make for a pleasant dining experience. Food is colorful, artfully prepared, and fabulous. Dessert is a must!
Upper East Side, 33 E. 60th St. (bet. Madison and Park Aves.), (212) 906-9177. Open M 11:30am-10pm, T-Sa 11:30am-12am, Su 3pm-10pm. MC, V, AmEx, Entrées: $25-$30, N R 4 5 6 to 59th St.- Lexington Ave.

Manana Restaurant

Delicious and reasonably-priced Mexican food lies behind this otherwise unassuming First Avenue facade. The atmosphere is cute, if a little cheesy, but the main draw here is the food. Everything is good across the board, but the Yucatan-style carnitas are worth a trip all by themselves.
Upper East Side, 1136 First Ave. (between 62nd and 63rd Sts.), (212) 371-8023. Open M-Su 12pm-12am. MC, V, Amex. Entrees: $8-$16, 4 5 6 to 59th St.

Maya

Excellent cuisine, excellent service, and a comfortable atmosphere make dining at this "Gourmet Mexican" truly a euphoric experience. The food is that good. Colorful and flavorful, the dishes are inventive with surprising combinations. Try the mango margaritas and the guacamole with fresh chips.
Upper East Side, 1191 First Ave. (at 64th St.), (212) 585-1818. Open M-Su 5pm-10pm, T-R 5pm-11pm, F-Sa 5pm-11:30pm. MC, V, AmEx, Entrées: $17-$27, N R 4 5 6 to 59th St.-Lexington Ave.

Merchants, NY

The East Side branch of a trio of sleek establishments of the same name, some actually order food here to go with their martini or cosmopolitan; check out the downstairs sofa scene for ultimate cushiness. The appetizer and dessert menus are excellent.
Upper East Side, 1125 First Ave. (at 62nd St.), (212) 832-1551. Open M-Su 11:30am-2am. MC, V, AmEx, DC, Entrées: $13-$19, N R 4 5 6 to 59th St.-Lexington Ave.

Mocca Hungarian

Throw your doctor's cholesterol warnings to the wind and dig into peasant staples like goulash and stuffed cabbage. The decor takes its cues from Communist functionalism.

Breakfast at Tiffany's, 1961

Audrey Hepburn plays Holly Golightly, a woman who believes that nothing can go wrong at Tiffany's & Co. (57th St. and Fifth Ave.); sometimes after a night out, she arrives at the store with breakfast in hand and window shops.Otherwise, shespends her days in her Upper East side apartment.

Upper East Side, 1588 Second Ave. (bet. 82nd and 83rd Sts.), (212) 734-6470. Open M-Su 11:30am-10:30pm. Cash Only, Entrées: $7-$14, 4 5 6 to 86th St.

Pamir

Savory pilaf complements the well-executed lamb and chicken dishes, from kebabs to quabilli palaw, at this cozy uptown en-clave of Afghan cuisine adorned with hand-tooled metalwork and bright Afghan rugs. Denim-clad patrons will feel self-conscious in the upscale atmosphere.

Upper East Side, 1437 Second Ave. (bet. 74th and 75th Sts.), (212) 734-3791. Open M-Su 5pm-11pm. MC, V, AmEx, Entrées: $11-$16, 6 to 77th St.

Payard Patisserie and Bistro

Payard's two-tiered restaurant, dim lighting and French service create an elegant, Upper East Side atmosphere. With an impressive wine list, traditional French cuisine and impeccable service, your meal will be well worth the bill. If you're not in the mood for big spending, skip straight to the dessert menu; their pastries truly melt in your mouth and most are under $10. The best dessert in New York.

Upper East Side, 1032 Lexington Ave. (bet. 73rd and 74th Sts.), (212) 717-5252, www.payard.com. MC, V, AmEx, DC, D, 6 to 77th St.

Penang Malaysia

This lively, decked out Malaysian is usually packed on weekends and reasonably so; the food is innovative and tasty, the crowd generally young and hip, and there's live music and a lounge in the bar downstairs. Try eating down there to avoid the wait upstairs.

Upper East Side, 1596 Second Ave. (at 83rd St.), (212) 585-3838, www.penangnyc.com. Open Su-M 12pm-12am, T-R 12pm-1am, F-Sa 12pm-2am. MC, V, AmEx, DC, Entrées: $11-$20, 4 5 6 to 86th St.

Rosa Mexicano

A well-heeled clientele sips pomegranate margaritas at the crowded bar while waiting for a taste of well executed classics. Guacamole is prepared table-side and desserts like the tamal en cazuela dulce, a sweetish, warm cornmeal swirled with a chocolate sauce, make this a must.

Upper East Side, 1063 First Ave. (at 58th St.), (212) 753-7407. Open M-Su 5pm-11:30pm. MC, V, AmEx, DC, D, Entrées: $17-$26, N R 4 5 6 to 59th St.-Lexington Ave.

♦ CAFES

DTUT

Ever want to hang out in a coffeehouse reminiscent of the one in Friends? Here's your chance. With deep couches, delicious coffee, and yummy goodies, you can spend hours just chatting with pals at this Upper East Side café. Be sure not to miss the do-it-yourself s'mores.

Upper East Side, 1626 Second Ave. (bet. 84th and 85th Sts.), (212) 327-1327. Open M-R 7:30am-12am, F 7:30am-2am, Sa 8:30am-2am, Su 8:30am-12am. Cash Only, Entrees: $5-$12, 4 5 6 to 86th St.

Lexington Candy Shoppe

Its antique malt-mix dispenser and shake machine have been churning since 1925, making a meal at this old-fashioned soda fountain and diner a historical event. Pay homage by ordering one of the burgers sizzling on a small griddle and a complicated dairy concoction.

Upper East Side, 1226 Lexington Ave. (at 83rd St.), (212) 288-0057. Open M-Sa 7am-7pm, Su 9am-6pm. MC, V, AmEx, Entrées: $6-$8, 4 5 6 to 86th St.

Serendipity 3

Famous for their frozen hot chocolates and ice cream sundaes that go on forever, leave your diet at the door when you visit. Though a bit overpriced, most concede that it's worth it when they taste the desserts here.

Upper East Side, 225 East 60th St. (bet. Second and Third Aves.), (212) 838-3531, www.serendipity3.com. Open Su-R 11:30am-12am, F 11:30am-1am, Sa 11:30am-2am. MC, V, AmEx, DC, D, Entrees: $12-$17, N R 4 5 6 to 59th St.-Lexington Ave.

Shopping

♦ CLOTHING & SHOES

Bally

One of the best-known and most reputed leather companies in the world, this tannery sells a vast selection of high-quality leather shoes, bags, belts, and other ready-to-wear accessories.

Upper East Side, 628 Madison Ave (at 59th St.), (212) 751-9082, www.ballyswiss.com. Open M-F 10am-6:30pm, Sa

10am-6pm, Su 12pm-5pm. MC, V, AmEx, DC, N R 4 5 6 *to 59th St.-Lexington Ave.* ♿

Betsey Johnson

In-your-face girly chic means Betsey's not afraid to flaunt lace alongside faux leather, or pair zebra stripes with fuschia fishnets. Straightforward, sexy slip dresses are surprisingly affordable on sale.

Upper East Side, 251 East 60th St. (bet. Second and Third Aves.), (212) 319-7699, www.betseyjohnson. com. Open M-Sa 11am-7pm, Su 12pm-7pm. MC, V, AmEx, N R 4 5 6 *to 59th St.-Lexington Ave.*

Also at:

Upper East Side, 1060 Madison Ave (at 80th St), (212) 734-1257, www.betseyjohnson.com. Open M-Sa 11am-7pm, Su 11pm-6pm. MC, V, AmEx, 6 *to 77th St.* ♿

Calvin Klein

Pay tribute to the commercial master who made a young American public hunger for androgyny, kiddie-porn, and denim trashiness. Along with its refined, simple men's and women's wear, this flagship megastore boasts roomfuls of classically styled home accessories and a full staff of the predictably trendy, long-limbed photo-session specimens.

Upper East Side, 654 Madison Ave. (at East 60th St.), (212) 292-9000. Open M-W, F-Sa 10am-6pm, R 10am-8pm, Su 12pm-6pm. MC, V, AmEx, DC, D, N R 4 5 6 *to 59th St.-Lexington Ave.* ♿

Calypso

Fun and funkily printed fabrics abound in this boutique which successfully attempts to bring an international-island aesthetic to the neighborhood. While the inspiration for the clothing styles may be other-wordly, though, the prices all-too-closely mirror those of other East Side fashion boutiques. Paradise doesn't come cheap, after all, for the true fashion elite.

Upper East Side, 935 Madison Ave. (at 74th St.), (212) 535-4100. Open M-F 10am-7pm, Sa 10am-6pm, Su 12pm-6pm. MC, V, AmEx, DC, 6 *to 77th St.* ♿

Club Monaco

This Canadian Company has transformed New York. They have basics with a Trendy kick. Check out their CMX sports line.

Upper East Side, 1111 Third Ave., (at 65th St.) (212) 352-0936, www. clubmonaco.com. Open M-R 10am-7pm, F-Sa 10am-8pm, Su 12pm-6pm. MC, V, AmEx, DC, N R 4 5 6 to 59th St.-Lexington Ave. ♿

Cole Haan

Shoes of the very finest materials and nicest design are available in this Upper East Side foot haven. The store utilizes its space so as to display the merchandise (including

other leather goods) quite well.

Upper East Side, 667 Madison Ave. (at 61st St.), (212) 421-8440. Open F-W 10am-7pm, R 10am-8pm. MC, V, AmEx, D, N R 4 5 6 *to 59th St.-Lexington Ave.* ♿

Diesel

Two stories worth of youth culture in all its incarnations. Pump your well-toned system full of caffeine with a visit to the cappuccino bar before ravaging the aisles of shoes, underwear, outerwear, and accessories.

Upper East Side, 770 Lexington Ave. (at 60th St.), (212) 308-0055, www. diesel.com. Open M-Sa 10am-8pm, Su 10pm-6pm. MC, V, AmEx, DC, D, N R 4 5 6 *to 59th St.-Lexington Ave.*

Givenchy

Audrey Hepburn and Givenchy helped make each other even more famous back in their heyday. Today, their designs are still very French and very chi-chi, though there's probably no movie star today that could carry them off like Hepburn.

Upper East Side, 710 Madison Ave. (at 63rd St.), (212) 688-4338. Open M-Sa 10am-6pm. MC, V, AmEx, N R 4 5 6 *to 59th St.-Lexington Ave.* ♿

Hanae Mori

Vibrantly colorful and irreverently patterned, the shop's collection of women's fashion is among the most cutting edge in contemporary design. Dazzle the senses even further with an eyeful of the storefront's striking stucco front and off-center chrome cylinder, designed by Hans Hollein.

Upper East Side, 27 East 79th St. (bet. Madison and Fifth Aves.), (212) 472-2352. Open M-Sa 10am-6pm. MC, V, AmEx, DC. 6 *to 77th St.* ♿

Nicole Miller

This designer is known for her detailed bold silk patterns. They are on everything from eyeglass cases to bow ties to umbrellas. She carries dresses for all occasions with interesting fabrics. While you are there be sure to check out the sale rack.

Upper East Side, 780 Madison Ave. (bet. 66th and 67th Sts.),

One of the few charms that Manhattan has for me is its nearly complete freedom from one of the most annoying of American habits: impertinent curiosity about other people's affairs.

—Sir Denis Brogan

(212) 288-9779, www.nicolemiller.com. Open M-T, F 11am-7pm, R 9:30am-8pm, Sa-Su 9:30am-6pm. MC, V, AmEx, D, ❻ to 68th St.-Hunter College.

Prada

This sleek, green-walled store is great for window shopping, even if you don't have the bucks to buy. Prada's conservative yet trendy style isn't as popular as it used be , but they still hold rank in the Pantheon of labels people know without owning a single item.

Upper East Side, 841 Madison Ave. (at 70th St.), (212) 327-4200. Open M-W, F-Sa 10am-6pm, R 10am-7pm. MC, V, AmEx, DC, ❻ to 68th St.-Hunter Colleg. ♿

TSE

With modern styles , this is the best spot for young cashmere-o-philes. Offering blends as well, come for suits, jackets, and other must-haves. Don't miss the goat's-hair blankets.

Upper East Side, 827 Madison Ave. (at 69th St.), (212) 472-7790. Open M-Sa 10am-6pm, R 10am-7pm. MC, V, AmEx, ❻ to 68th St.-Hunter College.

Urban Outfitters

This hipster playground for urban youth packs its industrial interior with racks of multicolored, funky kid fashion, suitable for an array of day or evening urban outings. Weave through aisles of vintage clothing, sassy sundresses, and trendy housewares while swaying to the smooth rhythms of ambient music played in the background.

Upper East Side, 127 East 59th St. (bet. Lexington and Park Aves.), (212) 688-1200, www.urbanoutfit ters.com. Open M-W 11am-10pm, R-Sa 11am-11pm, Su 1pm-9pm. MC, V, AmEx, D, ⓃⓇ❹❺❻ to 59th St.-Lexington Ave.

Valentino

The name speaks for itself - Haute couture for those who can afford it. Need we say more?

Upper East Side, 747 Madison Ave. (at 65th St.), (212) 772-6969. Open M-Sa 10am-6pm. MC, V, AmEx, DC, ❻ to 68th St.-Hunter College. ♿

♦ BOOKS, MAGAZINES & RECORDS

Bookberries

Coffee table books are the specialty of this store — huge volumes loaded with pictures, especially of travel and food. In the rear is a children's section.

Upper East Side, 983 Lexington Ave. (at 71st St.), (212) 794-9400. Open M-Sa 10am-6:30pm, Su 10:30am-5:30pm. MC, V, AmEx, ❻ to 68th St.-Hunter College

The Corner Bookstore

What a bookstore should be. You won't find trendy cafes or a music section here, just a carefully chosen selection of books of all genres. In addition, they host a neighborhood Christmas Party, an annual "Canine Buffet" (a sidewalk dog party), as well as frequent readings. By far the store's most impressive resource, however, are the people who work there – all true lovers of books, they won't just shove the current bestseller at you to make a sale, but assist each customer like a (well-read) friend.

Upper East Side, 1313 Madison Ave. (at 93rd St.), (212) 831-3554. Open M-R 10am-8pm, F 10am-7pm, Sa-Su 11am-6pm. MC, V, AmEx, ❹❺❻ to 86th St., ♿

Kitchen Arts & Letters

With a fabulous selection of over 10,000 cookbooks, the definitive answer to "what's cooking?" for either the novice or the gourmet.

Upper East Side, 1435 Lexington Ave. (bet. 93rd and 94th Sts.), (212) 876-5550. Open M 1pm-6pm, T-F 10am-6:30pm, Sa 11am-6pm. MC, V, ❻ to 96th St. ♿

The Lenox Hill Bookstore

Several years ago, while independent bookstores were closing left and right, the owners of the beloved Corner Bookstore in Carnegie Hill opened this small shop on Lexington Avenue. Like its older sibling, the Lenox Hill Bookstore employs a friendly and knowledgeable staff, holds frequent readings, and hosts its own "Canine Buffet" (an annual party for neighborhood dogs). To anyone who has been to either shop, it's no mystery why they continue to thrive despite the advent of the superstore – this is the pleasurable type of shopping experience that Barnes & Noble can never offer.

Upper East Side, 1018 Lexington Avenue (bet. 72nd and 73rd Sts.), (212) 472-7170. Open M, F 10am-7pm, T-R 10am-8pm, Sa-Su 11am-6pm. MC, V, AmEx, ❻ to 77th St. ♿

Logos Bookstore

Located within the residential splendor of York Ave, Logos Bookstore has that simple wooden décor that makes a reader feel at ease. The extensive religious and philosophical works on display complement the true focus of this store:

high quality fiction. Rounded off by a helpful and knowing staff, this relaxing shop is worth the trip to the East Side.
Upper East Side, 1575 York Ave. (bet. 83rd and 84th Sts.), (212) 517-7292. Open M-F 10am-9pm, Sa 10am-6pm, Su 12pm-6pm. MC, V, AmEx, 4 5 6 to 86th St.

Shakespeare & Co.
One of four locations left after the recent demise of the Upper West Side store, offering a diverse selection of books, and the soul of an actual bookstore, too.
Upper East Side, 939 Lexington Ave. (bet. 68th and 69th Sts.), (212) 570-0201, www.shakespeare-nyc. com. Open M-F 9am-8pm, Sa 10am-7pm, Su 10am-5pm. MC, V, AmEx, D, 6 to 68th St.-Hunter College.

Chicago City Limits
No alcohol is served at New York's best improv theater, but you may get a buzz from the audience participation.

Upper East Side, 1105 First Ave. (at 61st St.), (212) 888-5233, www.chicagocitylimits.com. Showtimes W-R 8:30pm, F, Sa 8pm, 10:30pm. MC, V, AmEx, N R 4 5 6 to 59th St.-Lexington Ave.

♦ GROCERY, GOURMET & SPECIALTY

Ecce Panis
A bread store with an extra (and expensive!) flair, they most definitely have bragging rights to the best chocolate bread in NYC. Go for the generous selection of free samples.
Upper East Side, 1120 Third Ave. (at 66th St.), (212) 535 2099. Open M-F 8am-8pm, Sa 8am-7pm, Su 8am-6pm. MC, V, AmEx, DC, 6 to 68th St.-Hunter College. ♿

Also at:
Upper East Side, 1260 Madison Ave. (at 90th St.), (212) 348-0040. Open M-F 8am-7pm, Sa 8am-6pm, Su 8am-5pm. AmEx, D, MC, V, 4 5 6 to 86th St. ♿

Eli's Vinegar Factory
An ex-mustard and vinegar factory converted into a gourmet food warehouse with retail prices, including the best deals on imported caviar in the city. Exotic imports beckon from between stacks of fresh produce and gourmet delights.
Upper East Side, 431 East 91st St. (bet. First and York Aves.), (212) 987-0885, www.elizabar.com. Open M-Su 7pm-9pm. MC, V, AmEx, D, 4 5 6 to 86th St.

Elk Candy
Resist, if possible, the urge not to eat the cute, stylized treats at this confectioners, renown for more than sixty years for its marvelous marzipan.
Upper East Side, 1628 Second Ave. (bet. 84th and 85th Sts.), (212) 650-1177. Open M-W 9am-8pm, R-Sa 9am-10pm, Su 10am-7pm. V, MC, AmEx, 4 5 6 to 86th St. ♿

La Maison du Chocolat
As one might guess, chocolate is this store's specialty, and it comes in many shapes and sizes, none of which even approach being healthy or veer far from being absolutely divine.
Upper East Side, 1018 Madison Ave. (bet. 78th and 79th Sts.), (212) 744-7117, www.lamaisonduchocolat.com. Open M-Sa 10am-7pm, Su 12pm-6pm. MC, V, AmEx, 6 to 77th St. ♿

M. Rohrs House of Fine Teas & Coffee
Satiating the ever-fluctuating caffeine addictions of locals for over 100 years with its wide selection of refined tea leaves and coffee beans. Wooden counters and aged tea canisters with beveled mirrors retain the shop's original, old-world charm, an anomaly among slick coffee bars.
Upper East Side, 303 East 85th St. (at Second Ave.), (212) 396-4456, www.rohrs.com. Open M-Sa 7am-10pm, Su 8am-10pm. MC, V, AmEx, 4 5 6 to 86th St. ♿

Petak's
This Carnegie Hill specialty deli may be overpriced, but residents don't seem to mind. You may think you'll never have to cook again as you eye their many ready-made salads and entrees. Petak's also has a small eat-in area with a salad bar and waitress service, so customers can sit and have lunch while they order what they won't be cooking for dinner.
Upper East Side, 1246 Madison Ave., (bet. 90th and 89th Sts.), (212) 722-7711. Open M-Sa 7:30am-8pm, Su 9am-8pm. MC, V, AmEx, D, 4 5 6 to 86th St. ♿

♦ MISCELLANEOUS

Barney's New York
Power dressers, and those looking for something more elegant, put dents in their substantial bank accounts at this airy, beautiful legend, which still holds its head high despite the closure of the original Chelsea store. Head to the top floor for the lowest prices and most casual wear.
Upper East Side, 660 Madison Ave. (at 61st St.), (212) 826-8900. Open M-Sa 10am-7pm, Su 11am-6pm. MC, V, AmEx, N R 4 5 6 to 59th St.-Lexington Ave. ♿

Bloomingdale's
Although the trademark perfume arcade is usually a zoo, the upper floors are open, bright, and filled with helpful salespeople eager to successfully match people with outfits bearing three (or four!) digit price tags.
Upper East Side, 1000 Third Ave. (bet. 59th and 60th Sts.), (212)

705-2000, www.bloomingdales.com. Open M-F 10am-8:30pm, Sa 10am-7pm, Su 11am-7pm. MC, V, AmEx, NR456 to 59th St.-Lexington Ave. ♿

Boyd's

It's expensive, but this is the Upper East Side. This pharmacy has so many hair products you'll find whatever you're looking for. They also carry many make-ups you might not find in your local Rite-Aid. Just tell yourself the prices are justified by the selection.

Upper East Side, 655 Madison Ave. (bet. 60th and 61st Sts.), (212) 838-6558, www.boydsnyc.com. Open M-F 8:30am-7:30pm, Sa 9:30am-7pm, Su 12pm-6pm. MC, V, AmEx, D. NR456 to 59th St.-Lexington Ave. ♿

Face Stockholm

This Sweden-based company excels at the basics. Personal attention is easy to come by within the airy boutique; the $9 nail polish selection makes you wish you had more fingers. A favored stop for fashionistas and actresses, you might even spot a celeb or two au naturel!

Upper East Side, 687 Madison Ave. (at 62nd St.), (212) 207-8833, www. beauty.com. Open M-Sa 10am-7pm, Su 12pm-6pm. MC, V, AmEx, NR456 to 59th St.-Lexington Ave. ♿

Mackenzie Childs

Be careful not to break anything as you browse through this Upper East Side housewares and knickknacks store. Famous for its one of a kind, hand-painted items and window displays that are sure to keep you from walking on by, nearly everything in this store is appealing. The prices are high, but it's still a fun place to visit.

Upper East Side, 824 Madison Ave. (at 69th St.), (212) 570-6050, www.mackenzie-childs.com. Open M-Sa 10am-6pm. MC, V, AmEx, D, 6 to 68th St.-Hunter College. ♿

Arts & Recreation

♦ LEISURE

Ballet Academy East

Itching to test those dancing shoes? Drop in here and for $12 you can sample one of the jazz, ballet, or tap classes.

Upper East Side, 1651 Third Ave. (bet. 92nd and 93rd Sts.), (212) 410-9140. Open M-F 8:30am-9:30pm, Sa-Su 8:30am-5pm. 6 to 96th St.

New York Zendo Shobo-ji

New Yorkers looking to escape urban chaos seek out this serene temple, complete with rock gardens, instructions on

correct breathing, meditation, posture, etiquette, and Oriental floor cushions. Hard-core enthusiasts can partake of a purer experience on one of the weekend retreats held at an affiliated monastery in the Catskills.

Upper East Side, 223 East 67th St. (bet. Second and Third Aves.), (212) 861-3333, www.zenstudies.org. 6 to 68th St.-Hunter College. ♿

♦ PERFORMANCE

The Comic Strip Live

New York's most famous comedy theater regularly plays host to mainstream big-name performers and other crowd-pleasers. No cover Mondays.

Upper East Side, 1568 Second Ave. (bet. 81st and 82nd Sts.), (212) 861-9386, www.comicstriplive.com. Showtimes M-R 8:30pm, F-Sa 8pm, 10:30pm, 12:30 am, Su 8pm. MC, V, AmEx, D, 456 to 86th St. ♿

Harkness Dance Center at the 92nd St. Y

The Upper East Side's cultural mecca hosts professional performances as well informal shows of works-in-progress or new works.The dance workshops are a good reason for visiting, with programs like Argentine Tango Party, boasting Madonna's Evita coaches as instructors, and Israeli folk dancing classes occurring regularly.

Upper East Side, 1395 Lexington Ave. (bet. 91st and 92nd Sts.), (212) 415-5552. MC, V, AmEx, 456 to 86th St. ♿

♦ MUSEUMS & CULTURAL CENTERS

Alliance Française

Brush up on the language of love at Tuesday's $7 screenings of French flicks ($5.50 for members). Dance classes and more than 200 language courses are also available. Members enjoy free films, culinary and wine tastings, travel seminars, art excursions, discounts on French perform-

ances around the city, and the use of the multimedia library.
Upper East Side, 22 East 60th Street (bet. Madison and Park Aves.), (212) 355-6100, www.fiaf. org. Open M-R 9am-8pm, F 9am-6pm, Sa 9am-1:30pm. N R 4 5 6 to 59th St.-Lexington Ave. ♿

Americas Society
Inter-American policy issues come up for debate at the conferences and study groups organized by the Society's Western Hemisphere Department; the Cultural Affairs department offers an extensive arts library, lectures in conjunction with special exhibits, and concerts with receptions for the white wine crowd.
Upper East Side, 680 Park Ave. (at 68th St.), (212) 249-8950, www. Americassociety.org. Open T-Su 10am-6pm. 6 to 68th St.-Hunter College ♿

Asia Society
Celebrate Asian cultural awareness with notable film series, lectures, and an art collection featuring sculpture, paintings, ceramics, prints and bronzes from across Asia. Prominent authors and public leaders speak regularly here; other programs for the public include dance performances, well-attended art exhibits usually gathered from private collections, and receptions involving community and professional organizations.
Upper East Side, 502 Park Ave. (at 59th St.), (212) 288-6400, www. asiasociety.org. MC, V, AmEx, 6 to 68th St.-Hunter College. ♿

Sotheby's
Don your most expensive dress and pretend you're an heiress at Manhattan's other leading auction house; collectibles sold here range from

rare coins, jewels, and vintage wine to decorative and fine arts. Admission here is free, but the glossy catalog will set you back about $20 bucks.
Upper East Side, 1334 York Ave. (at 72nd St.), (212) 606-7000, www. sothebys.com. Open: M-F 10am-5pm. MC, V, Admission:

China Institute
America's oldest bi-cultural organization focusing on China promotes awareness of the country's culture, history, language, and arts through semester-long classes in Mandarin, Cantonese, Tai Chi, calligraphy, cooking, and painting. Seminars, lecture series, and film screenings with Chinese and Chinese-American themes are also regularly scheduled.
Upper East Side, 125 East 65th St. (bet. Lexington and Park Aves.), (212) 744-8181, www.chinainstute. org. 6 to 68th St.-Hunter College.

The Cooper-Hewitt Museum
The Smithsonian's National Museum of Design utilizes its 11,000 square feet to present landmark historic pieces as well as pioneering contemporary designs. Attention is paid to both the one-of-a-kind and the mass-produced. The building itself, once the Carnegie Mansion, boasts an eye-catching ceiling and an intricate staircase. Come free from 5pm-9pm, Tuesdays.
Upper East Side, 2 East 91st St. (at Fifth Ave.), (212) 849-8400, www. si.edu/ndm. Open: T 10am-9pm, W-Sa 10am-5pm, Su 12pm-5pm. MC, V, AmEx, Admission: $5-$8, 4 5 6 to 86th St.

Czech Center
Exhibits on Czech culture and contemporary art; one recent show included photographs taken by blind children.
Upper East Side, 1109 Madison Ave. (at 83rd St.), (212) 288-0830, www.czechcenter.com. Open: T, W, F 9am-5pm, R 9am-7pm. Cash Only, Admission (suggested): $3, 4 5 6 to 86th St. ♿

Frick Collection
Steel kingpin Henry Clay Frick built this mansion with his fine art collection and a future museum in mind. The museum's been realized and now offers a rare chance to view masterpieces displayed in a residential setting. Highlights include portraits by El Greco, Rembrandt, and Renoir, and waterscapes by Turner. One of the most soothing spots in the city is the sun-lit, virtually sound-proof indoor courtyard with marble benches and a drizzling fountain. The mail-in procedure for free tickets to Sunday concerts is an ordeal, but no tickets are required to listen in from the courtyard. Children under ten are not admitted.
Upper East Side, 1 East 70th St. (at Fifth Ave.), (212) 288-0700, www. frick.org. Open T-Su 10am-6pm. MC, V, AmEx, Admission: $5-$7, 6 to 68th St.-Hunter College. ♿

Gracie Mansion
The official residence of all New York mayors since LaGuardia, Archibald Gracie built Gracie Mansion 1799 on the site of a former Revolutionary fort. It was bought by the city in 1887. The mansion became part of Carl Schurz Park and was the home of the Museum of the City of New York from 1924-30. Tours are by appointment every day except Wednesday, but you can stop by anytime for a nice view of the Harlem River. $4 suggested admission.
Upper East Side, East 88th St (at East End Ave.), (212) 570-4751. 4 5 6 to 86th St.

The International Center for Photography
Founded in 1974, one of the youngest members of Museum Mile showcases over 45,000 photographs and serves as a

learning center for budding photographers of all levels of expertise.
Upper East Side, 1130 Fifth Ave. (at 94th St.), (212) 860-1777, www.icp.org. Open T-R 10am-5pm, F 10am-8pm, Sa-Su 10am-6pm. Cash Only, Admission: $4-$6, ❻ *to 96th St.* ♿

Istituto Italiano di Cultura
The Italian consulate operates this center for the dissemination of the country's culture; attend concerts, exhibits and lectures occurring frequently, or just swing by to flip through Italian mags for some insight into the Pope or haute couture.
Upper East Side, 686 Park Ave. (bet. 68th and 69th Sts.), (212) 879-4242, www.italcultny.org. ❻ *to 68th St.-Hunter College.* ♿

Jewish Museum
The largest collection of Judaica in the world outside of Israel, housed in an imperious French Renaissance structure, boasts over 27,000 works in its permanent collection. Works detail the Jewish experience throughout history and feature archeological pieces, ceremonial objects, modern masterpieces by Marc Chagall and Frank Stella, and even an interactive computer program based on the Talmud. The first two floors host temporary installations and exhibits. Admission is free for children under 12 and for everyone Tuesdays 5pm-8pm.
Upper East Side, 1109 Fifth Ave. (at 92nd St.), (212) 423-3200, www.the jewishmuseum.org. Open Su-R 11am-5:45pm, T 11am-8pm, MC, V, AmEx. Admission: $5.50-$8, ❻ *to 96th St.* ♿

The Metropolitan Museum of Art
Where to begin? The Met seems to be as big and sprawling as the city itself, and similarly the trick is finding the hidden (or not so hidden) treasures. Favorites include the spectacular Temple of Dendur, the American Wing Garden Court, the Medieval section, and in the summer, the Roof Garden where an older crowd sips white wine and ponders the sculptures (out loud). Don't do too much or follow a strict plan — this is the best place to get lost in the City.
Upper East Side, Fifth Ave. (at 82nd St.), (212) 535-7710, www.metmuse um.org. Open: T-R, 9:30am-5:30pm, F-Sa 9:30am-9:00pm, Su 9:30am-5:30pm. MC, V, AmEx, Admission (suggested): $5-$10, ❹❺❻ *to 86th St.* ♿

Mount Vernon Hotel Museum and Garden
John Adams' daughter wanted to replicate Mount Vernon here, but ended up with this 1799 carriage house. Formerly a hotel, it later became offices for Standard Oil. Now the museum displays classic American memorabilia from the 1820s-40s in reconstructed rooms — a tavern, kitchen, bedroom, and several parlors. There are lectures regularly, along with live music and an outdoor café open during the summer months.
Upper East Side, 421 East 61st St. (bet. First and York Aves.),

The Museums of the Museum Mile

♦ Cooper-Hewitt National Design Museum
Andrew Carnegie asked for a modest building to house his art and got this mansion of high ceilings and great art that even has a curator just for its wall coverings.

♦ The Frick Collection
A lot of money can buy a lot of great art and that's just what's happened at the Frick gallery where one old white guy's collection makes for a museum.

♦ International Center of Photography
Relocating soon, catch their thorough collection of some of the greatest photographers, while you still can.

♦ The Metropolitan Museum of Art
The Godfather of art in America. All the greatest hits of the last couple of centuries can be found here.

♦ National Academy of Design
Art varies, but a strong slant towards portraiture assures visitors they will know exactly who's been involved with the museum.

♦ Solomon R. Guggenheim
Frank Lloyd Wright's multi-story parking lot/gigantic toilet bowl houses sometimes good, sometimes bad exhibitions.

(212) 838-6878. Open: Tu-Su 11am-4pm. MC, V, AmEx, Admission: $2-$3, N R 4 5 6 *to 59th St.-Lexington Ave.*

Museum of American Illustration

View the work of key illustrators like Norman Rockwell and N.C. Wyeth at the home of the elite Society of Illustrators, which claims a long history of service to none other than the United States Army. Educational opportunities include sketch classes and lectures.

Upper East Side, 128 East 63rd St. (at Lexington Ave.), (212) 838-2560, www.societyillustrators.org. Open T 10am-8pm, W-F 10am-5pm, Sa 12pm-4pm. Admission: free, N R 4 5 6 *to 59th St.-Lexington Ave.*

National Academy of Design

Founded in 1825 to promote the art of design in America through painting, sculpture, architecture, and engraving, the academy still strives to meet its same purpose through training young artists and serving as a fraternal organization for other distinguished American artists. Its permanent exhibit features works by such 19th Century masters as Winslow Homer, John Singer Sargent, and Thomas Eakins, and such contemporary artists as Robert Rauschenberg, Isabel Bishop, and Phillip Johnson.

Upper East Side, 1083 Fifth Ave. (bet. 89th and 90th Sts.), (212) 369-4880, www.nationalacademy.org. Open W-R, Sa-Su 12pm-5pm, F 10am-6pm. MC, V, AmEx, Admiss-ion: $4.50-$8, 4 5 6 *to 86th St.* ♿

Mo's Caribbean Bar and Mexican Grill

Mo's is a garish and festive East Side anachronism. It'll probably strike you as super-cheesy until your second or third stiff mai tai.

Upper East Side, 1454 Second Ave. (Bet. 76th and 77th Sts.), (212) 650-0561. Open M-F 4pm-4am, S-Su 1130am-4am. MC, V, AmEx, D, DC. 6 *to 77th St.*

92nd Street Y

One of New York's most valuable cultural resources serves as an umbrella for a multitude of classes, workshops and speak and reading series. The Unterberg Poetry Series is by far the city's most star-studded, consistently drawing the finest poets and authors, both national and international, established and emerging.

Upper East Side, 1395 Lexington Avenue (at 92nd St.), (212) 996-1100, 6 *to 96th St.,* ♿

Solomon R. Guggenheim Museum

It's now hard to imagine upper Fifth Ave. without Frank Lloyd Wright's famous spiral of a building, home to one of the most remarkable 20th century art collections in the world. Special exhibits wind their way down interior ramps.

Upper East Side, 1071 Fifth Ave. (at 89th St.), (212) 360-3500, www.guggenheim.com. Open Su-W 10am-6pm, F-Sa 10am-8pm. MC, V, AmEx, Admission: $7-$12, 4 5 6 *to 86th St.* ♿

The Spanish Institute

Exhibitions, events, and lectures acquaint visitors with Spanish culture. Semester-long language classes include the perks of access to both the reference collection and reading room with current publications. Go, Iberia, go!

Upper East Side, 684 Park Ave. (bet. 68th and 69th Sts.), (212) 628-0420, www.spanishinstitute.org. 6 *to 68th St. - Hunter College.* ♿

Temple Emanu-El

Founded in the mid-nineteenth century when Jews began to arrive in New York in significant numbers, Temple Emanu-El is the first Reform congregation in NYC and the largest Jewish house of worship in the world. The temple conducts religious school, nursery school and continuing education supported by an extensive library and Judaica collection. Sabbath services Fridays at 5:15pm and Saturday at 10:30am.

Upper East Side, 1 East 65th (at Fifth Ave.), (212) 744-1400. www.emanuelnyc.org. N R *to Fifth Ave.*

The Whitney Museum of American Art

A mother lode of American avant-garde and post-modern art. Provocative shows are the rule: the ever-controversial Biennial, an exhibit of contemporary works held in odd-numbered years, never fails to rile critics.

Upper East Side, 945 Madison Ave. (at 75th St.), (212) 570-3676, www. whitney.org. Open: W, F, Sa-Su 11am-6pm, R 1pm-8pm. MC, V, AmEx, Ad-mission: $7-$9, 6 *to 77th St.* ♿

♦ GALLERIES & LIBRARIES

Acquavella

Uptown gallery hoppers never overlook this mother lode of 19th and 20th century European masters and postwar European and American pieces.

Upper East Side, 18 East 79th St. (bet. Fifth and Madison Aves.), (212) 734-6300, www.acquavella galleries.com. Open M-F 10am-5pm. 6 *to 77th St.* ♿

Christie's

Scope out the goods at the free public viewing five days before an auction at this New York branch of the London legend; 19th and 20th century European art, traditionally favored here, is still a strong suit.

Upper East Side, 219 East 67th St. Park Ave. (bet. Second and

Third Aves.), (212) 606-0400, www. christies.com. Open M-F 9:30am-5:30pm. ❻ to 68th St.

Gagosian

A vast gallery filled by established artists who are often eager to take advantage of the space. As such, large paintings, three-dimensional pieces, and sculpture often come into play, and the results can be more absorbing than a similar show executed in a smaller area. Even when this physical potential isn't realized, the art is usually worth checking out.

Upper East Side, 980 Madison Ave. (bet. 76th and 77th Sts.), (212) 744-2313, www.gagosian.com. Open T-Sa 10am-6pm. ❻ to 77th St. ♿

Knoedler Gallery

Not to be missed by art historians or art historians in-the-making, the oldest New York-based art gallery, established in 1846, exhibits such modern greats as Nancy Graves, Robert Motherwell, Frank Stella, and Robert Rauschenberg.

Upper East Side, 19 East 70th St. (bet. Madison and Fifth Aves.), (212) 794-0550, www.artnet.com. Open M-F 9:30am-5:30pm. ❻ to 68th St.-Hunter College. ♿

New York Society Library

George Washington, James Feni-more Cooper, Henry Thoreau, and Herman Melville all frequented the oldest circulating library in New York, founded in 1754. Nowadays you'll have to fork over 90 bucks ($135 for non-students) for the privilege of perusing literature in the luxurious reading rooms. Non-members are accommodated in the ground floor's reference room.

Upper East Side, 53 East 79th St. (bet. Madison and Park Aves.), (212) 288-6900, www.nysoclib.org. Open M,W,F-Sa 9am-5pm, T,R 9am-7pm. ❻ to 77th St.

Salander-O'Reilly Galleries

Twentieth century Mod-ernist American paint-ers of the Stieglitz group are exhibited alongside a new generation of similarly daring, young artists.

Upper East Side, 20 East 79th St. (bet. Madison and Fifth Aves.), (212) 879-6606, www.salander. com. Open M-Sa 9:30am-5:30pm. ❻ to 77th St.

William Secord Gallery

While the occasional feline or barnyard theme sneaks in, this anomalous uptown gallery is known for its carefully (and very seriously) curated and meticulously selected dog art. True canine addicts not fully satiated by this gallery alone need not distress: a similar showcase, the Dog Museum, once directed by Secord as well, exists in St. Louis.

Upper East Side, 52 East 76th Street, 3rd Floor (bet. Park and Madison Aves.), (212) 249-0075, www.dogpainting.com. Open M-Sa 10am-5pm. ❻ to 77th St.

Nightlife

♦ BARS

American Trash
Bikers and bankers meet without colliding at this East Side dive; its subtitle —"professional drinking establishment" — suggests democracy among lushes.
Upper East Side, 1471 First Ave. (bet. 76th & 77th Sts.), (212) 988-9008. Open M-Su 12pm-4am. MC, V, AmEx, ❻ to 77th St. ♿ 🚬

Auction House
Mature customers populate this pricey, baroque lounge, a microcosm of the Upper East Side. Good-looking, fashionable women encouraged.
Upper East Side, 300 East 89th St. (bet. First and Second Aves.), (212) 427-4458. Open M-Su 7:30pm-2am. MC, V, AmEx, DC, D, ❹❺❻ to 86th St. 🚬

American Spirits
There's something vaguely terrifying about the lighting situation in this dive. It's popular with the mid-20s set, probably due to karaoke on Tuesday and Thursday nights, and an epic daily happy hour.
Upper East Side, 1744 Second Ave. (at 91st St.), (212) 289-7510. Open Su-T 3pm-4am, F-Sa 12pm-4am. MC, V, AmEx, DC, D, ❹❺❻ to 86th St. 🚬

Amsterdam Billiard Club
More genteel than most pool halls, the ABC is the kind of place that's full of old men and dark wood. Weekends can get feisty, but mostly the scene is laid-back, with lots of regulars, such as actor/owner Paul Sorvino.
Upper East Side, 210 E. 86th St. (bet. Second and Third Aves.), (212) 570-4545. Open Su-W 12pm-2am, R-Sa 12pm-3am. MC, V, AmEx, D, ❹❺❻ to 86th St. 🚬

Big Sur
If the shenanigans of the young working crowd enjoying rock music in comfortable seating doesn't suit you, check out the alternate social scene near the unisex bathrooms.

An INY Interview with Upper East Side Resident Holden Caufield

NYU Student Holden Caufield in 1958

INY: Holden what have you been doing for the last fifty years?

HC: Therapy mostly. There was a point in the 60s when I got really good at squash, but it didn't pan out.

INY: Tell us about the red hat.

HC: I started balding when I was sixteen. More than anything this was the reason for my insecurities and non-stop whining.

INY: You used to want to save children, do you have children?

HC: No, I hate children. Those years were the worst of my life.

INY: How about phony, do you still think people are phony?

HC: I think you're phony. I think this interview's over too. God, I miss my brother.

The Upper East Side of Manhattan . . . is the province of Let's Pretend.
—Gail Sheehy

Upper East Side, 1406 Third Ave. (at 80th St.), (212) 472-5009. Open M-Su 5pm-4am. MC, V, AmEx, DC, ⑥ to 77th St.

Brother Jimmy's

Anyone from below the Mason-Dixon line will feel at home in this southern theme bar. Post-collegiates pre-professionals come for the generous bartenders and Sunday special: $18.95 for unlimited beer and all the ribs you can stomach.

Upper East Side, 1461 First Ave. (at 76th St.), (212) 288-0999, Open M-F 5pm-2am, Sa-Su 12pm-??. MC, V, AmEx, ⑥ to 77th St.

The Cocktail Room

Painted in neon colors and furnished with '60s mod dinettes, the Cocktail Room looks like something out of "A Clockwork Orange." No moloko synthemesc here, though. Instead, enjoy an impressive array of extremely well-made cocktails. The prices are a bit steep, but the pours are generous. Light tapas menu available.

Upper East Side, 334 East 73rd St. (bet. First and Second Aves.), (212) 988-6100. Open M-Sa 5pm-4am. MC, V, AmEx, D, ④⑤⑥ to 72nd St.

Hogs & Heifers East

While a little tamer than its downtown cousin, Hogs East is still a raunchy, good-times country & western bar. The beers are always cold and cheap, and the music is always live, whether there's a band playing or just a bunch of drunks singing along to Willie Nelson on the juke.

Upper East Side, 1843 First Ave. (bet. 92nd and 93rd Sts.), (212) 722-8635. Open M-Su 2pm-4am. Cash Only, ⑥ to 96th St.

Lexington Bar and Books

This pricey, high-class cigar bar offering great ambience and fantastic martinis is a nice place to pretend you're all grown up with the white-collars here. College students beware: "proper attire is required". Live jazz on Fridays and Saturdays.

Upper East Side, 1020 Lexington Ave. (at 73rd St.), (212) 717-3902. Open Su-R 4pm-2am, F-Sa 5pm-4am. MC, V, AmEx, DC, ⑥ to 77th St.

Oke Doke

Rumor has it that not even Jack Nicholson can always get past the octogenarian proprietor Elsie, the toughest door-woman around, at this intimate, after-hours spot.

Upper East Side, 307 East 84th St. (bet. First and Second Aves.), (212) 650-9424. Open M-Su 9:30pm-4am. Cash Only, ④⑤⑥ to 86th St.

Subway Inn

It's right across the way from Bloomingdale's, but you'll seldom see shoppers take a load off their Blahniks at this perfect dive bar. Dark, smelly, dirty, and cheap, Subway is heroically antithetical to the glittering, artificially chipper retail stores surrounding it. Drink up and then tumble down the conveniently proximate subway entrance.

Upper East Side, 143 East 60th St. (at Lexington Ave.), (212) 223-8929. M-Sa 8am-4am, Su 12pm-4am. Cash Only, NR456 to 59th St.-Lexington Ave.

♦ MUSIC

The Sun Music Company

A new version of the famous but recently-defunct Fast Folk Cafe, The Sun Music Company is more for the performer than the audience. Weekend shows regularly feature touring artists and indie-label acts, and Mondays host a workshop series on things such as guitar playing, song-writing, vocal technique, and music business issues. Wine, beer, and snacks are available.

contemporary acoustic

Upper East Side, 340 East 71st St. (at First Ave.), (212) 396-9521, www.sunmusiccompany.com. Open 8:30pm-12am. Cash Only, Cover: $10, ⑥ to 68th St.-Hunter College.

Upper East Side

Alternative Dining

Let's face it: if you have special dining requirements, whether you keep kosher, or are a vegetarian or a vegan, you are often a frustrating dining partner. To eat with anyone who does not share your dining practice of choice has always been an annoyance. You often have to choose between two equally unfulfilling options: awkward apologies for dragging everyone else to a specialty restaurant or settling for a regular restaurant with the ubiquitous "green salad with nothing, thank you."

But now you are in New York, and all of that is about to change. In a city with more restaurants than anyone can keep track of, there are quite a few places geared to any kind of alternative diet. And, quite a few great ones for you and your more carnivorous friends to enjoy. So stop apologizing and enjoy the culinary possibilities of the greatest city in the world.

Word of mouth is probably the best way to find out about good places, as other alternative diners can give you their reviews. Citysearch's New York website is updated fairly regularly, and it has vegetarian and kosher categories. Check out **Shamash's** index (**www.shamash.org/kosher**) for kosher listings that are good, if a bit slow to catch up. **Vegeats** (**www.vegeats.com**) has links to several good vegetarian and vegan restaurant indexes.

Vegetarians have it slightly easier than those with other restrictions, as there are so many vegetarian restaurants in the city. Most regular restaurants have a good (and often less expensive than the regular entree) vegetarian option on the menu, assuming that you are not in a steakhouse.

If you are looking for great veg dining, however, try a restaurant that specializes in preparing great vegetarian dishes. **Zen Palate** has three locations in the city and an interesting mix of vegetarian Asian cuisines (the Broadway branch is a favorite with many kosher Upper West Siders as well). If you know where to look, good vegetarian restaurants often turn up in unlikely places.

The laid-back atmosphere of **Spring Street Natural** is a refreshing contradiction to its SoHo location, and **Zenith**, with its untouristy menu, somehow finds itself in the theater district. **Ozu** is another rare find; this tiny little macrobiotic house resides just below Spanish Harlem. In Brooklyn, check out one of the two branches of **Henrietta's** (**Healthy Henrietta's** on Henry Street and **Henrietta's on the Slope** in Park Slope), which serves mostly good vegetarian Mexican food, but has other options as well.

Vegans will have a harder time finding specifically vegan restaurants, but most vegetarian restaurants will have several vegan options on their menu. If you don't see them on the menu, ask. But be careful — not every waiter, even in hardcore vegetarian places, necessarily knows what vegan means. Better to ask them to check with the chef or head waiter. The most famous of the restaurants that are entirely vegan and organic is the **Angelica Kitchen**, but try to avoid the mealtime crowds. **Vege Vege** on Third Avenue serves fantastic Asian vegan food. **Bachue** is a tiny find on 21st Street that serves many kinds of vegan dishes. And be sure to check out **Organica**, in Brooklyn, who's been getting rave reviews for the last two years.

Kosher restaurants in the City tend to cluster on the Upper West Side, especially on 72nd Street between West End and Columbus. The ribs at **Dougie's** have become quite famous, but think twice before bringing a date as the food is pretty messy. Go down the block to **Provi Provi**, an excellent and quiet dairy restaurant, or **Eden Wok**, which has the only kosher hibachi tables in New York.

The real treasures in kosher city dining, though, are the ones that are hiding in other neighborhoods, away from the kosher strip on the Upper West Side. The priciest is **Levana**, where you can sample delicacies that you might not find kosher anywhere else in the world, like bison and venison. Also expensive, but well worth it, **Va Bene** and **Tevere 84** are, respectively, the dairy and meat incarnations of an Upper East Side Italian restaurant. Try **Haikara** on Second Avenue for kosher sushi.

If you are with non-kosher friends who are willing to spend the money, take them to **Le Marais** in the theater district, an authentic Parisian-style steakhouse that you wouldn't know was kosher unless you were told. Ditto for the cluster of kosher Indian restaurants on Lexington in the 20s, which are consistently ranked among the best Indian places in the city. They are reasonably priced and most are vegetarian as well, so everyone can be happy together at one place. This is also true at **Caravan of Dreams**, a unique find in the East Village that is both vegetarian and kosher, and features beautiful décor and live music.

The best thing about these specialty restaurants, though, is the unique culture that they engender. Those with dining restrictions seem to have an unspoken bond between them, and this makes eating at these places a much friendlier experience. It is not uncommon for a fellow diner at Ozu to ask your opinion of the sautéed tofu with black bean sauce in exchange for a full account of the steamed root vegetable dumplings or the tofu raspberry pie.

Do not be surprised if a fellow kosher diner cheerily and without warning volunteers the location of a great new kosher Mexican place that just opened up. You've all had to eat a plain green salad at one time or another, and now, even with all these options, you retain that precious connection. Use it to your full advantage to find the best dishes and the best places, as no guide or website can ever compare to the word of mouth of your fellow New York alternative diners.

Central Park

If New York's a little bit safer and less prone to riots than other cities, it's because of Central Park. Central Park keeps New Yorkers from losing their heads. Who knows whether Frederick Law Olmstead knew this when he submitted his design of the park to the city in 1857. All we know is that he wanted to create a park where New Yorkers of all classes could relax in a life size imitation of pastoral England.

Central Park is 843 acres of 270,000 trees, shrubs and vines and ten million cart loads of rock. None of it was here when Olmstead started and it's testament to New York's spirit that they created such a perfect imitation of nature with the same facility they put buildings over what was once all nature. The park took sixteen years to build, displaced 1,600 squatters and cost the modern equivalent of $20 million.

That said, Central Park is visited by 20 million people a year and for a city notorious for draining cash, provides a welcome relief. While the antique castle carousel costs a dollar per ride, almost all the Park's attractions and events are free: including Belvedere Castle, the Swedish Cottage Marionette Theater, The Conservatory Garden, and Shakespeare in the Park.

Olmstead was let down when the park opened. It was the place the rich came to relax and lower classes weren't accepted. No longer true. Grazing in Sheep's Meadow was discontinued in 1934 and now you can stand in the middle of the field with crews of graffiti writing teenagers to the north and yuppies playing frisbee to the south.

In 1965, the park was declared a national historic landmark, and as a part of urban renewal and countercultural movements during the 60s, the park hosted rock concerts and "be-ins." Deterioration during the 1970s led to a revival of the Greensward Plan by the Central Park Conservancy in the 1980s, reinstating the park as the public respite it was constructed to be and is.

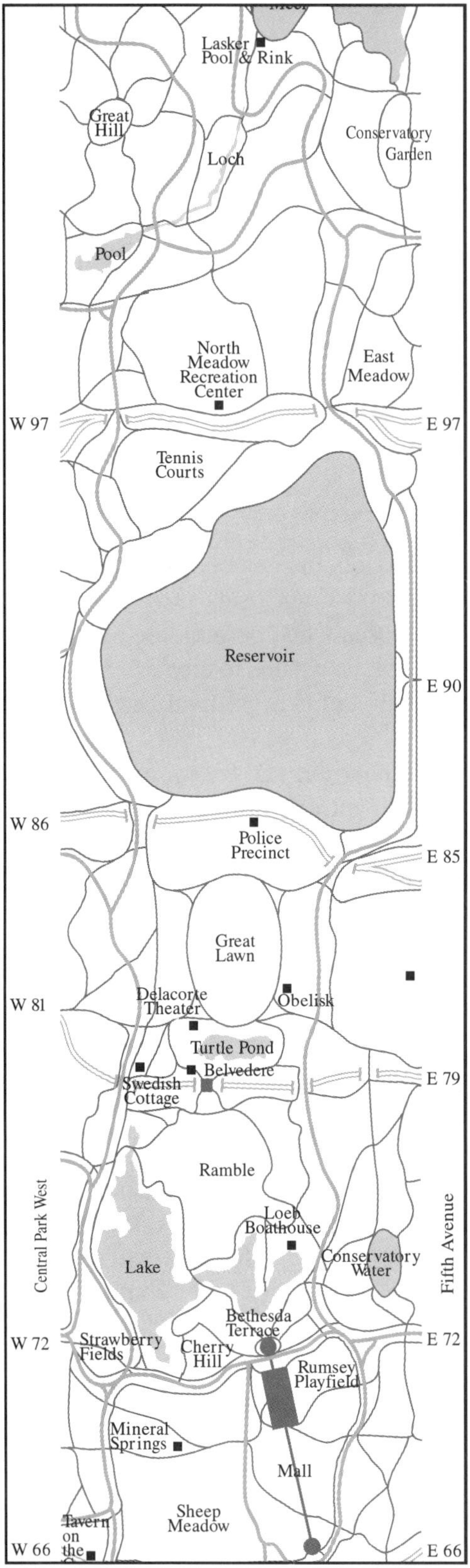

Dining

♦ RESTAURANTS

Tavern on the Green

Only the well-connected score the best seats, but the crystal chandeliers and tranquil setting are impressive, if a tad garish, from any area of this legendary Central Park outpost. The oysters and steak, along with a mind-boggling wine list, help to solidify the Tavern's reputation as one of New York's most prestigious restaurants; in winter, twinkling lights on the surrounding trees make for quite a Yuletide scene.

Central Park, Central Park West (at 67th St.), (212) 873-3200, www.tavern onthegreen.com. MC, V, AmEx, D, Entrées: $13-$25, B C to 72nd St. ♿

Arts & Recreation

♦ LEISURE

Bike Rentals

The cost is $8 - $14 per hour, depending on the bike; ID required. Open from the end of March to the end of October.

East Dr. (at 74th St.), (212) 861-4137, www.centralpark.org. MC, V, AmEx, DC, D, 6 to 77th St.

Bird-Watching at the Charles A. Dana Discovery Center

Over 270 different species of birds have been sighted in the park; expect to see about 150 species in the course of a year. The Central Park Conservancy and the Audubon Society (212-691-7483) organize bird-watching walks in May.

Central Park, 110th St. (bet. Fifth and Lenox Aves.), (212) 860-1370. Open M-Su 11am-5pm. 2 3 to 110th St. (Central Park North). ♿

Board Games

Chess players are welcome at the Chess and Checkers House at 64th St., west of the Dairy.

East Side of Park, 6 to 68th St.-Hunter College.

Central Park Zoo and Wildlife Center

Although the original Central Park zoo dates back to 1864, the current wildlife center opened in 1988 and covers 5 fi acres. Over two-dozen species including some endangered and threatened species like the Tamarin monkeys and red pandas live here. The staff also offers wildlife stories for

PLACES TO GO:

The Wildlife Conservation Center
Every half-hour make sure to be near the animal parade that dances around the clock. Then go inside and catch the feeding of sea lions and polar bears.

The Ramble
Weekend night's the rambles are a gay oasis of single men of all ages.

Claremont Riding Academy
This is your only chance to be an urban cowboy and not the sad desperate way of the movie, but literally you can ride a horse around the park.

kids, a wildlife theater in the summertime and wildlife chats. There are guided tours daily at 2:30, penguin feeding at 10:30 and 2:30 and sea lion feedings at 11:30, 2 and 4. If you're a Manhattanite who can't make it up to the Bronx, consider the Central Park Wildlife Center as a smaller alternative.
Central Park, 64th St. (at Fifth Ave.), (212) 861-6630, www.wcs.org. Open M-Su 10am-5pm, winter 10am-4:30pm, N R to Fifth Ave.

Claremont Riding Academy
Horses are $35 per hour for experienced riders only. A half-hour private lesson is $42. Stables are on Central Park West (bet. 89th and 90th Sts.). For the more sedentary, horse-drawn carriages leave from 59th St. on the east side.
Central Park, 175 W. 89th St. (at Amsterdam Ave.), (212) 247-5100. Open M-F 6:30am-10pm,Sa-Su 6:30am-5pm, MC, V, B C to 86th St., 1 9 to 86th St.

Fishing
The Harlem Meer stocks large-mouthed bass for fishing on a strictly catch-and-return basis. Bamboo rods and other equipment are available free of charge at the Charles A. Dana Discovery Center.
Central Park, 110th St. (bet. Fifth and Lenox Aves.), (212) 860-1370. Open M-Su 11am-5pm. 2 3 to 110th St. (Central Park North). ♿

Horse and Carriage Rides
A Central Park tradition, the horse and carriage ride is an emblem of old Manhattan. Year round, buggies pick up

tourists along 59th Street for variable-length tours around midtown and the park. The super friendly drivers know it's a romantic's must-do, and jack up the prices accordingly. Blankets are provided in the winter months.
Central Park, 59th St. (at Fifth Ave.) N R to 59th St.-Fifth Ave.

Organized Tours
The Central Park Conservancy (212-360-2726), Columbia University's Big Onion Walking Tours (212-439-1090), and The New York Historical Society (212-873-3400) all give historical tours of the park.
Call (718) 291-6825 for info.

Park View at the Boathouse
The Boathouse rents boats at $10 per hour plus a $30 deposit; model boat regattas and races are held on weekends on Conservatory Water. Open March-October.
Central Park, Fifth Ave. (at 72nd St.), (212) 517-2233, www.parkviewrestaurant.com. Open M-Su 10am-dusk. MC, V, 6 to 68th St.-Hunter College.

Shakespeare in the Park

Productions can be uneven and the star-studded casts underwhelming and overblown, but what better way to spend a balmy summer evening than sitting under the night sky in this intimate theater-in-the-round watching the best dramas by the best writer in the Western world? Tickets are free, but working folks will have to take a personal day to line up at sunrise to obtain seats to the more popular shows. (The bigger the stars, the longer the queue.) Tickets are distributed the day of the performance beginning at 1pm at the Delacorte and Public Theaters.
Central Park (at West 79th St.), 212-539-8500, Open: T-Su, June-September

Wollman Ice Rink

A New York tradition. If you're renting skates or bringing your own, Wollman rink is open in the season to figure skaters and ice hockey players at all levels. Lessons are available for a hefty fee, and most skaters are willing to fall over on the ice as long as they look great in their pea-coats. *Central Park, (at S. end of Park off Sixth Ave.), (212) 396-1010, www.wollmannrink.com. Open M-T 10am-3pm, W-R 10am-9:30pm, F-Sa 10am-11pm, Su 10am-9pm. $7 adults, $3.50 children and seniors. Skate rental $3.50.* A B C D 1 9 *to 59th St.-Columbus Circle*

♦ PERFORMANCE

Delacorte Theater

Shakespeare in the Park lures stars like Patrick Stewart and Andre Braugher to its leading roles. Tickets are free at the box office at 1pm on the day of the show. Be prepared to arrive as early as 4am on

weekends for the most popular shows, though you can sleep later on weekdays.

Central Park, W. side of park (near 81st St.), (212) 861-7277. B C *to 81st-Musuem of Natural History.*

Dana Discovery Center

A performance space for multicultural dance and music where the Harlem Meer Performance Festival is held.

Central Park, 110th St. (bet. Fifth and Lenox Aves.), (212) 860-1370, 2 3 *to 110th St. (Central Park North).* ♿

Metropolitan Opera

Bring wine and a picnic basket in June and listen to arias as the stars come out and the skyline lights up; arrive early for a good seat. People seated farther from the stage treat the opera as background music for their conversations so be prepared to shush. Admission is free.

Central Park, Great Lawn, (212) 362-6000. B C *to 81st St.-Museum of Natural History.*

SummerStage

A summer-long program of concerts, poetry readings, modern dance shows, and other events.

Central Park, mid-park at 72nd St. (at Rumsey Playground), (212) 360-2777. B C *to 72nd St.*

Swedish Cottage Marionette Theater

Performances take place on Saturday afternoons; call for reservations.

Central Park, W. Park (at 84st St.), (212) 988-9093. Cash Only, Admission $4-$5, B C *to 81st St.*

♦ SITES

Belvedere Castle

One of the main attractions at the Castle, apart from the view, is the Henry Luce Nature Observatory, which identifies local bird and plant life. Also located here is the Weather Center, the source for New York local weather forecasters. *Central Park, mid-park near 79th St.*

The Carousel

Open for slow-paced spinning year round.

Central Park, mid-park (at 64th St.), (212) 879-0244.

The Conservatory Garden

This garden is one of New York's best examples of formal landscaping in the European tradition, with fountains, flowers, and shaded pathways.

Central Park, E. side (near 105th St.)

The Dairy

The Dairy, overlooking Wollman Rink, has visitor information about Central Park including a reference library and historical exhibit. You can also find a 12-foot model of the

Central Park Summer Stage

Central Park SummerStage is New York's premier free performing arts festival. Through out the summer expect events from all genres. It could be a personal concert with Ani De Fracnco or a Hip Hop retrospective featuring Biz Markie and Doug E. Fresh or Manu Chao or Middle Eastern Drumming. The New York Grand Opera has been doing eight years of Verdi and this is probably the only chance to see more than ten people show up for probably the best spoken word in town. Events are throughout the summer, check out their web page, www.summerstage.org, for listings.

entire park as well as an interactive touch-screen display.
Central Park, mid park (at 65th St.), (212) 794-6564. Open M-Su 11am-5pm, winter 11am-4pm, ❶❾ to 66th St.

The Reservoir
The Reservoir lies directly to the north of the Great Lawn, recently refurbished by the Parks Department. It is circled by the park's main running track, which is about a mile-and-a-half around and named for Jacqueline Onassis.
Central Park, mid-park (be. 86th and 96th Sts.)

The Mall
A stately avenue lined with trees and statues of great literary figures leads up to the bandshell and fountain at Bethesda Terrace.
Central Park, E. side (bet. 65th-72nd Sts.)

The Ramble
This 37-acre natural woodland has winding paths and open lawns; the perfect place to bring a book and read in the shade.
Central Park. NE. side of the lake.

The Shakespeare Garden
Leading upwards to Belvedere Castle, The Shakespeare Garden is reminiscent of the villa gardens of Northern Italy. In this formal garden grows every species of flower or plant mentioned in Shakespeare's plays.
Central Park, W. side (at 80th St.)

Sheep Meadow
The hot spot for sun-worshippers, Frisbee-players, and kite-flyers of all ages, sizes, and shapes. On sunny afternoons in summer, the grass cannot be seen for all the bodies, hence the nickname "Gettysburg."
Central Park, W. side (at mid-60's.)

Strawberry Fields
The heart-shaped grove, a memorial to John Lennon, is right across from the Dakota Building where Lennon was shot. The name references a famous Beatles song.
Central Park, W. side(at 72nd St).

The Wildlife Conservation Center
Open year-round, this zoo features fun for the whole family.
Central Park, Fifth Ave. (at 64th St.), (212) 861-6030.

Nightlife

♦ BARS

Loeb Boathouse
It's probably the only place to get a cocktail in Central Park; luckily, it's a gorgeous one. Come and pass a warm afternoon at one of the outside tables and watch city slickers haplessly plying the oars on rental dinghies. Hours vary with the season (and weather) and rarely extend past nine, so call ahead. Adjacent cafe serves food.
Central Park, Central Park Lake (at 74th St.), (212) 517-2233. Open W-Sa 6pm-10pm, Buffet/Brunch Sa-Su 11:00am-3:00pm. MC, V, AmEx, DC, D, Ⓑ Ⓒ to 72nd St.

Running

Thousands of runners converge on Central Park nearly everyday and many meet on weekends for a road race sponsored by the New York Road Runners Club. Over 30,000 runners from around the globe run the New York City Marathon every November. If running's your thing Central Park's the place, and if company's what you need, here's who you should get in touch with.

♦ New York Road Runners Club, Inc.
212-860-4455

♦ Achilles Track Club
An international club for athletes with disabilities. 212-354-0300

♦ Front Runners
A gay and lesbian running group. 212-724-9700

♦ Millrose Athletic Association
Ideal for the amateur looking to get serious. ($20 membership fee) 212-663-5641

♦ Warren Street Social and Athletic Club
Training and competition. 212-807-7422

Upper West Side

It's 6pm and taxis head South on Broadway, past institutions like the gourmet store Zabars, towards the restaurants across the street from Lincoln Center—the city's most esteemed venue for the arts. Diners tell the waiter more times than he can stand that they have to make a show by 7:30.

Twenty blocks North, it's happy hour and the Upper West Side's thriving ghetto of young bankers are packed in Amsterdam and Columbus Avenue's bars, drinking anything from $2 beers to $11 martinis. Things move a little slower in this neighborhood and tomorrow there'll be no sign of a hang over, just an army of parents out with their kids headed towards Central or Riverside Park, with maybe a stop for brunch on the way.

The Upper West Side's growth has been the well-paced, well-rounded growth of someone born into a good family. A hundred years ago it was a good suburb called Bloomingdale where many New Yorkers rushed to to get away from the pace of the still hectic downtown life. The completion of the Ninth Avenue elevated train in 1879 brought things closer, but the neighborhood still stood on its own, closer to downtown, but just as far away in attitude. The Dakota, the famous apartment building and site of John Lennon's assassination, received its name because it was so far from downtown it might as well have been in the Dakotas.

The area did not truly become the Upper West Side until the development of Central Park from 1856 to 1873. Its completion spurred a wave of construction, and by the turn of the 20th Century, institutions like the American Museum of Natural History moved into the neighborhood along the Park's exterior. The extension of the Inter-borough Rapid Transit in 1904 spurred the construction of many new residential buildings and the population skyrocketed over the next 25 years.

It hasn't changed much since then; while not as hypersocial as Greenwich Village, the Upper West Side replaces the dowtown pace with a more mature mixture of work and play. Traditionally it's associated with moderate-to-liberal intellectuals, but there are just as many young professionals East of Broadway. West End Avenue is as close to complete calm as there is in the city, the only danger is side-stepping all the dogs and baby carriages.

Dining

◆ RESTAURANTS

Ayurveda Café

Upper Westsiders swear by this quaint Indian restaurant with a daily prix-fixed menu. The food is vegetarian and based on the Hindu philosophies of Ayurveda. What that boils down to is simple, healthful, holistic food that satisfies without being too filling.

Upper West Side, 706 Amsterdam Ave. (bet 94th and 95th Sts.), (212) 932-2400. Open M-Su, 11:30am-11pm, MC, V, AmEx, D, Entrees: $9-16, 2 3 1 9 *to 96th St.* ♿

Boulevard

A fun family restaurant with Sesame Street-style murals and all-you-can-eat specials on Monday nights; screaming babies covered in mashed potatoes, platefuls of enormous dinosaur ribs, and the Maryland crabcakes are all part of the charm. You'll have to request the aptly named "Liquid Hell" barbecue sauce, which is kept hidden in back.

Upper West Side, 2398 Broadway (at 88th St.), (212) 874-7400. Open M-F 11:30pm-11pm, Sa-Su 11am-12am. MC, V, AmEx, Entrées: $7-$18, 1 9 *to 86th St.*

Bruculino

Sicilian seafood cooked to perfection is served in the soothing wood and wave interior of this West Side culinary treasure. Dishes are inventive and colorful. Outdoor seating is available on the terrace. Try the specials of the evening and leave room for coffee and dessert!

Upper West Side, 225 Columbus Ave. (at 70th St.), (212) 579-3966. Open M-Sa 12pm-3pm, 5pm-11pm, Su 12pm-3pm, 5pm-10pm. MC, V, AmEx, Entrées: $10-$20, B C *to 72nd St.*

Cafe Des Artistes

You'll feel glamorous at this classic New York restaurant. Don't get addicted to that feeling though, because visiting this romantic rendezvous too often will clean out your wallet as seductively as it filled you up.

Upper West Side, 1 W. 67th St. (bet. Columbus Ave. and Central Park West), (212) 877-3500, www.cafedesartistes.com. Open 12pm-3pm, 5:30pm-12am, Sa 11am-3pm, 5:30pm-12am, Su 10am-3pm, 5:30pm-11pm. MC, V, AmEx, DC, Entrées: $30-$40, 1 9 *to 66th St.-Lincoln Center.* ♿

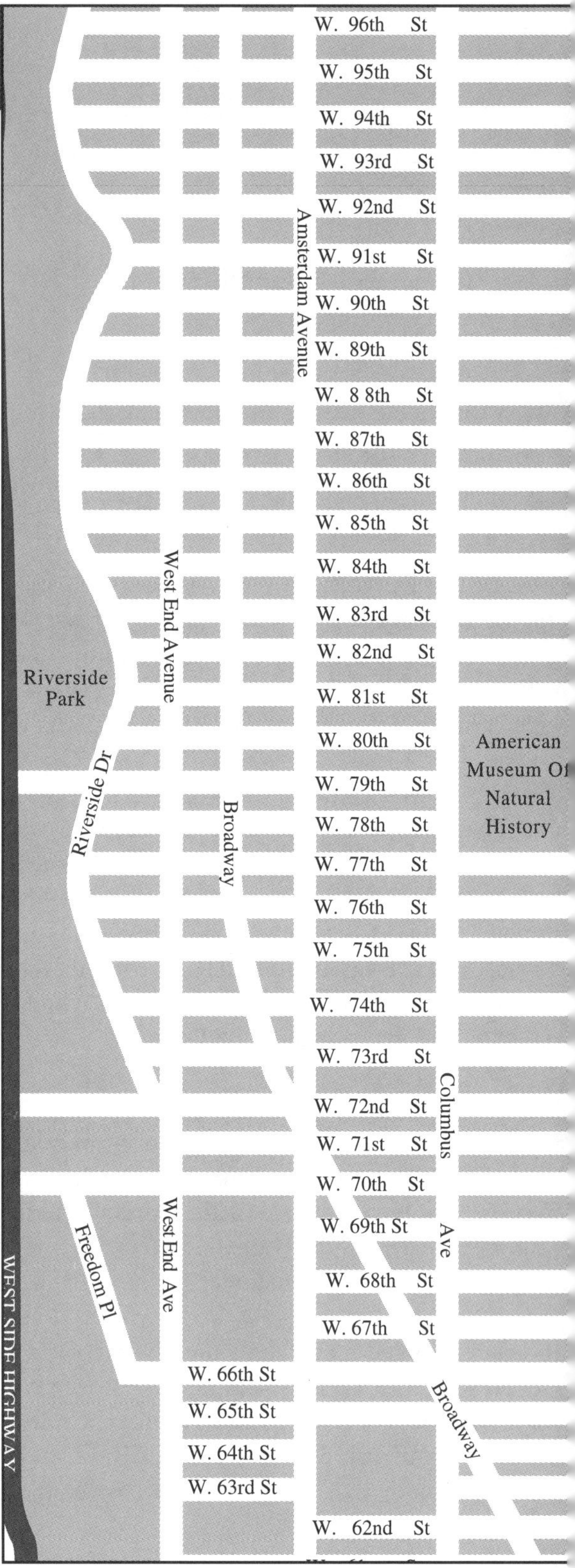

PLACES TO GO:

Ayurveda Café
Reasonably priced vegetarian Indian food, served simply in steaming steel bowls full of the sort of food that fills without hurting.

Citarella
No produce has better names than fish: halibut, monkfish, grouper, snapper, flounder, large mouth bass, all fresh at Citarella's.

Stand-Up NY
Unlike Caroline's in midtown, which features big name talent, for big time money, Stand-Up NY is the real deal, where people get booed, cheered and sometimes make it.

Carmine's
Come with a group of friends and order up a storm of family-style Italian. Seating is slow, so a visit to this enormous darkwood institution happily mandates a stop at the lovely bar.
Upper West Side, 2450 Broadway (bet. 90th and 91st Sts.), (212) 362-2200. Open M-R 11:30am-3pm, 5pm-11pm. F 11:30am-3pm, 5pm-12am, Sa 11am-12am, Su 2pm-10pm. MC, V, AmEx, Entrées: $15-$25, 1 2 3 9 to 96th St.

Deli Kasbah
Orthodox patrons fill the dining room, while take-out satisfies folks of all faiths with amazingly fresh meats and stellar entrées, like the jumbo pastrami burger. The menu has a Middle Eastern slant, with lots of hummus, babaganoush, and falafel; sample all three of them in the Kasbah Combination.
Upper West Side, 251 W. 85th St. (bet. Broadway and West End Ave.), (212) 496-1500. Open Su-R 12pm-10pm. MC, V, D, Entrées: $8-$20, 1 9 to 86th St.

Gabriel's
Among the crème de la crème of the bevy of restaurants around Lincoln Center, the combination of casual and class here is just about perfect. Beautiful decor, an astonishing, seasonal menu (order the delectable butternut squash ravioli if on the menu!), and a refined yet informal staff all account for why this is one of New York's hottest spots for dinner. Come after 7:45 pm to avoid the pre-concert crowd.
Upper West Side, 11 W. 60th St. (bet. Broadway and Columbus Ave.), (212) 956-4600. Open M-R 12pm-3pm, 5:30pm-11pm, F-Sa 5:30pm-12am. MC ,V, AmEx, D. Entrées: $25-$27, A B C D 1 9 to 59th St.-Columbus Circle.

Gennaro
Native Italian chef Gennaro Picone graced several upscale Manhattan establishments before opening his own place where he serves unpretentious, truly Italian (not Italian-American) dishes in a tiny, unassuming space. The decor may seem a little rough around the edges, but the food is most definitely not (try the gnocchi), and the prices are so reasonable that they impose a $20 minimum. But be warned, the waits are long and the space is cramped.
Upper West Side, 665 Amsterdam Ave. (bet. 92nd and 93rd Sts.), (212) 665-5348. Open M-F 5pm-11pm, Sa-Su 5pm-11:30pm. Cash Only, Entrées: $8-$15, 1 2 3 9 to 96th St.

Good Enough to Eat
The line to get into this popular brunch spot can often be seen from a few blocks away (no reservations accepted). Those who stick it out choose from ample portions of old-fashioned favorites and enjoy the warm, cozy atmosphere. "Just like Mom used to make" specialties include Cinnamon Swirl French Toast ($8.50) and Lumberjack breakfast ($8.00).

Lincoln Center's Midsummer Night Swing

For two decades Lincoln Center has given New Yorker's a chance to dance in the open air, to live music of all genres. Basically you have two options: If you're not sure about your skills arrive at 6pm and, for $11, get a free dancing lesson. It doesn't matter if you don't have a partner, there are plenty of other singles very willing to dance with you. If you know how to dance arrive later, anytime after 8pm, that's when the live band starts up. On any given night during the summer you can dance anything from Merengue to Mambo to Swing to Tango to Irish Jig. They also have food.

Dinner is served nightly.

Upper West Side, 483 Amsterdam Ave. (bet. 83rd and 84th Sts.), (212) 496-0163. Open M-F 8am-4pm, 5:30pm-10:30pm, Sa-Su 9am-4pm, 5:30pm-10:30pm. MC, V, AmEx, Entrées: $18-$21, 1 9 to 86th St. ♿ 🚲

Jean Georges

Undoubtedly one of the best in New York. The food's like a narcotic in your blood stream meaning you don't realize how good the food is until later when no other food compares. Sublime's the word. Enjoy. Be warned: despite the three dining areas, it's still hard to get in.

Upper West Side, 1 Central Park West (bet. 60th and 61st Sts.), (212) 299-3900, www.jean-georges.com. Open M-F 12:30pm-2:30pm, 5:30pm-11pm, Sa-Su 12pm-3pm, 5:30pm-11pm. MC, V, AmEx, DC, Entrées: $24-$32, A B C D 1 9 to 59th St.-Columbus Circle. ♿

Merchants, NY

The West Side branch of a trio of sleek establishments of the same name, some actually order food here to go with their martini or cosmopolitan; check out the downstairs sofa scene for ultimate cushiness. The appetizer and dessert menus are excellent.

Upper West Side, 521 Columbus Ave. (bet. 85th and 86th Sts.), (212) 721-3689. Open M-Su 11:30am-2am. MC, V, AmEx, DC, Entrées: $10-$18, B C to 86th St. ♿

Niko's Mediterranean Grill and Bistro

Nearly always crammed to capa\city, this tavern offers a range of delicacies that take cues from all over the Mediterranean, particularly Greece and Lebanon. Noteworthy are the stuffed grape leaves and the rodos yuvetsi, a lamb stew. Afterwards, choose from among the array of authentic honey-drenched desserts.

Upper West Side, 2161 Broadway (at 76th St.), (212) 873-7000, www. nikosgrill.com. Open Su-R 11am-12am, F-Sa 11am-1am. MC, V, AmEx, D, Entrées: $10-$18, 1 2 3 9 to 72nd St. ♿ 🚲

Ozu

Though prompt seating can be a problem, this small, Japanese macrobiotic, near-organic restaurant wins points for its creative tofu, grain, noodle, tempura, and vegetable dishes. The ambitious side orders will transport you to new levels of sensual awareness, especially the three-root sesame salad with carrot, burdock root, and daikon radish.

Upper West Side, 566 Amsterdam Ave. (at 87th St.), (212) 787-8316. Open M-Su 11:30am-10:30pm. MC, V, AmEx, Entrées: $7-$12, 1 9 to 86th St. 🚲

Penang Malaysia

This lively, decked out Malaysian is usually packed on weekends and rightfully so; the food is innovative and tasty, the crowd generally young and hip, and there's live music and a lounge in the bar downstairs. Try eating down there to avoid the wait upstairs.

Upper West Side, 240 Columbus Ave. (at 71st St.), (212) 769-3988, www.penangnyc.com. Open M-R 12pm-12am, F-Sa 12am-1am, Su 12pm-11pm. MC, V, AmEx, DC, Entrées: $11-$20, B C to 72nd St. 🚲

Popover Cafe

New England charm meets New York savvy at this convivial spot, one of the most popular brunch venues in the neighborhood. Feast upon gourmet omelets and excellent griddle specialties — and don't forget the popovers.

Upper West Side, 551 Amsterdam Ave. (bet. 86th and 87th Sts.),

(212) 595-8555. Open M-R 8am-10pm, F 8am-11pm, Sa 9am-11pm, Su 9am-10pm. MC, V, AmEx, Entrées: $13-$22, 1 9 *to 86th St.* ♿

Rain

Delicious pan-Asian fusion cuisine and a vibrant, attractive crowd make this one of the Upper West Side's hottest dining spots. On Friday and Saturday nights, the bar overflows with 20-somethings trying to get a table, but the Asian canopy and exotic beers make it worth the wait.
Upper West Side, 100 W. 82nd St. (at Columbus Ave.), (212) 501-0776. Open M-R 12pm-11pm, F-Sa 12pm-12am, Su 12pm-10pm. MC, V, AmEx, D, Entrees $12-22, 1 9 *to 79th St..* ♿

Rikyu

The freedom to choose can be mind-boggling for early-bird diners taking advantage of the $9.95 prix fixe, with 17 dinner options. You can't go wrong with remarkably fresh sushi or any combination involving tempura, teriyaki, or cooked fish.
Upper West Side, 483 Columbus Ave. (bet. 83rd and 84th Sts.), (212) 799-7847. Open M-Su 12pm-11:30pm. MC, V, AmEx, D, Entrées: $10-$17, 1 2 3 9 *to 72nd St.* ♿

Ruby Foo's

Fun, cool, hip pan-Asian with everything from dim sum to sushi and a popular Sunday brunch.
Upper West Side, 2182 Broadway (at 77th St.), (212) 724-6700. Open M-Su 11:30am-4pm, MC, V, AmEx, Entrées: $25, 1 9 to 79th St. ♿

Saigon Grill

One of the tastiest and best-priced Vietnamese restaurants in the city, and a favorite of Upper West Siders. Not much elbow room, so go early to avoid the crowds.You'll be craving the fresh summer rolls for days afterward.
Upper West Side, 2381 Broadway (at 87th St.), (212) 875-9072. Open M-Su 11am-12am. MC, V, AmEx, D, Entrées: $7-$13, 1 9 *to 86th St.*

Sarabeth's

This cheerful, yellow cafe is brimming with old-fashioned goodness. Sarabeth's serves hearty breakfasts and light, sophisticated lunches, but for a special treat, drop in for afternoon tea between 3:30 and 5:30. You'll feel like the Queen of England as you sip tea and nibble on finger sandwiches, cookies, and scones.
Upper West Side, 423 Amsterdam (bet. 80th and 81st Sts.), (212) 496-6280. Open M-Su am-10:30pm, Su 8am-9:30pm. 1 9 *to 79th St.* ♿

Time Cafe

Around mealtimes there are rarely many free tables in this vast, lofty space, and it's no wonder, since this is one of the better places filling the niche between greasy coffee shop and fancy restaurant. Health-conscious organic food and an extensive menu with selections like fancy tuna sandwiches and pan roasted penne are sure to satisfy nearly any craving.
Upper West Side, 2330 Broadway (at 85th St.), (212) 579-5100. Open M-R 10am-12am, F-Su 10am-1am. MC, V, AmEx, Entrées: $12-$22, 1 9 *to 86th St.* ♿

Shun Lee

Quite possibly New York's finest upscale Chinese, spitting distance from Lincoln Center; its glamour is defined by old-school, bejeweled Upper West Side matrons and their wizened escorts, complemented by excessive mirrors and a tiered dining floor. Exquisite dishes are served family-style in silver bowls; the chicken is tender and savory. All complemented by a heated towelette proffered by the white-suited waitstaff.

Upper West Side, 43 W. 65th St. (bet. Central Park West and Columbus Ave.), (212) 595-8895. Open M-Sa 12pm-12am, Su 12pm-10:30pm. MC, V, AmEx,

Under the Stairs

This bar/restaurant has been around for as long as anyone in the neighborhood can remember, and they still pack them in for happy hour. Come for the lively crowd, the loud jazz on weekends, and Wednesday's bargain shrimp night.
Upper West Side, 688 Columbus Ave. (bet. 93rd and 94th Sts.), (212) 663-3103. Open M-Su 11am-12am. MC, V, AmEx, Entrées: $10-$25, B C *to 96th St.* ♿

♦ CAFES

Café Con Leche

Cramped or cozy, depending on how tolerant you are of the neighboring conversation, this Cuban café pulses with upbeat salsa music and chatter. Standard dishes are perfectly prepared, from empañadas to "filet de pollo al limon."
Upper West Side, 424 Amsterdam Ave. (bet. 80th and 81st Sts.), (212) 595-7000, www.cafeconleche.com. Open M-Su 8am-12am. MC, V, AmEx, 1 9 *to 79th St.* ♿

Also at:
Upper West Side, 726 Amsterdam Ave. (bet. 95th and 96th Sts.), (212) 678-7000, www.cafeconleche.com. Open M-W 10am-11pm, R-F 10am-12am, Sa 8am-12am, Su 8am-11pm. MC, V, AmEx, 1 2 3 9 *to 96th St.* ♿

Cafe Lalo
This bright and lively European café serves night owls until 2am Sunday through Thursday, and until 4am on weekends. Come for the vast menu of decadent drinks and desserts; Sunday brunch available.
Upper West Side, 201 W. 83rd St. (bet. Broadway and Amsterdam Ave.), (212) 496-6031, www.cafe lalo.com. Open M-R 8am-2am, F 8am-4am, Sa 9am-4am, Su 9am-2am. Cash Only, 1 9 to 86th St.

Cafe Mozart
A slice of Europe on the Upper West Side, perfect after a show or for late morning paper perusal.
Upper West Side, 154 W. 70th St. (bet. Broadway and Columbus Ave.), (212) 595-9797. Open M-R 8am-1am, F 8am-3am, Sa 10am-3am, Su 10am-1am. MC, V, AmEx, 1 2 3 9 to 72nd St.

Drip
This coffee bar also has its liquor license so you can speed on caffeine, then come down with a micro-brewed beer. Singles can leaf through binders chock full of bios while sipping lattes and nibbling on oversized Rice Krispies treats. Atmosphere is casual, friendly, and relaxed unless, of course, you do find a match!
Upper West Side, 489 Amsterdam Ave. (bet. 83rd and 84th Sts.), (212) 875-1032, www.dripcafe.com. Open Su-R 8am-1am, F-Sa 9am-2am. MC, V, 1 9 to 86th St. ♿

French Roast
Art Nouveau dominates the decor at this airy, bustling café. Brunch and lunch available; try the consistently delicious soups.
Upper West Side, 2340 Broadway (at 85th St.), (212) 799-1533. Open M-Su 24hrs. MC, V, AmEx, D, 1 9 to 86th St. ♿

H&H Bagel
To certain New Yorkers, these bagels are good enough to qualify as a delicacy. The poppy and everything varieties go quickly, but the basic plain sourdough is something special, too. Call 1-800-NY-BAGEL to have mail orders delivered anywhere in the world.
Upper West Side, 2239 Broadway (at 80th St.), (212) 595-8003, www. hhbagel.com. Open M-Su 24hrs. Cash Only, 1 9 to 79th St. ♿

Shopping

◆ CLOTHING & SHOES

Betsey Johnson
In-your-face girly chic means Betsey's not afraid to flaunt lace alongside faux leather, or pair zebra stripes with fuschia fishnets. Straightforward, sexy slip dresses are surprisingly affordable on sale.
Upper West Side, 248 Columbus Ave. (bet. 71st and 72nd Sts.), (212) 362-3364, www.betseyjohnson. com. Open M-Sa 11am-7pm, Su 12pm-7pm. MC, V, AmEx, 1 9 to 72nd St. ♿

Club Monaco
This Canadian Company has transformed New York. They have basics with a trendy kick. Check out their CMX sports line.
Upper West Side, 2376 Broadway (at 87th St.), (212) 579-2587, www.clubmonaco.com. Open M-Sa 10am-8pm, Su 12pm-6pm. MC, V, AmEx, DC, 1 9 to 86th St.

Filene's Basement
This bargain staple superstore carries Calvin Klein, Perry Ellis, Kenar, and other designer names, and is worth a look for shoes, lingerie, coats, suits, and evening wear. Check out the occasional clearance sales where many prices are slashed to below $5.
Upper West Side, 222 Broadway (at 79th St.), (212) 873-8000, www.file nesbasement.com. Open M-Sa 10am-9pm, Su 11am-6pm. MC, V, AmEx, D, 1 9 to 79th St. ♿

Lord of the Fleas
So popular that they're currently operating several outlets within spitting distance of each other. This is the place to go to add a few trendy pieces to your existing wardrobe or to find something appropriate for a night of club-hopping. The prices and quality are both generally pretty low which is ideal for stuff that's in now but probably won't be next year.
Upper West Side, 2142 Broadway (at 75th St.), (212) 875-8815. Open M-Su 11am-8:30pm. MC, V, AmEx, D, 1 2 3 9 to 72nd St. ♿

Sacco
Trendy, retro, and classic, this chic shop carries it all. Make this store your first stop for well-made, eclectic women's footwear. Shoes tend to be dressy and relatively expensive, but there are always sale selections. Clearances offer an additional 20 percent off the sale price.
Upper West Side, 324 Columbus Ave. (bet. 75th and 76th Sts.), (212) 799-5229, www.sacco.com. Open M-F 11am-8pm, Sa 11am-7pm, Su 12pm-7pm. MC, V, AmEx, D, B C to 72nd St. ♿

It is one of the great charms of New York that at the Met [Metropolitan Opera] one may still see bejeweled Grandes Dames, rouged like crazy, wearing what at first glance appears to be black fur stoles, but then turn out to be their enervated sons slung across their mamas' magnificent shoulders; one may still see Elderly Patricians hanging from boxes by the heels, with their opera glasses pointing like guns right down the décolletage of a huge soprano.

—Tyrone Guthrie

♦ BOOKS, MAGAZINES & RECORDS

Applause Theatre and Cinema Books
Scripts, books, and plays. Perfect for the cinephile who has time to browse.
Upper West Side, 211 W. 71st St. (bet. Broadway and West End Ave.), (212) 496-7511, www.applausebooks.com. Open M-Sa 10am-9pm, Su 12pm-6pm. MC, V, AmEx, D, ❶❷❸❾ to 72nd St.

Book Ark
Relief for those weary of superstores. Fiction offerings are solid, as are the foreign language and rare book selections.
Upper West Side, 173 W. 81st St. (bet. Amsterdam and Columbus Aves.), (212) 787-3914, www.bookark.com. Open Su-R 11am-9pm, F-Sa 11am-11pm. MC, V, AmEx, ❶❾ to 79th St, ⒷⒸ to 81st St.

Dina News
Though the staff tends to frown upon browsing, try to sneak a peek at this impressive selection of periodicals, including a number of foreign magazines and newspapers.
Upper West Side, 2077 Broadway (bet. 71st and 72nd Sts.), (212) 875-8824. Open M-Su 6am-1am. MC, V, AmEx, D, ❶❷❸❾ to 72nd St.

Gryphon
Crowded shelves of used books climbing almost to the ceiling and piled on the floor. "I'd like it more if I could actually turn around in the aisles," complains one regular. There are books here which can be found nowhere else in Manhattan: you just have to look real hard.
Upper West Side, 2246 Broadway (bet. 80th and 81 Sts.), (212) 362-0706. Open M-Su 10am-12am. MC, V, ❶❾ to 79th St.

Murder Ink
This specialty bookstore featuring new and used mystery fiction is every aspiring sleuth's dream. Their stock includes many classic whodunnits as well as novels featuring elements of espionage and suspense. A Mecca for the City's true mystery buffs, this shop has frequent book-signings.
Upper West Side, 2486 Broadway (bet. 92nd and 93rd Sts.), (212) 362-8905, www.murderink.com. Open M-Sa 10am-10pm, Su 11am-7pm. MC, V, AmEx. ❶❷❸❾ to 96th St. ♿

Tani
Looking for footwear with a little pizzaz? Tani offers everything from funky, square-toed sneakers to elegant, open-toed heels, available in neons, neutrals, plastic, suede or silk. A special treat for shoe shoppers tired of super-chunky platforms a la Steve Madden. The only eyesores in this store are the prices, which range from $80 to $300.
Upper West Side, 2020 Broadway (bet. 69th and 70th Sts.), (212) 873-4361. Open M-F 10am-8pm, Sa 10am-7:30pm, Su 12pm-7pm. ❶❷❸❾ to 72nd St.

West Side Judaica
This haven of Judaica supplies music, art, decorations, and children's educational tools as well as a number of books dealing with Jewish issues. Closes at 3pm on Fridays for Shabbat and doesn't reopen until Sunday.
Upper West Side, 2412 Broadway (bet. 88th and 89th Sts.), (212) 362-7846. Open M-R 10:30am-9pm, F 10:30am-3pm, Su 10:30am-6pm. MC, V, ❶❾ to 86th St. ♿

♦ GROCERY, GOURMET & SPECIALTY

Citarella
With humble beginnings as a small fish market, this gourmet grocers now boasts a full range of fresh fish, meats, and pastas. Best known for its extensive selection of fresh local and imported seafood, Citarella also carries a sampling of foie gras, caviar, and cheeses for all your dinner party needs both here and in the Hamptons.
Upper West Side, 2135 Broadway (at 75th St.), (212) 874-0383. Open M-Sa 7am-9pm, Su 9am-7pm. MC, V, AmEx, ❶❾❷❸ to 72nd St. ♿

Ecce Panis
A bread store with an interesting (and expensive!) flair, they most definitely have bragging rights to the best chocolate bread in NYC. Go for the generous selection of free samples.
Upper West Side, 282 Columbus Ave. (at 73rd St.) , (212) 362-7189. Open M-Sa 8am-8pm, Su 8am-7pm. MC, V, AmEx, D, ⒶⒸ❶❷❸❾ to 72nd St. ♿

Fairway

"Like no other market" reads the awning, and this is indeed the most popular, largest, and lowest-priced produce and gourmet market on the West Side. A full deli counter offers prepared hot and cold dishes, the cheese department stocks an array of imports, and the bakery sells over a million bagels every year.

Upper West Side, 2127 Broadway (at 74th St.), (212) 595-1888. Open M-Su 24hrs. MC, V, AmEx, ❶❷❸❾ *to 72nd St.* ♿

Gourmet Garage

With its original location a converted garage in SoHo, Gourmet Garage was a pioneer in delivering gourmet goods at wholesale prices to the public. This Upper West Side location offers the same selection of breads, cheeses, organic produce, daily prepared foods, and a whole Kosher Cellar downstairs.

Upper West Side, 2567 Broadway (at 96th St.), (212) 663-0656. Open M-Su 7am-10pm. MC, V, AmEx, D. ❶❷❸❾ *to 96th St.* ♿

Zabar's

A name with impressive caché in uptown circles, this long-time Upper West Side institution is the prime source for gourmet meats, cheese, breads, and produce. Upstairs is an equally well-stocked kitchenware department featuring at least 30 kinds of whisks. The store can get shoulder-to-shoulder crowded on the weekends and holidays.

Upper West Side, 2245 Broadway (at 80th St.), (212) 787-2000, www.zabars.com. Open M-Sa 8am-7:30pm, Su 9am-6pm. MC, V, AmEx, ❶❾ *to 79th St.*

♦ MISCELLANEOUS

Bath Island

For the olfactorally-oriented comes this boutique of bath products. With 90 essential oils, customers can create their own custom-scented soaps and suds. Sample a couple of the most popular scents, "China Rain" and "Island," and pick up a few aromatherapy candles from the gift section while you're at it.

Upper West Side, 469 Amsterdam Ave. (at 82nd St.), (212) 787-9415. Open M-F 12pm-8pm, Sa 10am-8pm, Su 12pm-8pm. MC, V, AmEx. ❶❾ *to 79th St.* ♿

Hudson Dry Goods

Specializing in architectural ant-iques from trade shows across the country, Hudson Dry Goods is the place to pick up a piece of Americana. Browse through their catalog selection or consult with a friendly and helpful staff about custom redesigned pieces for your own brand of eclectic country chic.

Upper West Side, 112 W. 72nd St. (bet. Broadway and Columbus Ave.), (212) 579-7397. Open M-R 10am-9pm, F-Sa 10am-10pm, Su 10am-8pm. MC, V, AmEx, D, ❶❷❸❾ *to 72nd St.*

♦ LEISURE

Body Strength Fitness

Want a hard body and a calm mind? BSF offers free weights, personal training, aerobic classes, as well as massage, body sculpting, kick boxing, Pilates, and energy healing. Customize a workout plan to suit your needs.

Upper West Side, 250 W. 106th St. (at Broadway), (212) 316-3338, www.lifeinmotion.com. Open M-R 6:20am-10pm, F 6:20am-9pm, Sa-Su 8:30am-8pm. MC, V, AmEx, DC, D, ❶❾ *to 103rd St.*

Extra Vertical Climbing Center

Extra Vertical's wall offers routes ranging from easy to absurd, and it's not too pricey. Regulars are happy to help first timers "learn the ropes."

Upper West Side, 61 W. 62nd St. (at Broadway), (212) 586-5382. Open M-F 11am-10pm, Sa 9am-10pm. MC, V, AmEx, D. ⒶⒷⒸⒹ❶❾ *to 59th St.-Columbus Circle.*

Lincoln Plaza Cinemas

Down the street but still in the shadow of its titan neighbor Sony, this smallish theater doesn't want to do the big-budget Hollywood schtick anyway, preferring foreign and independent film festival standouts and a few surprises.

Upper West Side, 1886 Broadway (at 62nd St.), (212) 757-2280. ⒶⒷⒸⒹ❶❾ *to 59th St* ♿

Sony IMAX at Lincoln Square

By far the multiplex's coolest attraction: Nature films, which were always amusing for their magnificent underwater

Rose Center for Earth and Space

This newest addition to the Museum of Natural History produces riveting 3D effects that puts you where

Galileo said you ain't - the center of the universe. The most sophisticated star projector in the world shoots you and your queasy stomach under Saturn's rings and into a place where the sun doesn't shine: a black hole. Don't miss the Hall of the Universe that wraps around the central sphere.

Upper West Side, 81st St. (bet. Central Park West and Columbus Ave.), (212) 769-5100. Open F-Sa 10am-8:45pm, Su-R 10am-5:45pm. ⒷⒸ *to 81st St.*

action shots and close-ups of snouts and bug eyes, have given way a bit to plot-oriented pieces (the term 'plot' is used very liberally). The impressive show on New York City's history always draws a crowd.
Upper West Side, 1992 Broadway (at 68th St.), (212) 336-5000, www.enjoytheshow.com. 1 9 *to 66th St.-Lincoln Center.* ♿

Walter Reade Theater/Film Society of Lincoln Center
Since 1985, this luxurious theater has been the home of NYC's elite film club, which screens everything from Jim Carrey to Jean Luc Godard, with an emphasis on the latter end of the spectrum. New Directors/New Films, in conjunction with MoMA, has premiered work by such directors as Pedro Almodóvar and Peter Greenaway, while film festivals sport titles like "Rendez-Vous with French Cinema Today."
Upper West Side, 165 W. 65th St. (bet. Broadway and Amsterdam Ave.), (212) 875-5600, www.film linc.com. 1 9 *to 66th St.-Lincoln Center.* ♿

Arts & Recreation

♦ SITES

The Dakota
After its recent renovations, it is harder to picture the Dakota as the haunting backdrop for the film Rosemary's Baby. As one of four famous twin towered building so distinctive on Central Park West - the others being the Majestic, Sam Remo and Eldorado - this exclusive apartment building attracts celebrity residents. Since 1980, the doormen have spent most of their time answering questions about the exact spot where John Lennon was assassinated.
Upper West Side, 1 W. 72nd St. (at Central Park West) B C *to 72nd St.*

♦ PERFORMANCE

American Ballet Theater
This dance giant, once led by legends like Lucia Chase, Oliver Smith, and Mikhail Baryshnikov, and now headed by former Principal Dancer Kevin McKenzie, continues to stage staggering performances at its home in Lincoln Center. Classical ballet had its first renaissance here, and new works have been commissioned specifically for the ballet by key composers such as Balanchine, Antony Tudor, and Agnes de Mille. Call for schedules.
Upper West Side, W. 66th St. (at Broadway), (212) 362-6000. MC, V, AmEx, 1 9 *to 66th-Lincoln Center.* ♿

Symphony Space's Wall-to-Wall

While different institutions in New York specialize in unique dance, or original movies or plays you wouldn't see anywhere else, Symphony Space specializes in all of the above. Besides being home to NPR's broadcast of selected short stories it's also home to Wall-to-Wall. What started thirty years ago as a review of different classical musicians has turned into a celebration of any musician/genre that's produced enough work to warrant 12 hours of free music. In 1996, it was Wall-to-Wall folk music which brought folk musicians from all over the world to the stage and ended in a multicultural performance of "Good Night Irene". Last year it was Wall-to-Wall Miles Davis. Other Wall-to-Wall's include Duke Ellington and Bach.

Avery Fisher Hall
Over a hundred virtuosos led by Kurt Masur play Western classics, with an emphasis on European standards and American innovations. Home to the New York Philharmonic.
Upper West Side, 10 Lincoln Center Plaza (bet. 64th and 65th Sts.), (212) 875-5030, www.lincolncenter.org. 1 9 *to 66th St.-Lincoln Center.* ♿

Centerfold Coffeehouse at Church of St. Paul & St. Andrew
Poetry readings are free but hit or miss, so prepare to indulge some neophyte bards; evening jams with folk and jazz bands provide dependable, cheap weekend entertainment.
Upper West Side, 263 W. 86th St. (bet. Broadway and West End Ave.), (212) 362-3328. Cash Only, 1 9 *to 86th St.*

Lincoln Center Theater

A bastion of New York theater, its dramatic offerings make up the largest non-profit theater in the country. Artistic director Andre Bishop consistently presents high-profile premieres and revivals with top-name actors and directors. Consisting of two theaters — the Broadway-sized Vivian Beaumont and the smaller Mitzi Newhouse — recent seasons at Lincoln Center Theater have seen Helen Hunt and Paul Rudd in "Twelfth Night" and Kevin Kline in Chekhov's "Ivanov." In addition, international theatrical works of all kinds are presented every summer as part of Lincoln Center's annual festival.

Upper West Side, 150 W. 65th St. (bet. Broadway and Amsterdam Aves.), (212) 362-7600, www.lct.org. MC, V, AmEx, ❶❾ *to 66th St.-Lincoln Center.* ♿

Metropolitan Opera

When the Carnegies were the nouveau riche, Old Money's monopoly on the city's theater boxes frustrated the family so much that they went and built their own opera house. Though the original Met was further downtown, its current location retains a historic stodginess. A safely classical though consistently outstanding repertory. Check out the Chagall tapestries in the lobby.

Upper West Side, Lincoln Center (at 66th St. and Broadway), (212) 362-6000, www.metopera.org. MC, V, AmEx, ❶❾ *to 66th St.-Lincoln Center.* ♿

New York State Theater

Home to two of the city's artistic treasures. First, the New York City Ballet, a top-notch company which produces a particularly breathtaking Nutcracker, with champagne galore and lots of six-year-olds made up like dolls. In addition, the theater houses the New York City Opera, which renews and redefines the soul of the genre through stellar, innovative performances of both forgotten and familiar works.

Upper West Side, 20 Lincoln Center Plaza (at 64th St. and Broadway), (212) 870-5570, www.nycballlet.com, www.nyc-opera.com. MC, V, AmEx, ❶❾ *to 66th St.-Lincoln Center.* ♿

Stand-Up NY

Brett Butler and Dennis Leary cut their teeth here years ago and still swing by to pay their respects when in the neighborhood.

Upper West Side, 236 W. 78th St. (bet. Amsterdam Ave. and Broadway), (212) 595-0850, www.standupny.com. Showtimes Su-R 7pm, 9pm, F-Sa 8pm, 10pm, 12:15pm. MC, V, AmEx, D, ❶❾ to 79th St. ♿

Symphony Space

Playing host to an incredible range of talent, this spacious theater consistently offers up unique programs, often incorporating disparate genres into a unifying theme. Home to such ongoing favorites as "Selected Shorts," where actors and authors read short stories; an annual Bloomsday celebration; "Wall to Wall" music festivals devoted to individual artists; and World Music Institute shows of international performers.

Upper West Side, 2537 Broadway (at 95th St.), (212) 864-5400, www.symphonyspace.org. MC, V, AmEx, ❶❷❸❾ to 96th St. ♿

♦ MUSEUMS & CULTURAL CENTERS

American Folk Art Institute

Classes and workshops are offered in all manners of media. Lectures and other panels are also held here.

Upper West Side, 2 Lincoln Sq. (Columbus Ave. bet. 65th and 66th Sts.), (212) 977-7170, www.folkmuseum. org. ❶❾ *to 66th St.-Lincoln Center.* ♿

American Museum of Natural History

A taxidermist's paradise and proud owner of a fantastic floor of dinosaurs. The museum also houses a Hall of Human Evolution and Biology, chronicling human development from ape to homosapiens. Eat lunch under the big blue whale.

Upper West Side, 79th St. (at Central Park West), (212) 769-5100, www.amnh.org. Open Su-R 10am-5:45pm, F-Sa 10am-8:45pm. MC, V, AmEx, Admission (suggested): $4.50-$8.50, Ⓑ Ⓒ *to 81st St.-Museum of Natural History.* ♿

Children's Museum of Manhattan

Apartment-bred kids get a taste of nature in the Urban Tree House, see what makes TV tick at the Time Warner Media Center, and read about the life and works of Dr. Seuss at this creative, interactive museum for children of all ages. Lots of wild water fun when it gets hot.

Upper West Side, 212 W. 83rd St. (bet. Broadway and Amsterdam Ave.), (212) 721-1234, www.cmom. org. Open W-Su 10am-5pm. MC, V, AmEx, Admission: $6, ❶❾ *to 86th St.* ♿

New York Historical Society

An imposing building across from the Park houses both a library and a museum with a wealth of information and images of New York up to the turn-of-the-century. The museum features a permanent installation of 19th century paintings.

Upper West Side, 2 W. 77th St. (at Central Park West), (212) 873-3400, www.nyhistory.org. Open T-Su 11am-5pm. Admission: $5 adults, $3 students/seniors. Ⓑ Ⓒ *to 81st St. - Museum of Natural History.* ♿

♦ GALLERIES AND LIBRARIES

Makor

A vibrant cultural center that warmly embraces traditional and progressive Judaism, Makor's programs offer everything from weekly parties to Shabbat services. You can browse their art gallery, watch a Jewish film like The Commissar or eat kosher food at the café. Don't worry, every evening offers a different choice of classes, even ones on Jewish meditation.

Upper West Side, 35 W. 67th St. (bet. Columbus Ave. and Central Park West), (212) 601-1000, www.makor.org, Open M 2pm-6pm, T-R 2pm-10pm, Su 2pm-6pm. Call for times and schedules of films, V ❶❾ to 66th St.

Nightlife

♦ BARS

The All State Cafe

Once the Upper West Side's best singles bar, the All State is still a great place to grab a steak or a beer and perhaps a date. The menu features a fine array of hearty American offerings, and the draughts run cool with several good ales. The regular clientele is a mixed bag of young professionals and old-timers.

Upper West Side, 250 W. 72nd St., (bet. West End Ave. and Riverside Dr.), (212) 874-1883. Open M-Su 11:30am-4am. Cash Only, ❶❷❸❾ to 72nd St.

Blondies

Mounted televisions offering an impressive range of sporting events play continuously above the batenders, whose blonde coifs explain this boisterous sports bar's name. Try the "world-famous atomic wings."

Upper West Side, 212 W. 79th St. (bet. Broadway and Amsterdam Ave.), (212) 362-4360. Open Su-R 12:30 pm-1am, F-Sa 12:30pm-4am. MC, V, AmEx, DC, ❶❾ to 79th St.

Bourbon Street

This mostly college bar is known for women dancing on the bar and drinking heavily. It's not so classy, but the atmosphere is great for getting drunk and partying. A DJ plays Wednesdays through Saturdays. On Wednesdays women drink draft beer and hurricanes for free, and every Thursday is karaoke night.

Upper West Side, 407 Amsterdam (bet. 79th and 80th Sts.), (212) 721-1332. Open M-Su 5pm-4am. MC, V, AmEx, ❶❾ to 79th St.

Dive Bar

Sure, it's got dive written all over it, literally, but this clean haunt is actually quite tame. Even the resident pool sharks won't intimidate. Chug till 4am every day and don't overlook a menu strong enough to support a free delivery service.

Best and Worst Bar on Amsterdam Avenue

Worst Bar

Alligator Alley

It's not that the service is bad or the place is unnecessarily overpriced, it's just that this is the most boring bar ever invented.

Best Bar

Brother Jimmy's

One of those bottom line get drunk and have a good time bars, which is rare in a city that makes you feel like bars exist for some other reason.

Rosemary's Baby, 1968

If you're lucky enough to be one of the most famous, successful and beautiful of the city's residents, you might live in the Dakota building at 72nd at Central Park West. Home to numerous movie stars and big shots, the Dakota's most recent claim-to-fame is the location where John Lennon was assassinated. But before then, Rosemary's Baby (which takes place at the famous apartment building) provides the horrifying evidence that if your little old foreign lady neighbor makes smelly food, wears weird necklaces and has babies crying from her apartment; she might not be as sweet as she seems.

Upper West Side, 732 Amsterdam Ave. (at 96th St.), (212) 749-4358. Open M-Su 11am-4am. MC, V, AmEx, ❶❷❸❾ to 96th St., Ⓑ Ⓒ to 96th St.

Dublin House

While not a traditional Irish bar, the Dublin House is nevertheless a blessing to the Upper West Side. Its unpretentious atmosphere and straight-up bar politics attract the authentic old-timer and college student alike.

Upper West Side, 225 W. 79th St. (bet. Broadway and Amsterdam Ave.), (212) 874-9528. Open M-Su 8am-4am. Cash Only, ❶❾ to 79th St.

420 Bar and Lounge

This swank member of the Amsterdam scene, populated with the requisite clothes hangers and well-heeled single malt sippers, could teach the SoHo lounges a thing or two. Local scenesters, spared the cab fare downtown, don't seem to mind the pricey cocktails. But if you've come for the strip's notorious drink specials, you may be better served up the street.

Upper West Side, 420 Amsterdam Ave. (at 80th St.), (212) 579-8450. Open M-Su 5pm-4am MC, V, AmEx, DC, D, ❶❾ to 79th St.

The Evelyn Lounge

This spacious bar that is crowded most days of the week. It's sort of romantic, with fireplaces and comfortable chairs and couches in the back rooms. On the other hand, it's kind of cheesy: the Evelyn is a singles scene with men outnumbering women at least 3 to 1. There is live music several nights a week but not enough room to dance, which only increases the meat-market feel.

Upper West Side, 380 Columbus Ave. (at 78th St.), (212) 724-5145. Open M-Su 6pm-4am. MC, V, AmEx, DC, ❶❾ to 79th St.

The Gin Mill

So you're sitting around your fraternity and you've been talking for an hour about what you're going to do tonight. Well pile Steve, Rob and Trainwreck into a cab and head to the Gin Mill. It exists because you do and it's full of the sort of ladies that like you. Shots with silly names abound, never a Jaegermeister shortage and for some, always a good time.

Upper Westside, 442 Amsterdam Ave. (bet. 81st and 82nd Sts.), (212) 580-9080. Open M-F 11:30am-4am, Sa-Su 12pm-4am. MC, V, AmEx, ❶❾ to 79th St.

Jake's Dilemma

So by now you and the boys are pretty tanked and ready for a new bar. Head one block south to Jake's Dilemma where the only dilemma is what method you'll be using to destroy your diction. This is the bar to make proclamations and drunken surveys in. It doesn't pay to talk here, just scream what's on your mind and someone will scream something back at you.

Upper Westside, 430 Amsterdam Ave. (bet. 80th and 81st Sts.), (212) 580-0556. Open M 5pm-4am, T-F 4pm-4am, Sa-Su 1pm-4am. MC, V, AmEx, ❶❾ to 79th St.

Parlor

This Irish bar has good drinks and especially fine Guinnesses for the Upper West Side. The traditional Irish ambiance makes the parlor unique for the neighborhood and keeps the yuppie Upper West Siders at bay. Jeans are okay here even on the weekends. The ample seating and downstairs dance area provide for a relaxed night with friends.

Upper West Side, 250 W. 86th St. (bet. Broadway and Riverside Drive), (212) 580-8923. Open M-F 12pm-4am, Sa-Su 11am-4am. MC, V, AmEx, ❶❾ⒷⒸ to 86th St.

The P & G

You may know the P&G from its cameo roles in Taxi Driver, Seinfeld, or Donnie Brasco, but it's still an unassuming place. An old neighborhood bar dating back to the 1940s, the P&G is the real deal, filled with locals and old-timers drinking to tunes from the classic rock jukebox.

Upper West Side, 279 Amsterdam Ave. (bet. 73rd and 74th Sts.), (212) 874-8568. Open M-Su 11am-4am. Cash Only, ❶❷❸❾ to 72nd St.

Potion

Potion has cool décor, with an outside wall marked by portholes of blue bubbles. Their special drinks called "potions" are decent but also, at $10, expensive. It is frequently crowded with young yuppie types, and there are too few places to sit. Also, the doormen and the bartenders are obnoxious.

Upper West Side, 370 Columbus Ave. (bet. 77th and 78th Sts.), (212) 721-4386. Open T-Sa 7pm-4am. MC, V, AmEx, 1 9 to 79th St.

Prohibition

Although not worth a long travel, this bar is good for hanging out with friends. There is little style and the live music is often amateurish, but the atmosphere is not pretentious. There is plenty of seating and a pool table.

Upper West Side, 503 Columbus Ave. (bet. 84th and 85th Sts.), (212) 579-3100. Open M-Su 5:30pm-4am. MC, V, AmEx, DC, D, 1 9 B C to 86th St.

Raccoon Lodge

You'll get just what you'd expect from a bar with this name-it's a dive. The patrons are not your typical Upper-West Siders; men with cowboy hats and motorcycles frequent this bar. Maybe it's the video and electronic poker games. There is little seating and what there is resembles picnic tables. The alcohol is cheaper than the average for the neighborhood, which is a plus.

Upper West Side, 480 Amsterdam Ave. (at 83rd St.), (212) 874-9984. Open M-F 11am-4am, Sa-Su 1pm-4am. MC, V, AmEx, D, 1 9 to 86th St.

Shark Bar

A well-known, upscale hangout. Low lighting and polished wood accents make this hideaway a romantic alternative to the other more raucous local bars. Bring a date to ward off the post-collegiate singles hovering around the bar.

Upper West Side, 307 Amsterdam Ave. (bet. 74th and 75th Sts.), (212) 874-8500, www.sharkbar.com. Open Su-T 5pm-1:30pm, W 12pm-12am, R 12pm-12:30am, F 12pm-1:30am, Sa 5pm-1:30am. MC, V, AmEx, 1 2 3 9 to 72nd St. ♿

Time Out

For the true sports fanatic: know your stats and be ready to talk some serious trivia. The crowd of cheering, jeering, thirty-something men ignores the pool table in favor of the twenty three televisions. New York home of the Celtic's soccer supporter club, so know what you mean when asking about the "football" game.

Upper West Side, 349 Amsterdam Ave. (bet. 76th & 77th Sts.), (212) 362-5400. Open M-F 5pm-4am, Sa-Su 12pm-4am. MC, V, AmEx, D, DC, 1 9 to 79th St.

Triad

Both floors of this lounge/restaurant stage acts of surprisingly high quality seven nights a week. Check out the upstairs theater for Off-Broadway productions and jazz, blues, and comedy acts. Head downstairs to the relaxed Dark Star Lounge for open-mic on Mondays.

Upper West Side, 158 W. 72nd St. (bet. Broadway and Columbus Ave.), (212) 799-4599. Open M-Su 5pm-4am. MC, V, AmEx, 1 2 3 9 to 72nd St.

Venue

For lounging or dancing, Venue is a great Upper West Side option. Though the big plush couches fill up quickly and the upstairs is often impossible to navigate, the good drinks and clientele make the crowded atmosphere bearable. There are two DJs, and the downstairs lounge/dance floor is covered with fur and lava lamps.

Upper West Side, 505 Columbus Ave. (bet. 84th and 85th Sts.), (212) 579-9463. Open M-Su 7pm-4am. MC, V, AmEx 1 9 B C to 86th St.

♦ MUSIC

Dark Star Lounge

Clean and cozy, with a grand piano and an even grander menu. Its setting, uptown and away from the trendiness of the East and West Villages, has made it attractive to neighborhood musicians of some stature, such as Jeff Gollub, Holly Palmer and Shawn Pelton. Sunday nights host the popular Michael Raye's Soul Gathering. Full menu, full bar.

acoustic, blues, country, jazz, R&B

Upper West Side, 158 W. 72nd St. (bet. Broadway and Columbus Ave.), (212) 362-2590. Open M-Su 5pm-4am. MC, V, AmEx, D, Cover: $5-$10, 1 2 3 9 to 72nd St. ♿

Hip-Hop in New York

All the trouble started, as it too often does, in the South Bronx. Jamaican born DJ Kool Herc brought his reggae party here in the early 70s, and found Lady New York playing hard to get. Aloof as usual, she resisted Herc's attempts to woo her with his island style, so he started mixing and extending the breaks of disco and James Brown records. Disco DJs had been doing this for awhile, but not with the beats Herc used and no one spoke over them. The sound was new, the girl was got and hip-hop was born.

What started as parties in the park grew into singles of moderate success and a big dance scene at clubs like the Fever, Latin Quarter and Union Square. Other mediums besides Djing got involved and in the late 70s Afrika Bambata laid down the law on what hip-hop's four pillars were and are: Djing, Mcing, graffiti and break dancing.

Hip-hop culture, whether or not the city's willing to admit it, is a defining part of New York. Listen on a subway to the rap blasting out of headphones; walk out at one of the major subway stops and see kids, years after it was the thing to do, still break dancing. It's 3pm and a car hits a stop light outside a middle school, Jay Z fuming out the windows. Witness the block party of seventh graders who rap every word until the light turns green. Or, ask Brooklyn residents what their favorite Notorious B.I.G. song is and an argument ensues.

One rapper observed: "It's going down on my island of Manhattan/ the Bronx, Brooklyn, Queens or Staten/where shit happens." And if the news has reached Staten Island, you've for sure got no excuse. Just ask the legions of suburban fans to name every member of Staten Island's own Wu Tang Clan.

So, if you want to be the coolest kid in town by the end of the day, you've got some work to do. First off, replace the James Taylor CD collection with some better music. The best selection of hip-hop on CD is at **Mondo Kim's** at Astor Place, the biggest of the beloved Kim's stores scattered across the city.

But, if you're a purist and only have eyes for vinyl head to **Fat Beats** on 406 Sixth Avenue or **All the Right Records** on Junction Boulevard in Queens. Their collections range as far back as the early 80s and they have a decent graffiti magazine selection where you can study up on the competition before you wander down the train tracks. All the Right Records also stocks graffiti paraphernalia like fat caps and markers as well as a host of b-boy gear.

Later on that night your going to want to catch a show; and this being New York and New York being the most amazing city in the world, you have a host of options. Major venues like **Irving Plaza**, the **Knitting Factory**, **S.O.B.'s**, **Joe's Pub** and **Bowery Ballroom** have some of the best acts hip-hop has seen. More intimate run-ins with more underground performers can be had at smaller spaces like **CB's Gallery** and the **Nuyorican Poet's Cafe**. Of course, before you make any rash decisions consult the *Voice* or a website like www.graphonic.com/plugaction for an up-to-date listing of hip-hop related events.

After the show, especially if it's getting towards that early part of the morning, take the E or F train one stop into Queens. There lies the **Phun Factory**, a factory the size of a small airport covered in graffiti. You need permission to write anything, but there's a great view of the city and it's a good place to cut open a cigar.

Stumble home and for a night cap pop in Charlie Ahearn's 1983 Classic ***Wild Style***, which crystallizes the pre-Run DMC moment in hip-hop's life when heavies like Grandmaster Flash and the Rock Steady Crew ran the city. Or, if it's early Thursday morning, tune into **CM-Fam-A-Lam Radio Program** on 89.9 WKCR FM. From 1-5, let DJ Cucumberslice, aka Bobito the Barber, and Lord Spear spin you to sleep with the best radio show in town. While you drift off plan your next epic day of adventuring New York style.

Because as rapper Rakim said, "No other place gets as deep/whose parks release some the greatest atheletes/ DJs and MCs and graffiti artistes/ who use walls and subway trains for marquees/ we go back to b-boys, breakdancing, break beats/ and it'll never cease." Ever.

Morningside Heights

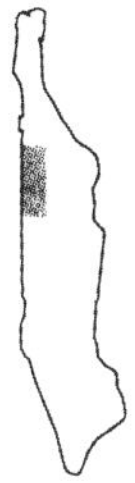

Outside the perimeter of most sightseers' travels is a welcome reprieve from city noise and congestion. Wedged between Harlem and the Upper West Side, Morningside Heights is something of a stepchild that's inherited the best from its parents—the neighborhood is both a home to some of the city's biggest intellectuals and a thriving ethnic community.

Here the business of education harmonizes with the restful quiet of a largely residential area. Small neighborhoods exist within the larger academic ones of Columbia University's many colleges.

Sandwiched between Morningside and Riverside Parks, Columbia University, the neighborhood's largest landholder, is by far the biggest influence. The Ivy League air of the campus, carries over into buildings like Riverside Church, General Ulysses S. Grant's Tomb and the as-yet incomplete Episcopal Cathedral of St. John The Divine. During the week, bookbag-toting students rush in and out of Columbia Bagels or Koronets for a meal on the run in between classes. At night they stumble out of one of Amsterdam Avenue's Bermuda Triangle of bars.

Down the hill and east of Broadway a highly visible Hispanic community wanders in and out of barber shops, bodegas and other flourishing businesses. Block parties and cars blasting music late into the night aren't uncommon, neither is a small drug problem. Things are getting better though, the gates of Columbia, once testament to the universities disinterest in the rest of the neighborhood, are slowly being opened. New building and community initiatives have done their best to unite the two sides. Whether they'll ever completely get along, who knows? A good place to be though, no matter what side you're on.

Dining

♦ RESTAURANTS

107 West
This restaurant's eclectic menu and décor waffle between southwestern, Italian, and New York chic themes, but the food is consistently good (especially the rigatoni with chicken and capers). A cozy interior and glassed-in porch provide the classy atmosphere for a perfect date, without incurring the debilitating costs often associated with fine dining.
Morningside Heights, 2787 Broadway (at 107th St.), (212) 864-1555. Open M-R 5pm-11pm, F-Sa 5pm-12pm, Su 5pm-10:30pm. MC, V, Amex, D, Entrees $8-18, 1 9 to 110th St.

Alouette
This intimate bi-level French bistro serves up savory and inventive cuisine in a rich, warm atmosphere — an anomaly for the Upper West Side. Wearing red velvet drapery and lace-curtained windows, Alouette is a romantic option in West Side dining. The prices are great in exchange for this culinary and atmospheric decadence.
Upper West Side, 2588 Broadway (bet. 97th and 98th Sts.), (212) 222-6808, www.alouettenyc.com. Open M-Su 5:30pm-11pm. MC, V, AmEx, DC, Entrées: $16-$22, 1 2 3 9 to 96th St.

Amsterdam Café
Friendly neighborhood feel with a good menu of classic bar items and pastas. Their weekend brunch for $4.95 is the best deal in the area, the cute bartenders another plus!
Morningside Heights, 1207 Amsterdam Ave. (bet. 119th and 120th Sts.), (212) 662-6330. Open M-F 7:30am-4am, Sa-Su 9am-4am. MC, V, AmEx, DC, D, Entrées: $7-$10, 1 9 to 116th St.-Columbia University.

Awash
Ethiopian restaurants aren't exactly ubiquitous, so it's a thrill just to find one, especially one as good as Awash. Order any of the numerous delectable meat or vegetable dishes and learn to eat Ethiopian-style, using a piece of injera (a thin teff pancake) to pick up your food. If you're brave try the kitfo, a delicious mix of raw ground beef and exotic spices.
Morningside Heights, 947 Amsterdam Ave. (bet. 106th and 107th Sts.), (212) 961-1416. Open M-R 1pm-11:30pm, F-Su 12pm-12am. MC, V, AmEx, Entrées: $7-$13, 1 9 to 103rd St.

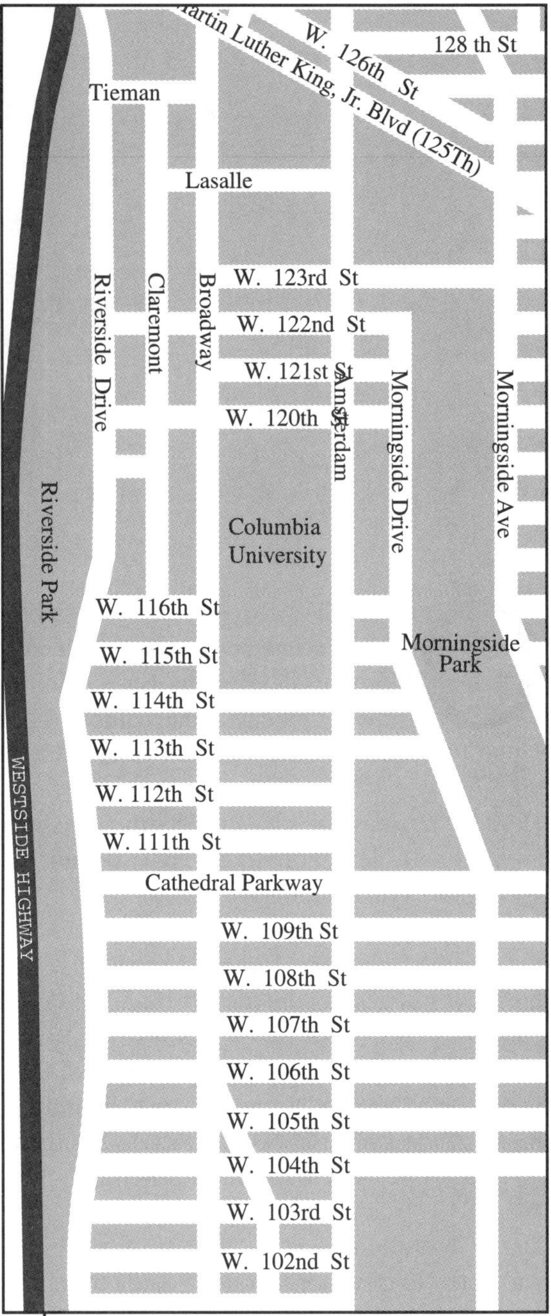

Cafe Amiana
This reasonably priced restaurant specializes in Middle Eastern and Continental fare. The bar is well stocked with wine and beer and stays open long after the kitchen closes.
Morningside Heights, 2737 Broadway (at 105th St.), (212) 663-7010. Open M-F 9am-12am, Sa-Su 9:30am-12am. Cash Only, Entrées: $12-$15, 1 9 to 103rd St.

PLACES TO GO:

Turkuaz
Excellent Turkish food in this restaurant starved neighborhood, and the occasional belly dancer.

Metisse
The menu's pretty static, but good enough as the food's excellent. Their crème brulee is the best in town.

General Ulysses S. Grant Memorial
The largest mausoleum in the country and a beautiful columned structure, filled with the solemnity only a dead president, he's on the $100 bill, could inspire

Caffé Pertutti
Bright and breezy, with a hard-tiled floor and marble-topped tables, this neighborhood café hosts intellectual tête-à-têtes while serving up Italian standards which hardly merit their above-average prices. The salads, however, are enormous and tasty, and the desserts usually taste as good as they look.
Morningside Heights, 2888 Broadway (bet. 112th and 113th Sts.), (212) 864-1143, www.barnardwalks.com/pertutti.menu. Cash Only, Entrées: $7-$12, ❶❾ to Cathedral Parkway (110th St). ♿

Caffé Taci
Crowds of Columbia students eat adequately prepared Italian basics in the mock-ruin interior of this popular, dimly-lit eatery. Manhattan School of Music students sing live opera on Wednesday, Friday and Saturday nights; due to slow service, diners can theoretically hear one in its entirety.
Morningside Heights, 2841 Broadway (at 110th St.), (212) 678-5345. Open M-R 10am-1am, F-Sa 10am-2am, Su 10am-1am. Cash Only, Entrées: $5-$14, ❶❾ to Cathedral Parkway (110th St.) ♿

Camille's
Named after the owner's mother, this cozy Columbia magnet is reliably good. Pizzas are a bargain at $4.25, and the hearty pasta dishes are topped with light and flavorful sauces. It's difficult to eat this well for less money; breakfast is a particularly cheap alternative to bacon 'n egg grease-balls at area diners.
Morningside Heights, 1135 Amsterdam Ave. (at 116th St.), (212) 749-2428. Open M-F 7:30am-8pm, Sa 8:30am-5pm. MC, V, AmEx, Entrées: $3-$9, ❶❾ to 116th St.-Columbia University.

Famous Famiglia's
Come for the photos of celebrities on the wall, the jocular service, and the delicious and greasy pizza. The 'hood's finest garlic twists and the pizza's garlicky tomato sauce will keep the vampires away.
Morningside Heights, 2859 Broad-way (at 111th St.), (212) 865-1234, www.famousfamiglias.com. Open M-Su 10am-2am. MC, V, AmEx, D, Entrées: $14.50, ❶❾ to Cathedral Parkway. (110th St.) ♿

Jerusalem Restaurant
Step off the grungy street and into Jerusalem's Arab quarter in this small Middle Eastern hot spot. Amidst the cook's frantic Arabic exclamations and the sultry music you'll find some of Manhattan's best shawarma and falafel - the perfect spot for a sumptuous late night meal or a snack on the run.
Morningside Heights, 2715 Broadway (bet. 103rd and 104th Sts.), (212) 865-2295. Open M-Su 10am-4am. Cash only, Entrees $3-9, ❶❾ to 103rd St. ♿

Ghostbusters, 1984

Possibly the zaniest New York movie of all time is Ghostbusters. From the first frame, this movie is filled with the Manhattan landscape – the more you watch, the more you catch. It's a must-see for anyone who believes in architectural restoration or has a thing for marshmallows. See if you can recognize, among other places, Columbus Circle, Columbia University and the New York Public Library.

Mama Mexico

The food isn't out of this world, but evenings it's packed, with a giant mariachi band blaring boleros to hungry diners. Ask for a tequila shot, and you'll think an alarm went off in the back of the restaurant. Service suddenly picks up, and, a couple of shots later, the owner's pouring booze down your throat.

Morningside Heights, 2672 Broadway (bet. 101st and 102nd Sts.), (212) 864-2323. Open M-R 12pm-12am, Sa-Su 12-2. MC, V, AmEx, Entrees: $10-20, 1 9 *to 109th St.,* ♿

Metisse

Ooh la la! With this rich, delicious, reasonably priced food, you might blink and think you've found Paris in New York.

Upper W. Side, 239 W. 105th St. (at Broadway), (212) 666-8825. Open M-R 6:30pm-10:30pm, F-Sa 5:30pm-11pm, Su 5:30pm-10pm. MC, V, AmEx, Entrées: $12.50-$18.50, 1 9 *to 103rd St.* ♿

Metro Diner

Unique to the world of diners, this veggie-friendly establishment offers all the standard diner fare — only fresh! — with a splash of Mediterranean dishes including a variety of salads and vegetarian plates. Grab a booth and soak in its streamlined train car decor. A great post-movie hangout.

Upper West Side, 2641 Broadway (at 100th St.), (212) 866-0800. Open M-Su 6am-1am. MC, V, AmEx, Entrées: $10-$14, 1 2 3 9 *to 96th St.* ♿ 🚲

Miss Mammie's Spoonbread Too

Bottom line, Mammie's has the sort of soul food that will make you say daaaaaaaamn. How do you want your soul food: barbecued, blackened, deep-fried, smothered in sauce? It's all here. Save room for some banana bread pudding, coconut pineapple cake, or sweet potato pie. The laid-back staff, who take just long enough to make you appreciate your meal, will be more than happy to serve you any of the above.

Morningside Heights, 366 W. 110th (at Columbus Ave.), (212) 865-6744. Open M-Su 11am-10pm. MC, V, AmEx, Entrees: $10-17, B C 1 9 *to 110th St.*

The Heights

This slick restaurant-bar now has a rooftop garden which is heated in the cooler months. Potent margaritas, fresh salsa with tricolored chips, and an eager waitstaff make this a favorite among Columbia students. Start early by slurping $2.50 margaritas during happy hour between 5pm-7pm and 12am-1am.

Morningside Heights, 2867 Broadway (at 111th St.), (212) 866-7035. Open M-Su 11:30am-11:30pm. MC, V, Entrées: $8-$15, 1 9 *to Cathedral Parkway (110th St.)*

La Rosita

For years, New Yorkers have claimed that this place serves the best cup of coffee. The service is well-paced (read "slow") so that food usually arrives as you're about to crack, but devouring your meal is always worth the wait. Probably the most authentic cooking and definitely the best Latin food in the neighborhood.

Morningside Heights, 2809 Broadway (bet. 108th and 109th Sts.), (212) 663-7804. Open M-Su 7am-12am. MC, V, AmEx, D, Entrees: $3-15, 1 9 *to 110th St.,* ♿

Saji's Kitchen

This hole-in-the-wall is one of Morningside Heights' hidden gems. Behind a tiny counter that blares rock music lies uptown's best Japanese food at amazingly low prices. This is mainly a take-out / delivery place, but the food is so good that going anywhere else seems like a waste.

Morningside Heights, 256 W. 109th St. (at Broadway), (212) 749-1834. Open M-F 11:30am-10:30pm, Sa-Su 12pm-10:30pm. Cash only, Entrees: $2-11, 1 9 *to 110th St.,* ♿

Sophia's Bistro

Downtown style has been creeping into the local neighborhood during the last year. This little bistro leads the onslaught, offering hip, romantic dining. Pale yellow and red brick, flickering candlelight, and wine-colored drapery create a laid-back atmosphere.

Upper West Side, 998 Amsterdam Ave. (bet. 109th and 110th Sts.), (212) 662-8822. Open M-Su 11am-12am. MC, V, AmEx, Entreés: $6-$10, 1 9 *to Cathedral Parkway (110th St).* ♿

Terrace

The exquisite view of upper Manhattan from this upscale dining room may finally convince your parents that living

next to Harlem isn't so bad, or it may impress your date by revealing your uncanny ability to find romance in the most unexpected places. After trying the house risotto or grilled salmon, visit the rooftop garden. The open air and a much-needed cocktail will help you recuperate from the bill.
Morningside Heights, 400 W. 119th St. (bet. Amsterdam Ave. and Morningside Dr.), (212) 666-9490. Open T-R 12pm-2:30pm, 6pm-10pm, F-Sa 6pm-11pm. MC, V, AmEx, DC, D, Entrées: $25-$38, ❶❾ to 116th St.-Columbia University. ♿

Tomo
Enjoy good sushi and Japanese fare in this upbeat Morningside Heights eatery. The place tends to fill up quickly and the tables are packed close together, but the prices are reasonable, though not cheap.
Morningside Heights, 2850 Broadway (bet. 110th and 111th Sts.), (212) 665-2916. Open M-Sa 12 pm-11:30pm, Su 12pm-11pm. MC, V, AmEx, Entrees: ($6-$14), ❶❾ to 110th St, ♿

Tom's Restaurant
Once you push through the occasional crowd from a Kramer's Reality tour (the southern façade serves as a cut-away shot in *Seinfeld*), you'll be surprised to see what the fuss is all about. Though recent renovations have jacked the prices up a bit be sure to find huge platters, late hours, and thick "Broadway" shakes that keep kids coming back to this greasy spoon.
Mornigside Heights, 2880 Broadway (at 112th St.), (212) 864-6137. Open Su-R 6am-1:30am, F-Sa 24hrs. Cash Only, Entrées: $3-$10, ❶❾ to Cathedral Parkway (110th St.) ♿

Turkuaz
With the restaurant's artistically draped fabric ceiling that evokes a breezy Ottoman tent and the waiters' red satin balloon pants, you might think you've stepped into a tale from the Arabian nights. Enjoy the traditional dishes and desserts at this Upper West Side Turkish delight, which offers both Turkish and Western style food. Almond pudding is especially good.
Upper West Side, 2637 Broadway (at 100th St.), (212) 665-9541. Open M-Su 12pm-11pm. MC, V, AmEx, D, Entrees: $10-15, ❶❾ to 103rd, ♿

Zula
Being cheap and slightly run down, Zula has the comfort level of your average diner, but since they offer tasty, vegan-friendly Ethiopian food instead of grease-sodden French fries, it's a better bet.
Morningside Heights, 1260 Amsterdam Ave. (bet 121st and 122nd Sts.). Open M-Su 10am-10pm. MC, V, AmEx, Entrees: $6-8, ❶❾ to 125th St.

♦ CAFES

Hamilton Deli
The true New York experience awaits at this popular deli. Hefty heroes with names like "The Lewinsky" are served up dripping with onions and mustard by a whirlwind staff of no-nonsense locals. Grab a drink or candy bar from the convenience store in the back and you're ready to go.
Morningside Heights, 1129 Amsterdam Ave. (at 116th St.), (212) 749-8924. Open M-F 6am-12am, Sa-Su 7am-9pm. Cash only, ❶❾ to 116th St.

The Hungarian Pastry Shop
The cafe's enduring reputation as Columbia University's intellectual hangout par excellence has suffered somewhat since the citywide smoking ban. Still the place of choice, however, to ostentatiously discuss Fellini or Godard, or write that dissertation on the hermeneutics of the Marquis de Sade while sipping chamomile tea and nibbling on a linzer torte.
Morningside Heights, 1030 Amsterdam Ave. (bet. 110th and 111th Sts.), (212) 866-4230. Open M-F 7:30am-11:30pm, Sa 8:30am-11:30pm, Su 8:30am-10pm. Cash Only, ❶❾ to Cathedral Parkway (110th st.).

Nussbaum & Wu
Not your ordinary coffee stop — a Chinese pastry shop and deli collided to form this one. Well-lit with a great wrap-around counter, you just may decide to stay a while. Fresh sandwiches and yummy pastries, both Asian and non, are available here, not to mention bagels and, of course, coffee too.
Morningside Heights, 2897 Broadway (at 113th St.), (212) 280-5344. Open M-Su 6am-12am. MC, V, AmEx, ❶❾ to Cathedral Parkway (110th St.). ♿

Shopping

◆ CLOTHING & SHOES

Aerosoles

A brand new Morningside Heights branch of this shoe chain boasts a clean and well-lit store of men's and women's footwear. Offering contemporary styles at affordable prices, these shoes specialize in comfort for the walk-weary Manhattanite.

Morningside Heights, 2913 Broad-way (bet. 113th and 114th Sts.), (212)665-5353, www.aerosoles.com. Open M-Sa 10am-8pm, Su 12pm-6pm. MC, V, AmEx, D, ❶❾ to 116th St. ♿

Renell

The neighborhood lingerie store, this two-sectioned boutique also offers a selection of moderately priced women's clothing and apparel. In a humble and comfortably rustic atmosphere, take a few minutes from a lazy afternoon to browse for that summer sundress or boxy shirt to knock around in.

Morningside Heights, 2931 Broadway (bet. 114th and 115th Sts.), (212) 749-4749. Open M-F 11am-8pm, Sa 10am-6:30pm, Su 12pm-5pm. MC, V, AmEx, D, ❶❾ to 116th St. ♿

◆ BOOKS, MAGAZINES & RECORDS

Bank St. Bookstore

Serving the fledgling schoolteachers of the nearby Bank St. College with an extensive selection of children's books, educational theory, and planning guides. Flip through old faves like *Madeleine* and *Where the Wild Things Are*.

Morningside Heights, 2879 Broadway (at 112th St.), (212) 678-1654, www.bankstreetbooks.com. Open M-R 10am-10pm, F-Sa 10am-6pm, Su 12pm-5pm. MC, V, AmEx, ❶❾ to Cathedral Parkway (110th St.) ♿

Columbia Bookstore

Columbia's new bookstore has more than just coursebooks. They have a full selection of books you may never see in a class description, along with magazines and enough university parephenalia to dress you from head to toe. Don't worry if you see long lines; thanks to a ton or registers, lines always move quickly.

Morningside Heights, 2920 Broadway (bet. 114th and 115th Sts.), (212) 854-4131, www.bkstore.com/ columbia. Open M-F 9am-7pm, Sa-Su 11am-5pm. MC, V, AmEx, D, ❶❾ to 116th St.-Columbia University. ♿

Kim's Mediapolis

The new. installment of the Kim's stores boasts videos, DVDs, music and books. The video selection remains their strong suit; there's an enormous collection of Hollywood and Independent movies. It's difficult to browse, so come with some idea of what you want. The impressive book section overshadows their weaker music selection. Don't expect to get much assistance, either: the staff brings the daydreaming, careless attitude all the way from the Village branches.

Morningside Heights, Broadway (bet. 113th and 114th Sts.), (212) 864-5321, www.kimsvideo.com. Open M-Su 9am-12am, ❶❾ to 116th St.-Columbia University.

Labyrinth Books

Professors and students alike applaud this recent addition to Morningside's healthy population of bookstores, made possible in part by the rare generosity of its landlord (Columbia). Relying on a strong selection of academic titles rather than coffee and comfy furniture, Labyrinth is a wel-

Where the Students Are

◆ Hungarian Pastry Shop

Graduate students arguing, "You're Wrong!" "No, you're wrong. Heidegger never ate a berry tart that way!"

◆ Kim's Mediapolis

The sort of place stocked with CDs that make you feel hip being around

◆ Koronets

Pizza slices the size of Columbia's endowment. Best late at night when eating this much food magically makes sense.

◆ 1020 Bar

While other neighborhood bars strive to be something they are not, 1020 is happy being just a straight-up good bar.

come retreat for hard-core bibliophiles.
Morningside Heights, 536 W. 112th St. (bet. Broadway and Amsterdam Ave.), (212) 865-1588. Open M-F 9am-9pm, Sa 10am-8pm, Su 11am-7pm. MC, V, AmEx, D, ❶❾ to Cathedral Parkway (110th St.) ♿

Papyrus
Though its hegemony was slightly infringed upon with the introduction of Labyrinth Books, this smallish store stocks a little bit of everything. The literature and travel sections are excellent, as is the selection of textbooks, which often run cheaper than at Columbia University's bookstore.
Morningside Heights, 2915 Broadway (at 114th St.), (212) 222-3350, www.papyrusnyc.com. Open M-F 9:30am-11pm, Su 11am-10pm. MC, V, AmEx, D, ❶❾ to 116th St.-Columbia University. ♿

Universal News
Newly opened to further cater to the literary needs of the Columbia crowd, this in-dustrial looking, no-frills newsagent carries a large selection of national and international newspapers, journals, and magazines.
Morningside Heights, 2873 Broadway (bet. 111th and 112th Sts.), (212) 531-1042. Open M-F 5am-1am, Sa-Su 6am-1am. MC, V, AmEx. ❶❾ to Catherdral Parkway (110th St.) ♿

♦ GROCERY, GOURMET & SPECIALTY

Mondel Chocolates
Florence Mondel has been catering to Morningside Heights chocoholics for more than 50 years. Her modest store is filled with homemade fudge and marzipan, as well as a dozen different kinds of truffles.
Morningside Heights, 2913 Broadway (at 114th St.), (212) 864-2111. Open M-Sa 11am-7pm, Su 12pm-6pm. MC, V AmEx, ❶❾ to 116th St.-Columbia University.

Somads
Located beneath The Heights restaurant and bar, Somads offers some of the best coffee in the neighborhood. Delicious homemade soups and muffins along with Mediterranean-influenced fare make this gourmet deli one of Morningside's hidden gems.
Morningside Heights, 2867 Broadway (bet. 111th and 112th Sts.), (212) 749-7555, Open M-F 7am-9:30pm, Sa-Su 8am-8pm. Cash only, ❶❾ to 110th. ♿

West Side Market
Morningside's neighborhood grocery store, West Side's claim to fame is its round-the clock hours, which make it a perfect spot for watching rowdy fraternity brothers, glassy-eyed alcoholics and night shift construction workers intermingle at 3am.
Morningside Heights, 2844 Broadway (bet. 110th and 111th Sts.), (212) 222-3367. Open 24 hours. MC, V, ❶❾ to 110th-Catherdral Pkwy

♦ MISCELLANEOUS

Cardomat
You'll be amazed how much you'll be able to spend on stationery and candles at this Morningside Heights cards tore. With everything from stuffed animals to frames to hand creme, Cardomat is always a fun place to stop in and kill time. Be careful, though, the cooler the cards, the higher the prices.
Morningside Heights, 2884 Broadway (bet. 112th and 113th Sts.), (212) 663-2085. Open M-Sa 10:30am-9pm, Su 11am-7pm. MC, V, AmEx, D, ❶❾ to Cathedral Parkway (110th St.) ♿

Lechters Housewares
Yet another branch of the national houseware chain, this Lechters is always a good resource in the fall for new Columbia University students needing a laundry hamper or extra self-adhesive hooks. Come mid-year, you'll walk in for a vase because a new boyfriend brings flowers and suddenly you're feeling domestic.
Morningside Heights, 2875 Broadway (bet. 111th and 112th Sts.), (212) 864-5591, www.lechtersonline.com. Open M-Sa 10am-8:30pm, Su 11am-6pm. MC, V, AmEx, D, ❶❾ to Cathedral Parkway (110th St.) ♿

Arts & Recreation

♦ SITES

Columbia University
Architecturally and financially the centerpiece of the neighborhood, this heavily symmetrical creation of McKim, Mead and White appears uncannily like a walled city from the outside; recent construction and renovation projects solidify this Ivy's presence just under Harlem. Low Library (now an administrative building) was once voted one of the most beautiful buildings in North America. The plaza below "the steps" is a grassy playground for co-eds and families alike.
Morningside Heights, From 114th to 120th Sts. (bet. Broadway and Amsterdam Aves.), (212) 854-1754,❶❾ to 116th St.-Columbia University. ♿

General Grant Ashley Memorial
America's largest mausoleum, this tomb, once marred by graffiti, is now in prime condition. Recently, residents of the neighborhood fought to preserve mosaic benches around its perimeter.
Morningside Heights, Riverside Drive (at 122nd St.), (212) 666-1640, ❶❾ to 116th St.-Columbia University.

♦ MUSEUMS AND CULTURAL CENTERS

New York Buddhist Temple
This branch of the Japanese Buddhist sect Jodo Shinshu welcomes all visitors to the Sunday services, which are conducted in both Japanese and English, and to meditation workshops.
Morningside Heights, 331-332 Riverside Dr. (bet. 105th and 106th Sts.), (212) 678-0305, 1 9 to 110th St.

St. John the Divine Cathedral
When you're standing in the crossing of the largest Gothic Cathedral in the world, it's hard to remember you are in Morningside Heights. St. John the Divine features a Gothic nave and Romanesque choir along with over 150 stained glass windows celebrating not just religious scenes - at a closer look the windows depict an early television, a human skeleton and Michelangelo carving the David. Tapestries dating back to the early 17th century along with cloisonné vases, mosaics and a sculpture garden make the Cathedral seem as if it's an uptown annex to the Metropolitan Museum of Art. Services, tours and workshops daily.
Morningside Heights, 1047 Amsterdam Ave. (at 112th St.), (212) 316-7540, www.stjohndivine.org. $2 sightseeing fee, $1 for students and seniors. 1 9 to 110th St.-Cathedral Pkwy.

♦ PERFORMANCE

Manhattan School of Music
Prodigies at one of the country's most prestigious conservatories perform, usually for free.
Morningside Heights, 120 Claremont Ave. (at 122nd St.), (212) 749-2802. Cash Only, 1 9 to 125th St.

Miller Theater
The student price of five bucks buys a consistently impressive line-up, from readings by poet demigods such as Pulitzer prize winners Richard Howard and Louise Glück to performances by established professionals like Yo Yo Ma and Ann Bogart's SITI troupe. The theater's curators also present film retrospectives featuring hard-to-find directors and actors.
Morningside Heights, 2960 Broadway (at 116th St.), (212) 854-7799, www.millertheater.com. MC, V, AmEx, D, 1 9 to 116th St.-Columbia University. ♿

♦ PARKS

Morningside Park
The city has cleaned up this park in recent years. From the top of the hill benches look eastward over breathtaking views of Harlem. Softball fields around the base provide community sports activities, and the daffodills cover the top of the hill in springtime.
Morningside Heights, Morningside Dr. (bet. 110th and 123rd Sts.), www.nycparks.org. 1 9 to Cathedral Parkway (110th St.)

Riverside Park
Continuing up to 158th Street, the upper end of Riverside Park offers beautiful sunset views at the edge of the Hudson. Running trails, ball fields, tennis courts, dog runs, and even a café draw New Yorkers to this narrow strip of nature.
Morningside Heights, Riverside Dr. (bet. 72nd and 158th Sts.), www.nycparks.org.

♦ GALLERIES & LIBRARIES

Miriam and Ira D. Wallach Art Gallery
Located on the eighth floor of Schermerhorn Hall, Columbia University's gallery presents traveling exhibitions throughout the year, curated by professors and students who ensure an academic tilt to the line-up. Lectures and receptions are often sponsored in conjunction with exhibits.
Morningside Heights, 2960 Broadway (at 116th St.), (212) 854-7288, www.columbia.edu/cu/\wallach. Open W-Sa 1pm-5pm. 1 9 to 116th St.-Columbia University. ♿

Nicholas Roerich Museum
Discreetly hidden among a row of brownstones, this museum honors Nicholas Roerich, the artist who designed an international peace symbol during World War II.
Upper West Side, 319 W. 107th St. (bet. Broadway and Riverside Dr.), (212) 864-7752, www.roerich.org. Open: T-Su 2pm-5pm. Admission: Free, 1 9 to 110th St.

Nightlife

♦ BARS

1020 Bar
While most of the bars in Morningside Hegihts pretend to be something they are not, 1020 is just a bar, and quite content that way. During the week, come with a good friend to throw back a few in peace; on the weekends, watch the artsy kids take their first fumbling steps towards skankiness at a nascent pick-up scene. The drinks are okay and prices are friendly.
Morningside Heights, 1020 Amsterdam Ave. (bet. 110th and 111th Sts.), (212) 531-3468. Open M-Su 4pm-4am. MC, V, AmEx, 1 9 to Cathedral Parkway (110th St.) ♿

Abbey Pub
Both the food and the atmosphere are comforting at this ideal neighborhood bar where older locals mingle easily with the collegiate (and younger) crowd. A perfect spot to meet for beers and a shared basket of fish 'n chips.
Morningside Heights, 237 W. 105th St. (bet. Broadway and Amsterdam Ave.), (212) 222-8713. Open M-Su 4pm-4am. MC, V, AmEx, 1 9 to 103rd St.

> As a boy in Harlem, I and many of my friends saw Columbia as a gateway to opportunity and hope. Columbia still provides those same elusively essential ingredients for our city.
>
> —David Dinkins

Amsterdam Café

This local favorite, espicially of AEPI, is a great place to visit either alone, at the padded bar, or in large thirsty groups. Columbia students and locals alike come for cheap pitchers, pub grub and sports TV in a relaxed restaurant atmosphere.

Morningside Heights, 1207 Amsterdam Ave. (bet. 119th and 120th Sts.), (212) 662-6330. Open M-Su 11am-2am. MC, V, D, AmEx, DC, 1 9 to 116th St.-Columbia University.

Saints

Columbia's requisite gay bar has been getting kind of shady on the weekends lately. It's still good for the occasional raucous karaoke throwdown, but this dark, comfortable bar is facing some kind of identity crisis, after enabling so many more through the years.

Morningside Heights, 992 Amsterdam Ave. (at 109th St.), (212) 222-2431. Cash Only, 1 9 to Cathedral Parkway (110th St.)

SoHa Bar & Lounge

"I never want to grab anyone's ass, except when I come here," muses one bespectacled Columbia student. Weekends see a hedonistic pick-up scene at SoHa, with coeds often dancing on the bar; weeknights are more relaxed, good for sinking into a couch with a cosmo and surveying the room.

Morningside Heights, 998 Amsterdam Ave. (bet. 108th and 109th Sts.), (212) 678-0098. Open M-Su 4pm-4am. MC, V, AmEx, 1 9 to Cathedral Parkway (110th St.)

The West End

Hanging out at the West End is a rite of passage for Columbia freshmen with bad fake IDs. It's gone downhill since the days when Kerouac and Ginsberg made this their haunt, now attracting a loyal clientele of frat boys in cologne.

Morningside Heights, 2911 Broadway (bet. 113th and 114th Sts.), (212) 662-8830. Open M-Su 11am-3am. MC, V, AmEx, DC, D, 1 9 to 116th St.-Columbia University.

Ding Dong Lounge

The best bar in the neighborhood. Ding Dong works because it's neither gentrified or collegey or ritzty. And, that doesn't make it an Irish bar or dive, just a bottom line great bar. It's brand new and on a

block of the neighborhood that has yet to be defined. That means you get to make whatever of the time at the bar you want. It could be great, but if you wanted a place to sulk it works just as well. Either way it's yours, so enjoy.

Morningside Heights, 929 Columbus Ave. (bet. 105th and 106th Sts.), (212) 663-2600. Open M-Su 4pm-4am. Cash Only, B C 1 9 to 103rd St.

What Bar

The new addition to this block of bars, What Bar amazes without gimmicks. The deep leather banquettes and oak bar make it comfortable for schmoozing. The large wall of stuff-bras, bad pictures, worse poetry-invites patrons to make a donation for a free drink, providing fun for the mostly college crowd. The shockingly good menu makes it a must for anyone whoever wanted a well-rounded bar.

Morningside Heights, 995 Amsterdam Ave. (at 109th St.), (212) 866-1030. M-Su 5pm-4am. MC, V, AmEx 1 9 to 110th St.

♦ MUSIC

Postcrypt Coffeehouse

Located in the basement of a chapel on the Columbia University campus and seating only fifty, the Postcrypt is one of the most unique rooms in the city. No electronic equipment is allowed on the stage and the only lighting is from candles stuck in wine bottles and chandeliers. Suzanne Vega played her first gig here when she was a student at Barnard College across the street. Snacks and bottled beer available.

acoustic, country, folk, jazz

Morningside Heights, Columbia University (at 116th St. and Broadway), (212) 854-1953, www.columbia.edu/-crypt/. Open F-Sa 9pm-12am (during school year only). Cash Only, Cover: free, 1 9 to 116th St.-Columbia University.

Smoke

This is the classiest and best bar in the neighborhood, and one of the best places for good, intimate jazz. Replacing the Morningside ficture Augie's in 1999, Smoke quickly made a name for itself with jazz acts like George Coleman, Slide Hampton, Cecil Payne, Leon Parker, Eric Alexander and a legendary cameo by George Benson, just to name a few. Don't miss the Wednesday Blues night. Not a college bar at all.

jazz, blues

Morningside Heights, 2751 Broadway (bet. 105th and 106th Sts), (212) 864-6662, www.smokejazz.com. Open: 5pm-4am. MC, V, Cover: $8-$15 ($10 drink minimum), 1 9 to Cathedral Parkway (110th St.)

Harlem

Fine. Harlem is unsafe and a lot of its streets are dark. Everyone knows that and too often it's these disclaimers that hold people back from some of the most beautiful architecture and the most condensed center of culture in New York. Harlem is Manhattan's largest neighborhood and in the past few years has seen some of the economic prosperity its rich history has long deserved.

The Dutch named it Nieuw Haarlem and the neighborhood was farmland until it was linked to downtown by the Harlem railroad. Buildings were constructed in a matter of days and mostly German Jews moved uptown from the Lower East Side in the late 1800s. But, the real estate boom predicted for Harlem never took off and cheap rents and empty buildings attracted New York's African-Americans. The white exodus started.

This is the time of the Harlem most people idealize, when jazz was perfected in Harlem's clubs and the Harlem Renaissance redefined the rules of American expression. When writers like Zora Neale-Hurston, Countee Cullen and Lanston Hughes who said, "as goes Harlem, so goes Black America," lived here. And, jazz clubs like the Cotton Club, Savoy Ballroom, Apollo Theater, and Smalls Paradise were filled with white audiences and not a trace of prohibition.

After the renaissance, Harlem ends as an ideal in history books, though it continued as an ideal in the minds of African-Americans who migrated from the South through the 50s. This was when Malcolm X arrived, and this was when Puerto Ricans arrived by the boatload and turned East Harlem into El Barrio. Heavy redevelopment kicked in in the 70s and this, coupled with the recent economic boom, has put Harlem on the rise. For better or worse Starbucks, has arrived, along with a Pathmark, a huge NYSC gym, Magic Johnson's mutiplex theater and more. Bill Clinton now keeps an office on 125th Street.

The best day to enjoy Harlem is on Sunday. Catch a gospel choir at one of Harlem's many Baptist churches and grab brunch at a soul food restaurant like Miss Maude's or Sylvia's. From there it's all walking, down 125th Street or Strivers Row, through stretches of green like Nicholas or Marcus Garvey Parks. Finish with drinks at one of Harlem's many rowdy-to-laid back bars.

Dining

♦ RESTAURANTS

Amy Ruth's
Menu offerings like the Rev. Al Sharpton Chicken and Waffle special give new meaning to the concept of soul food. The traditional southern food is nothing to write home about, but hearty portions ensure you won't leave hungry.
Harlem, 113 W. 116th St., (212) 280-8779. Open M-Su 7:30am-11 pm. MC, V, AmEx, Entrees: $9-18, ❷❸ *to 125th St.,* ♿

Café Largo
This intimate, dimly lit restaurant has a trendy feel to it, but the crowd remains diverse. Ask for the orange glazed steak, a worthwhile special that doesn't appear on the menu.
Harlem, 3387 Broadway (bet. 137th and 138th Sts.), (212) 862-8142. Open M-Sa 12pm-11:30pm, Su 10:30am-10:30pm. MC, V, AmEx, Entrees: $10-24, ❶❾ *to 137th St.*

Copeland's
A rich and varied menu offers everything from braised oxtails and gumbo to grain-fed catfish and shrimp Creole. The atmosphere is for serious eating; Sunday's gospel brunch is among the neighborhood's finest.
Harlem, 547 W. 145th St. (bet. Broadway and Amsterdam Ave.), (212) 234-2357, www.copelandsrestaurant.com. Open Su-R 8am-11pm, F-Sa 8am-12am. MC, V, AmEx, D, Entrées: $9-$25, ❶❾ *to 145th St.* ♿ 🚲

Jimbo's Coffee Shop
This tiny greasy spoon is always crowded and confused with people clamoring for the phenomenal, $3 bacon cheeseburger.

PLACES TO GO:

Perk's Fine Cuisine
Soul food to the sounds of a soul singer. When you're plate of ribs arrives you'll tell yourself, "If Loving you is Wrong I don't want to be Right."

El Museo del Barrio
A must see. El Museo is incredibly well run and offers exhibits and events that chronicle the lives of Latinos in the U.S.

Lady Luci's Cocktail Lounge
A throwback to when bars were big, the bandstand was bigger and the music blew the place out the water.

Harlem, 1345 Amsterdam Ave. (bet. Hancock and 127th Sts.), (212) 865-8777. Open M-Su 5am-9pm. Cash only, Entrees: $3-5, 1 9 to 125th.

Londel's
Owner Londel Davis greets customers at the door of his sophisticated new Strivers Row supperclub, a harbinger of gentrification in this quickly changing neighborhood. Harlem's hottest restaurant serves delicious, painstakingly prepared Southern food like smothered pork chops and pan-seared red snapper to the neighborhood's most upwardly mobile.
Harlem, 2620 Frederick Douglass Blvd. (bet. 139th and 140th Sts.), (212) 234-6114. Open T-Sa 11am-11pm, Su 12am-5pm. MC, V, AmEx, D, Entrées: $9-$20, A B C D to 145th St.

Miss Maude's
Newly opened by the owners of Miss Mammie's on 110th, Miss Maude's is bigger and better. You can't find better soul food for a lower price. Summers, it's a great place to sip lemonade and get fat; winters, it's a great place to sip something warmer and stay fat.
Harlem, 547 Lenox Ave. (bet. 137th and 138th Sts.), (212) 690-3100. Open M-Sa 12pm-9pm, Su 11am-9pm. MC, V, AmEx, Entrees: $10-17, 2 3 to 135th St.

Perk's Fine Cuisine
"Every third person's a gangsta and the other two are buppies," said one Harlemite about this Harlem hangout. Savor succulent baby back ribs while vocalist Robert Fox serenades the ladies with his super-slick renditions of "Me and Mrs. Jones" and other R&B standards. Terrific bar menu; gracious waitstaff in the plush, expensive dining room downstairs.
Harlem, 553 Manhattan Ave. (at 123rd St.), (212) 666-8500. Open M-Sa 4pm-4am. MC, V, Entrées: $13-$22, A B C D to 125th St.

Sylvia's
Although the most venerable soul food restaurant in New York, Sylvia's succeeds on more than reputation. The crispy and flavorful fried chicken will leave you wishing for more, while sides like collard greens and candied yams will leave you begging for more. Come Sunday for the spectacular after-church gospel brunch (yes, there's singing). And don't forget to leave space for sweet potato pie.
Harlem, 328 Lenox Ave. (bet. 126th and 127th Sts.), (212) 996-0660. Open M-Sa 8am-10:30pm, Su 11am-8pm. MC, V, AmEx, D, Entrees: $9-$18, 2 3 to 125th St.

♦ CAFES

Krispy Kreme
A southern import, these donuts melt in your mouth so fast and taste so good that it's impossible to eat fewer than three.
Harlem, 280 W. 125th St (bet. Seventh and Eighth Aves.), (212) 531-0111, www.krispykreme.com. Open M-Su 6am-10pm. Cash Only, A C D to 125th St.

> Every layover night in Harlem, I ran and explored new places . . . I combed not only bright-lit areas, but Harlem's residential areas from best to worst . . . beggars, sleazy bars, store front churches . . . "bargain" stores, hock-shops, undertaking parlors, greasy "home cooking" restaurants. But New York was Heaven to me. And Harlem was seventh heaven.
>
> —Malcolm X

On the Park Cafe

Filling the vacuum left behind by the sorely missed Harlem Cafe next door, this stylish little coffeehouse promises to be Harlem's answer to the Jackson Hole chain further downtown. Smack dab in the middle of fashionable Striver's Row.

Harlem, 301 W. 135th St. (at Frederick Douglass Blvd.), (212) 694-5469. Open Su-R 7am-11pm, F-Sa 7am-2am. Cash Only, B C to 135th St. ♿ 🚲

Shopping

♦ CLOTHING & SHOES

Sugar Hill Thrift Shop

This excellent option for high-quality vintage clothing, used household merchandise, and jewelry has a purpose: It provides job-training for the formerly homeless. The stock is continually replenished.

Harlem, 409 W. 145th St. (bet. Convent and St. Nicholas Aves.), (212) 281-2396. Open M-F 10am-6pm, Sa 11am-6pm. MC, V, A B C D to 145th St.

♦ BOOKS, MAGAZINES & RECORDS

Liberation Book Store

One of the country's lar-gest and best selections of books about black history and culture. Posters, calendars, and greeting cards are also available.

Harlem, 421 Lenox Ave. (at 131st St.), (212) 281-4615. Open T-F 3pm-7pm, Sa 12pm-4pm. Cash Only, 2 3 to 135th St.

♦ GROCERY, GORMET & SPECIALTY

Fairway

It's not a mirage - it's an honest to goodness supermarket with a parking lot in the middle of Manhattan. A little of suburbia in NYC, Fairway's loaded with a vast array of your favorite foods and the best selection of produce short of a farmer's grove stand. A step up from Stop N' Shop with the best prices.

Harlem, 2328 Twelfth Ave. (at 133rd St.), (212) 234-3883. Open M-Su 8am-11pm. MC, V, AmEx, 1 9 to 125th St.

Make My Cake

A popular bakery whose goods are better recommended for their taste than their looks. Go for the homestyle cupcakes, cakes, breads, and banana pudding, or splurge on a sheet cake with your picture airbrushed on the frosting.

Harlem, 103 W. 110th St. (at Lenox Ave.), (212) 932-0833. Open M 12pm-7pm, T-F 7am-7pm, Sa 10am-7pm, Su 9-4pm. AmEx, 2 3 to 110th St.

♦ MISCELLANEOUS

African Paradise

Paradise is right! Nearly 2000 square feet of crafts and clothing from all over Africa. As Harlem's main street continues undergoing a local renaissance, stores like this are great places to stop in and get a feel for the local identity.

Harlem, 27 W. 125th St. (bet. Lenox and Fifth Aves.), (212) 410-5294. Open M-Sa 10am-7:30pm, Su 12pm-6:30pm. MC, V, AmEx, 2 3 to 125th St.

Cynergy Spa Spa

The only day spa in Harlem, Cynergy provides skin treatments, massage, full body waxing, manicure and pedicure, hair consultations and styling in addition to full body treatments using seaweed, mud, sea salt and herbal wraps in their basement Jacuzzi. Most products are prepared onsite using fresh herbs, vegetables and fruit. The staff is friendly and enthusiastic. Customers can sip tea and eat cake while admiring the Pan-African décor. A placard instructs you to "relax, read, and if you must speak, speak softly."

Harlem, 207 W. 135th St. (bet. Frederick Douglas and Adam Clayton Powell Blvds.), (212) 491-7880. Open M-Sa 9am-7pm, Su 12pm-6pm. MC, V, AmEx. B C to 135th St.

Kaarta's Imports

If you're looking for extraordinary fabrics, do not avoid Kaarta's Imports. They carry stunning African material and clothing for men and women. The entire store is filled with authentic imports.

Harlem, 121 W. 125th St. (bet. Seventh and Lenox Aves.), (212) 866-4062. Open M-Sa 10am-8pm, Su 12pm-7pm. MC, V, AmEx, D, 2 3 to 125th St. ♿

La Marqueta
Spanish for "The Market," La Marqueta offers its customers a large selection of African and Caribbean foods. Products range from bacalao (dried salted codfish) to tropical fruits to cellular and tailoring services. "The best place for Spanish products at the best prices."
Harlem, 1607 Park Ave. (at 116th St.), (212) 534-4900. Open M-Sa 8:30am-6pm. ❻ *to 116th St.* ♿

Mart 125
Enclosed, but far too interesting to feel like a mall, this neighborhood staple sells African dress, crafts, cosmetics, and accessories. The food court upstairs offers good, reasonably priced soul food.
Harlem, 260 W. 125th St. (bet. Adam Clayton Powell, Jr. and Frederick Douglass Blvds.), (212) 316-3340. Open M-Su 8am-10pm. ⒶⒷⒸⒹ *to 125th St.* ♿

Arts & Recreation

♦ PERFORMANCE

Apollo Theater
Fostering such performers as Josephine Baker, the Supremes, and Bill Cosby, since it started integrating black audiences and performers in 1935, this multi-use theater is in full swing thanks to a revival effort in the '80. The televised "Amateur Night" rages on Wednesdays, and both comedians and children's flicks find space here; the stage even hosted James Brown's post-prison comeback concert.
Harlem, 253 W. 125th St. (bet. Adam Clayton Powell Jr. and Frederick Douglass Blvds.), (212) 749-5838. MC, V, AmEx, D, ⒶⒷⒸⒹ *to 125th St.*

Boys Choir of Harlem
This well-known performing arts institution fosters discipline and integrity in young boys and girls through development of academic and artistic talents. Performances include classical music to jazz, contemporary songs, gospels, spirituals, and commissioned works by leading African-American composers.
Harlem, 2005 Madison Ave. (at 117th St.), (212) 289-1815, www.boyschoirofharlem.org. Open M-F 8:30am-4:30pm. ❷❸❹❺❻ *to 125th St.*

Dance Theater of Harlem
This world-renowned, neo-classical company, founded in 1969 as a school and now one of the country's most competitive, dabbles in a bit of everything: jazz, tap dance, modern ballet, and ethnic genres. Students of all ages and at all

The Apollo Theater

The Apollo Theater was built in 1913, and originally a white's only strip show called the Hurtig Seamon's Burlesque Theater. The owner died in 1932 and in 1934 it was bought out, desegregated and renamed the Apollo Theater. The Apollo Theater has, at one time or another, played host to virtually every major black entertainer over the last 70 years.

From Duke Ellington's 1932 performance of "It Don't Mean Thing if it Ain't got that Swing" to Count Bassie up through Smokie Robinson and Stevie Wonder to Parliament to rap and R and B acts now, they've all been here. Most famous of all is the Apollo's Amateur Night, started in 1935. Sarah Vaughn, Ella Fitzgerald and Billy Holiday are all past winners.

More legendary than Amateur Night is Amateur Night's audience who reserves the right to boo anyone off the stage. The Theater went bankrupt briefly but was bought back and given to the community as a gift. The Theater's since been declared a national landmark. Amateur night is every Wednesday, check their website for other events, www.apolloshowtime.com.

The Entertainers Basketball Classic

Master P goes up for a shot, misses and now the ball's in Ron Artest's hands. Puff Daddy , standing at the sidelines, screams at him to pass. There's only one person in the front court, Allen Iverson, who catches the ball and makes the basket. This is the EBC.

Across the street from the projects that replaced the old Polo Grounds, home of the New York Giants, is Rucker Park, home of New York's biggest playground legends. In the 60s and 70s this is where Wilt Chamberlain, Connie Hawkins and Julius Erving spent their off seasons battling locals like Joe Hammond and Pee Wee Kirkland. By the early 80s NBA players were making too much money to risk injury hooping in the playgrounds and the EBC was invented.

The EBC is made up of teams, many owned by hip-hop impresarios like Puff Daddy and Russell Simmons, that serve as a sort of basketball camp for NBA, NCAA and rising high school talents. The small court, technically built for 500 people, is filled with upwards of 1,000 fans from July through mid-August for the tournament. The EBC's schedule trades off with the equally fun-to-watch Rucker League. Rucker Park is located on 155th Street and Eighth Avenue.

levels perform in a monthly open house, usually with accompanying performances by guest artists.
Harlem, 466 W. 152nd St. (bet. St. Nicholas and Amsterdam Aves.), (212) 690-2800. MC, V, AmEx, D, ⒶⒷⒸⒹ *to 155th St.*

National Black Theatre
Founded by Dr. Barbara Ann Teer, the theatre is the only revenue-generating black theater in the United States. A prominent force in perpetuating the richness and beauty of black lifestyle and black culture, the theatre has nurtured great talents, producers, award-winning plays, workshops, lectures, international tours, research projects, and films.
Harlem, 2031-33 Fifth Ave. (bet. 125th and 126th Sts.), (212) 722-3800. Open F 7:30pm, Sa 2pm and 7:30pm, Su 3pm. ⒶⒸⒷⒹ②③④⑤⑥ *to 125th St.* ♿

♦ SITES

Hamilton Grange National Memorial
When Alexander Hamilton commissioned this house from one of City Hall's architects, John McComb, Jr., the location was far removed from the heart of New York. Today, it serves as a public museum operating under the auspices of the National Park Service in the heart of Hamilton Heights.
Harlem, 287 Convent Ave. (at 141st St.), (212) 283-5154, Open F-Su 9am-5pm, ⒶⒷⒸⒹ *to 145th St.*

Theresa Hotel
A tall, white, terra cotta building across from the State Office Building, the old Theresa Hotel has provided rooms to many prominent figures. Fidel Castro and Nikita Khruschev were residents at the hotel when they came to New York City after the Cuban Revolution. The hotel is now a converted office building housing many small firms and offices.
Harlem, 2090 Adam Clayton Powell Jr. Blvd. (bet. 124th and 125th Sts.), (212) 866-0494. Open M-F 9am-10pm. ②③ *to 125th St.* ♿

Strivers' Row
No visit to Harlem is complete without seeing Strivers' Row, two blocks of some of the most elegant row houses in New York City. The first occupants were white millionaires like Randolph Hearst. Since the 1920s, the row has housed prominent black doctors, lawyers, and entertainers, the "strivers" of the community, from which the streets derive their name. Come take a look at the well-kept shrubbery and the clean sidewalks and experience the elegance of Harlem's architecture.
Harlem, 138th and 139th Sts. (bet. Adam Clayton Powell Jr. and Federick Douglass Blvds.). ②③ *to 135th St.* ♿

♦ MUSEUMS & CULTURAL CENTERS

Abyssinian Baptist Church
Pastor Adam Clayton Powel, Sr., built this church from 1920-23 to serve the needs of the growing numbers of blacks on the Upper West Side, naming it for its first worshippers, Abyssinian merchants who wanted to maintain their connection with Africa. The congregation has grown to over 4,000 and is known for its community involvement.
Harlem, 132 W. 138th St. (bet. Adam Clayton Powell Jr. and Malcolm X Blvds.), (212) 862-7474, ❷❸ *to 135th St.* ⅊

African American Wax Museum and History Museum of Harlem
Nelson Mandela and Magic John-son, together at last in life-size wax sculpture. Opened in 1989, the museum also features busts, statues and all the art work of owner Raven Chanticleer.
Harlem, 316 W. 115th St. (bet. Manhattan Ave. and Frederick Douglass Blvd.), (212) 678-7818. Open by appointment only. Cash Only, Admission (suggested): $5-$10, ❽❸ *to 116th St.* ⅊

El Museo del Barrio
Located at the tippy top of Museum Mile, this museum establishes a forum that preserves and projects the cultural heritage of Puerto Ricans and all Latin Americans in the U.S. The museum hosts bilingual public programs, educational activities, and festivals.
Upper East Side, 1230 Fifth Ave. (at 104th St.), (212) 831-7272, www.elmuseo.org. Open W-Su 11am-5pm. MC, V, AmEx, Admission (suggested): $2-$4, ❻ *to 103rd St.* ⅊

Museum of the City of New York
In light of its ego, it's fitting that New York was the first city to get its own museum. Exhibits glorify New York's vast history, and include photographs, furniture, costumes, and toys. The Sunday concert series and the Big Apple Film series make the trip worthwhile.
Upper East Side, 1220 Fifth Ave. (bet. 103rd and 104th Sts.), (212) 534-1672, www.mcny.org. Open W-Sa 10am-5pm, Su 12pm-5pm. Cash Only, Admission (suggested): $4-$5. ❻ *to 103rd St.* ⅊

Schomburg Center for Research in Black Culture
World-famous for its extensive research facilities, this branch of the New York Public Library is an invaluable resource for scholars of black history and culture.
Harlem, 515 Malcolm X Blvd. (at 135th St.), (212) 491-2200, www.nypl.org. Open M-W 12pm-8pm, R-Sa 10am-6pm. ❷❸ *to 135th St.* ⅊

Studio Museum in Harlem
From its origins as a rented loft back in 1967, this intriguing museum has burgeoned into one of the most innovative, focusing on arts from Africa and Black America. The artists-in-residence program gives emerging artists gallery space, and the Cooperative School Program puts professional artists in Harlem schools.
Harlem, 144 W. 125th St. (bet. Adam Clayton Powell Jr. and Malcolm X Blvds.), (212) 864-4500, www.studiomuseuminharlem.org. Open W-R 12pm-6pm, F 12pm-8pm, Sa-Su 1pm-6pm. Cash Only, Admission: $3-$5, ❹❽❻❸ *to 125th St.* ⅊

♦ GALLERIES & LIBRARIES

De La Vega
James De La Vega is best known for the positive messages he writes in chalk on sidewalks throughout the city. If you find those obnoxious, his Spanish Harlem gallery will be intolerable.
Harlem, 1651 Lexington Ave. (bet. 104th and 105th Sts.), (212) 876-8649. Open M-Su 12pm-7pm. Cash Only. ❻ *to 103rd St..*

Galeria Morivivi
This nonprofit gallery located in the heart of El Barrio makes up for its small size with big projects with a multicultural focus. The Galeria changes its exhibits frequently and sponsors performances and side shows during the year.

> Come,
> Let us roam the night together
> Singing.
>
> I love you.
>
> Across
> The Harlem roof-tops . . .
> —Langston Hughes

Harlem, 1671 Lexington Ave. (bet. 104th and 105th Sts.), (212) 663-0672. Open W-F 3pm-7pm, Sa 1pm-6pm. 6 *to 103 St.* ♿

Taller Boricua

Sharing a building with El Museo, this space provides a workshop for community artists. The creative part of Taller Boricua consists of a group of five professional artists, who, in addition to their own projects, help mentor kids from around the neighborhood.

Harlem, 1680 Lexington Ave. (bet. 105th and 106th Sts.), (212) 831-4333. Open T-Sa 12pm-6pm. 6 *to 103 St.*

Countee Cullen Branch of NYPL

Housing the largest collection of African-American materials in the system, the library offers a large circulating and reference collection of books for all ages. Available resources include a newly enlarged reference collection on the third floor, a well-equipped auditorium on the lower level, and a large gallery exhibiting works by local artists on the mezzanine.

Harlem, 104 W. 136 St. (bet. Seventh and Lenox Aves.), (212) 491-2070, www.nypl.org. Open M-T 10am-6pm, W 12pm-8pm, R-F 12pm-6pm, Sa 10am-5pm. 2 3 *to 135th St.* ♿

Gallery M

This non-profit gallery may be small but its size is in no way representative of its art collection. This gallery offers interesting African-American themed paintings, small collectables, hand-made jewelry, glass, and a variety of decorative home accessories. All proceeds from sales go to broaden Gallery M's self-help training program from the community.

Harlem, 123 W. 135 St. (bet. Lenox and Powell Aves.), (212) 234-4106. Open T-Sa 12pm-6pm. 2 3 *to 135th St.* ♿

Nightlife

♦ BARS

Lady Luci's Cocktail Lounge

This spacious neighborhood lounge brings in an older crowd with live jazzmost nights. Monday nights are the best, when a 17-piece big band takes the stage.

Harlem, 2306 Eighth Ave. (bet. 124th and 125th Sts.), (212) 864-8760. Open M-Su 4pm-3am. Cash only, A B C D *to 125th St.* ♿

Lenox Lounge

Unlike other historic bars (like The West End, the Beat enclave turned frat-boy heaven), the Lenox Lounge still has it. There's live jazz most nights, and, with a

recent half mil of renovations, it looks as cool as it sounds.

Harlem, 288 Lenox Ave. (bet. 124th and 125th Sts.), (212) 427-0253. Open M-Su 12pm-4am. MC, V, AmEx, DC, D, 2 3 to 125th St. ♿

Nikki's

A raucous local hangout, Nikki's packs them in every night. Live jazz is featured several nights a week.

Harlem, 289 St. Nicholas Ave. (bet. Dr. Martin L King Blvd. and W. 124th St.), (212) 690-0565. Open M-Su 2pm-4am. Cash only, A B C D *to 125th* St.

Nick's Pub

Definitely a place with a loyal clientele: if a regular is a no-show, the manager calls to see what's wrong. Renowned jazz musicians play to this low-key crowd, and allow local musicians to join in (no, you can't bring your recorder). \

Harlem, 773 St. Nicholas Ave. (at 149th St.), (212) 283-9728. Open Su-F 2pm-2am, Sa 2pm-1am. Cash Only, A B C D *to 145th St.*

Showman's

"Everything is copacetic" at this laid-back haunt, according to the Copasetics, Harlem's brotherhood of tap dancers, which makes this popular club its headquarters. Come for the live jazz Wednesday through Saturday.

Harlem, 375 W. 125th St. (bet. Morningside and St. Nicholas Aves.), (212) 864-8941. Open M-Sa 12pm-4am. MC, V, AmEx, 1 9 *to 125th St.* ♿

♦ MUSIC

Cotton Club

A Harlem legend since before you were born, the Cotton Club is still kicking through the ongoing Harlem renaissance and will probably be around for a few more. Show times vary widely and you must call for reservations. The "don't miss": $25 gospel brunches every weekend. Full southern menu and full bar.

Harlem, 656 W. 125th St. (bet. Broadway and Riverside Dr.), (212) 663-7980, www.cottonclubny.com. Call for schedule and showtimes. MC, V, Cover: $15-$30, 1 9 *to 125th St.*

Fleeing Danielle Steele

"I was waiting for a friend to meet me for coffee the other day, and he was late. So I started doing my French homework while I waited. And I was doing that for a few minutes, before I realized that I was alone, in a coffee shop, reading Proust. In French," relates one undergrad. "And then I realized, Oh my God, I'm that guy."

The bespectacled, black-clad twenty-something hunched over a cup of coffee and sheaf of papers is certainly a New York archetype, and not for nothing. New York has produced a list of famous writers deeper than Santa Claus' sack and if you, an aspiring writer or just a fan of literature, want to know where to go, you've come to the right place.

"Wise Men Fish Here" states the sign swinging in front of the **Gotham Book Mart**, and with good reason. The shelves of this narrow and musty store offer an abundance of great new and used books. The film and poetry sections alone make it worth the visit.

Even mustier than Gotham, the venerable **Strand** is famous for its eight miles of new and used books. But the million titles within are organized by a strange logic more confusing than Finnegans Wake. Our advice: never enter Strand looking for a specific book. Instead, mosey aimlessly through the aisles and see what turns up. If Strand's organization leaves you baffled, flee to **St. Mark's Bookshop** and discover a tasteful selection of chic new titles, from the entire corpora of Derrida and Deleuze to the latest issue of Motorbooty.

If collecting is more your yen, **Argosy Book Store, Inc**. is abundant with ancient (and pricey) volumes of nearly everything in the Western canon. Here first editions of Tennyson mingle with old German Bibles the size of a couch. Be sure to explore the map and poster room on the second floor.

Specialty bookstores abound in Manhattan. **Hacker Art Books** houses a comprehensive collection of books on art, photography, and architecture. Beuys shares shelf space with Botticelli, Malevich with McCarthy; nothing separates them from one another but their dust-jackets. Hacker also carries criticism and artists' biographies.

The **Librarie de France**, **Lectorum**, and **S.F. Vanni** carry only French, Spanish, and Italian books respectively. Librarie de France has one bonus; instructional books on learning any language under the sun and a variety of bilingual dictionaries cram its basement. In due time you too could be reading Proust in the original.

Washington Heights

Of all the neighborhoods in New York City undergoing a renaissance, Washington Heights is perhaps the most deserving and overdue. Throughout the late 1970s and into the 80s, its name served as a synonym for crack-cocaine, after then-U.S. District Attorney Rudy Giuliani and future U.S. Senator Alfonse D'Amato went undercover to prove how easy such purchases were. This event, immortalized on the front page of the *New York Post*, has dogged the area's image for years.

Now Washington Heights, its reputation on an upswing, is on the cusp of trendiness. A walk through the hopping shopping districts of 181st Street and 207th Street confirms just how vibrant and healthy the area can be. Inwood, Manhattan's northern-most neighborhood, continues onward from 207th Street up to the Harlem River Ship Canal, just north of Fort Tryon Park, home to the Cloisters (the Metropolitan Museum of Art's medieval art complex), as well as stunning vistas to the west towards the New Jersey Palisades. Nestled in the north-eastern reaches of the island is the wild and woolly Inwood Hill Park, where you can still find artifacts from the Algonquin village that once stood there.

For much of the 20th century, Washington Heights and Inwood have welcomed large and lively immigrant communities: German, Irish, Jewish, and Greek settlements all strung along Broadway. The last twenty years have seen a massive influx of Dominican immigrants that's made Washington Heights the biggest Dominican community in the U.S. Then there are the hipsters and flocks of twenty something's moving uptown for the luxury of cheap rent in Manhattan. This last influx has led real estate agents to cynically rename the area west of Fort Washington Avenue as "Hudson Heights," attempting to circumvent negative associations with Washington Heights.

Dominating the eastern section of the mid-Heights is Yeshiva University, founded as the first Jewish parochial school in the country. Ten blocks to the south is High Bridge Watch Tower, an architectural leftover from the city's Roman-inspired 19th century aqueduct system. The tower's adjacent to the graceful George Washington Bridge, the only bridge linking New Jersey and Manhattan. Another Heights feature is the newly developed Audubon Biomedical Science and Technology Park, built behind the preserved facade of the Audubon Ballroom, site of Malcolm X's assassination.

This area has always accommodated the blend of middle- and working-class, old world and new, urban and parkland, a scene which is leading outsiders to understand what locals have always known — Washington Heights and Inwood are an authentic microcosm of the city experience.

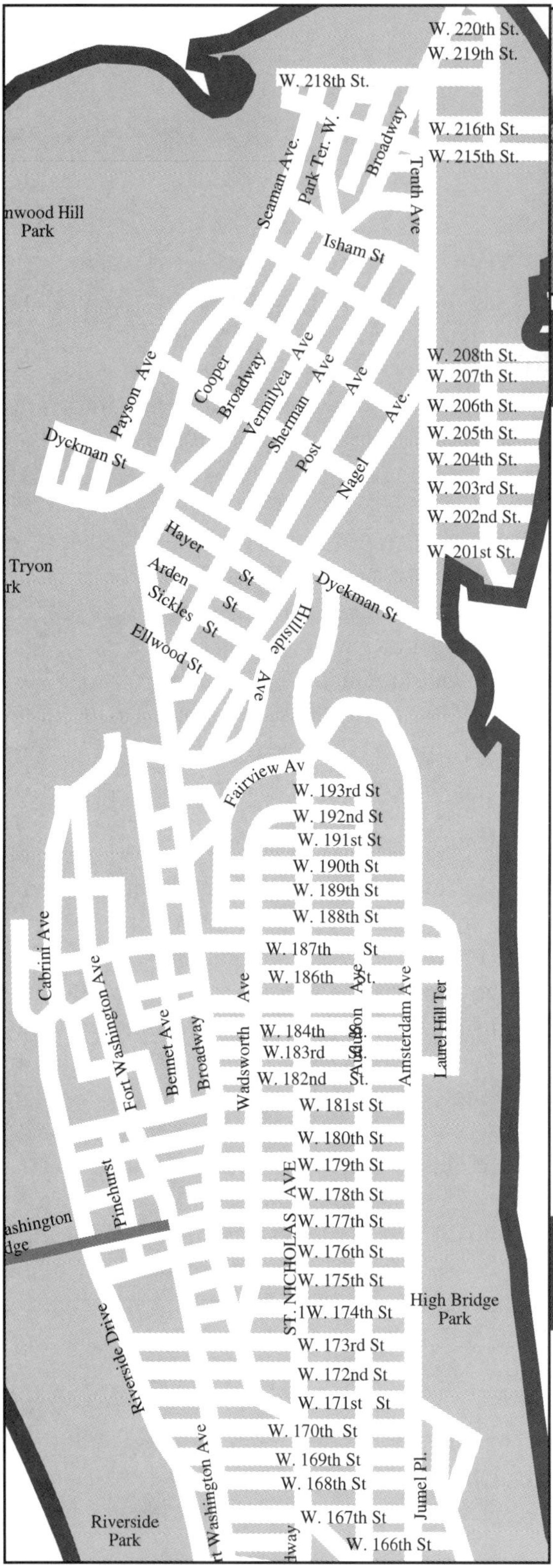

Dining

◆ RESTAURANTS

Bleu Evolution

The food and setting will justify the trek uptown. There's a lovely garden to eat in and a lounge that stays open long after the kitchen closes. Despite its out-of-the-way location, this place is undeniably hip. Some say it's the best part of the neighborhood.

Washington Heights, 808 W. 187th St. (at Fort Washington Ave.), (212) 928-6006. Open M-F 5pm-11pm, Sa-Su 10am-3pm, 5pm-11pm. MC, V, AmEx, D, Entrees: $12-$15, A to 184th St.

Coogan's Restaurant

Latinos and Irish congregate at this upscale pub to partake of classics such as shell steak, shrimp scampi, French onion soup, and roast beef au jus. Karaoke nights on Tuesdays and Thursdays enhance the eclecticism of this popular local hangout, just down the street from the Columbia Presbyterian Medical Center.

Washington Heights, 4015 Broadway (at 168th St.), (212) 928-1234, www.coogans.com. Open M-Su 11am-12am. MC, V, AmEx, DC. Entrées: $9-$17, A B C 1 9 to 168th St.-Washington Heights.

Shopping

◆ CLOTHING & SHOES

Mister Roger

"Italian styles for men" is the only way to view this small boutique. Prices are steep, but the establishment has managed to maintain a beautiful day in the

neighborhood for 14 years.
Washington Heights, 565 W. 181st St. (bet. St. Nicholas and Audubon Aves.), (212) 795-1774. Open M-Sa 10am-8pm, Su 12am-6pm. MC, V, AmEx, D, 1 9 to 181st St., A to 181st St. ♿

Arts & Recreation

♦ MUSEUMS & CULTURAL CENTERS

The American Academy of Arts and Letters
Recent initiates, Oliver Sacks and Elie Wiesel included, attest to the prestige of this exclusive society created to honor American artists, writers, and composers. Check out samples of honorees' works inside the gallery. For a good look at the neighboring Trinity Church Cemetery, stop by the South Gallery, but call ahead — the Academy is only open to the public three times a year.
Washington Heights, 633 W. 155th St. (bet. Broadway and Riverside Dr.), (212) 368-5900. 1 to 157th St. ♿

The American Numismatic Society
If you had one of those penny books as a kid, this is your chance to see what you may have had if you'd only stuck with it. Numismatics has been practiced in these hallowed halls since 1858, and their library maintains over 70 thousand volumes. Other pursuits include a fellowship program for grad students and museum professionals, publishing monographs and journals, and running the annual conference on coinage in America.
Washington Heights, Audubon Terrace, 155th St. (at Broadway), (212)234-3130, www.amnumsoc.org. 1 to 157th St. ♿

The Cloisters
A smorgasbord of old-style Euro-pean glories, not to mention the finest picnicking in the city. The Met has their famed medie-val collection here, including the breathtaking Unicorn tapestries, and medievalthemed readings and concerts keep hobbyists and scholars busy. The Cloisters themselves are a collection of European chapels and buildings in the Gothic and Romantic styles that were dis-assembled and shipped overseas stone by stone by John D. Rockefeller, Jr. and George Barnard, then reassembled way uptown.

PLACES TO GO:

The Cloisters
The Met built the cloisters with pieces from European castles. Seen from afar the building is surreal and the brain rushes to the memory of some movie or other point of reference that doesn't exist.

Bar Hideway
The kind of rowdy bar that could once be found all over the city, in places like Hell's Kitchen, now lives uptown.

The American Academy of Arts and Letters
Maybe it's strange that an organization like this would end up this far uptown, but the Academy, a sort of secret society of art, likes it that way.

Washington Heights, Fort Tryon Park, (212) 923-3700, www.metmu seum.org. Open T-Su 9:30am-5:30pm. Cash Only, Admission (suggested): $5-$10, A to 190th St.

Dyckman Farmhouse Museum
A museum of 18th century farmhouse life, located in one of

A Perfect Murder, 1998

In this 1998 remake of Alfred Hitchcock's Dial M For Murder, humane heiress Gwyneth Paltrow searches for answers at the derelict Washington Heights home of a man she killed when he broke into her sprawling Museum Mile apartment.

Manhattan's oldest residences, reminds urbanites that the city did not simply spring from the soil full-grown. Period furnishings and quiet gardens maintain the mood. Benches out front are ideal for catching rays or hanging out with the area's elderly population (and no, none of them actually lived here).
Washington Heights, 4881 Broadway (at 204th St.), (212) 304-9422, www.astroatlas.com/dyckmanfarmhouse. Open T-Su 11am-4pm. Admission: free, A to 207th St.

Dyckman Street Marina
This marina at the western end of Dyckman St. - the only point above 145th St. where river access isn't blocked - is one of the latest steps in recent revitalization plans for the waterfront. The marina development has sparked a clean-up movement - rumor has it, Bette Midler has recently rolled up her sleeves and joined the litter patrol.
Washington Heights, Dyckman St. on the Hudson River 1 to Dyckman 200 St.

The Hispanic Society of America
Described by a delighted visitor as "one of the city's hidden gems," the museum focuses on the art, literature, and cultural history of Spain; it also offers a reference library which is open to the public.
Washington Heights, 613 W. 155th St. (at Broadway), (212) 926-2234, www.hispanicsociety.org. 1 to 157th St.

Inwood Hill Park
This uptown expanse of woodland boasts cross-country ski trails, caves that were once inhabited by a local tribe, and the island's last remnant of primeval forest. Park Rangers organize tours of the caves during the summer; safety concerns dictate that you not explore them alone.
Washington Heights, Entrance at 207th St., (at Seaman Ave.), (212) 260-1311, A to 207th St.

Morris-Jumel Mansion
Down from the remaining farmhouse is the area's extant Georgian mansion, where Washington kept his headquarters during the Revolution.
Washington Heights, 65 Jumel Terrace (at 160th St.), (212) 923-8008, www.preserve.org/htt. Open W-Su 10am-4pm. Cash Only, Admission: $3, A B C to 163rd St.-Amsterdam Ave.

Yeshiva University Museum
The country's oldest Jewish institution of higher learning regularly holds exhibits on historical and contemporary Jewish themes, such as "Sacred Realm: The Emergence of the Synagogue in the Ancient World." A must see for all.
Washington Heights, 2520 Amsterdam Ave. (bet. 185th and 186th Sts.), (212) 960-5390, www.yu.edu/museum. Open M-R 10am-5pm. Cash Only, Admission: $2-$3, 1 9 to 181st St.

Nightlife

♦ BARS

Bar Hideaway
Things are rowdy at this neighborhood hangout, thanks in large part to the efforts of the lovely Krystal, whose drinks show little of the crippling dependency on mixers that so many 'tenders have.
Washington Heights, 3880 148th St. (at Broadway). Open M-Su 12pm- 3am. Cash only. 1 to 145th St.

Coogan's
Coogan's, whose layout recalls the set of "Cheers," hosts a bustling, after-work crowd from Columbia Presbyterian Medical Center, as well as a loyal and mixed neighborhood clientele. The atmosphere is always festive, especially on karaoke nights (Saturday and Tuesday). It also serves food from an extensive menu.
Washington Heights, 4015 Broadway (bet. 168th and 169th Sts.), (212) 928-1234. Open Su-Sa 11am-4am. MC, V, AmEx, A C 1 9 to 168th St.

Goldbrick Inn
This vaguely posh pub is a little bit out of place in the neighborhood. They seem to know this, though, half-heartedly closing around one many nights.
Washington Heights, 1965 Amsterdam Ave. (bet. 157th and

Ethnic Enclaves:

Washington Heights

The Dominican Republic has been New York City's number one source of new faces since the 70s, when large numbers of Dominicans fled their Caribbean home for the less-than-tropical barrios of the Northeastern United States. Almost a quarter of the immigrant flow has settled in Manhattan's Washington Heights district, where the flavor of Dominican culture is for sale at the scores of tiny eateries located up and down Broadway and St. Nicholas Avenue. Menus at local luncheonettes boast bistec encebollado, octopus salad, guanabara shakes, and cold Presidente beer, served to the beat of merengue music bumping from every available speaker.

Another tip-off that the area is the Dominican Republic's uptown annex is the proliferation of travel agencies offering ticket specials to Santo Domingo and the beach resort of Puerto Plata (only $318!). The community keeps one collective foot in the DR and one in New York City, shuttling back and forth with such regularity that the lines between old world and new seem purely geographical. Even though Washington Heights has strong Russian, Jewish, and Greek presences, it's the slang from the streets of Santo Domingo (and Santiago and Higuey) that rises above the international fugue.

158th Sts.), (212) 281-8171. Open M-Su 12pm-1am. Cash only. A C *to 155th St.*

Irish Brigade Pub
A feisty female bartender serves a much older crowd interested in letting loose. Beers start at $1.50, pitchers at $6. Sometimes as a special treat there's a DJ for dancing.

Washington Heights, 4716 Broadway (at Arden St.), (212) 567-8714. Open M-Su 10am-4am. Cash Only, A *to Dyckman St. (200th St.)*

The Piper's Kilt
The best neighborhood bar in Washington Heights serves odd multi-ethnic food (try "Nachos à la Piper's Kilt") in a plush setting. Specials include a $10 weekend brunch with lots of food and bottomless drinks between noon and 3pm, a weekday lunch special between 11am and 3pm and dinner specials every night between 5pm and 10pm. The wide selection of beer starts at $2, pitchers at $6.50.
Washington Heights, 4944 Broadway (at 207th St.), (212) 569-7071. Open M-Su 11am-2am. MC, V, AmEx, DC, D, A *to 207th St.-Inwood.*

Rose of Kilarney Bar
This dive is beloved by Columbia Med students for its friendly, down-to-earth atmosphere and starving-student prices.
Washington Heights, 1208 St. Nicholas Ave. (bet. 170 and 171st Sts.), (212) 928-4566. Open M-Su 8am-3am. Cash only. 1 9 *to 168th St.-Washington Heights.*

The Little Red Lighthouse and the Great Gray Bridge, 1942

One of those children's books that has developed a large cult of nostalgia, this charming story features the eponymous lighthouse, still extant and set in Fort Washington Park along the Hudson, and its new neighbor, the great, gray George Washington Bridge.

The Bronx

The Bronx is the only NYC borough named after a person, Jonas Bronck, a Swedish sailor who cleared 500 acres and built himself a farmhouse. By 1700, Bronck's farm was destroyed and most of the land was split between four large manors: Pelham, Morrisania, Fordham, and Philipsburg.

The Bronx became famous for its landscaping attractions. In the late 19th Century, the Grand Concourse was built, modeled after tree-lined French boulevards. In 1891, the New York Botanical Gardens opened, followed by the Bronx Zoo; at 2,764 acres, Pelham Bay Park is still the city's largest oasis. The borough was consolidated into New York City in 1898.

Most think of the Bronx and think of an extra large bad neighborhood not worth visiting. It's true to an extent, the South Bronx is arguably the city's worst ghetto, but the Bronx is much more and most people deny themselves of the Bronx's many faces. Riverdale, tucked away west of Van Cortlandt Park, is one of New York's wealthiest areas. Opulent mansions line Fieldston Road and Riverdale Avenue; people often bike through the neighborhood to catch a glimpse of its luxurious houses.

Southeast of Riverdale, the Fordham area is the geographical and demographical center which holds the Bronx together: Latino, Afro-Caribbean, and African-American cultures mix here, allowing meringue to mingle peacefully with hip-hop, Add a long history as a haven for European immigrants and a few Fordham students from Long Island and the mix is complete.

As for the South Bronx and every movie that ever gave it a bad name: Remember that this is where hip hop was invented and, this is the home of Yankee Stadium. So every time a World Series is won (and they've won a bunch), remember that the world comes here.

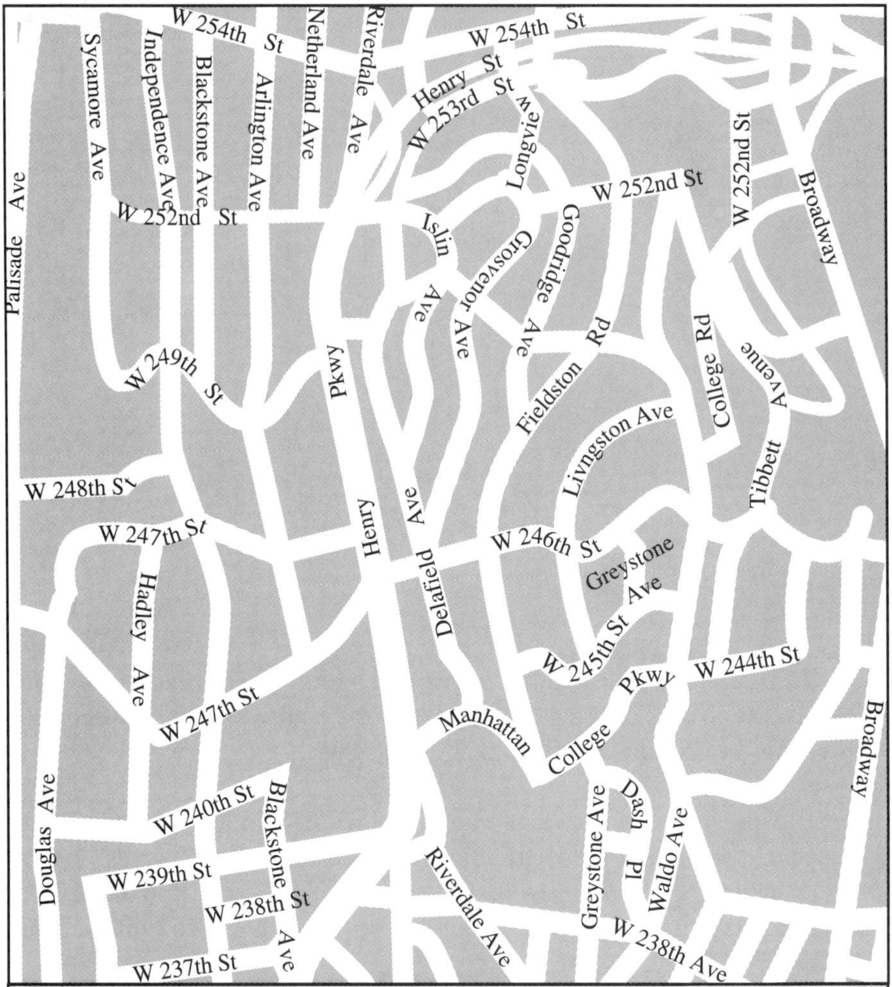

Riverdale

Dining

♦ RESTAURANTS

Bellavista

Riverdale has a bunch of good restaurants, but most residents enjoy this one. It's got a warm environment with a menu of your basic basic Italian fare--pizza and pasta. The sort of basic Italian fare that never did anybody wrong.

Riverdale, The Bronx, 554 W. 235th St. (bet. Oxford and Johnson Aves.), (718) 548-2354. Open M 5pm-10pm, T-Su 12pm-10pm. MC, V, AmEx, DC, D, Entrees: $12-$24, 1 9 *to 231st St.* ♿

Dominick's

There's a reason for the Sunday evening wait, this grandfather of Bronx restaurants is the blueprint for all of the Bronx's other Italian restaurants. There's no menu, just be patient while the waiter tells you exactly what it is you need.

East Tremont, The Bronx, 2335 Arthur Ave. (at 187th St.), (718) 733-2807. Open W-M 12pm-10pm. Cash Only, Entrées: $15-$30, C D *to 182nd-183rd Sts.* ♿

Il Boschetto

The place to see huge portions of food on big ass plates. Bring the beano and an appetite. Bring a bunch of friends too. Forget the conversation, just concentrate on the large portion of food in front of you and proceed to hurt yourself.

Baychester, The Bronx, 1660 E. Gun Hill Rd. (at Tiemann Ave.), (718) 379-9335. Open Su-R 12pm-10pm, F-Sa 12pm-12am. MC, V, AmEx, DC, D, Entrées: $25-$35, 5 *to Gun Hill Rd.* ♿

PLACES TO GO:

Jimmy's Bronx Café

Jimmy's is the essence of the Latino experience in New York. It's a gigantic restaurant, perched on a hill, with amazing food and a dance floor with lives bands that play the best Salsa outside of Puerto Rico.

The Bronx Zoo

The largest urban zoo in the country is so up-to-date and such a great imitation of different animal habitats that the animals still aren't sure where exactly they are.

Skate Key Roller Rink

Old school fun. Gives visitors the chance to throw on the skates and race, hold hands and do the Electric Slide.

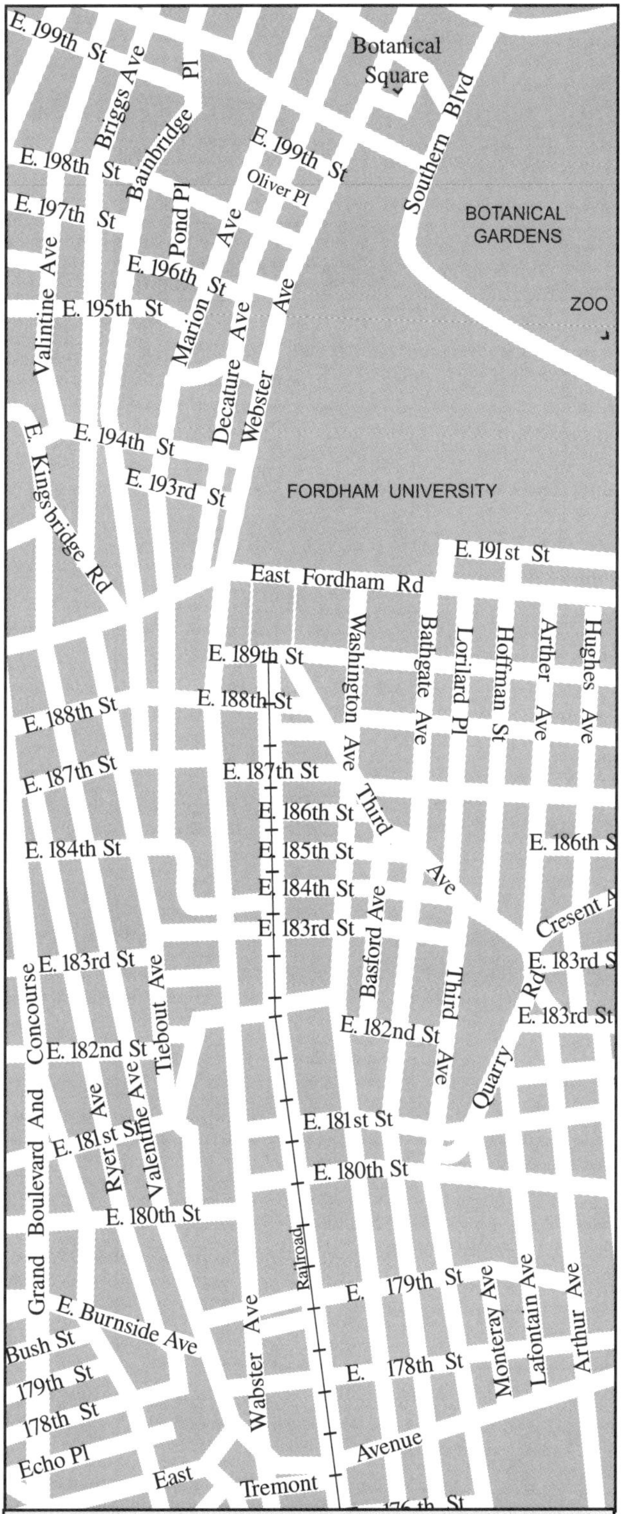

Fordham

Jimmy's Bronx Café

After just four years in the Bronx, this "Latin Restaurant and Entertainment Complex" has become the nucleus for nightlife in the borough's Latino community. Upstairs, seafood is served into the wee hours as patrons watch boxing and baseball on the large TVs. Downstairs, the dance floor resembles a hotel ballroom, built for high capacity. As at other Latin clubs, there's no such thing as overdressing, though casual seems prevalent. Salsa dancing on Tuesday nights.

Fordham, The Bronx, 281 W. Fordham Rd. (at Major Deegan Expressway), (718) 329-2000, www.jimmysbronx-cafe.com. Open Su-R 11am-2am, F-Sa 11am-4am. MC, V, AmEx, Entrées: $8-$18, 1 9 to 207th St.

Le Refuge Inn

You'll be tempted to stay the night at this bed and breakfast. Whoever thought the words, "I think I'd like to live in the Bronx" would cross your mind. Well they will when you sit down to the delicous French food and great service, staring the whole time at the stairs leading to the rooms above.

City Island, The Bronx, 620 City Island Ave. (at Sutherland St.), (718) 885-2478. Open W-Su 6pm-10pm. AmEx, Entrées: $45-$55, 6 to Pelham Bay Park.

Lobster Box

Though not what it used to be, the Lobster Box still provides the amazing view of the water it's always boasted. The lobster's great, the fish mediocre. What it amounts to is a good place to go with family or the answer to an overwhelming lobster craving.

City Island, The Bronx, 34 City Island Ave. (bet. Belden and Rochelle Sts.), (718) 885-1952. Open Su-R 12pm-11pm, F-Sa 12pm-12:30am. MC, V, AmEx, DC, D, Entrées $25-$35, 6 to Pelham Bay Park.

Mario's

After visiting the Botanical Gardens a lot of people amble over to this Arthur Avenue institution that's been around since 1919. A near oppressive amount of tourists mingles with locals, but it's worth the pasta.

East Tremont, The Bronx, 2342 Arthur Ave. (bet. 184th and 186th Sts.), (718) 584-1188. Open Su, T-R 12pm-10:30pm, F-Sa 12pm-11:30pm. MC, V, AmEx, Entrées: $16-$25, C D to 182-183 Sts.

Shopping

♦ CLOTHING & SHOES

Loehmann's

As legendary as Century 21 in designer junkie circles, this discount outpost rewards the shopper who makes the trek: lots of big-name labels and high stock turnover justify frequent trips.

Riverdale, The Bronx., 5740 Broadway (at 236th St.), (718) 543-6420, www.loehmanns.com. Open M-Sa 10am-9pm, Su 11am-6pm. MC, V, D, 1 to 238th St.

♦ BOOKS, MAGAZINES & RECORDS

DJ Specialty

Trying to make it as a DJ and need music to accomplish your goal? DJ Specialty carries CDs, tapes, and vinyl of the best in hip-hop, reggae, R&B, house, salsa, and merengue. At least you'll have the music right.

The Bronx, 1154 Castle Hill Ave. (at Powell Ave.), (718) 829-4000. Open M-W 11am-6pm, R 11am-7pm, F 11am-8pm, Sa 10am-7pm. MC, V, AmEx, D, 6 to Castle Hill Ave.

Paperbacks Plus

One of few Riverdale bookstores, Paperbacks Plus fits in nicely on Riverdale Avenue. They feature books for adults and children, with a wide selection of contemporary fiction.

Riverdale, The Bronx, 3718 Riverdale Ave. (bet. 236th and 238th Sts.), (718) 796-3119. Open M-Sa 9:30am-6:30pm, Su 11am-5:30pm. MC, V, AmEx, 1 to 238th St.

Wow Comics

Those who can't always make it to Manhattan's larger comic stores take heart in this comfortable mainstay — remember, even Peter Parker lived in an outer borough at first, commuting into town to do his crimefighting as Spiderman! New and old releases from a variety of both mainstream and independent companies are sold alongside baseball cards, action figures, and other memorabilia.

Parkchester, The Bronx, 1491 Williamsburg Rd. (at Eastchester Ave.), (718) 829-0461, www.wow comics.com. Open M-Su 8am-7pm. MC, V, AmEx, D, 6 to Zerega Ave.

♦ GROCERY, GOURMET & SPECIALTY

Bancardi's

This meatshop is over 60 years old, but you can be sure that what you buy is very fresh. You can purchase excellent pork, beef, and especially veal, and at Bronx prices.

East Tremont, The Bronx, 2350 Arthur Ave. (at 187th St.), (718) 733-4058. Open M-Su 8am-6pm. Cash Only, C D to 182nd-183rd Sts.

Delillo Pastry Shop

Treat yourself to sweet Italian pastries next time you're in the neighborhood. Delillo Pastry Shop offers delicious Italian eats, and even Italian ices.

East Tremont, The Bronx, 606 E. 187th. St. (at Arthur Ave.), (718) 367-8198. Open M-Su 8am-7:30pm. Cash Only, ⓒⓓ *to 182nd-183rd Sts.* ♿

♦ MISCELLANEOUS

Macy's

"The Largest Store in the World" often resembles the chaos of the Thanksgiving Day parade they sponsor, especially after work and around Christmas. Most items are lower priced than other department stores, but the service and bathrooms reflect this reduction.

Parkchester, The Bronx, 1441 Metropolitan Ave. (bet. Wood Ave. and Metropolitan Oval), (718) 828-7000, www. macys.com. Open M-W 10am-7pm, R 9am-8pm, F-Sa 9am-7pm, Su 12pm-6pm. MC, V, AmEx, D, ⑥ *to East 177th St.-Parkchester.*

Arts & Recreation

♦ LEISURE

The Bronx Zoo

The largest urban zoo in the country, The Bronx Zoo has over 6,000 animals covering every neighborhood of the world, from tigers of the Himalayan Highlands to bats flying straight at your head in The World of Darkness (don't worry, there's a glass window). Beware, just because you paid to get in doesn't mean the rest is free - be expected to pay an extra $3 admission to see the gorillas in the Congo, $2 to ride the monorail or safari gondola plus marked-up snack and fast foods. Still a must-do for all ages.

Bronx, 2300 Southern Blvd., (at Pelham Parkway), (718) 367-1010. www.wcs.org. Open M-F 10am-5pm, Sa-Su 10am-5:30pm, Holidays 10am-5:30pm. R-T $9 adult, $5 child 2-12, $5 seniors 65+, Free admission Wednesdays. ②⑤ *to Pelham Parkway*

The New York Botanical Garden in the Bronx

"Flowering" in the shadow of the inimitable Bronx Zoo is the 250-acre sprawl of gorgeousness. It's a great place to get lost on a spring day, whether you choose to educate yourself on an eco-tour, or just to lounge and marvel at it all.

Bronx, 200th St. (at Kazimiroff Blvd.), (718) 817-8700, www.nybg.org. Open T-Su 10am-6pm. ⒷⒹ *to Bedford Park Blvd.*

Skate Key Roller Rink

Skate Key is a modern roller-skating rink that has managed to stay in touch with its old school roots. Skaters still use four track skates, still munch on microwave pizza from an overpriced concession stand, and still dance the hokey-pokey. With rates of six dollars for one tour hour session, Skate Key is well worth its price.

Bronx, 220 138th St. (bet. Grand Concourse and Third Ave.), (718) 401-1387. Open R-F 8pm-12am, Sa 4pm-2am, Su 4pm-1am. MC, V, AmEx, ④⑤ *to 138th St.*

Wave Hill

This Riverdale estate and public garden is one of New York's best-kept sight-seeing secrets. Overlooking the Hudson River and the Palisades, Wave Hill offers a number of breathtaking views to inspire even the most jaded New Yorker. Within its 28 acres are meticulously manicured gardens and nature trails highlighting the estate's diverse flora. Guided walks are offered every Sunday; art and nature are celebrated year-round with concerts, nature hikes and educational programs.

Bronx, 675 W. 252nd St. (entrance at W. 249th St. and Independence Ave.), (718) 549-3200, Cash Only, Admission: $2-$4 (free Nov-Mar.), Open T-Su 9am-5:30pm (Oct-Apr. closed 4:30pm), ①⑨ *to 231st St.*

Yankee Stadium

A true American experience. Down to the peanuts and crackerjacks, Yankee Stadium fulfills the dream for every 8-year-old boy in the country. Even though the notoriously uproarious crowds have tamed down since the no-beer mandate in the bleachers, Yankee games are still fun for all ages. Even if you're not the world's biggest baseball fan, this is an experience you just can't miss.

I grew up in a ghetto called Morrisania, which, had its own Black Belt on Boston Road, and a strip of bodegas under the trucks of Southern Boulevard, a wall of Irish surrounding Crotona Park, and a heartland of Italians and Jews, poor as hell, except for a handful of furriers, accountants, lonely physicists, and our congressman, who lived on Crotona Park East.

—Jerome Charyn

Bronx, 161st St. (at River Ave.). BD4 *to 161st St-Yankee Stadium*

♦ SITES

Edgar Allen Poe Cottage
Situated on little more than a median strip, this tiny cottage where the godfather of gloom lived out the last years of his life and penned "Annabel Lee" and "The Bells" will nonetheless delight Poe admirerers. Open only on weekends or by appointment, the tour includes a video presentation.
Bronx, Grand Concourse Rd. (at E. Kinsbridge Rd.), (718) 881-8900. Open Sa 10am-4pm, Su 1pm-5pm. Cash Only, Admission $2, CD *to Knightsbridge Rd.*

♦ PARKS

Pelham Bay Park
New York's largest park offers fun on land and off. Find your sea-legs at Orchard Beach, the lagoon, or a canoe and kayak launch. If none of these float your boat, opt for one of two full-size or miniature golf courses, the driving range, tennis courts, the mansion-museum, stables and bridle trails, or the two wildlife centers and trails. What more could you ask?
City Island, The Bronx, E. of the Hutchinson River (bet. Park Dr. and Eastchester Bay), (718) 430-1890. 6 *to Pelham Bay.*

Van Cortlandt Park
Van Cortlandt Park features three golf courses, tennis courts, a swimming pool, nature trails, equestrian center and a certified forest - it's hard to remember you're still in New York City. With a large number of public recreational fields, Van Cortlandt's always good for a soccer or rugby game. There's also a scenic cross-country trail; and at six miles, it's the largest of its kind in the city.
Van Cortlandt Park (bet. Broadway and Jerome Ave.) 19 *to 242nd St.*

♦ MUSEUMS & CULTURAL CENTERS

Bartow-Pell Mansion Museum
If ever motivated to go all the way out to this museum, you'll enjoy this mansion's beautiful interior and gardens. Victorian, all of it, full of chairs you can't sit on and ugly statues. Be advised: it is waaaay out there.
Bronx Shore Rd. (at Pelham Bay Park), (718) 885-1461, Open: W, Sa-Su 12pm-4pm, Admission: $2.50 Adults, $1.25 Senior Citizens, Children under 12 Free 6 *to Pelham Bay Park.*

Bronx Museum of the Arts
True to its slogan,"It's more than just a museum," the space serves not only as a site for visual arts exhibitions, but also as a performance space, an artists' forum, and a center for "art making workshops." Its commitment to multicultural programming is evident in its diverse array of shows and weekly events.
Fordham, The Bronx, 1040 Grand Concourse Rd. (at 165th St.), (718) 681-6000. Open W 3pm-9pm, R-F 10am-5pm, Sa-Su 12pm-6pm. Admission (suggested): $2-$3, CD4 *to 161st St.-Yankee Stadium* ♿

Van Cortlandt House Museum
Once a plantation estate, Van Cortlandt House Museum is now testimony to beautifully maintained colonial architecture and groundskeeping. Here you'll find parlors, bed chambers, a slave chamber and various other rooms with their original furnishings.
Van Cortlandt Park, Bronx, Broadway (at W. 246th St.), (718)543-3344, www.vancortlandthouse.org. Open T-F 10am-3pm, Sa- Su 11am-4pm. Admission: Adults: $2, Senior Citizens and Students: $1.50, Children: Free,. 19 *to end of line (Van Cortlandt) and walk to Park.*

♦ GALLERIES AND LIBRARIES

Bronx River Art Center
A great spot to browse local artists from culturally diverse backgrounds (the latest exhibit features tapestries and Vodoo art from Haiti) or pick up the brush yourself. The Center offers gallery space, art lessons and an outdoor sculpture garden.
Bronx, 1087 E. Tremont Ave. (at E. 177th St.), (718) 589-5819, www.bronxriverart.org. Open Gallery M-F 3pm-6pm, Sa 4pm-5pm by appointment only, 25 *to Tremont Ave.* ♿

Nightlife

♦ BARS

The Warehouse
A gay dance club in the Bronx is somewhat anachronistic. The Warehouse reflects its roots by laying the focus on the dancing, not on profiling, and offering an ecstatically blue-collar menu of fried meat by-products.
The Bronx, 41 E. 40th St. (bet. Walton Ave. and Grand Concourse Rd.), (718) 992-5974. Open Sa 11pm-7am. Cover: $15; cash only. 2 *to 149th St.-Grand Concourse*

Long Island's Beaches

Long Island has long served as a playground for New Yorkers and is easily accessible by the Long Island Railroad (LIRR) and offers a variety of recreational possibilities.

Hamptons

In the summer, celebrities, society notables, and others head out to the, a conglomeration of small towns on the island's eastern end. The beaches in the Hamptons are beautiful, and some are relatively deserted. There are trendy shops and galleries to browse through in town, and for a truly guilty pleasure, walk or drive through the residential blocks and stare at the mansions.

Montauk

Sample some of the tastiest lobster you've ever had from one of the many roadside seafood restaurants in this town just East of the Hamptons. For more mansions and spectacular views head to Old Westbury Gardens (516-333-0048) and visit the replica of a Charles II-style mansion on 150 landscaped acres, or the Sands Point Preserve (516-571-7900)

Shelter Island

For a trek off the beaten path, take a day trip to this secluded, 12 square mile island nestled between the north and south forks of Long Island's eastern end. The island can only be reached by ferry, which ebbs the tide of tourism. Rent a sailboat and go fishing, or hike over the varied terrain and enjoy the peace and quiet. Take the Sunrise Express Bus Service (631-477-1200) from Manhattan.

Oyster Bay

A charming rustic town home to Sagamore Hill National Historic Site (516-922-4447), the former residence of original roughrider Theodore Roosevelt. This three-story, 22 room Victorian House is an impressive sight (the guided tours frequently sell out on weekends, so get there early).

Jones Beach

By far the most popular beach (516-785-1600, for information) and reached by the ubiquitous LIRR. The beach is inundated with sunseekers on summer weekends, when people from all boroughs leave the city for some serious beach bumming. Long Island's most famous boardwalk is found here, and it offers such amenities as 1930s bath houses, outdoor eateries, miniature golf, and swimming pools.

Queens

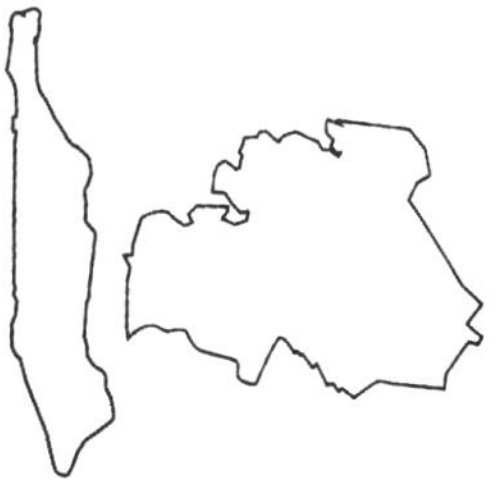

If New York is still the city for immigrants to make a living in, the dream lives on in Queens. No ships stop at Ellis Island anymore, instead planes land by the hundred thousand at La Guardia or JFK in Queens. Many, suitcase in one hand, address of a far off friend in the other, don't make it further than New York's largest borough.

Queens boasts residents from 100 backgrounds who speak over 120 languages. Forest Hills, Kew Gardens and Rockaway have long been predominantly Italian and Jewish, while the Irish live in Woodside and Long Island City. Astoria is something of a little Greece; Jamaica and Elmhurst boast a huge West Indian population; and Jackson Heights is home to Latin Americans and South Asians alike.

The 1939-40 World's Fair solidified Queens' role as one of New York's primary locales for recreation, arenas, and beautiful parks. Preparation for the Fair converted Flushing Meadows from a dumpsite to the city's largest landscaped recreation area after Central Park. La Guardia Airport and bridges were built, streets were widened, and sports stadiums were constructed.

It's a less hectic life in Queens. Tree lined rows of modest brick and wood houses, all with backyards—the sort of place to raise a family. Still city though, edge and everything. Check out Queens Boulevard at night or try a Mets game at Shea where the fans are rowdier than their cross town rivals in the Bronx. Queens, for the most part, is a middle and working class paradise. Residents affirm it's an inexpensive place to live, work and play. That's why so many people fly in from somewhere far away, look around, and decide things look fine right here.

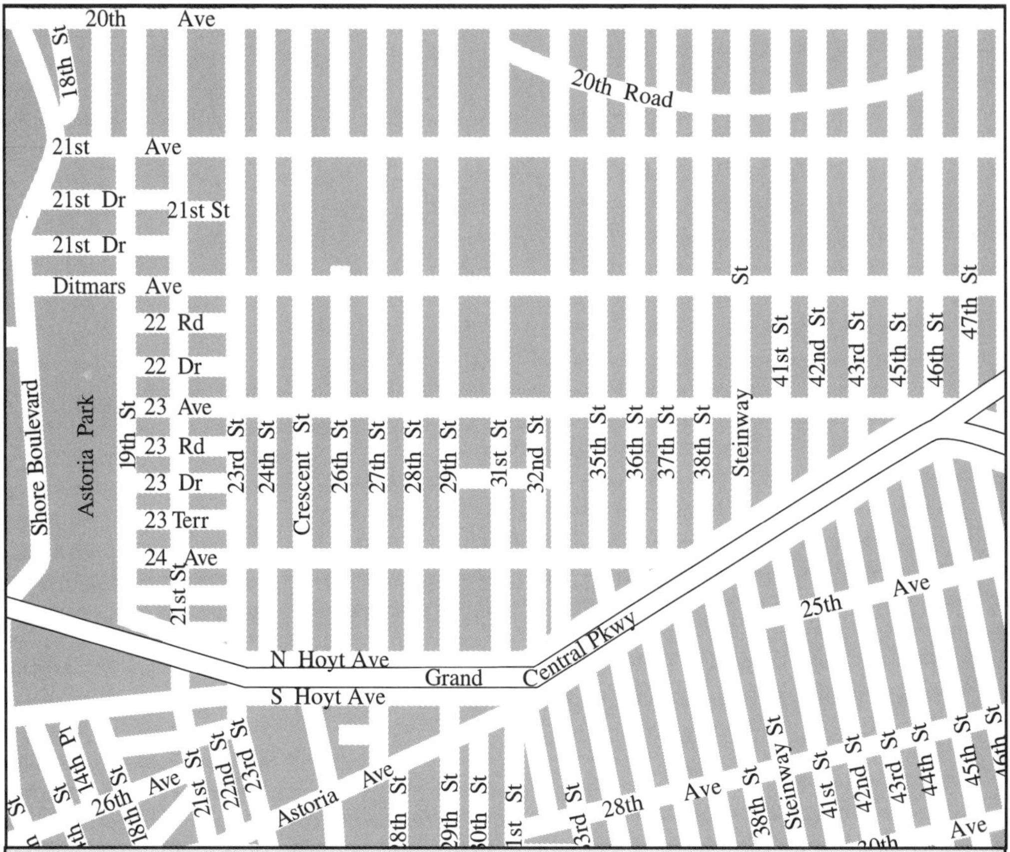

Astoria

Dining

♦ RESTAURANTS

Annam Brahma Restaurant

The eclectic menu's only unifying thread is that everything is prepared sans meat, meaning everything from Indian ratia to tofu omelets to chapatti roll-ups may grace your table. Thursdays the cooks rally around pasta for Italian day; Tuesdays put Chinese vegetarian mainstays center stage. Check out the books, tapes, and other items for sale in the back of the restaurant.

Jamaica, Queens, 84-43 164th St. (at Eighty Fifth Ave.), (718) 523-2600. Open M-T, R-F 11am-10pm, W 11am-4pm, Su 12pm-10pm. Cash Only, Entrées: $4-$8, F *to Parsons Blvd.*

Carmichael's

Wizened locals fill up on soul food after Sunday's sermon at this slightly derelict, though cozy, neighborhood favorite. The fried chicken is amazing.

Jamaica, Queens, 117-08 Guy R. Brewer Blvd. (at One Hundred Eighteenth Ave.), (718) 723-6908. Open M-Su 6am-8pm. Cash Only, Entrées: $6-$10, E *to Jamaica Center-Parsons/Archer.*

Dante Restaurant

Mature crowds of businessmen and nearby St. John's University professors and athletes visit this dimly lit Italian bistro and bar. After hours it's a good place for big hair and big fun.

Flushing, Queens, 168-12 Union Turnpike, (718) 380-3340. Open M-F 11:30am-10pm, Sa 2pm-10pm, Su 1pm-9:30pm. Entrées: $9.95-$19.95, MC, V, AmEx, D, E F *to Union Turnpike-Kew Gardens.*

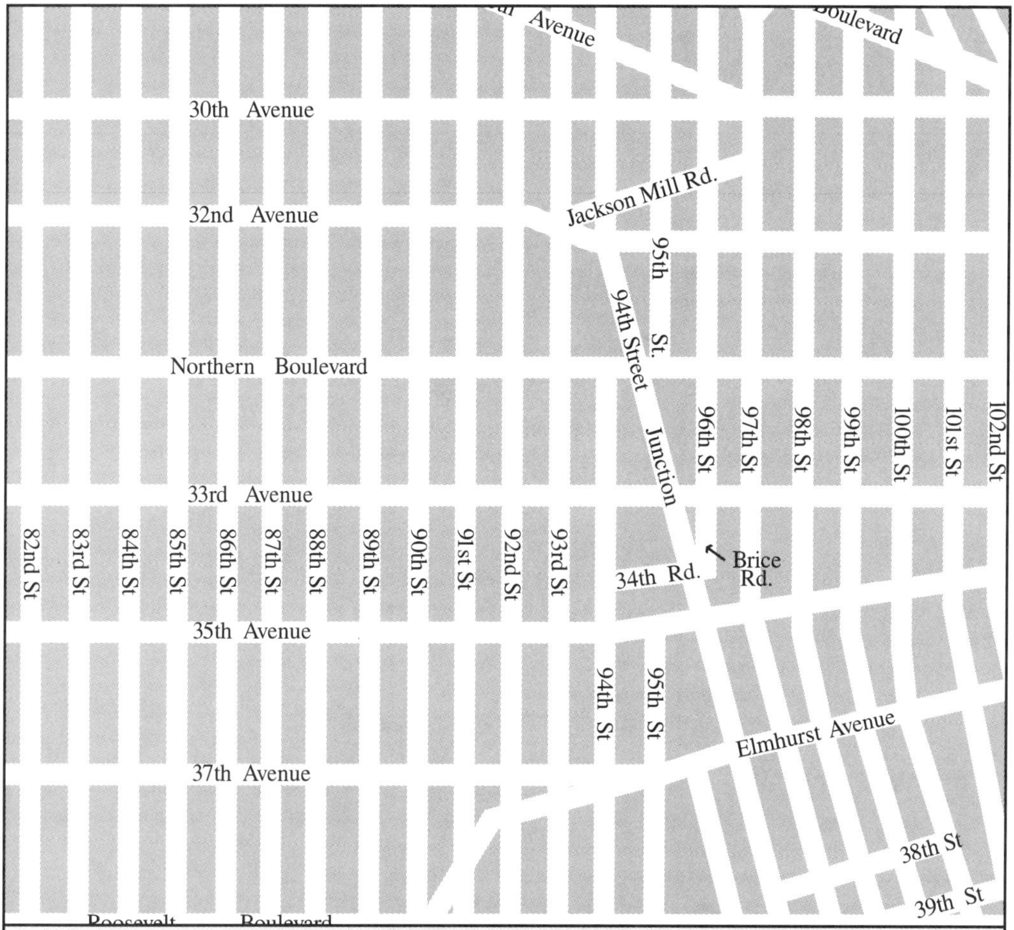

Jackson Heights

PLACES TO GO:

Rib Shack
Soooooooooooooul food. A finger licking, fattening, greasy version of paradise.

Von's School of Hard Knocks
So you just got out of prison and you want a line of clothing that represents what you've been through. Or, maybe you're just a tough guy. This is the place to go.

Kaufman-Astoria Studios
In the 30s movies weren't only made in Hollywood. Giants like Charlie Chaplin and the Marx Brothers made as many movies here as they did in that other town.

I lay puzzle as I back track to earlier times. Nothing's equivalent, to the New York State of Mind."

—Nas

Manducatis

Wine buffs and locals alike frequent Manducatis, a friendly family-run restaurant with fresh ingredients and a vast wine cellar reflecting serious dedication to Italian imports. Fireplaces and lavender tablecloths dress up the exposed brick walls. The menu standards astound, particularly the homemade pasta, but if nothing appeals, you can create your own dish.

Queens, 13-27 Jackson Ave. (bet. 21st St. and Forty Seventh Ave.), (718) 729-4602. Open M-F 12pm-3pm, 5pm-10pm, Sa 5pm-10pm, Su 2pm-8pm. MC, V, AmEx, DC, D, Entrees: $8-$19, G to 21st St. (Van Alst).

El Sitio de Astoria

Set the mood for truck-stop romance with your table's jukebox, although deals like the bandejas completas — a massive serving of meat, rice, beans, plantains, and croquettes —aren't among the wisest first-date choices. Getting a little tipsy on the sangria should take care of this.

Long Island City, Queens, 35-55 31st St., (718) 278-7694. Open Su-R 11am-11pm, F-Sa 11am-12am. MC, V, AmEx, Entrées: $7-$13, N to Thirty Sixth Ave. (Washington Ave).

Elias Corner

You'll have to read the reviews on the wall or point at fish in the glass case — there are no menus — but either way Elias Corner will stuff you silly. Across the street from its old location, this seafood pleasure house features rough charm and primitive décor, but no matter: Delicious red snapper, octopus, and squid, along with bottles of cheap but effective wine make this completely worth the trip to Astoria.

Astoria, Queens, 24-02 31st St. (at Twenty Fourth Ave.), (718) 932-1510. Open M-Su 4pm-12am. Cash Only, $8-$16, N to Astoria Blvd. (Hoyt Ave.).

Joe's Shanghai

Tourists, locals, and suburban Chinese flock here for the juicy crabmeat buns for which Joe's is deservedly famous. Friendly service and the savory quality of the rest of the fare keeps customers coming back for more.

Queens, 136-21 Seventh Ave. (bet 138th and Main Sts.), (718) 539-3838. Open M-R 11am-11:00pm, F-Sa 11am-12pm. Cash Only, Entrées: $5-$18, 7 to Main St.

Rib Shack

This venue's offerings of sweet potato pie, collard greens, and fried chicken will move the hearts of devoted soul food lovers. The employees are so friendly that they regularly garner tips, a wow considering that customers are only allowed to order take-out.

Jamaica, Queens, 157-06 Linden Blvd. (bet. Sutphin and Guy Brewer Blvds.), (718) 659-7000. Open Su-R 11am-11pm, F-Sa 11am-12am. MC, V, AmEx, Entrées: $6-$8, EJZ to Sutphin Blvd.-Archer Ave.

Richard's Place

Something about church just makes you hungry sometimes. Forget all you learned about gluttony and gorge yourself at Richard's scrumptious all-you-can-eat Sunday brunch. Prices leave enough for tithings.

Jamaica, Queens, 200-05 Linden Blvd. (bet. Francis Lewis and Farmers Blvds.), (718) 723-0041, www.richardsplace.com. Open W-R 11:30am-9:15pm, F 11:30am-10:15 pm, Sa 8:15am-10:15pm, Su 8:30 am-7:15pm. MC, V, Entrées: $8-$12, EJZ to Jamaica Center-Parsons/Archer.

Zum Stammtisch

While German cuisine hardly qualifies as in vogue to chic Manhattan critics, its heartiness goes over well with the locals in this quiet neighborhood. Stained glass windows and dim lights bring to mind stodgy
19th century German intellectuals debating Hegel over steins.

Glendale, Queens, 69-46 Myrtle Ave. (at Cooper Ave.), (718) 386-3014, www.zumstammtisch.com. Open Su-F 12pm-10pm, Sa 12pm-12am. MC, V, AmEx, Entrées: $7-$16.

♦ CAFES

Cafe Kolonaki

The fun and cozy split-level coffee shop is fairly new to the Steinway shopping area. The decor is contemporary, and the staff has young and perky nipples.

Astoria, Queens, 33-02 Broadway (at 33rd St.), (718) 932-8222. Open M-Su 6:30am-3am. MC, V, AmEx, D, N to Broadway.

Omonia Café

Enjoy a piece of Greece at Astoria's best liquor, coffee, and pastry bar. Lounge at a table among a multilingual crowd, or choose what to order from the vast selection of standard and exotic pastries behind the glass counter up front including five shelves of different kinds of baklava.

Queens, 32-20 Broadway (at 33rd St.), (718) 274-6650. Open M-Su 6:30am-3am. MC, V, AmEx, D, N to Broadway.

♦ CLOTHING & SHOES

Bang Bang
This is a basic store if you are into the New York club scene. They have the typical club clothing that you don't want to spend a lot of money on because they only cover one-third of your body. The only problem is that you may see someone wearing the same thing on Friday night.
Elmhurst, Queens, Queens Center Mall, 90-15 Queens Blvd. (at 90th St.), (718) 760-0114. Open M-Sa 10am-9:30pm, Su 11pm-7pm. MC, V, AmEx, DC, D, GR to Woodhaven Blvd. ♿

Also at:
Flushing, Queens, 136-41 Roosevelt Ave. (at Main St.), (718) 886-8585. Open M-W 10am-8pm, R-Sa 10am-9pm, Su 11am-7pm. MC, V, AmEx, DC, D, 7 to Main St. ♿

Jackson Heights, Queens, 3708 82nd St. (bet. Thirty Seventh and Roosevelt Aves.), (718) 446-9711. Open M-R 10am-8pm, F-Sa 10am-9pm, Su 10am-6pm. MC, V, AmEx, DC, D, 7 to 82nd St. ♿

Marshall's
Find brand names for less at this Queens Marshall's. Sort through the racks of junk and you might find some great bargains from Calvin Klein, Esprit, Polo, Express, and Tommy Hillfiger. Finding two of the same shoes can sometimes be a challenge, and the perfume bottles may be half full, so if you don't find what you're looking for at Marshall's, try next door at Old Navy or Conway.
Queens, 34-27 48th St. (at Northern Blvd.), (718) 626-4700. Open M-Sa 9:30am-9:30pm, Su 10am-6pm. MC, V, AmEx, D. ♿

Von's School of Hard Knocks
Over six years ago a father-and-son sneaker and men's sportswear business spawned the School of Hard Knocks, a men's line with a large hip-hop influence. Everything from jackets and caps, to sneakers and knapsacks can be had for relatively low prices; women's and children's lines recently introduced.
Corona, Queens 106-11 Northern Blvd. (bet. 106th and 107th Sts.), (718) 898-1113, www.hardknocks usa.com. Open M-Sa 10am-8pm. MC, V, AmEx, D, 7 to 103rd St.-Corona Plaza. ♿

♦ BOOKS, MAGAZINES & RECORDS

The Music Factory
The latest in contemporary music including hip-hop, gospel, jazz, reggae and soul. Cassettes, vinyl, CD's, and even videotapes are available at very affordable prices at this local DJ hang-out.
Jamaica, Queens, 162-01 Jamaica Ave. (at 162nd St.), (718) 291-3135, www.musicfactory.com. Open M-Su 9:30am-8pm. MC, V, AmEx, D, EJZ to Jamaica Center.-Parsons/Archer. ♿

♦ GROCERY, GOURMET & SPECIALTY

Corona Heights Pork Store
This old school butcher shop carries every cut of the other white meat that you could possibly desire. Come for great cold cuts, prosciutto, and sausages.
Corona Heights, Queens, 107-04 Corona Ave. (bet. Fifty First and Fifty Second Aves.), (718) 592-7350. Open M-Su 10am-6pm. Cash Only, 7 to 103rd St.-Corona Pl.

Patel Brothers
Trying to make that Asian specialty on your own? You'll need a place like Patel Brothers. This is the spot for South Asian foods. The enormous store is filled with all the spices, nuts, and rice you'll need to try to imitate your favorite Indian restaurant at home. Don't overlook the rose-flavored ice cream.
Queens, Jackson Heights, 37-46 74th St. (at Thirty Seventh Ave.), (718) 898-3445. Open M-Su 10am-9pm. MC, V, AmEx, D, 7 to 74th St.-Broadway.

♦ MISCELLANEOUS

Bed Bath and Beyond
An obsessive-compulsive's dream, this moderately priced emporium of all things domestic fits the bill for convenience - a rarity in Manhattan, to be sure. The perfect stop for decorating dorm rooms or first apartments, the convenience of everything in one store sometimes lets you forget you could get what you're buying elsewhere for cheaper.
Flushing, Queens, 9605 Queens Blvd, (718)459-0868.

Also at:
Chelsea, 620 Sixth Ave. (bet. 18th and 19th Sts.), (212) 255-3550. Open M-Sa 9:30am-9pm, Su 10am-8pm. MC, V, AmEx, D, FNR to 23rd St.

Closeout Paradise
Street-fair meets thrift-store at Closeout Paradise. Their selection runs the gamut from rugs, socks, shampoo, non-perishable imported food-products, porch furniture to miniature sculpture. Find great deals on anything you might need to outfit a dorm room or serve a tea party. In case this isn't enough, cross the street for Pergament or Home Depot.
Queens, 34-41 48th St. (bet. Northern Blvd. and Thirty Seventh Ave.), (718) 545-3547. Open M-Sa 9:30am-9:30pm, Su 10am-8pm. MC, V, AmEx, D.

Arts & Recreation

♦ LEISURE

Chan Meditation Center
The goal of the Chan Meditation Center is to educate the Western world about Buddhism. The Center offers classes on Buddhism, meditation, and Tai Chi as well as weekly chants and other spiritual events. The helpful staff is always willing to answer any questions regarding Buddhism. The Chan Center offers an enlightening cultural experience to those who visit. See their website for an updated schedule of hours and activities.
Elmhurst, Queens, 90-56 Corona Ave., (718) 592-6593, www.chan1.org, G R to Grand Ave. ♿

Queens Wildlife Center
If you like zoos, you'll like Queens Wildlife Center. It's everything a zoo should be. It's full of animals ... should a zoo be anything more? Queens Wildlife Center specializes in North and South American wildlife and is geared towards families.
Flushing, Queens, 53-51 111th St., (718) 271-1500. www.wcs.org. Open M-Su 10am-4:30pm, $2.50 admission. 7 to 111th St., ♿

Shea Stadium
A good example of the sort of gaudy, lunar-minded ballparks built in the mid 1960's, Shea has seen the best of times (1969, 1986) and the worst of times (1962, 1977, 1992). Having served as stomping grounds for names like Thronberry, Seaver, Staub, Gooden, Carter and Hundley, the fate of this facility has been sealed, as the Mets are planning to build a new stadium across the street, modeled after Brooklyn's old Ebbett's Field.
Flushing, Queens, 123-01 Roosevelt Ave. (at 126th St.), (718) 507-8499, MC, V, AmEx, D. Tickets: $10-$30 7 to Willets Point-Shea Stadium ♿

♦ PERFORMANCE

The African Poetry Theater, Inc.
Fledgling poets, playwrights, directors, and actors all do shows regularly. For those in need of more structured training, various dance, drum and Shakespeare classes are available.
Jamaica, Queens, 176-03 Jamaica Ave. (at 176th St.), (718)523-3312. Showtimes F-Sa 8pm, Su 5pm. Cash Only, F to 179th St.-Jamaica. ♿

Black Spectrum Theater Company, Inc.
Three to five large-scale productions a year, with directors fav-oring socially conscious works by both emerging and established writers. Kids and teens get in on the action with their own productions at this Roy Wilkins park-based company.
Jamaica, Queens, 119-07 Merrick Blvd. (bet. 177th St. and Baisley Blvd.), (718) 723-1800, www.black spectrum.com. Cash Only, E J Z to Jamaica Center-Parsons/Archer. ♿

Colden Center For the Performing Arts at Queens College
The oldest, largest arts presenter in Queens, with over 300,000 visitors annually. Features classical, pop, jazz, theater, opera, and children's events weekly.
Flushing, Queens, 65-30 Kissena Blvd. (at the Long Island Expressway), (718) 793-8080, www.coldencenter.com. MC, V, AmEx, D, 7 to Main St.-Flushing.

Jamaica Center for Arts & Learning
A neo-Italian Renaissance structure built in 1898, houses a non-profit community cultural center dedicated to making all genres of the performing arts accessible to the Jamaica community.
Jamaica, Queens, 161-04 Jamaica Ave. (at 161st St.), (718) 658-7400. Cash Only, E J Z to Jamaica Center-Parsons/Archer ♿

Langston Hughes Community Library and Cultural Center
The spirit Langston Hughes brought to Harlem almost 100 years ago lives on in Queens. Year-round readings and performances, as well as a wealth of reference materials in the on-site library.
Corona, Queens, 102-09 Northern Blvd. (at 102nd St.), (718) 651-1100, www.queenslibrary.org. Open M, F 10am-6pm, T 1pm-6pm, W, R 1pm-8pm, Sa 9:30am-5pm. Cash Only, 7 to 103rd St.-Corona Plaza.

Queens Theatre in the Park
Find diverse theatrical and artistic offerings in beautifully manicured Corona Park. Look for summer Shakespeare festivals, the Latino Arts Festival, and the Independent Film Showcase, and independent film festival. Programs are curated by the Queens Council on the Arts.
Flushing Meadow, Corona Park, Queens (at the New York State Pavilion), (718)760-0064, www.queenstheatre.org, Call for schedule and admission (varies), AmEx, MC, V. 7 to Willets Point/Shea Stadium ♿

Thalia Spanish Theater
One of New York's hottest stages for established and new Hispanic playwrights, actors, and directors. Three productions yearly, as well as three ongoing showcases in music,

dance, and special events.
Sunnyside, Queens, 41-17 Greenpoint Ave. (bet. 41st and 42nd Sts.), (718) 729-3880, www.queesnew york.com/cultural/thalia. MC, V, AmEx, 7 to 40th St. (Lowery St.). ♿

♦ SITES

Kaufman-Astoria Studios
Valentino, the Marx Brothers and Paul Robeson have all made films at this popular studio, which has been at the heart of New York's movie industry for years.
Queens, 34-12 36th St. (bet. Thirty Fourth and Thirty Fifth Aves.), (718) 392-56000, G R to Steinway St.

♦ PARKS

Flushing Meadows-Corona Park
The park's claim to fame is the Unisphere, site of the 1964 World's Fair, Will Smith's alien showdown of "Men In Black" and unofficial icon of Queens. The park itself was once beautiful but is now run-down and in need of some revitalization. Though Flushing's residents may be proud of the Unisphere, it simply isn't exciting enough to warrant a visit to Flushing Meadows.
Flushing, Queens, 7 to Willets Point/Shea Stadium

♦ MUSEUMS & CULTURAL CENTERS

American Museum of the Moving Image
"One has the sense of being transported from the everyday world straight to the set of a modern-day Oz," wrote Stephen Holden in *The New York Times*, referring to "Behind the Screen," one of the permanent exhibits at this museum devoted to the art, history, technique, and technology of the visual media and its influence on culture and society. Housed in the old Paramount Studios at the heart of Queens' old movie district, the museum is a treasure trove of movie memorabilia from the '30s through the '60s. Regular film series at the Riklis Theater screen over 500 movies a year, shown on weekends, free with admission.
Long Island City, Queens, 3601 Fifth Ave. (at 36th St.), (718) 784-4520, www.ammi.org. Open T-F 12pm-5pm, Sa-Su 11pm-6pm. Cash Only, Admission: $4.50-$10, N to Thirty Sixth Ave. (Washington Ave.). ♿

The Isamu Noguchi Garden Museum
More than 300 works in granite, steel and marble, including the famous Akari paper light sculptures by Isamu Noguchi, who also designed the twelve galleries and the outdoor sculpture garden. Open April to October. A shuttle runs from 70th St. and Park Ave. on weekends.
Long Island City, Queens, 32-37 Vernon Blvd.(at 33rd St.), (718) 204-7088, www.noguchi.org. Open W-F 10am-5pm, Sa-Su 11am-6pm. Cash Only, Admission: $2-$4, N to Broadway. ♿

Ethnic Enclaves: Jackson Heights

If Queens is the Asia of New York City, Jackson Heights is the Indian Subcontinent. It's got curry houses. It's got sari shops. It's got bookstores stocked with Sanskrit dictionaries and deluxe editions of the *Kama Sutra.* It's even got a movie theater showing epic family sagas.

The nucleus of the community is 74th Street. A collection of colorful stores — Sagar Sari Palace, Shri Krishna Jewelers, Ayurvedic Herbal Centre — draw their clientele from the surrounding neighborhood of South Asians. It's the kind of place where women swathed in silk saris push baby carriages, where the sound of spoken Hindi and Urdu sets the street abuzz, and a piece of Bengali milk fudge is never too difficult to find.

King Manor Museum
Home of Rufus King, delegate to the Constitutional Convention. The oldest house in southeast Queens has been restored to reflect the King family's tenancy in the early 19th century. Visitors can tour King's library and read pages from his diary, account books, and letters; guided tours are available in English and Spanish. Exhibit galleries are devoted to local history and to village life in Jamaica during the early 1800s.
King Park, Jamaica, Queens, Jamaica Ave. (bet. 150th and 153rd Sts.), (718) 206-0547. Open Mar.-Dec. Sa-Su 12pm-4pm. Cash Only, Admission: $2, E J Z to Jamaica Center-Parsons/Archer.

New York Hall of Science
While designed primarily for kids, this playground of hands-on exhibits appeals to the science nut in everyone. The newly expanded exhibition hall boasts a Technology Gallery, with access to the Internet and a wide range of CD-ROMs. Thursday and Friday are free 2pm-5pm.
Corona, Queens, 47-01 111th Street (in Flushing Meadows Corona Park), (718) 699-0005, www.nyhall sci.org. Open M-W 9:30am-2pm, R-F 9:30am-5pm. MC, V, AmEx, Admission: $5-$7.50, 7 to 111th St. ♿

P.S. 1
If the name didn't give you a clue P.S.1. is housed in an old school building, three stories high. The museum has plenty of

> I began to like New York, the racy, the adventurous feel of it at night, and the satisfaction that the constant flicker of men and women and machines gives to the restless eye . . . The city seen from the Queensboro Bridge is always the city seen for the first time, in its first wild promise of all the mystery and beauty in the world.
>
> —F. Scott Fitzgerald

nooks and crannies, all of which are filled with interesting and enlightening contemporary art exhibits. All of the museum's exhibits are temporary — so you can visit P.S.1. again and again. Summer weekends a fake beach, saunas, good beer and a DJ makes for a party full of hipsters.
Long Island City, Queens, 22-25 Jackson Ave. (at Fourty Sixth Ave.), (718) 784-2084, www.ps1.org. Open W-Su 12pm-6pm. Admission (suggested): $2-$5, EF to 23rd St. (Ely Ave.), G to Court Sq. ♿

The Queen's Country Farm Museum
Dating back to 1772, this farm covers 52 acres of land and is the only working farm of its era that has been restored and reopened to the public. Check out the hayrides, $2 a pop! Open year-round.
Kew Gardens, Queens, 73-50 Little Neck Pkwy (bet. Seventy Fourth Ave. and 73rd Rd.), (718) 347-3276, www.queensfarm.org. Open M-F 9am-5pm, Sa-Su 10am-5pm. Admission: free, EF to Union Turnpike-Kew Gardens. ♿

Queens Museum of Art
The must-see exhibit of this small museum, which is located right opposite the Unisphere and housed in the original U.N., is the scale model of New York City, the largest of its kind.
Flushing, Queens, Flushing Meadows Corona Park (at Grand Central Pkwy.), (718) 592-9700, www.queensmuse.org. Open W-F, 10am-5pm, Sa-Su 12pm-5pm. Cash Only, Admission (suggested): $2-$4, 7 to Willets Point-Shea Stadium. ♿

♦ GALLERIES AND LIBRARIES

Louis Armstrong Archives
Interested in knowing Louis Armstrong's dieting secrets? Visit the Archives. They have just about everything related to Satchmo, from personal recordings and writings to trophies and instruments. The Archives cater especially to students researching Armstrong. Call ahead to make an appointment.
Flushing, Queens, 65-30 Kissena Blvd., Queens College's Benjamin Rosenthal Library, Rm. 332, (718) 997-3670, www.satchmo.net. Open M-F 10am-5pm, 7 to Main St. ♿

Nightlife

♦ BARS

Bohemian Hall and Park
Come for the beer; stay for the beer. And the atmosphere, of course. This European-style beer garden (complete with polka stage) will fool you into thinking that you didn't just step off the N train after all. This place is legendary for a reason.
Astoria, Queens, 29-19 Twenty Fourth Ave. (bet. 29th and 31th Sts.), (718)728-9776. Open M-F 5pm-2am, Sa-Su 12pm-2am. Cash Only, N to Astoria Blvd. ♿

Cafe Bar
This is one of those places that will become a favorite the first time you walk in. The funky decor and laid-back atmosphere make it a good place to spend hours over coffee, dessert, or a drink. It's especially good for people watching on Friday and Saturday nights when the old country locals mix with club kids.
Astoria, 32-19 36th St. (bet. 32nd and 33rd Sts.), (718) 204-5273. Open Su-R 9:30am-3am, F-Sa 9:30am-4am. Cash Only, N to Thirty Sixth Ave. ♿

Irish Rover
The Irish Rover draws a mean pint of Guinness and a proffers pretty good shepherd's pie to a mostly local clientele. As one might guess, the regulars are mostly Irish, but the crowd is always mixed. Occasional live performances liven up the joint.
Astoria, Queens, 37-18 Twenty Eighth Ave. (bet. 38th and 37th Sts.), (718) 278-9372. Open M-Su 8am-4am. Cash Only, N to Thirteeth Ave., GR to Steinway St.

♦ CLUBS

Krash
No doubt its parent club in San Juan would be proud of the Latin music this cavernous dance emporium serves up Mondays, Thursdays, Fridays, and Saturdays. Worth the tokens if you crave this beat.
Astoria, Queens, 34-48 Steinway St. (at Thirty Fifth Ave.), (718) 937-2400. MC, V, Cover: $1-$10, GR to Steinway St.

Apartments in NYC

The perfect (or perfectly located) apartment does not exist. There are, however, plenty of places that will suffice, and the real estate market will seem more manageable if approached with an open mind. Here are a few guidelines to assist with the search:

Finding your Bracket

Take a look first at your bank account and then, if you can, at your parents' bank account. This is your bracket and if it's low, and that's most people's story, you won't be living in Chelsea, or the Village. Studios there are upwards of $1,200 a month. Besides, anyone in the city can tell you everything there is to know about the popular neighborhoods. If you're really going to discover the city, do it by discovering a neighborhood not too many other people have, like people did to Williamsburg, Brooklyn, Astoria, Queens and Washington Heights a couple of years ago.

Brokers

They can be pushy, and they'll ask for all sorts of forms and maybe a cosigner if you're not making enough, and always, at least 12 percent of the first year's rent. They will however find you an apartment, and a good one, fast.

Open Houses

These rarely work and waiting outside a building with like fifteen other chatty, tense people is no fun. You'll have a better chance getting into a club with sneakers and a Phish t-shirt on. If you do try, get there early and bring a checkbook.

Subletting and Sharing

If you just arrived, especially if it's the beginning of the summer, this is a great way to save money and buy yourself some time while you search for an apartment. Sublets are best found looking at listings on college campuses or on those colleges' web pages. If all you want services like Roommate Finders (212-489-6862) will find one for you for a fee of around $250.

The Real Estate Section

With a little patience and luck this works. However you should learn the lingo first:

♦ cozy — Very, very small.

♦ EIK — Eat-in kitchen. Don't be fooled into thinking this means a spacious chef's space. Rather, it could mean room enough for anything from a stool at a counter to a bona fide breakfast nook.

♦ exposed brick — Realtors have somehow suckered renters into believing that unfinished red brick walls are a desirable urban feature. Maybe they do it for you. Knock yourself out.

♦ floor-through (often "flrthru") — An apartment that takes up the entire floor of a building, often a brownstone.

♦ garden apartment — A ground-floor apartment with access to an unspecified amount of outdoor lawn or patio space.

♦ No Fee — Rented directly by an owner, so no broker's fee charged for rental. This means big savings, as much as $1,800 for an apartment renting for $1,000/month.

♦ one-month's security — Standard collateral toward any damage you might inflict on an apartment during your lease, which may or may not be returned in full when you move out, depending on the condition of the rental.

♦ Rent Stabilized — If an apartment is listed as "Rent Stabilized," rent hikes for one-year leases subsequently signed are limited to 2%, as of September, 1998. For complete information regarding issues of rent increase, contact the New York City Rental Guidelines Board at www.nycrgb.com.

♦ walk-up — No elevator here, so don't kid yourself about how in shape you are; a 4th floor walk-up will make or break you.

♦ wbfp — Wood burning fireplace.

Brooklyn

When Lauren, a writer, moved to Brooklyn three years ago, Carroll Gardens was mostly Hispanic. Weekend nights Dominican men stumbled out of the social club lined streets and salsa was everywhere. "Now there is only one of these social clubs and its squeezed between a sleek new bar and a tiny expensive clothing shop. There might be another but I can't seem to find it."

Up in Williamsburg the same changes are happening. Around 5pm hipsters pour out of the L train in t-shirts of high school sports teams they were never on and perfectly messy hair. Same goes for D.U.M.B.O., Clinton Hill, Fort Greene and Cobble Hill. But further east, Bedford-Stuyvesant and Bushwick are as tough as they've ever been. Bensonhurst is as Italian as it ever was; kids play stick ball and some clothing stores specialize in velvet sweat suits. The Cyclone at Coney Island is a life or death experience and a walk down Brighton Beach is a great collection of outrageous Russian dinner theater. Hasidic Jews and West Indian immigrants in Crown Heights. The wall of Reggae during Summer Splash. No matter the changes Brooklyn remains beyond definition.

Brooklyn likes it that way. The upswing now is a notch in a long history of ups and downs that Brooklyn has seen through with optimism and fierce independence. Before Brooklyn became a borough of New York City it was the fourth largest city in the country. The close vote that consolidated it into the city has been called the "Great Mistake" by writer Peter Hamill and today Brooklyn remains, for the most part, Democratic because it was Republicans that made the vote for unity.

That said, Brooklyn started as a Dutch settlement of three villages linked together in 1642 as "Breuckelen" or "Broken Land." The opening of the Brooklyn Bridge in 1883 brought an influx of industry that died after WWII when most of the factories and manufacturers were closed. These abandoned spaces are now being filled. Brooklyn is still the most populated borough. It's home to the Brooklyn Botanical Gardens, the Brooklyn Academy of Music, Nathan's Famous hot dogs, the Brooklyn Museum of Art, the most beautiful brownstones anywhere, Peter Luger's Steakhouse, the amazing view of the city from Brooklyn Heights and, always, the 1955 Brooklyn Dodgers—World Champions.

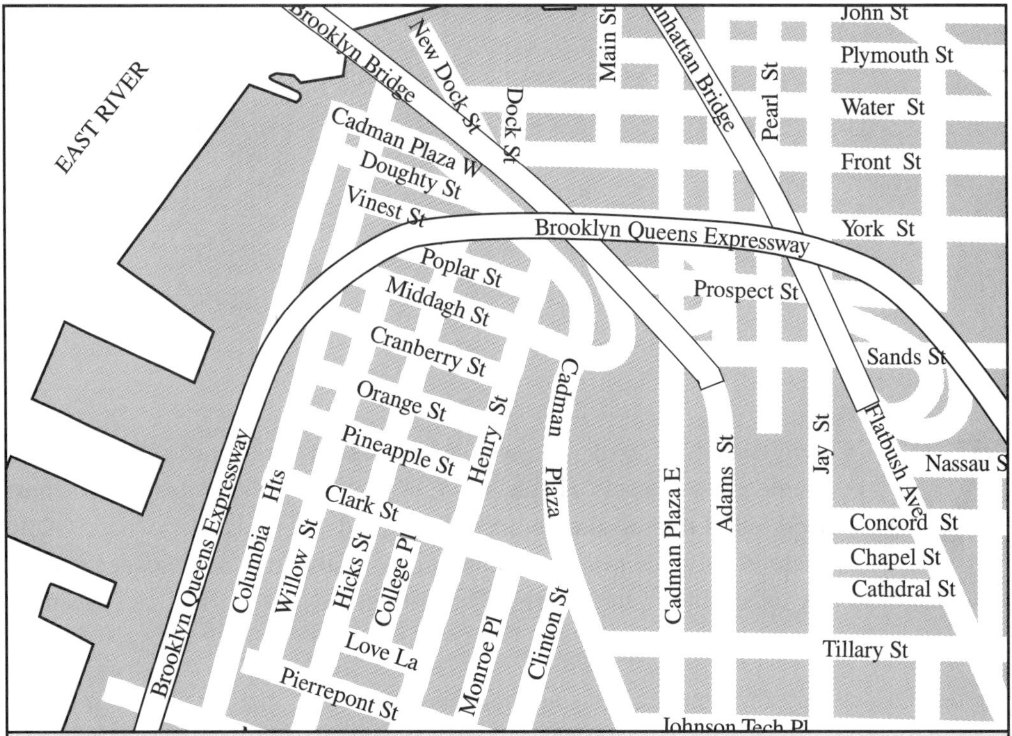

brooklyn heights

Dining

♦ RESTAURANTS

Bar Tabac

This relaxing and moderately priced French Bistro features magnificent Duck, confit cigars, luscious desserts, and an attentive waitstaff. You could spend several hours lounging around the back room - designed to resemble the inside of a fin de siecle Paris subway train - as you sip wine and sample savory selections like mouth watering steak frites and scrumptious sea bass.

Carroll Gardens, Brooklyn, 128 Smith St. (at Dean St.), (718) 923-0918. Open Su-R 11am-2am, F-Sa bar open till 4am. AmEx, Entrees: $11-$16, F G *To Bergen St.*

Coco Roco

You might someday ask yourself, where can I get tasty Peruvian food in Brooklyn? Here it is, equipped with spicy Peruvian chicken and amazing sangria. It's also a fun, sprightly place that hustles and bustles.

Park Slope, Brooklyn, 392 Fifth Ave, (718) 965-3376. Open M-T 12pm-10:30pm, F-Sa 12pm-11:30pm. MC, V, Amex, F *train to 4th Ave.* R *train to 9th St.*

Cucina

One of the best restaurants in New York and it's not even in Manhattan. Everything is great here, but the risotto is what people rave about. The antipasto is the best this side of Tuscany and the wine and dessert menus are superb. Plus there is valet parking on weekends! In a word: perfect.

Park Slope, Brooklyn, 256 Fifth Ave. (bet. Garfield Pl. and Carroll St.), (718) 230-0711, www.cucinarestaurant.com. Open T-R 5:30pm-10:30pm, F-Sa 5:30pm-11pm, Su 5pm-10pm. MC, V, AmEx, DC, D, Entrées: $15-$28, M N R *to Union St.*

The Downtown Brooklyn Diner

It's late and you're lost somewhere between the gas station and the party you were going to, driving around Brooklyn. Chances are you are on Atlantic Ave. and a good suggestion is stopping at this 24 hour diner, ordering breakfast, lunch or dinner, and figuring out where the hell you are.

Downtown Brooklyn, 515 Atlantic Ave. (at Third Ave.), (718) 243-9172. Open M-Su 24hrs. MC, V, Entrées: $6/$8, D Q 2 3 4 5 *to Atlantic Ave.*

Giardini Pizza and Restaurant

Some of the best pizza and straight up Italian food in New York, which is no small feat considering there's a pizza joint on every corner. This place delivers (literally, too) with great plain and topping slices and a nice array of the old standards - spaghetti, stuffed shells, parmigianas, and big,

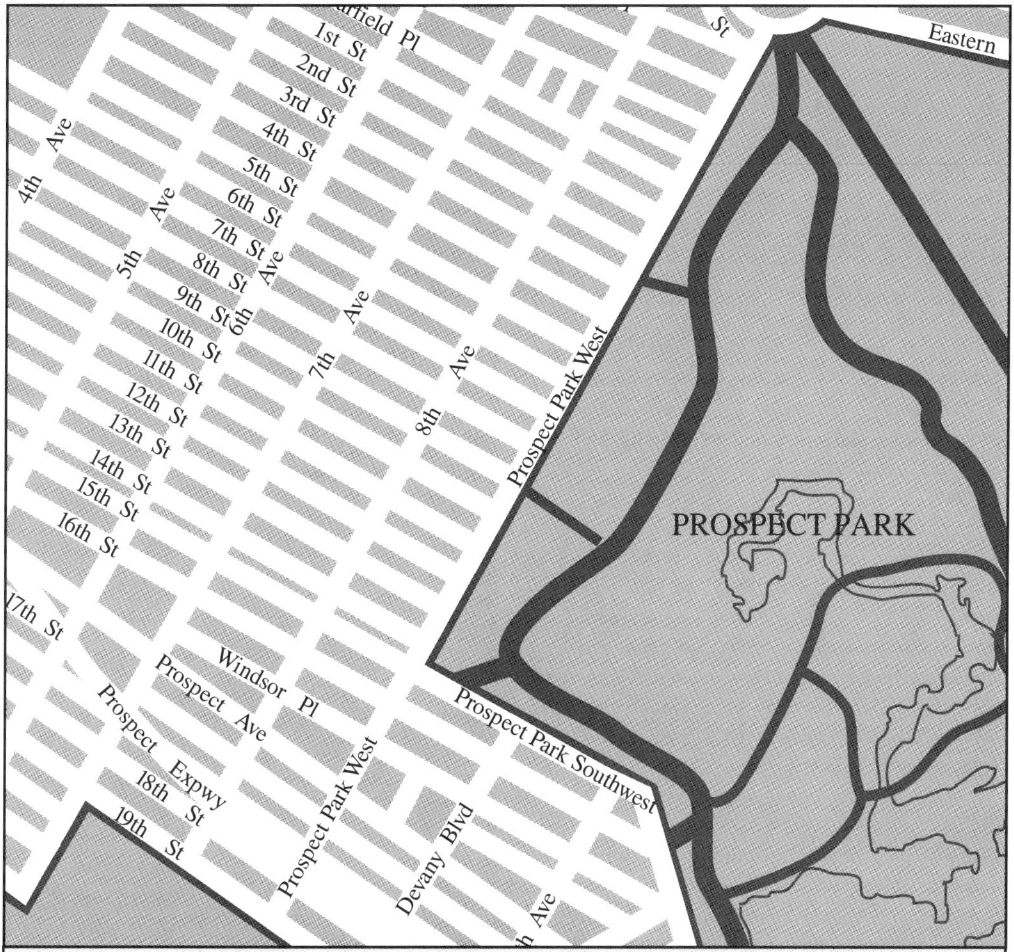

park slope

PLACES TO GO:

Rising Café
This for-the-most-part Lesbian bar is a welcome relief from the standard gay scene of Manhattan.

Prospect Park
Bordered by institutions like the Botanical Gardens and the Brooklyn Museum of Art, this is a more beautiful, less hectic park then that one in the middle of Manhattan.

New York Transit Museum
The stuff of elementary school trips, if you're going to figure out how to get around you might as well figure out where it started.

Sparky's Ale House
If a heaven is a laid back bar with more kinds of beer than you can count, this is it. And, if this is heaven, don't offend the bartender because you don't want to be kicked out.

tasty heroes. It's cheap, fast, and deeply satisfying.
Carroll Gardens, Brooklyn, 363 Smith St. (at Carroll St.), (718) 596-5320. Open M-Su 11am-10pm, F 11am-11pm. Cash only, Entrees: $1.25-9.00, F train to Carroll St.

Grimaldi's
Every New Yorker claims to know the best pizzeria in the city, but Grimaldi's may be the real thing. Old Brooklyn ambiance is enhanced by Sinatra and Bennett crooning as you savor crisp, thin-crust pizza that will satisfy even the most discriminating pizza lovers.
Fulton Ferry Landing, Brooklyn, 19 Old Fulton St. (bet. Water and Front Sts.), (718) 858-4300. Open M-R 11:30am-11pm, F 11:30am-12am, Sa 12pm-12am, Su 12pm-11pm. Cash Only, Entrées: $12-$20, A C to High St.-Brooklyn Bridge.

Junior's
Sample "New York's Best Cheesecake" (don't confuse it with the cheese pie!) or just about anything else you can imagine at this monster diner/bar, open till 2am on weekends. Busy bar, with eclectic group of patrons. Speedy service, but sometimes a wait for a table on weekends.
Downtown Brooklyn, 386 Flatbush Ave. (at DeKalb Ave.), (718) 852-5257. Open Su-R 6:30am-12:30am, F-Sa 6:30am-2am. MC, V, AmEx, DC, D, Entrées: $10-$28, D M N Q R to DeKalb Ave.

Mabat
Like any ethnic neighborhood restaurant in the outer boroughs, this place may not be as fancy as its Manhattan counterparts, but it makes up for it in authenticity and price. Nearly everything here is very good.
Midwood, Brooklyn, 1809 E. 7th St. (bet. Quentin Rd. and Kings Highway), (718) 339-3300. Open Su-R 12pm-12:30am, Sa 10pm-12:30am. Cash Only, Entrées: $14-$16, D Q to King's Highway.

New Prospect Café
A diminutive cutie, the light menu here features some excellent seafood vegetable dishes and nice, reasonably priced wine. Not for New York's night owls, the kitchen closes by 10pm; on the other hand, brunch is excellent and always crowded.
Prospect Heights, Brooklyn, 393 Flatbush Ave. (bet. Plaza St. and Sterling Pl.), (718) 638-2148. Open M-Su 11:30am-3pm, 5pm-10:30pm. MC, V, AmEx, Entrées $9-$16, 2 3 to Grand Army Plaza, D Q to Seventh Ave.

Ethnic Enclaves:

BRIGHTON BEACH

When the going got tough in the waning years of the Soviet Union, the Russians got going, en masse. A huge influx of émigrés — almost 9,000 in the early '90s alone — has turned the Brighton Beach area of Brooklyn into a lively miniature of the Black Sea port city Odessa. Today, this faded stretch of the Brooklyn Riviera is home to the largest Russian population in the U.S., boasting enough pierogi shops and lavish discotheques to make even the most Americanized transplant pine for home.

Ride the D or Q line to its terminus and you'll emerge on a different continent, a place where signs advertise European fashions in fancy Cyrillic lettering and newspapers divulge the latest Moscow gossip with incredible accuracy. Along the wide beach boardwalk, Gucci-clad hostesses beckon passersby into cafés whose tables are filled with boisterous groups of locals. Typical of most Russian social gatherings, the revelers feast on shashlik and pilmeni, toasting each other with such exaggerated gestures of jollity that you'll be tempted to join in. The sandy side of the boardwalk sees more sedate action as dozens of simultaneous chess matches are staged here all day long, reputations rising and falling with the tide.

Conclude your tour along Brighton Beach Avenue, the community's main street, where you'll pass bakeries, restaurants, boutiques, nightclubs, and grocery marts, predominantly owned, operated, and frequented by Russian immigrants. The walk is a voyage through another world; everywhere, emblems of the Russian culture underscore the community's collective nostalgia for a country changing faster than the ruble is falling. Forgo Aeroflot for the subway and see for yourself.

Oznot's Dish

This quirky restaurant has become a premiere site for nouveau ethnic cuisine, combining Mediterranean flavors and French presentation. With bright mosaics covering the walls and a year-round sunroom, Oznot's is elegantly hip: the waitstaff is down-to-earth but knowledgeable, the ambience laid back but classy, and the food superior but moderately priced. The expansive menu, offering outrageous meat dishes as well as vegetarian delights, boasts a selection of 300 wines.

Williamsburg, Brooklyn, 79 Berry St., (at N. 9th St.), (718) 599-6596. Open M-F 11am-12am, Sa-Su 10am-12am. MC, V, Entrées: $11-$18, L to Bedford Ave.

Red Rail

Come one, come all to this busy and popular breakfast/lunch spot and enjoy a nice prix fixe brunch that includes coffee, tea, and all the mimosas you can handle. Try the big, nicely presented omelets, grilled squid salad with basil, red onion and tomato, or tasty avocado salad with tomatoes and goat cheese. If the architecture appears familiar, you may remember it from a heated romantic spat between Nicolas Cage and Cher in Moonstruck.

Carroll Gardens, Brooklyn, 502 Henry St. (at Sackett St.), (718) 875-1283. Open S, T, R 6pm-10pm, F-S 6pm-10:30pm, T-F 7:30am-4pm, brunch 10am-4pm. MC, V, AmEx, F train to Carroll St.

Patois

This French restaurant joins a host of new ventures on Smith Street and doesn't disappoint with favu leek and goat cheese tart, tasty duck breast, and excellent grilled salmon served over lentils. Good wines compliment most of the food, whether it be the tripe stew or beer-drenched mussels. Bon appetit, mon ami!

Carroll Gardens, Brooklyn, 255 Smith St. (bet. Degraw and Douglas Sts.), (718) 855-1535. Open T-S 6pm-10:30 pm, F-Sa 6pm-11:30pm, Sun brunch 11am-3pm. MC, V, AmEx, Entrees: $12-18, F to Bergen St.

Peter Luger Steak House

Simply the superlative steakhouse in New York City. Not for the faint of heart (and definitely not for vegetarians), the menu is limited to steak, salmon, and lamb chops, as well as an amazing array of à la carte side-dishes. Informal, given the price of a meal, a reservation on a Friday or Saturday can be weeks in the waiting. Worth the wait, worth the cost, just plain worth it!

Williamsburg, Brooklyn, 178 Broadway (between Bedford Ave. and Driggs St.), (718) 387-7400, www.peterluger.com. Open M-R 11:45am-9:45pm, F-Sa 11:45-10:45pm, Su 12:45pm-9:45. Cash Only, Entrées: $50-$60, J M Z to Marcy Ave.

Petite Crevette

Ignore the decor, which is in transition, and step inside this roomy Brooklyn Heights restaurant where a friendly and comfortable ambience is promoted by the staff and patrons alike. For the best bites, ask waiter Lynn, who runs the dining room like "a big dinner party," for a suggestion from the fish, stews, or pastas and sit back to enjoy some of the freshest fish available. FYI, it's BYOB.

Brooklyn Heights, Brooklyn, 127 Atlantic Ave. (at Henry St.), (718) 858-6660. Open M-R 11am-4pm, 5pm-10:30pm, F-Sa 11am-4pm, 5pm-11pm, Su 5pm-10pm. Cash Only, Entrées $8-$19, 2 3 4 5 to Borough Hall

Queen Italian Restaurant

Downtown Brooklyn's pasta of choice for local suits and shoppers; try anything on the menu since it's difficult to go wrong, especially with the spicy, crisp pizza.

Downtown Brooklyn, 84 Court St. (bet. Livingston and Schermerhorn Sts.), (718) 596-5954. Open M-R 11:30am-10pm, F 11:30am-11pm, Sa 4pm-11pm, Su 4pm-10pm. MC, V, AmEx, Entrées: $15-$25, M N R to Court St., 2 3 4 5 to Borough Hall.

Red Rail

Come one, come all to this busy and popular breakfast/lunch spot and enjoy a nice prix fixe brunch that includes coffee, tea, and all the mimosas you can handle. Try the big, nicely presented omelets, grilled squid salad with basil, red onion and tomato, or tasty avocado salad with tomatoes and goat cheese. If the architecture appears familiar, you may remember it from a heated romantic spat between Nicolas Cage and Cher in Moonstruck.

Carroll Gardens, Brooklyn, 502 Henry St. (at Sackett St.), (718) 875-1283. Open S, T, R 6pm-10pm, F-S 6pm-10:30pm, T-F 7:30am-4pm, brunch 10am-4pm. MC, V, AmEx, F train to Carroll St.

Rose Water

Vegetarian cuisine coming at ya, loaded with organic seasonal ingredients that combine to make delectable, low-priced meals. Get the fine cheese plate accompanied by slices of pears, black grapes, and squishy (in a good way) bread, or try the seared diver scallops with roasted butternut squash.

Park Slope, Brooklyn, 787 Union St. (at Sixth Ave.), (718) 783-3800. Open M-R 6pm-10:30pm, F-S 6pm-11pm, Sun 6pm-10pm. MC, V, AmEx, R train to Union St.

Second Street Cafe

This bastion of Park Slope café culture serves up light meals and an appealing array of desserts, including chocolate cookies that would put mom's to shame. The café is packed during lunch hours, seven days a week; on weekend evenings, however, seats are plentiful.

Park Slope, Brooklyn, 189 Seventh Ave. (at 2nd St.), (718) 369-6928. Open M-R 8am-10:30pm, F 8am-12am, Sa 8:30am-12am, Su 8:30am-10:30am. MC, V, AmEx, Entrées: $6-$12, F to Seventh Ave.-Park Slope.

Sotto Voce

Cool Décor fills this tiny neighbor restaurant, which is always hopping with happy diners eating crab cake antipasto, homemade fettuccine in rosemary cream sauce, and veal medallions. Great for the meat lover in you. If you've got room, go for the delicious cheesecake with strawberries. You won't regret it.

Park Slope, Brooklyn, 225 Seventh Ave. (at 4th St.), (718) 369-9322. Open M-Su 3pm-11pm, S-Su brunch, 11am-4pm. Cash only, Entrees: $10-$22, F train to Seventh Ave.

Tom's Diner

"I came, I sat, I wrote" reads a note from Suzanne Vega on the wall of this venerable luncheonette, suggesting that it is this Prospect Heights favorite, not Tom's on 112th St. in Manhattan, immortalized in Vega's "Tom's Diner." Worthy of immortality, Tom's is a charmer, founded in 1936 with prototypical Brooklyn fare, great egg creams, and terrific service. Closes at 4pm.

Prospect Heights, Brooklyn, 782 Washington Ave. (at Sterling Pl.), (718) 636-9738. Open M-Sa 6am-4pm. Cash Only, Entrées: $3-$8, 2 3 to Eastern Pkwy.-Brooklyn Museum.

Victory Kitchen

Chef Tanya Holland cooks up standard fare with a flare, giving beef ribs the spice-glazed treatment and succulent roasted chicken a nice side of delightful dumplings, accompanied by an array of mouthwatering appetizers and salads. Nice brunch too, and pretty cheap. Good food that satisfies all your carnal desires

(well, maybe not all), outdoor dining, and a place to have that satisfying after-dinner cigarette.

Carroll Gardens, Brooklyn, 116 Smith St. (bet. Dean and Pacific Sts.), (718) 858-8787. Open T-F 5:30pm-10:30pm, Sa-Su 1:30 pm-3:30 pm. MC, V, AmEx, F train to Bergen St.

♦ CAFES

Fall Cafe

Settle into a cushy couch and finish a physics problem set or dig into your debut novel. Sustenance comes at starving student prices: $3 or less for soups, and a small coffee for less than $1.

Carroll Gardens, Brooklyn, 307 Smith St. (bet. President and Union Sts.), (718) 403-0230. M-F 7:30am-9pm, Sa 9am-9pm, Su 10am-8pm. Cash Only, F G to Carroll St.

L Café

The food - standard American café fare - is mediocre, but the eclectic crowd will hold your attention as you wine and dine inside this tiny brick enclave or in the sunny, outdoor garden. Service can be inefficient at times.

Brooklyn, 189 Bedford Ave., (718) 302-2430. Open M-F 9am - 12am, Sa-Su, 10am - 12am. MC, V, AmEx, L to Bedford Ave.

Omonia Café

You won't be sorry when you come here for dessert or a sweet snack. With delicious cakes and coffees, and two locations in Queens and Brooklyn, these cafes are lovely places to sit and savor yummy pastries and delicious coffees late into the evening.

Brooklyn, 7612 Third Ave. (bet. 76th and 77th Sts.), (718) 491-1435. Open M-Su 8am-2am. MC, V, AmEx, Entrees: $12-$16, R to 79th St.

Sweet Melissa Patisserie

A reasonably priced café for sweets, salads, and French food. It's becoming increasingly popular among local residents, with a building reputation for good food at the right prices. The place may be small, but as the name promises, it's sweet.

Brooklyn, 276 Court St. (bet. Butler and Douglass Sts.), (718) 855-3410. Open Su-R 8am-10pm, F-Sa 8am-12am. Cash Only, Entrees: $4-$6, F to Bergen St.

The Brooklyn I was born in was still a city of churches, with their great bronze bells walloping to the faithful from early dawn . . . Gentlemen and deer ran wild in Prospect Park. I was born in a world of much more sunlight and less smoke than now, a world of rining horse cars, ragtime music, cakewalks and Floradora sextets.
—Mae West

Shopping

♦ CLOTHING & SHOES

Beacon's Closet
Many of the hipsters of Williams-burg are avid thrift shoppers and this is the neighborhood outlet for such diversions. A wide assortment of used clothing fills the racks and it doesn't take too much hunting to find something really nice like a suede jacket or a pair of perfectly worn boot-cut Wranglers. The prices tend to be a little expensive, but are still about one-third what you'd pay in Manhattan. Plus, they'll buy your unwanted clothes or take them in trade.
Williamsburg, Brooklyn, 110 Bedford Ave. (at N. 11th St.), (718) 486-0816. Open M-F 12pm-9pm, Sa-Su 11am-9pm. MC, V, AmEx, DC, D, Ⓛ to Bedford Ave.

Century 21
Determined shoppers will find designer items for up to 80 percent off; the other departments attract a slightly less bloodthirsty crowd.
Bay Ridge, Brooklyn, 427 86th St. (bet. Fourth and Fifth Aves.), (718) 748-3266, www.c21stores.com. Open M-W, F 10am-8pm, R 10am-9pm, Sa 10am-9:30pm, Su 11am-7pm. MC, V, AmEx, D, Ⓡ to 86th St. ♿

Domsey's
Four stories of mostly second-hand clothing for women, men, and kids, this store even carries some (new!) housewares.
Williamsburg, Brooklyn, 431 Kent Ave. (at S. 9th St.), (718) 384-6000, www.domsey.com, Open M-F 9am-5:30pm, Sa 9am-6:30pm, Su 11am-5:30pm. MC, V, D, ⒿⓂⓏ to Marcy Ave. ♿

Eidolon
Four of Brooklyn's young designers sell their work at Eidolon, a boutique that brings SoHo's stylish looks across the East River. The name is Greek for "ideal image," and the clothing caters that idea to the unpretentious, fashion-hungry Brooklynites. The staff, primarily the designers themselves, is eager and friendly.
Brooklyn, 233 Fifth Ave. (at President St.), (718) 638-8194. Open W-Su 12pm-8pm. MC, V, AmEx, ⓃⓇ to Union St.

Loehmann's
As legendary as Century 21 in de-signer junkie circles, this discount outpost rewards the shopper who makes the trek: lots of big-name labels and high stock turnover justify frequent trips.
Sheepshead Bay, Brooklyn, 2807 E. 21st St. (at Eammons Ave.), (718) 368-1256, www.loehmans. com. Open M-Sa 10am-10pm, Su 11am-6pm. MC, V, D, Ⓓ to Sheeps-head Bay Road. ♿

Max + Roebling
Showcase for some of New York's hippest young designers, including Cake and Living Doll, with prices that even Williamsburg's starving artists can swing.
Williamsburg, Brooklyn, 189 Bedford Ave. (bet. No. 6th and N. 7th Sts.), (718) 387-0045. Open T-Sa 12pm-9pm, Su 12pm-8pm. MC, V, AmEx, D, Ⓛ to Bedford Ave.

Pop's Popular Clothing
This store has been in business for over 50 years. They carry a full line of new and used clothes. You'll find what you're looking for at lower prices than you'd pay at a Manhattan counterpart.
Greenpoint, Brooklyn, 7 Franklin St. (at Mezzoro Ave.), (718) 349-7677. Open M-F 8am-5pm, Sa 9am-4pm, (Oct-Dec also Su 12pm-5pm). MC, V, AmEx, Ⓛ to Bedford Ave. ♿

♦ BOOKS, MAGAZINES & RECORDS

A Novel Idea
Sit back in one of their easy chairs and thumb through your selections of new books to buy or old favorites. This charming family bookstore even features a selection of used books in the back.
Bay Ridge, Brooklyn, 8415 Third Ave. (bet. 84th and 85th Sts.), (718) 833-5115. Open M-Sa 10am-8pm, Su 12pm-5pm. MC, V, AmEx, D, Ⓡ to 86th St. ♿

Booklink
Come for quality fiction and children's books; also a sampling of intellectual and academic periodicals. Specializes in Scottish and Middle Eastern Literature.
Park Slope, Brooklyn, 99 Seventh Ave. (bet. President and Union Sts.), (718) 783-6067. Open M-F 10am-9pm, Su 11am-8pm. MC, V, AmEx, ⒹⓆ to Seventh Ave. ♿

Community Book Store and Café of Park Slope
This integral part of Park Slope's social life carries a mixture of current best-sellers and classic fiction, with a wonderful café and garden in the back. The owners also coax well-known authors out for readings, most recently Mary Gordon and Pete Hamill.
Park Slope, Brooklyn, 143 Seventh Ave. (bet. Garfield and Carroll Sts.), (718) 783-3075, www.community bookstore.com. Open M-F 9am-9:45pm, Sa 9am-10pm, Su 10am-10pm. MC, V, AmEx, D, DQ to Seventh Ave.

Kings Books
This bookstore serves the local schools: Kingsborough Community College and High School. Kings Books provides students with an alternative to school-run bookstores; here they can find many of the textbooks their classes demand, often at lower prices.
Kingsborough, Brooklyn, 1613 Oriental Blvd. (bet. Oxford and Norfolk Sts.), (718) 743-8582. Open M 9am-6pm, T-W 9am-7pm, R 10am-4pm, Sa 9am-3pm. MC, V, AmEx, D, DQ to Brighton Beach.

♦ GROCERY, GOURMET & SPECIALTY

Brooklyn Brewery
New York's closest approximation to a hometown beer is brewed here, and on weekends they open the place up. That means free brewery tours, beer tastings, and merchandise for sale. The hats and T-shirts make excellent gifts for any beer lover on your list. They've recently begun using the space as a gallery and performance space as well, making this a perfect day of cheap fun for a variety of different tastes.
Williamsburg, Brooklyn, 79 N. 11th St. (bet. Berry St. and Wythe Ave.), (718) 486-7422, www.brook lynbrewery.com. Open F 6pm-10pm, Sa 12pm-5pm. MC, V, AmEx, L to Bedford Ave.

Bruno Bakery
The key word for this bakery is fresh: their out-of-this-world canoli are made to order. They also feature delicious cookies, eclairs, and biscotti. They have a delivery service throughout New York City, and a top-rate catering service.
Brooklyn, 602 Lorimer St. (bet. Skillman Ave. and Conselyea St.), (718) 349-6524. Open M-F 7am-9pm, Sa-Su 7am-8pm. MC, V, AmEx, D. G to Metropolitan Ave. ♿

The Damascus Breads & Pastries Shop
Hands-down the best pita bread in Brooklyn, and it has recently caught on in Manhattan supermarkets. But why not buy it fresh here, where a six-pack goes for 55¢, and other staff-of-life items are equally cheap.
Cobble Hill, Brooklyn, 195 Atlantic Ave. (bet. Court and Clinton Sts.), (718) 625-7070. Open M-Su 8pm-7pm. Cash Only, 2345 to Borough Hall, MNR to Court St. ♿

Eagle Foods
Arguably second only to the East Village Meat Market, Eagle Foods is definitely worth the trek out to Brooklyn if you're a fan of Polish meats. Come for kielbasa, assorted smoked meats, and even a selection of low-cost groceries.
Prospect Park, Brooklyn, 628 Fifth Ave. (bet. 17th and 18th Sts.), (718) 499-0026. Open M-Sa 6am-7pm, Su 6am-5pm. MC, V, AmEx, D. R to Prospect Ave. ♿

♦ MISCELLANEOUS

Macy's
"The Largest Store in the World" often resembles the chaos of the Thanksgiving Day parade they sponsor, especially after work and around Christmas. Most items are lower priced than other department stores, but the service and bathrooms reflect this reduction.
Downtown Brooklyn, 420 Fulton St. (bet. Hoyt and Elm Sts.), (718) 875-7200, www.macys.com. Open M, R 10am-8pm, T-W, F-Sa 9am-8pm, Su 12pm-7pm. MC, V, AmEx, 23 to Hoyt St.-Fulton Mall.

Arts & Recreation

♦ LEISURE

Brighton Beach
A boardwalk lined with restaurants east of the Coney Island Amusement Park stretches along nearly three miles of sand in this Russian neighborhood. The surf is gentle, but the crowds can get wild, particularly on Friday nights when the beach hosts fireworks displays.
Brooklyn, Brightwater Ave. (near Coney Island Boardwalk East), (718) 946-1350. Lifeguard hours: Daily 10am-6pm. Q to Brighton Beach.

Coney Island
This All-American playground has seen its day come and go, but it's still there for visitors to see. The Cyclone still has a certain rickety appeal; and of course, Nathan's hot dogs will always be there. Sunbathing is better left to happier places; the appeal of Coney Island is the neo-noir charm of an urban ghost town.
Coney Island, Brooklyn. www.coneyisland.com. BDFB to Stillwell Ave.-Coney Island

Deep-Sea Fishing on the Pastime Princess
Party-fishing boat offers excursions to troll for bluefish, flounder, and mackerel.
Brighton Beach, Brooklyn, Eamons Ave., Pier 5 (bet. Mansfield Pl. and Bedford Ave.), (718) 252-4398, www.pastimeprincess.com. Open M-Su 7am. MC, V, AmEx, BDF to Stillwell Ave./Coney Island

Floyd Bennet Airfield
Now that the air traffic doesn't come through, this spacious airfield is used mostly for biking and blading. The hangar has become an exhibition hall, and visitors can golf, mini-golf and use batting cages at the nearby Gateway National Recreation Area.
Brooklyn, At Gateway National Recreation Area, (718) 338-3799 D to Ave. U

Manhattan Beach
Brooklyn's smaller and more intimate beach offers ocean views without the dazzle of Coney Island. The crescent nestles between Sheepshead Bay and the Atlantic, and a small boardwalk features great seafood restaurants. Two newly renovated playgrounds and tennis and handball courts provide leisure alternatives to sand and surf.
Brooklyn, Atlantic Ocean (at Oriental Blvd.), (718) 946-1373. Lifeguard hours: Daily 10am-6pm. By bus: B_1 *or* B_{49} *bus to Manhattan Beach/Oriental Ave.*

Metropolitan Pool
History and swimming in one: This indoor public pool situated between North & South Williamsburg was converted from an old 1920s bathhouse. A historical memento, it now serves primarily as a recreational swimming pool for the neighborhood's eclectic population. The $10 membership fee ensures access to this popular spot.
Brooklyn, 261 Bedford Ave. (bet. Metropolitan Ave. and N. 1st St.), (718) 599-5707. (Call for seasonal hours). L to Bedford. ♿

New York Aquarium
Over 350 aquatic species over 14 acres in Coney Island. With huge panoramic windows beneath the surface of the water, you can see eye-to-eye with Beluga Whales, Bottlenose Dolphins and Nurse Sharks. Don't miss the Aquatheater, a show that promises leaping dolphins and soaking audience members. Shows daily.
Brooklyn, Surf Ave. (at W. 8th St.), (718) 265-FISH, www.wcs.org. Open M-F 10am-5pm, Sa-Su 10am-5:30pm, holidays 10am-5:30pm. Admission: $9.75 for adults, $6 children and seniors. F D to West 8th St.

Ocularis
On Sunday evenings, this arts and performance space in a converted mayonnaise factory, screens non-commercial independent films, foreign films and classics together with short and medium length works by independent film makers. Though the folding chairs may leave you with a stiff back, the quality of the productions and the price ($5) are worth it. At Galapagos Art Performance Space.
Williamsburg, Brooklyn, 70 N. 6th St. (bet. Wythe and Kent Aves.), (718) 388-8713. Open Su-M, call for showtimes. L to Bedford Ave. ♿

Ethnic Enclaves:

GREENPOINT

The next time you crave your grandmother's kielbasa, don't fret. You can get all the Polish smoked sausage you want in Greenpoint, a quaint Brooklyn neighborhood that could easily be Warsaw's westernmost suburb. The "restauracjas" near the corner of Manhattan and Greenpoint Avenues serve up Poland on a platter with their buckwheat, stuffed cabbage, and pierogi specials, and the short-order cooks, taxi drivers, and market clerks deliver it, accent and all. Venture here on the Queens-bound G train, and you'll be slavicified by simple osmosis.

The Polish presence in New York isn't new; exiled Poles have been coming to the city since the 1830s. But among the post-WWII and post-Communism refugees, more and more began flocking to Greenpoint. The effect was a profusion of aptekas, rather than pharmacies, and "Produkts Polski" everywhere. Ads in the neighborhood began stringing more and more consonants together. Words like zloty, serdeczna, and pravda started swishing through the streets. The immigrants even imported some of their own architecture — an onion-domed church rises behind a schoolyard along Bedford Avenue. Its spiky spires are an apt reminder that you don't have to trek to another hemisphere for your grandmother's home cooking.

Where the Hipsters Are

♦ GAle GAtes et al.
40,000 square feet of warehouse space dedicated to pushing the envelope on every medium. It's never clear what you're seeing, only clear that you haven't seen it before.

♦ Halcyon
Like GAle GAtes above Halcyon combines different mediums, except it's a bar where you can drink, listen to records and buy furniture.

♦ Boat
The local bar for many Carroll Garden residents, Boat is the kind of bar you start or end you're evenings at.

♦ Patois
One of a string of French bistros popping up along Smith Street. This is the best one of them all.

♦ 31 Grand
Artistic furniture and fashion, in a gallery next to the water, makes for an experience that compares to nothing else.

Rockaway Beach
Urban living meets "Irish Riviera" where JFK's planes dwarf seagulls. Once a summer resort, Rockaway flaunts the old homes of Belle Harbor as a remnant of its nineteenth century glory. Today, this expanse of sand lined with boardwalk stores and seafood restaurants runs from 9th to 149th Streets.
Brooklyn, 90-14 Rockaway Beach Blvd. (bet. 90th and 91st Sts.), (718) 634-8058. Open 24 hours. Ⓐ *to Beach 90th St.*

♦ PERFORMANCE

Bargemusic
Excellent chamber music on the water in the moonlight; bring a date and get all mushy on this cozy converted coffee barge.
Fulton Ferry Landing, Brooklyn, Water St. (at River Sts.), (718) 624-4061. Cash Only, ⒶⒸ *to High St.-Brooklyn Bridge.*

The Brooklyn Academy of Music (BAM)
Although the Brooklyn Philharmonic has distinguished itself with its range and a repertoire that runs the gamut from European classics to selections from African-American traditions, its pet projects are clearly those rooted in the avant garde, which are best realized in BAM's provocative yearly "Next Wave" festival that consistently pushes the boundaries of classical music.
Fort Greene, Brooklyn, 30 Lafayette Ave. (at Ashland Pl.), (718) 636-4100, www.bam.org. MC, V, ⒹⓆ②③④⑤ *to Atlantic Ave.* ♿

Galapagos Performance Art Space
Housed in an old warehouse with a stylish bar and indoor pond, Galapagos provides a forum for performance art, dance, music, and films. A popular scene where you'll find listings for upcoming art exhibits and performances in the neighborhood.
Brooklyn, 70 N. 6th St. (bet. Wythe & Kent Aves.), (718) 782-5188. Open Su-R 6pm-2am, F-Sa 6pm-4am. Ⓛ *to Bedford.* ♿

♦ SITES

Williamsburg Bridge
Stroll, jog, bike, skate, or blade across this bridge for its spectacular Manhattan views. Or revel in the ghosts of early 20th-century immigrant life as you gaze across the river. Sunny weekends lure out the biggest pedestrian crowds.
Brooklyn, Entrance at Williamsburg Bridge Plaza (bet. Driggs St. and Broadway). ⒿⓂⓏ *to Marcy Ave.*

♦ PARKS

Grand Ferry Park
In the shadow of the Domino Sugar Refinery, lies a small, beautiful park with magical cobblestone charm. Have a picnic by the river or gaze at the sweeping Manhattan skyline and Williamsburg Bridge.
Brooklyn, East River Waterfront (bet. Grand and River Sts.) Ⓛ *to Bedford.*

McCarren Park
The biggest park in Williamsburg, McCarren provides a site for lounging, ballgames, or picnics. Neighborhood artists, kids, and families flock to this grassy hub, which hosts summer concerts and other events.
Brooklyn, N. 12th St (bet. Driggs, Union, and Manhattan Aves.). Ⓛ *to Bedford*

Monsignor McGolrick Park
A quaint European park in Greenpoint? Or perhaps New York's very own "small-town-square" with a mix of elderly Polish folks, kids, families, artists, and students in the

neighborhood looking for a quieter time. Definitely worth it if you seek charm in a park.
Brooklyn, Nassau Ave. (bet. Driggs Ave., Monitor, and Russell Sts.) (G) to Nassau Ave.

♦ MUSEUMS & CULTURAL CENTERS

The Brooklyn Museum of Art
A world-class museum with strong permanent collections and impressive special exhibitions. The American paintings are excellent, the Egyptian Collection is outstanding, and there's a lovely sculpture garden as well. Located next to the botanical garden, it's a great way to get away from it all while remaining in the city.
Prospect Heights, Brooklyn, 200 Eastern Parkway (at Washington Ave.), (718) 638-5000, www.brook lynart.org. Open W-F 10am-5pm, Sa-Su 11am-6pm. MC, V, AmEx, Admission (suggested): $1.50-$4, (2)(3) to Eastern Parkway-Brooklyn Museum. ♿

The New York Transit Museum
While you may consider the turnstiles in working stations antique, the originals are really housed in this authentic 1930s subway station. Vintage subway maps and mosaics comprise the permanent collection, along with exhibitions chronicling the development of rapid transit. Tag along with a school group for a field trip to somewhere great like the Metro North car-repair facility.
Downtown Brooklyn, corner of Boerum Pl. and Schermerhorn St., (718) 243-3060, www.mta.nyc.ny.us. Open T-F 10am-4pm, Sa-Su 12pm-5pm. Cash Only, Admission: $1.50-$3, (2)(3)(4)(5) to Borough Hall. ♿

Polish and Slavic Center
Located in an old Italian church, this community center provides social services for new and established Polish residents. In addition to its regularly scheduled cultural events, it hosts the high-spirited Festival of Polish Culture and the Polish Film Festival in the fall season.
Greenpoint, Brooklyn. 177 Kent St. (bet. Manhattan Ave. and McGuinness St.), (718) 383-5290. (G) to Greenpoint Ave.

Williamsburg Art & Historical Society
Whatever your tastes, this is one of Williamsburg's highlights. Located in a beautiful bank built in 1868, this non-profit art nexus hosts incredible music, readings, poetry, parties, film festivals, multimedia art exhibitions, and performances by artists both established and lesser-known.
Williamsburg, Brooklyn, 135 Broadway (bet. Grand St. and Flushing Ave.), (718) 486-7372, www.wahcenter.com. Open Sa-Su 12pm-6pm. (J)(M)(Z) to Marcy Ave. ♿

♦ GALLERIES & LIBRARIES

GAle GAtes et al.
A performance and visual arts company that both performs and exhibits fine art and installations in its 40,000 square foot space. Founded in 1995 by Michael Counts, the troupe's capacity to extend the definitions of theater, installations and music lead to highly imaginative exhibits that qualify as a new and yet to be labeled medium. Rotating curator programs which focus on local artists spotlight the growing art community in DUMBO.
DUMBO, Brooklyn, 37 Main St. (bet. Water and Front Sts.), (718) 522-4596, www.galegates.org, Call for Admission and schedule (varies), (F) to Front St. (A)(C) to High St. (2)(3) to Clark St.

Goliath Visual Space
Goliath is quickly becoming one of the most impressive art spaces in Brooklyn. Affiliated with a Goliath gallery in Japan, the curators here pay attention to promoting visual artists of all forms, (including performance and video art) and attempt to shy away from the more pretentious Soho/Chelsea scene. While the gallery tends to get crowded on weekends with these very types, make an appointment for the weekday and peruse the diverse exhibits at leisure.
Greenpoint, Brooklyn, 117 Dobbins St. (bet. Norman and Messerole Aves.), (718)389-0369, www.goliath777.com. Open Sa-Su 1pm-6pm, weekdays by appointment, (G) to Nassau

Holland Tunnel Arts Project
Art in a tool shed? Don't let the size of this tiny gallery fool you. Their shows are ambitious and big, featuring compelling work by hundreds of talented local and international artists, sometimes all at once.
Brooklyn, 61 S. 3rd St. (bet. Berry and Wythe Sts.), (718) 384-5738. Open Sa-Su 1pm-5pm, weekdays by appointment, (L) to Bedford. ♿

31 Grand
If you like avant-garde furniture and fashion, this gallery promises a rewarding visit. Located on the river, this unique gallery not only features traditional multimedia arts, from painting to video, but also exhibits "functional objects" as art.
Brooklyn, 31 Grand St. (bet. Kent and Wythe Sts.), (718) 388-2858, www.31grand.com. Open Sa-Su 1pm-7pm, weekdays by appointment, (L) to Bedford.

Cave
Known for its diverse range of mixed media and performance art, this renovated garage-turned-gallery is truly dedicated to the experimental arts. The gallery's mission is to provide a space for artists who are devoted to forming con-

nections with one another through creative expression which is what sets this gallery apart from the others.
Brooklyn, 58 Grand St. (bet. Kent and Wythe Sts.), (718) 388-6780. Ⓛ *to Bedford.* ♿

Momenta Art
The neighborhood's most grown-up gallery, yet still beyond the orbit of the conventional. The focus is on group shows featuring works by many artists reflecting a central, provocative theme, and the execution ranges from competent to brilliant. Well worth the trip for anyone looking for something beyond the played out Chelsea scene.
Williamsburg, Brooklyn, 72 Berry St. (bet. 9th and 10th Sts.), (718) 218-8058. Open F-M 12pm-6pm. Ⓛ *to Bedford Ave.*

Pierogi 2000
The name reflects the way the traditional Polish flavor of the community melds with the influx of forward-focused artists and others, and like most Williamsburg galleries, the art here is as far outside of the mainstream as the location. The gallery serves as everything from an outlet for resurrections of art treasures unseen for years to a center for many of the area's resident artists, many of whom can be found hanging out on its stoop.
Williamsburg, Brooklyn, 177 N. 9th St. (bet. Bedford and Driggs Aves.), (718) 599-2144, www.pierogi 2000.com. Open F-M 12pm-6pm. Ⓛ *to Bedford Ave.*

Roebling Hall
A gallery located in the very trendy artist locale of Williamsburg, Roebling holds its own with its hip neighbors without compromising quality curatorial standards. Expect conceptual works here with a mix of the conventional oil and canvas painting: the latest exhibition is a wonderfully accessible tribute to the ultimate tropical paradise, done with paints on vinyl squares.
Williamsburg, Brooklyn. 390 Wythe Ave. (at S. 4th St.), (718) 599-5352, www.brooklynart.com. Open Sa-M 12pm-6pm, Ⓛ *to Bedford Ave.*

Rotunda Gallery
The Rotunda Gallery showcases innovative artists with works in mixed media, sculpture and painting. Students and young children can often be found here, as the gallery is affiliated with numerous educational programs. The art, however, is often quite sophisticated. Past exhibits have included compartmentalized kitsch-oddities and mass-media responses to the lottery.
Brooklyn Heights, Brooklyn. 33 Clinton St. (bet. Pierrepont St. and Cadman Plaza W.), (718) 875-4047, www.brooklynx.org/rotunda. Open T-F 12pm-5pm, Sa 11am-4pm ②③④⑤ *to Borough Hall* ♿

Star 67
Experience interactive, experimental multimedia installations in this collaborative, artist-run space. The creativity of the group in charge comes through in their work. The friendly group of hosts deviates from the pretentious attitudes most of us expect to encounter in galleries.
Brooklyn, 67 Metropolitan Ave. (bet. Kent and Wythe Sts.), (718) 599-7339. Open Sa-Su 12pm-6pm. Ⓛ *to Bedford.*

Nightlife

♦ BARS

Black Betty
Black Betty dishes up cool live music and North African cuisine to a young crowd of new Brooklynites seven days a week. The jazz, world music,and trip-hop acts booked by the "Professor" have helped to make this one of Williamsburg's most popular nightspots. Be sure to call ahead for reservations.
Brooklyn, 366 Metropolitan Ave. (at Havemeyer St.), (718) 599-0243. Open M-Su 6:30pm-4am. MC, V, AmEx, Ⓛ *to Bedford Ave.,* Ⓖ *to Metropolitan Ave.*

Boat
Great jukebox, good drinks, friendly staff, nice design and layout-what more could you want of a neighborhood bar in Brooklyn or anywhere else for that matter? Located right off the F train, this place is usually busy early in the week, gets the night cap crowd on the weekends and is a "Cheers" kind of place for the locals.
Carroll Gardens, Brooklyn, 175 Smith St. (bet. Wyckof and Warren Sts.), (718) 254-0607. Open M-Su 5pm- 4am. MC, V, AmEx, Ⓕ *to Bergen St.*

Carriage House
Home away from home for Park Slope's cable-deprived in need of a Knicks fix. Had enough sports? Amuse yourself at the pool table or come by on karaoke night.
Park Slope, Brooklyn, 312 Seventh Ave. (bet. 7th and 8th Sts.), (718) 788-7747. Open M-Su 12pm-3am. MC, V, AmEx, D, Ⓕ *to Seventh Ave.-Park Slope.* ♿

Excelsior
Darkness shrouds this neighborhood gay bar until you step outside onto the cute veranda and descend the stairs into the even cuter large garden (which, unfortunately for us, closes at midnight). Mostly, although not exclusively, men are there to appreciate all this cuteness.
Park Slope, Brooklyn, 390 Fifth Ave. (bet. 6th and 7th Sts.), (718) 832-1599. Open M-F 6pm-4am, Sa-Su 2pm-4am. Cash Only Ⓕ *to Fourth Ave.,* ⓃⓇ *to 9th St.*

> If you want to make Brooklyn in words or film or paint, you must see the way the sun defines the silent streets on an early Sunday morning, sculpting trees, buildings, fire hydrants, stray dogs, and wandering people with an almost perfect clarity . . . If you have ever lived in Brooklyn or if you ever grew up on its streets, you carry that light with you forever.
>
> —Peter Hamill

Frank's Lounge

Frank's is the friendly neighborhood lounge in this part of Brooklyn. Come in and you'll be greeted with smiles and the sounds of smooth DJing. It gets crowded on weekends, but you can always expect to see regulars and the quality mixed drinks.

Fort Greene, Brooklyn, 660 Fulton St. (at S. Eliot St.), (718) 625-9339. Open Su-R 4pm-2am, F-Sa 4pm-4am. Cash only C *to Lafayette,* G *to Fulton St.,* D N R Q *to DeKalb Ave.,* 2 3 4 5 *to Nevins Ave.*

Halcyon

An of-the-moment spot that deserves the attention, Halcyon is a combination furniture store/record store/lounge/coffeeshop. Play with their turntables while you check out the foxy Brooklynites.

Brooklyn Heights, Brooklyn, 227 Smith St. (bet. Butler and Douglas Sts.), (718) 260-9299. Open M-Su 12am-12pm. MC, V, F G *to Bergen St.*

Last Exit

Last Exit is an oasis of cool in the sometimes-stuffy bar wasteland that is Brooklyn Heights. The low-key lounge serves delicious martinis and strong mixed drinks to a young, fresh clientele. A friendly staff, comfy couches, and an unpretentious crowd also await at Last Exit.

Brooklyn, 136 Atlantic Ave., (bet. Henry and Clinton Sts.), (718) 222-9198. Open M-Su 4pm-4am. MC, V, AmEx, DC, D, M N R 4 5 *to Borough Hall.*

Mugs Ale House

Baffled by so many good beers on tap, most people never investigate the vast selection of bottled imports. The colorful local contingent and a decent jukebox explain why Manhattanites schlep out here for a drink. Join 'em.

Williamsburg, Brooklyn, 125 Bedford Ave. (at N. 10th St.), (718) 486-8232. Open M-Su 2pm-4am. MC, V, AmEx, D, L *to Bedford Ave.*

Rising Café

Local place for gay women and a few men who love them. It's good if you're sick of travelling into Manhattan to visit the standard lesbian haunts. On Saturdays a DJ spins as the dance floor swells; on Wednesdays, Fridays and Sundays, the stage is ceded to local singer-songwriters and other performers.

Park Slope, Brooklyn, 186 Fifth Ave. (at Sackett St.), (718) 789-6340. Open M-Su 5pm-1am. Cash Only, N R *to Union St.,* B D *to Pacific St.,* 2 3 4 5 *to Atlantic Ave.*

Sparky's Ale House

24 cold taps and four hand drawn casks filled with a myriad of micro and macro brews from all over the world, poured along side such old favorites such as Guinness, Harp, Brooklyn and Stela, keep this popular bar in business. The pool table, dartboards, and jukebox don't hurt either.

Carroll Gardens, Brooklyn, 481 Court St. (bet. Nelson and Luquer Sts.), (718) 624-5516. Open M-Sa 4pm-4am, Su 12:30pm-3am F *to Carroll St.*

Teddy's Bar and Grill

The best bar food in Brooklyn. Try a burger or go for dessert — sample the ice cream smothered in homemade hot fudge. There's plenty of drinks to wash it down, too; Teddy's is of the few places offering pitchers of really good beer.

Williamsburg, Brooklyn, 96 Berry St. (at N. 8th St.), (718) 384-9787. Open M-Sa 11:30am-4am, Su 11:30am-2am. MC, V, L *to Bedford Ave.*

200 5th

An upscale crowd dines and drinks at one of Park Slope's most popular nightspots. Get there early on Friday nights for salsa dancing; other evenings are a bit more sedate. The cover varies and, more importantly, is negotiable.

Park Slope, Brooklyn, 200 Fifth Ave. (bet. Union and Berkeley Sts.), (718) 638-2925. Open M-Su 4pm-12am. MC, V, AmEx, DC, D, M N R *to Union St.*

Staten Island

Combining close proximity to the urban with the tranquility of the suburban, Staten Island, with only 400,000 residents, is the city's least populated and quietest borough, and one which most New Yorkers neglect. Most Staten Islanders like it this way and the history of the borough is filled with a stubborn resistance to any of the fast pace most see as defining New York.

Henry Hudson gave Staaten Eylandt its original name in 1609, when he sailed into the bay which now bears his name. In 1639, the Dutch opened Staten Island to colonization, but the area remained difficult to settle due to conflicts with indigenous inhabitants who'd been there for thousands of years. Things were calmer when the British took over in 1664, but no more easier to settle. The Island was reachable only by private boat and remained largely a secluded place for fishing and farming until 1713, when a public ferry began carrying passengers to and from Manhattan, and continues to do so today.

The Island's independent streak has persisted since it joined New York City in 1898 and saw the watershed 1964 construction of the Verrazano Narrows Bridge, which connects it to Brooklyn. Fed up with garbage dumps, filled largely with trash from elsewhere, the citizens of Staten Island voted in 1993, albeit unsuccessfully, to secede from New York City. Fresh Kills, the country's largest trash dump and visible from space, was closed last year. If that isn't enough appeasement the minor league affiliate of the Bronx's Yankees starts playing this summer.

Though the butt of more jokes than any place this side of Poughkeepsie, Staten Island's plethora of fine restaurants, historical sites, and shoreline contain some of New York's best-kept secrets and are a must at some point.

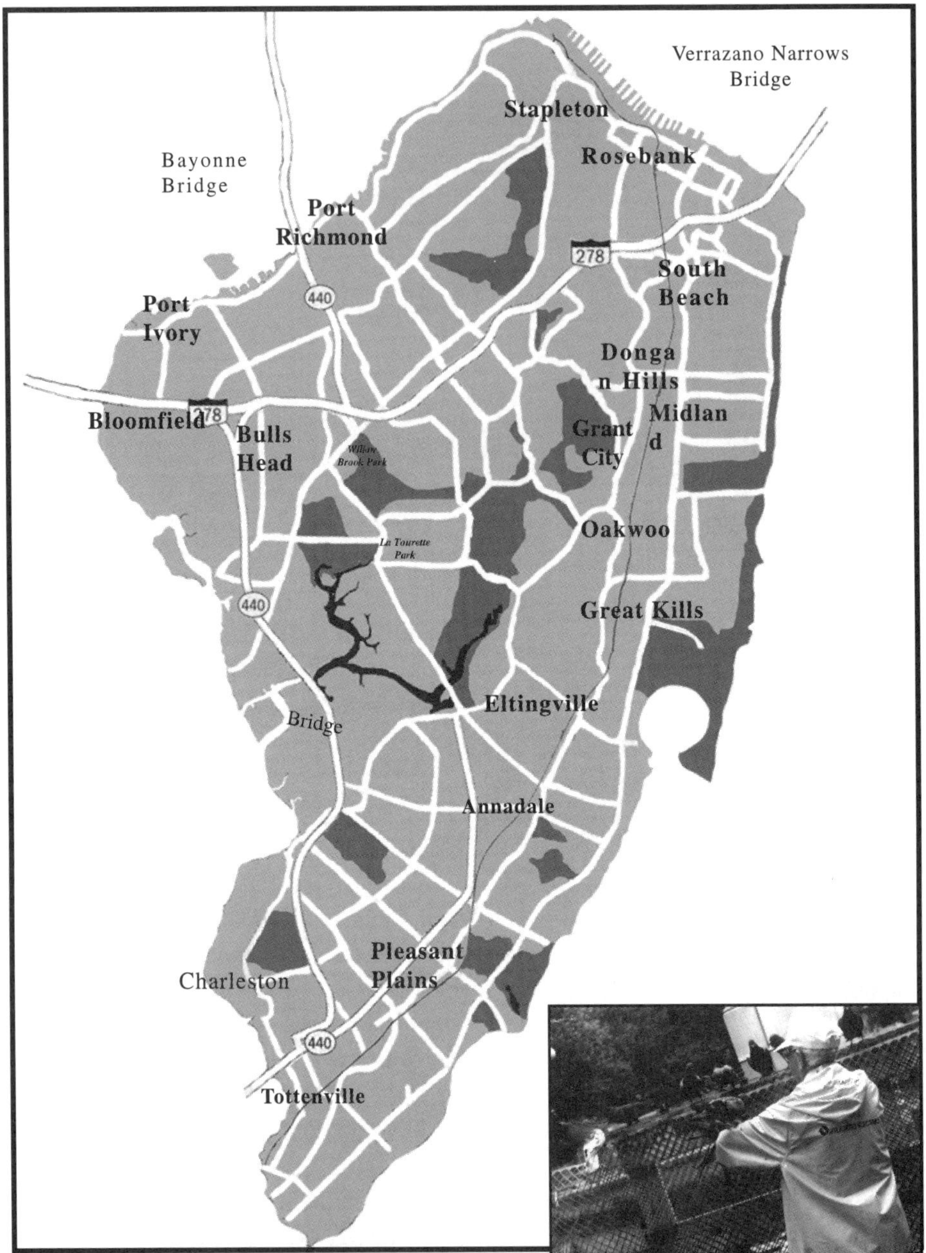

Verrazano Narrows Bridge
Stapleton
Rosebank
Bayonne Bridge
Port Richmond
278
South Beach
440
Port Ivory
Donga n Hills
Midlan d
Grant City
Bloomfield
278
Bulls Head
La Tourette Park
Oakwoo
Great Kills
440
Eltingville
Bridge
Annadale
Pleasant Plains
Charleston
440
Tottenville

Dining

♦ RESTAURANTS

Aesop's Tables
There's a lot you can do with the metaphor here. Aesops's Tables. Are the stories in the variations of new American food Aesop's Tables offers? Or, are the stories at your table where the décor provides hours of speculation. The moral-worth it if your in town, but don't go out of your way otherwise.
Staten Island. 1233 Bay St. (at Maryland Ave.), (718) 720-2005. Open T-Sa 5.30pm-10.30pm, Su 12pm-4pm, 5pm-9pm MC, V, AmEx, D, Entrees: $11-$17 ❶❾ to South Ferry

Carol's Café
Arguably the best restaurant in Staten Island, the worst thing about Carol's Café is that it's only open four days a week. That and the fact that despite its Staten Island location, the prices will make you think you're in Manhattan. Though the eclectic fare may take a while to get to your table (the service is known for being slow), you'll likely concede that it was worth the wait.
Staten Island, 1571 Richmond Rd. (bet. Four Corners Rd. and Seaview Ave.), (718) 979-5600. Open W-F 6pm-indefinite, Sa 5pm-indefinite. MC, V, AmEx, D, Entrées: $14-$35. ❶❾ to South Ferry

Basilio Inn
Housed in a 19th century stable imbued with a Tuscan rustic flavor, the Inn serves up incredible Italian — the red snapper Livornese is divine — the likes of which Manhattanites have never seen. Prices reflect the Island's low rent and low pretension.
Staten Island, 2-6 Galesville Court, (718) 447-9292. Open M-Su 12pm-3pm, 5pm-10pm. AmEx, Entrées: $12-$14. ❶❾ to South Ferry

Cargo Cafe
Just a stone's throw from the Staten Island Ferry terminal, this modern, trendy spot is hard to miss. A youngish local crowd congregates on the terrace in summer for delectable fresh fish specials like pan-seared tuna. Sandwiches, burgers, and salads make appearances as well. Local artists often showcase their work and live jazz cooks up Thursdays.
Staten Island, 120 Bay St. (at Flosson Terrace), (718) 876-0539. Open 11:30am-2am. MC, V, AmEx, D, Entrées: $10-$18. ❶❾ to South Ferry

Denino's Pizzeria and Tavern
As much a Staten Island institution as the ferry, if not more so. Denino's has been around since 1937, owned by the same family and serves some of the best thin crust pizza and fried calamari in the city. The décor isn't much but who cares, it's a pizza place, and the sort of place you go to with a big group, order a lot and get ugly.
Staten Island. 524 Port Richmond Ave. (bet. Hooker Pl. and Walker St.), (718) 442-9401. Open Su-R 11:30am-11pm, F-Sa 11:30-12am. Cash Only, Entrees: $8-$15 ❶❾ to South Ferry

Parsonage
The priest is gone, but this 150-year-old house of a priest serves food that is as close to divine as it gets on Staten Island. The food's American with twists-cherry peppers here, bunch of Italian stuff there, escargots wallowing in lots of garlic. The ambience completes the experience. Two floors of antiques in an antique house. And on your plate recipes so time tested they'll be around as long as the house you're eating them in.
Staten Island. 74 Arthur Kill Rd. (at Clark Ave.), (718) 351-7879. Open M-Su 12pm-10pm. MC, V, AmEx, D, Entrees: $16-$30 ❶❾ to South Ferry

Shopping

♦ CLOTHING & SHOES

Bang Bang
This is a basic store if you are into the New York club scene. They have the typical club clothing that you don't want to spend a lot of money on because they only cover one-third of your body. The only problem is that you may see someone wearing the same thing on Friday night.
Staten Island, Staten Island Mall, 2655 Richmond Ave. (at Platinum Ave.), (718) 982-8732. Open M-Sa 10am-9:30pm, Su 10am-6pm. MC, V, AmEx, D. ❶❾ to South Ferry

Dresses For Less Inc.
Got a last minute dinner function? This store has a great selection of beautiful dresses at a fraction of the cost of chain retailers. Bargain sportswear finds are located in the back half of the store. The selection changes weekly so if you see your dream dress, grab it!
Dongan Hills, Staten Island, 1462 Hylan Blvd. (bet. Benton and Cooper Sts.), (718) 351-8134. Open M-W 10am-6:30pm, R-F 10am-7:30pm, Sa 10am-6:30pm, Su 11am-5pm. MC, V. ❶❾ to South Ferry

Payhalf
A shopper's extravaganza, this relatively new store offers

> Staten Island combines advantages which, it is believed, are unrivalled in this country. Added to its proximity to the great commercial mart of the Western Hemisphere, it possess a beauty of location, extent of prospect, and salubrity of climate, that will in vain be sought elsewhere.
>
> —Henry Steinmeyer

designer clothing for men, women, and children for literally half price. Pick up the latest trends without breaking your piggybank.

New Springville, Staten Island, 2795 Richmond Ave., (bet. Richmond and Platinum Aves.), (718) 982-7728. Open M-Sa 10am-9pm, Su 11am-6pm. MC, V, AmEx, D. ❶❾ to South Ferry ♿

Time After Time

This consignment shop is perfect for buying some staple pieces or evening wear and vintage jewelry. You can even make an appointment to sell your unwanted, gently used clothing.

New Dorp, Staten Island, 59 New Dorp Plaza (bet. Rose Ave. and New Dorp Lane), (718) 987-0853. Open T-Sa 11am-5pm, R 11-6:30pm. MC, V, AmEx, D. ❶❾ to South Ferry

Wu Wear

Wu-tang Clan, the premier rap group of Staten Island, has placed itself on the fashion map with its own offerings of active menswear. View the platinum albums of Ol' Dirty Bastard and Method Man alongside brightly-hued jackets and oversized denim. Prices are moderate, at least for designer labels.

Staten Island, 61A Victory Blvd. (at Montgomery Ave.), (718) 720-9043, Open T-Sa 12am-7pm. MC, V, AmEx, D. ❶❾ to South Ferry ♿

♦ BOOKS, MAGAZINES & RECORDS

Infinity Records & Tapes

This small and inconspicuous store is brimming with great finds that other stores can't get. DJs seek this enclave out for the great up-to-date vinyl selection and CD singles of hits from the '50s to today. Even cassettes can still be snagged. Get underground bargains without going down to the basement.

Great Kills, Staten Island, 4203-B Hylan Blvd. (bet. Armstrong Ave. and Hylan Blvd.), (718) 967-4793. Open M-F 10am-8pm, Sa 10am-6pm, Su 11am-4pm. MC, V. ❶❾ to South Ferry ♿

Our Music Center

A landmark for some area residents, this is one of the few "real" record stores a-round. Top hits and hard-to-come-by records are their specialty. Take the time to browse their shelves for the tunes from today and yesterday you can't live without.

New Dorp, Staten Island, 2626 Hylan Blvd. (in the Hylan Shopping Plaza on Hylan Blvd. at Beach Ave.), (718) 667-8563, www.ourmusiccenter.com. Open M-R 9am-8:30pm, F 9am-9pm, Sa 9am-6pm, Su 11am-4pm. MC, V, AmEx, D. ❶❾ to South Ferry ♿

Zig Zag Records

Small on square footage but not on selection, this store is a must-see on your music-buying journey. Hurry over to get the soundtrack for the movie you just saw at the UA theater next door.

Staten Island, Travis, 4174 Victory Blvd., (at Victory Blvd. and West Shore Expressway), (718) 494-9019. Open M-Sa 11am-8pm, Su 11am-6pm. MC, V, AmEx, D. ❶❾ to South Ferry.

Arts & Recreation

♦ LEISURE

The Staten Island Botanical Garden

Probably a better walk than any of the city's parks, the botanical garden offers world after green world of rose gardens, Victorian replicas, a maze. Most impressive is the new Chinese Scholar's Garden, the only authentic Chinese garden of its type in the country. Based on a walled Ming Dynasty model and designed by China's foremost authority on classical garden design, the Scholar's Garden is filled with imported bamboo, courtyards, a great view of the 83 acre gardens and the benches perfect for marinating on some thoughts.

Staten Island, 1000 Richmond Terrace, (718) 273-8200. www.sibg.org. Open M-Su dawn to dusk, Chinese Scholar's Garden T-Su 10am-5pm. 1 9 *to South Ferry* ♿

South Beach Park

The fourth longest boardwalk in the country is always packed with cyclists, but this is primarily a bathing beach for families and other sun worshippers. It's not the best beach but if hanging out's all you want to do this place will do just fine.

Staten Island, 1 9 *to South Ferry* ♿

The Godfather House

Literally the house from the Godfather. The place where Don Corleone dies and where the last shot, with Kay looking at the closing door, happened. Visitors aren't allowed and it's not as big as you think, but still, it the

Godfather House.
Staten Island, 16 Longfellow Rd.

♦ SITES

Historic Richmond Town

The one hundred acres of historic buildings in Richmond Town date back as far as 1695. This is the stuff of elementary school trips and things to do with grandma. Its museum is packed with trinket after trinket - old kegs of beer, jewelry cases, butter churners, axes, nails - and the ground tours are led by motivated professionals dressed in full puritan regalia. You will be blown away by how much there is to know about Staten Island.

Staten Island, 441 Clarke Ave., (718) 351-1161, www.historicrichmondtown.org. Open W-Su 1pm-5pm MC, V., Admission: $.50-2.50. 1 9 *to South Ferry*

Staten Island Lighthouse

This secret gem is just up Lighthouse Hill in Richmondtown. Now located on private property, the interior of this picturesque 90-foot octagonal tower is closed to the public but you can get within 100 feet to snag some great photos. At night, bring a date to this romantic spot.

Lighthouse Avenue can be accessed from Richmond Road. 74 bus to Lighthouse Road. 1 9 *to South Ferry*

♦ MUSEUMS & CULTURAL CENTERS

Garibaldi Meucci Museum

This historic house museum is a great stop if you're on the island. Garibaldi played a major role in Italian Unification and Meucci was the original inventor of the phone. This museum houses artifacts from when they lived there.

Staten Island, 420 Tomkins Ave. (at Chesnut Ave.), (718) 442-1608, www.community.silive.com/cc/garibaldimeuci. Open T-F 1pm-5pm, Sa-Su 1pm-5pm. Cash Only, Admission (suggested): $3. 1 9 to South Ferry ♿

Jacques Marchais Museum of Tibetan Art

Housed in a two-story stone building resembling a Himalayan Budhist monastery and set in a terraced garden overlooking New York Bay, the museum features a permanent collection of Tibetan and other Buddhist art and ethnography. Notable past visitors include the Dalai Lama, who came in 1991.

Staten Island, 338 Lighthouse Ave. (at Richmond Rd.), (718) 987-3500, www.tibetanmuseum.com. Open by appointment only. Cash Only, Admission: $1-$3, 1 9 *to South Ferry*

Staten Island Children's Museum

Your average children's museum full of the kind of interactive, educational exhibits kids love. The wonders of water. Bugs and other insects. Pirates. If you're in Staten Island and your kid's restless this is the place to get your breath back.

Staten Island, 1000 Richmond Terrace, (718) 273-2060, Open: T-Su 12pm-5pm, Admission: $4 1 9 *to South Ferry* ♿

Nightlife

♦ BARS

Cargo Café
The décor is a bit perplexing: the solitary distraction on the ceiling, for example, is a forlorn-looking tuba. But the kitchen's open late and they have a nice pseudo-outdoors room, so the mostly local, slightly older crowd doesn't mind too much.
Staten Island, 120 Bay St. (at Slosson Ave.), (718) 876-0539. Open M-Su 12:30pm-2:30am. MC, V, AmEx, DC, ❶❾ *to South Ferry* *♿

Ruddy & Dean
Like a recent college grad, Ruddy & Dean is all dressed up and not sure where it's going. While he grapples with his existential crisis, patrons enjoy a great view of Manhattan from the patio. Of course, they could just go enjoy Manhattan instead.
Staten Island, 44 Richmond Terrace (bet. Day and Wall Sts.), (718) 816-4400. Open Su-R 4pm-2am, F-Sa 4pm-4am. MC, V, AmEx, DC, ❶❾ *to South Ferry* ♿

Sidestreet Saloon
High-schoolers in shiny pants pack this dive. Most nights a DJ spins hip-hop, but once a month there's an '80s party, at which you can score a badge claiming intimate knowledge of Molly or Duckie. Or both!
Staten Island, 11 Schuyler St. (bet. Richmond Terrace and Styvasen St.), (718) 448-6868. Open M-Su 11am-4am. MC, V, AmEx, DC, ❶❾ *to South Ferry*

♦ CLUBS

Atlantis
You'll feel like you're in a fishbowl at this unique spot. The decor makes it seem like you might really be under the sea, coral reef and all. the DJ spins mostly classics and dance music for a slightly older crowd. Dress to impress.
Staten Island, 2066 Hylan Blvd. (at Hunter Ave.), (718) 980-1111. Cash only, Cover: $0-$10. ❶❾ *to South Ferry*

Swimming

New York's longest boardwalk is on beautiful South Beach, Staten Island. If you can't make it, here are some other places to go. Two city pools are particularly clean and accessible, although they are invariably crowded on weekends, especially during the sweltering summer months: Carmine Street Pool (1 Clarkson St., 212-242-5228) and John Jay Park (East 77th St. and Cherokee Pl., 212-794-6566). New York City's other indoor and outdoor pools vary in popularity and cleanliness and are too numerous to list.

City beaches are open from Memorial Day through Labor Day on weekends from 10am to 6pm.

♦ **Orchard Beach**
The Bronx, 718-885-2275

♦ **Manhattan Beach**
Brooklyn, 718-946-1373

♦ **Coney Island and Brighton Beach**
Brooklyn, 718-946-1350

♦ **Rockaway Beach**
Queens, 718-318-4000

♦ **South Beach**
Staten Island, 718-816-6804

"The two moments when New York seems most desirable . . . are just as you are leaving and must say goodbye, and just as you return and can say hello."

—anonymous

D

E

F

G

H

I

J

K

L

Index

T

U

V

W

X

Y

Z